Gothic Revival in Europe and Britain: Sources, Influences and Ideas

Translated by Gerald Onn

Georg Germann

Gothic Revival

in Europe and Britain: Sources, Influences and Ideas

The MIT Press   Cambridge, Massachusetts

Copyright © 1972 Georg Germann

First U.K. edition 1972
Published by Lund Humphries, London

First American edition 1973
Published by MIT Press, Cambridge, Massachusetts

ISBN 0-262-07059-6
Library of Congress Catalog Card Number: 72-9999

Designed by Herbert Spencer and Christine Charlton
Made and printed in Great Britain by
Lund Humphries, Bradford and London

Contents

Author's acknowledgements

I wish to thank all those who have contributed to the preparation of this book for their generous assistance and advice, which I have found invaluable. Above all, I wish to thank Dr Alfred Anderau, Mr and Mrs Othmar Birkner, Dr and Mrs Bruno Carl, Dr Johannes Dobai, Miss Anne-Marie Dubler, Miss Marianne Fischer, Dr Alain Gruber, Mr Andreas Hauser, Dr Carlo Huber, Dr Dieter Koepplin, Dr Günter Krüger, Dr Peter Kurmann, Professor Hanspeter Landolt, Dr Andreas Morel, Professor Claude Pichois, Mr Hanspeter Rebsamen, Professor Hans Reinhardt, Professor Adolf Reinle, Dr Herbert Rode, Mr Dennis Sharp, Dombaumeister Arnold Wolff and Mr Peter Zürrer. My indebtedness to other scholars has been acknowledged in the notes. Unfortunately a number of new and important books, whose authors have covered some of the same ground, came to my attention too late for me to comment on them.*

I also wish to express my gratitude for the help accorded by the following institutions and libraries: the British Museum, the Victoria and Albert Museum, the Royal Institute of British Architects, the Kunstbibliothek Berlin, the Dombauarchiv in Cologne, the Öffentliche Bibliothek der Universität Basel, the Öffentliche Kunstsammlung Basel, and the Allgemeine Gewerbeschule in Basle.

I am especially indebted to Basle University, which gave me a grant for the year 1968, and to the Schweizerischer Nationalfonds zur Förderung der wissenschaftlichen Forschung, which gave me an additional grant for the years 1968–71. Thanks to the generosity of these institutions, I was able to travel widely and concentrate exclusively on my book throughout the whole of this period.

In Gerald Onn's English translation many a passage has become clearer than it was in the original; I owe a great deal to his sympathetic understanding. My sincere thanks are also due to Mrs I. Loeb-Müller, who read the page proofs and prepared an intelligent index, and to Mr John Taylor, Dr Herbert Spencer and Miss Charlotte Burri of Lund Humphries for their diligence, patience and constant assistance.

Unless otherwise stated, the photographs reproduced in this book are my own. But I am very grateful to those who have placed their photographic material at my disposal, particularly Dr Bruno Carl, Mr Andreas Hauser and the Library of the R.I.B.A. I am also indebted to the Deutscher Kunstverlag (publishers of *Karl Friedrich Schinkel: Lebenswerk*), the Staatliche Museen zu Berlin and Professor Willy Weyres for allowing me to reproduce drawings for which they hold the copyright.

*George L. Hersey, *High Victorian Gothic: a Study in Associationism* (The Johns Hopkins Studies in Nineteenth-Century Architecture), (Baltimore and London, 1972).
Robert Macleod, *Style and Society: Architectural Ideology in Britain, 1835–1914* (London, 1971).
Stefan Muthesius, *The High Victorian Movement in Architecture: 1850–1870* (London and Boston, 1972).
Gillian Naylor, *The Arts and Crafts Movement: a Study of its Sources, Ideals and Influences on Design Theory* (London, 1971).
Paul Thompson, *William Butterfield* (London and Cambridge [Mass.], 1971).
For bibliography see also Gertrud Klevinghaus, *Die Vollendung des Kölner Doms im Spiegel deutscher Publikationen von 1800 bis 1842* (Saarland thesis, 1971; printed in Cologne, n.d.).

Preface

When Eastlake wrote his *History of the Gothic Revival* it evidently did not occur to him that he needed to specify that he was writing of England alone or to do anything to relate the English movement to contemporary developments on the Continent. There was then, as there has been since, nothing exceptional in this insularity. Though a number of our Victorian architects – Street pre-eminently – were distinguished scholars of the mediaeval architecture of Europe, though Ruskin took so many of his examples from France and Italy, the actual progress of the Revival has always been seen in this country as something peculiarly English: we perhaps admit some early influence from Rousseau and even the German Romantic philosophers, but we stress that English architects won the competitions at Hamburg and Lille and were therefore internationally recognized as understanding their Gothic better than their French and German coevals.

We have not been alone, Dr Germann shows, in such habits of mind. In Germany in the late eighteenth and early nineteenth centuries it seems to have been widely believed that Gothic architecture (by then freed from pejorative associations) was actually a German invention, and even that *all* the great Gothic cathedrals had been built by German masons. So cultivated and knowledgeable a traveller as Didron thought the English revival hampered by a severe shortage of mediaeval churches in England. And so the Gothic Revival did develop in notably different national ways. On the whole the English archaeologists, led by Carter, Rickman and Willis, got going earlier, and then the influence of Pugin and the ecclesiologists became decisive, fusing the architectural and liturgical revivals, so that the first cannot be understood without the second. Like Pugin, Chateaubriand had a vision of Gothic as the architecture of a past golden age, but he lacked any appreciation of its formal qualities; and Viollet-le-Duc, unquestionably the leading French theorist of the Revival, had no theological impulses – was indeed an atheist – and stressed only the constructivist virtues of mediaeval buildings: 'The most important of all qualities in architecture . . . is that it should not conceal any needs, any necessities; on the contrary, it should display them, profit from them in the happiest manner possible, and deck them out with a beautiful form . . . Our conclusion is quite simply that French thirteenth-century architecture, which was fashioned from our materials and in our climate to suit our character, which is beautiful, often formally admirable, and not very costly, should be the only form of architecture studied in France; and it should be approached under three different headings: construction, art, and economy.' This, though obviously sharing important principles with Pugin, is not very like him in spirit; and the nationalist emphasis is striking.

Carl Schnaase on the other hand, writing in the *Annales archéologiques* in 1851, told his French readers that 'our German taste and attitudes differ somewhat from yours . . . We do not believe that the restoration of Gothic art pure and simple is possible, or even desirable. We would prefer, so to speak, to revive the ideas evolved in the Middle Ages; to vivify and christianize (if we may be allowed to use such expressions) our national taste by study and, within certain limits, by the imitation of mediaeval art. We hope that, as a result, a style will emerge that will be partly new and partly a mediaeval revival.' Yet the great effort of German Gothic art in the nineteenth century – perhaps the greatest single achievement of the Gothic Revival anywhere – was the completion of Cologne Cathedral; and the motives which prompted this formed a remarkable mélange and were certainly as much nationalistic as anything else.

Yet, as Dr Germann observes, 'there was a lively interaction between the ecclesiologists, the *archéologues* and the *Neugotiker* which transcended national borders', and its aim was to undermine the classically dominated or inclined academies and institutes. Certainly we have at best a partial, and probably a seriously misleading, impression of our own Gothic Revival if we think only in terms of England. The problem of style, which was so much at the heart of the choice of particular Gothic modes and forms, was an international one; but it was not only in the nineteenth century that people occupied themselves with trying to settle what is meant by style. So Dr Germann conducts a semantic enquiry into the usage of both 'style' and 'Gothic'. In trying to understand so historically-minded a movement as the Gothic Revival, the historical examination in depth is essential; and we now have here the basic materials for examining the prehistory of the Revival as well as its theoretical framework and background, for which of course the literary evidence, likewise examined by Dr Germann, is equally important.

The time seems to be approaching when a comprehensive critical history of the Gothic Revival will be possible: it is a major part of Dr Germann's achievement to demonstrate that such a work cannot be carried out within national boundaries even if we limit ourselves to revivalism in one country; for what does he know of England who only England knows?

Andor Gomme

I The Gothic in Vitruvianism

1 The Babel of Styles

The nineteenth century suffered more than any other, not only from a confusion of architectural styles, but also from a lack of understanding as to what actually constituted architectural style. At first people were quite unconcerned by this state of affairs. In 1802 for example, one year before he died, James Malton commended his services to the public in the following words:
'From his acquaintance with the various styles of architecture, Mr Malton will alter any sound old building, to any particular style desired, that it may be capable of being converted to; or he will extend any structure, strictly keeping, if desired, to the original style of construction.'[1]

But by 1830 the multiplicity of styles culled from different historical periods was felt to pose a definite threat. Karl Friedrich Schinkel (1781–1841) wrote at the time:
'Every major period has established its own architectural style, so why do we not try to establish a style for ours?
'Why should we always build in the style of another period? Whilst it is commendable that we should be able to grasp the essence and purity of each and every style – it is still more commendable to conceive a pure and comprehensive style which will not clash with the best qualities of any other style . . .
'Seen in these terms, the new style will not diverge from earlier or existing styles to the point of becoming a phantasm that people will find difficult to accept and understand; on the contrary, many will not even notice its novelty, for its principal virtue will derive, above all, from the consistent application of a number of discoveries made in the course of time, which heretofore it has not been possible to integrate into an artistic whole.'[2]

James Savage (1779–1852), who designed St Luke's, Chelsea (London) and was therefore the first architect to build a stone vault in a Gothic Revival church (1820–4), expressed himself in similar terms in the course of the general debate on the design of the new Houses of Parliament:
'It is said that every thing is already invented; that the age of invention is passed; and that all that art can now do, is to select and copy. But this is not the way in which any of the excellences which we admire has been produced, nor is the principle or practice admitted in other arts, or in literature. The degraded state of modern architecture is to be mainly

1 James Malton, *A Collection of Designs for Rural Retreats, as Villas, Principally in the Gothic and Castle Styles of Architecture . . .* (London, n.d. [1802]), advertisement following the title-page.

2 Karl Friedrich Schinkel, *Briefe, Tagebücher, Gedanken*, ausgewählt, eingeleitet und erläutert von Hans Mackowsky (Berlin, 1922), p.194: 'Warum sollen wir immer nur nach dem Styl einer anderen Zeit bauen? Ist das ein Verdienst, die Reinheit jedes Styls aufzufassen – so ist es ein noch grösseres, einen reinen Styl im allgemeinen zu erdenken, der dem Besten, was in jedem andern geleistet ist, nicht widerspricht . . .
'Dieser neue Styl wird desshalb nicht so aus allem Vorhandenen und Früheren heraustreten, dass er ein Phantasma ist, welches sich schwer allen aufdringen und verständlich werden würde, im Gegentheil, mancher wird kaum das neue darin bemerken, dessen grösstes Verdienst mehr in der consequenten Anwendung einer Menge im Zeitlaufe gemachter Erfindungen werden wird, die früherhin nicht kunstgemäss vereinigt werden konnten.' – For the dating of this statement see Goerd Peschken, 'Schinkels nachgelassene Fragmente eines Architektonischen Lehrbuches' in *Bonner Jahrbücher des Rheinischen Landesmuseums in Bonn (im Landschaftsverband Rheinland) und des Vereins für Altertumsfreunde im Rheinland*, CLXVI (1966), pp.293–315, esp. pp.293–4.

28, 29

attributed to this fatal opinion; and we see the consequence of tamely copying and repeating forms, which, so copied, are destitute of that living principle which first prompted them, and which still gives them their charm.'[3]

Friedrich Eisenlohr (1805–55), who was famous in his own day for the railway stations which he built for the Badische Eisenbahnen in the timbered style of rural Germany, sought a solution to this problem in 'spiritual forces':

'Harmony (without loss of genuine variety) can also be achieved in the field of modern architecture, provided our architects are prepared to concern themselves not only with the implications of living, climate, building materials, etc., but also with the higher spiritual forces, which are rooted in the religious life and in the life of the people, thus ensuring the continuous, natural and abundant growth of our art in this fertile soil. It is only by this act of surrender to the absolute forces that exist outside of ourselves . . . that we can achieve *true expression* and an integrated art form.'[4]

Eisenlohr dated what he regarded as the entirely pernicious onset of stylistic pluralism to *c.*1820. In this he differed from James Fergusson, the architectural critic (1808–86), who considered that this era of masquerade and deception had set in with the Renaissance.[5] The following statement by this rather inconsistent author testifies to his dislike of imitation:

'One great cause of this confusion which has arisen in applying principles of criticism, or in defining architecture, is to be found in persons applying to the constructive art of architecture principles derived from the imitative arts of painting or sculpture, whilst in fact no two things could in reality be more essentially different.'[6]

And yet the only solution that Fergusson himself could find to the problem posed by the 'babel of styles' was imitation. He recommended that the architecture of the Renaissance should be adopted as a universal model.[7]

Hermann Muthesius (1861–1927), the leading German expert on English architecture at the turn of the century and an opponent of 'Stilarchitektur', regarded the nineteenth century as the 'unartistic century'. But in his early period even he was unable to free himself from the popular view of architecture as a discipline composed of different genre styles. In fact, he considered that this view constituted a definite advance:

'And so today we even seek to characterize individual buildings by emphasizing the particular architectural category to which they belong. For example, in a town hall we try to express a civic quality, in a castle a majestic quality and in a country house a homely, residential quality.'[8]

It was not until some fifteen years later, in 1917, that Muthesius was able to smile both at 'Stilarchitektur' and at his own earlier attitude towards it:

'Today only the general public is obsessed with style. The architect is no longer concerned with the application of historical, foreign or so-called

3 James Savage, *Observations on Style in Architecture, with Suggestions on the Best Mode of Procuring Designs for Public Buildings* . . . London 1836, p. 27.

4 F[riedrich] Eisenlohr, *Ausgeführte oder zur Ausführung bestimmte Entwürfe...* (Karlsruhe, n.d. [1852–9]), sect. 2: 'Eine harmonische Einheit (ohne Beeinträchtigung einer wahren Mannigfaltigkeit) kann auch heutzutage in unserer Gesammtbaukunst errungen werden, wenn sie nicht nur den Einwirkungen der realen Gründe und Forderungen, die in dem wirklichen Leben, dem Klima, dem Baumaterial u.s.w. liegen, sondern auch den höheren idealen geistigen Triebkräften, welche in dem Leben aus Gott, sowie in der Volksthümlichkeit wurzeln, sich unbedingt hingiebt, so dass . . . ein flüssiges naturgemässes Werden aus dem immer reichen Quell solchen Naturgrundes unserer Kunst in Hülle und Fülle wie von selbst sich ergebe. Nur durch solche unbedingte Hingabe an das ausser uns Feststehende und Gegebene kann . . . *Wahrheit des Ausdrucks* und Einklang unserer Kunstformen gewonnen werden.'

5 James Fergusson, *The Illustrated Handbook of Architecture* . . . , 2 vols. (with consecutive page numbers), (London, 1855), I, pp. xxvi, lii and liii.

6 *Ibid.*, p. xxix.

7 *Ibid.*, pp. xxv and lvi.

8 Hermann Muthesius, *Stilarchitektur und Baukunst: Wandlungen der Architektur im XIX. Jahrhundert und ihr heutiger Standpunkt* (Jena, n.d. [1902]), p.39: 'So suchen wir heute, schon was die einzelnen Gebäudegattungen anbetrifft, die besondere Bestimmung durch die architektonische Gattung zu charakterisieren, indem wir z.B. in einem Rathaus etwas Bürgerliches, in einem Fürstenschloss etwas Majestätisches, in einem Landhause etwas Wohnliches und Trautes auszudrücken versuchen.'

"modern" styles. All he wants to do, apart from satisfying functional requirements, is to produce good architecture.'[9]

Eugène-Emmanuel Viollet-le-Duc (1814–79), who rebelled against the traditions of the Ecole des Beaux-Arts and tried in vain to reform it, was no more able to dissociate himself from the past than his traditionalist adversaries:

'To all those who say to us today "Choose a new art, an art of our time" we would reply, at the end of this [third] *Entretien* . . . "Let us not be the sons of our fathers. Let us refuse to believe that this century of doubt exists at all, that all our traditions have been undermined by this doubt, and all our systems overthrown . . . Above all, let us try to forget everything that was accomplished before our time. Then we will have a new art, and we will have done something, the like of which has never been seen before; for although it is difficult for man to learn, it is much more difficult for him to forget." '[10]

Tired of the great multiplicity of styles which had emerged and of the lack of precision with which the word 'style' was employed, Viollet-le-Duc began to use it in an absolute sense at a later stage in his career, and tried to set up new standards. In 1881, two years after Viollet-le-Duc's death, George Edmund Street (1824–81) quoted the following sentences from the *Entretiens* in a lecture at the Royal Academy:

'Style resides in nobility of form; it is one of the essential elements of beauty, although it does not in itself constitute beauty. Civilization enervates those human instincts by which man is moved to invest style in his works of art, but it does not destroy them. Those instincts operate in us in spite of ourselves.'[11]

But in the final analysis Viollet-le-Duc was unable to decide between this modern attitude and the traditional view, in which the nineteenth century was depicted as the one historical period in which man had fallen from grace:

'In primitive times *style* imposed itself on the artist; today the artist has to rediscover style.'[12]

2 The Word 'Style' in Italian

It is only in architecture that the concept of 'style' has such an iridescent quality, and it is only in architecture that this concept formed the focal point of theoretical discussion throughout the nineteenth century. Consequently, I now propose to carry out a semantic enquiry – the first of its kind in the field of architectural theory – in order to unravel the confusion which arose as a result of the continuous shifts of meaning to which this concept was subjected. In this enquiry, which begins with developments that took place long before the nineteenth century, I shall be dealing, above all, with the concept of 'Gothic style'.

As far as we know Filarete (Antonio Averlino; *c.*1400–69) was the first theorist to apply the word 'style' to the fine arts. In *c.*1460, when he published his treatise, he employed this word, whose use had previously

9 Hermann Muthesius, *Wie baue ich mein Haus?* (Munich, 1917), p.111: 'Nur das Publikum ist heute noch stilwütig. Was der Architekt, abgesehen von der Erfüllung des Bedürfnisses, erstrebt, ist nicht, einen historischen, einen ausländischen oder etwa den sogenannten "modernen" Stil anzuwenden, sondern gute Architektur zu machen.'

10 [Eugène-Emmanuel] Viollet-le-Duc, *Entretiens sur l'architecture*, 2 vols. of text (Paris, [1858–]1863 and 1872) and 2 vols. of plates (Paris, 1863–4); I, p.99: 'En finissant cet *Entretien* [the third discourse], à tous ceux qui nous disent aujourd'hui: "Prenez un art neuf qui soit de notre temps", nous répondrons: ". . . Faites que nous ne soyons pas les fils de nos aïeux. Faites que le siècle de doute n'existe pas, que toutes les traditions n'aient pas été sapées par ce doute, tous les systèmes renversés . . . Faites, enfin, que nous puissions oublier tout ce qui s'est fait avant nous. Alors nous aurons un art neuf, et nous aurons fait ce qui ne s'est jamais vu: car s'il est difficile à l'homme d'apprendre, il lui est bien plus difficile d'oublier".' – An English translation was published in 1877–81 and 1960.

11 *Ibid.* (French edition), I, p.180: 'Le style réside dans la distinction de la forme, il est un des éléments essentiels de la beauté, mais ne constitue pas la beauté à lui seul. La civilisation émousse les instincts de l'homme qui portent à mettre du style dans ces œuvres d'art, mais elle ne les détruit pas. Ces instincts agissent malgré nous.' – Arthur Edmund Street, *Memoir of George Edmund Street, R.A. 1824–1881* (London, 1888), p.343.

12 Viollet-le-Duc, *Entretiens sur l'architecture*, I (1863), p.179: 'Aux époques primitives, le *style* s'impose à l'artiste; aujourd'hui, c'est à l'artiste à retrouver style.'

13 Antonio Averlino, *Filarete's Treatise on Architecture, Being the Treatise by Antonio di Piero Averlino, Known as Filarete,* translated with an Introduction and Notes by John R. Spencer, 2 vols. (translation and facsimile), (New Haven and London, 1968), I, p.12 (corresponding to Book I, fol. 5v.): 'E così d'ogni facultà si conosce lo stile di ciascheduno.' – See also Peter Tigler, *Die Architekturtheorie des Filarete* . . . (Berlin, 1963), p.82.

14 Marco Treves, '"Maniera", the History of a Word' in *Marsyas, a Publication by the Students of the Institute of Fine Arts, New York University,* I (1942), pp.69–88. – Jan Białostocki, 'Das Modusproblem in den bildenden Künsten: zur Vorgeschichte und zum Nachleben des "Modusbriefes" von Nicolas Poussin' in *Zeitschrift für Kunstgeschichte,* XXIV (1961), pp.128–41; reprinted in J. B., *Stil und Ikonographie: Studien zur Kunstwissenschaft* (Dresden, n.d. [1966]), pp. 9–26, see esp. p.26, note 8.

15 E[vert] F. van der Grinten, *Enquiries into the History of Art-Historical Functions and Terms up to 1850* (Diss. Lett. Amsterdam, 1952; printed in Delft, n.d.; published under slightly different title in Amsterdam, 1952), p.12. – Heinrich Klotz, *Der Ostbau der Stiftskirche zu Wimpfen* . . . (n.p. [Munich and Berlin], 1967, pp.17–18. – E[vert] F. van der Grinten, *Elements of Art Historiography in Mediaeval Texts: an Analytic Study* (The Hague, 1969).

16 Erwin Panofsky, *Early Netherlandish Painting: Its Origins and Character,* 2 vols. (text and plates), (Cambridge [Mass.], 1953), I, p.135 and p.412, note 2.

17 Wilhelm Waetzold, 'Der Begriff des Barbarischen' in *Kunst und Künstler,* XIII (1915), pp.437–41. – Paul Frankl, *The Gothic: Literary Sources and Interpretations through Eight Centuries* (Princeton, 1960), pp.237–315.

18 Vitruvius, *De Architectura, Nachdruck der kommentierten ersten italienischen Ausgabe von Cesare Cesariano (Como, 1521),* with an Introduction and Index by Carol Herselle Krinsky . . . (Munich, 1969), Book I, fol. XVr. and v. – Cesariano described the Cathedral of Milan as being built 'Germanico more a trigono ac pariquadrato' and 'secundum Germanicam symmetriam'.

19 Erwin Panofsky, 'Das erste Blatt aus dem "Libro" Giorgio Vasaris: eine Studie über die Beurteilung der Gotik in der italienischen Renaissance, mit einem

been restricted to the sphere of rhetoric, as a synonym for 'maniera' (i.e. mode of handling):

'And in every discipline one is known by his style.'[13]

In sculpture and painting the word 'style' was not universally adopted until 'maniera' had acquired its present pejorative sense following the development of Mannerism. It then provided a neutral concept capable of denoting formal differences of every kind.[14]

But in the field of architectural theory things were very different.

In mediaeval architecture regional and historical characteristics were always far more prominent than the personal features incorporated into their buildings by individual architects. This is clearly demonstrated by the laconic 'opere romano', 'opere gotico' and 'opere francigeno' and by the occasional presence in mediaeval buildings of stylistic features which strike us as essentially modern.[15] The fifteenth-century Netherlandish artists distinguished quite specifically between Romanesque and Gothic buildings, identifying them iconographically with the old and the new covenants, with the synagogue and the church.[16]

In the fifteenth century, the Gothic and the Renaissance, the mediaeval theory of design and the Vitruvian theory of proportions, clashed head-on. Qualities which were still accepted unquestioningly north of the Alps as an integral part of the European tradition were already being decried in the south as ugly, barbaric and – since the Goths were held responsible for the destruction of the Roman Empire – Gothic.[17] In theory it was a relatively simple matter to reconcile mediaeval design and Vitruvian proportions. In his edition of Vitruvius's treatise, which appeared in Como in 1521, Cesare Cesariano (1483–1543) demonstrated the Vitruvian theory by reference to a cross-section of the original plans for Milan Cathedral, which he, as an expert, was allowed to consult for this purpose. His drawings provide an early record of Gothic triangulation.[18]

The completion of Gothic buildings, on the other hand, proved far from simple. The most famous example was furnished by the Church of San Petronio in Bologna.[19] Work began on this church in 1390 but came to a halt in 1440 after a temporary roof had been erected. From 1521 to 1600 drawings and written reports were commissioned by the church authorities in an attempt to provide a permanent roof and complete the principal façade. Numerous architects submitted designs for the façade including such famous men as Baldassare Peruzzi (1481–1536), Giulio Romano (1492–1546), Giacomo Barozzi da Vignola (1507–73) and Andrea Palladio (1508–80). The structural details of their designs, which were partly Gothic and partly Classical, need not concern us. But what does concern us is the fact that the word 'style' was first applied to architecture in connexion with the San Petronio project in 1578. Commenting on Palladio's design for a portico façade, which reflected this architect's predilection for Roman temples, Camillo Bolognino, a contemporary *dilettante,* argued that in such cases it would be better to follow the 'style' of modern Christian churches than that of heathen temples ('seguir più tosto il stilo delle fabriche moderne').[20]

Exkurs über zwei Fassadenprojekte Domenico Beccafumis' in *Städeljahrbuch*, VI (1930), pp.25–72; an English version of this article has appeared in E. P., *Meaning in the Visual Arts . . .* (Garden City New York, 1955), pp.169–235. – Richard Bernheimer, 'Gothic Survival and Gothic Revival in Bologna' in *Art Bulletin*, XXXVI (1954), pp.263–84. – Frankl, *The Gothic* (1960), pp.299–314. – James S[loss] Ackerman, 'Palladio's Lost Portico Project for San Petronio in Bologna' in *Essays in the History of Architecture Presented to Rudolf Wittkower . . .* (n.p. [New York], 1967), pp.110–15. – Wolfgang Götz, 'Historismus: ein Versuch zur Definition des Begriffes' in *Zeitschrift des Deutschen Vereins für Kunstwissenschaft*, XXIV (1970), pp. 196–212. – John Harris, 'Three unrecorded Palladio Designs from Inigo Jones' Collection' in *Burlington Magazine*, January 1971, pp.34–7.

20 Giovanni Gaye, *Carteggio inedito d'artisti, de' secoli XIV., XV., XVI., pubblicato ed illustrato con documenti pure inediti* dal Dott. G. G. con fac-simile, 3 vols. (Florence, 1839/40); facsimile edition (Turin, 1968), III: *1501–1672*, p.411. – Bolognino made a similar comment in the following year: 'quel stilo de' tempii antiqui'; see *ibid.*, p.426.

21 *Ibid.*, p.491.

22 *Ibid.*, p.492: 'per la perpetuità et per lo stile usato in simile fabriche, et per seguire anco la intentione dei primi architetti . . . Questa volta dovea essere dordine Tedesco et di arte composito, per non partorire una esorbitanza di ponere un capello Italiano sopra un habito Tedesco, essendo tutte l'altre sue volte di composito.' – 'Composito' = pointed?

23 *Ibid.*, p.493.

24 *Ibid.*, pp.496–7: 'Et continuando in questa confusione li Germani o pur li Gotti, come più piace a qualqu'uno, conservando una certa imitatione delle cose vedute a Roma, e massimamente dell'ordine Corinthio, mescolando il Greco col suo, fecero una terza specie d'architettura a suo modo, et la introdussero in Italia, che è questa apunto di S. Petronio, la qual si può dir più tosto architettura abusata che regolata della qualle trattano adesso queste oppinioni, fondandosi sopra un certo Cesariano, comentatore di Vitruvio, che parla de' triangoli . . . Et perchè noi non havemo ch'io sapia, regola determinata di questo ordine Tedesco, serà necessario nelle regole naturale communi regolare questa opera Tedesca con li precetti di Vitruvio, che ne ha scritto fondatissimamente.'

Francesco Terribilia (d.1603), who was put in charge of the construction work on the San Petronio site in 1568, described the church in 1589 as 'di architettura chiamata Tedesca, imitante l'ordine Corinthio' (so-called German architecture, which imitates the Corinthian order).[21] He favoured a vaulted roof:
'on account of continuity, on account of the style used in such buildings, and also on account of the intention pursued by the original architects, which we should also pursue . . . This vault should be executed in the German order and in a Composite form, so as to avoid the unwarranted extravagance of wearing an Italian hat with a German dress, for all the other vaults are Composite.'[22]

Although Terribilia knew 'molte altre chiese di buona architettura tedesca' (many other churches [executed] in good German architecture),[23] he none the less regarded the history of architecture in the period following the migration of peoples in much the same light as Giorgio Vasari (1511–74):
'And in this extremely confused state of affairs the Germans, or the Goths as some people like to call them, continued to a certain extent to imitate the things that they had seen in Rome, especially the Corinthian order. They mixed Greek characteristics with their own and so, in their own way, created a third kind of architecture and introduced this into Italy; it is the kind found in San Petronio, one which ought really to be designated as unorganized rather than organized, although the followers of a certain Cesariano, a commentator on Vitruvius, claim to have discovered its principles in triangles . . . But since, to the best of my knowledge, we have no specific rules for the German order, we shall have to organize this German work within the framework of our natural and universal rules according to the guide-lines laid down by Vitruvius, who has written at great length on this matter.'[24]

In his approach to the completion of San Petronio, Terribilia showed himself to be a true disciple of Vitruvius. Perhaps he was seduced by the crocket capital, perhaps he was misled by the slender proportions. But, at all events, he regarded the Gothic architecture of this church as a degenerate and unorganized derivative of the Corinthian order. He wavered between the partly accurate traditional version, according to which the Germans had introduced this type of architecture into Italy, and the later version based on an historical reconstruction, which ascribed this act to the Goths. He also wavered in his critical assessment, for on one occasion he referred to the Gothic as 'good German architecture', whilst on another occasion, as we have just seen, he complained that it was 'unorganized rather than organized'. In the end he recommended that San Petronio should be completed in a conformist style.

In the passages quoted above we find that, with the exception of 'genere' and 'maniera', Terribilia uses all the words and phrases which are related to, or synonymous with, 'stile'. Thus we find 'architettura', which is self-explanatory; 'ordine', which is employed for both the German and the Corinthian forms; 'arte', which appears in juxtaposition to 'composito'; 'specie d'architettura', which Terribilia evidently considered to be so inappropriate as a description of a building that he immediately qualified it by the phrase 'a sua modo'; and 'opera', which in this particular context could refer either to the incomplete *building* of San Petronio or to *the way in which it was built*.

'Stile' is linked with 'usato', which means that it was regarded as something that could be applied, something the architect had at his disposal. But both in Terribilia's report and in the reports submitted by other architects the phrase 'ordine Tedesco' is used to express what we today would call the 'Gothic style'.

It was only in the course of the sixteenth century that the word 'ordine' superseded Vitruvius's 'genere' and became the standard expression for classical columns (Ionic, Doric, Corinthian). Leon Battista Alberti (1404–72), who regarded the Classical orders as the most noble form of architectural ornamentation, used the word 'columnatio' when he wished to describe a column together with its entablature.[25] He also had occasional recourse to phrases such as 'opus doricum' and 'opus ionicum', but on such occasions the word 'opus' referred to the building and not the architectural style.[26]

Sebastiano Serlio (1475–1554) was the first writer to try to codify the five orders. In Book IV of his *Regole generali di architettura*, which appeared in 1537, he printed the various synonyms side by side in the chapter headings,[27] and on the title page he referred to the 'cinque maniere de gliedifici'. Book IV was intended to facilitate the 'cognition de le differenti maniere de gliedificij, et de i loro ornamenti',[28] while Book V was meant to deal with 'i molti modi de i tempii dessignati in diverse forme, cio è rotonda, quadrata, di sei faccie, d'otto faccie, ovale, in croce' (the various forms and shapes of the temples, namely circular, quadratic, hexagonal, octagonal, oval and cruciform).[29] But although Book IV was supposed to have been based on the 'meno ornato ordine; cio è dal Thoschano', Serlio later referred to the Tuscan order as 'l'opera Thoscana' and contrasted it with the 'maniera Corinthia'.[30] The chapters bear the following titles: 'De l'opera Thoscana et de i suoi ornamenti', 'De l'ordine Dorico', 'De l'ordine Ionico, et de i suoi ornamenti', 'Di L'ordine Corinthio, et de gliornamenti suoi' and 'De l'opera Composita'.[31] But Serlio's 'ordine' corresponds not only to Alberti's 'columnatio' (columns plus entablature), but also to his 'concinnitas' (harmony).[32] In a statement which anticipated the demands made by Jacques-François Blondel (1705–74), and by various nineteenth-century writers, Serlio argued that architects should be given ultimate control over their colleagues in the other branches of art, even over painters, for he feared that, otherwise, 'l'ordine de le Architetture' might be undermined.[33]

In this context the word 'ordine' acquires an authoritative significance which makes it difficult to understand how the phrase 'ordine Tedesco', which was quite common in the sixteenth century, could have been used in a pejorative sense. Presumably, the situation will have been similar to that obtaining around 1800 in respect of the

25 Leon Battista Alberti, *L'Architettura* (*De re aedificatoria*), testo latino e traduzione a cura di Giovanni Orlandi, introduzione e note di Paolo Portoghesi . . . , 2 vols. (with consecutive page numbers), (Milan, 1966), II, pp.521, 563 and 599.

26 *Ibid.*, pp.565 and 605.

27 [Sebastiano Serlio,] *Regole generali di architettura sopra le cinque maniere de gliedifici, cioè, Thoscano, Dorico, Ionico, Corinthio, et Composito, con gliessempi dell'antiquità, che, per la magior parte, concordano con la dottrina di Vitruvio* (Venice, 1537). – 'Libro quarto' appears as the running head.

28 *Ibid.*, fol. Vr.

29 *Ibid.*

30 *Ibid.*

31 *Ibid.*, fols. VIv., XIXr., XXXVIr., XLVIIv., and LXIv.

32 Alberti, *L'Architettura* (1966), II, p.447 etc. – Rudolf Wittkower, *Architectural Principles in the Age of Humanism* . . . (London, 1949). – The latest edition of Wittkower is the German translation by George Lesser (Munich, 1969). – It is a point worth noting that Wittkower does not deal with the architectural terminology of the Renaissance.

33 Serlio, *Regole* (1537), fol. LXIXv.

34 Filippo Baldinucci, *Vocabolario Toscano dell'arte del disegno* . . . (Florence, 1681), p.113: 'Dicesi quel modo di lauorare tenuto nel tempo de' Goti, di maniera Tedesca, di proporzione in niuna cosa simile a' cinque buoni Ordini d'Architettura antichi; ma di fazzione in tutto barbara, con sottilissime colonne, e smisuratamente lunghe, auuolte, e in più modi snervate, e poste l'vna sopra l'altra, con vn'infinità di piccoli tabernacoli, e piramidi, risalti, rotture, mensoline, fogliame, animali, e viticci, ponendo sempre cosa sopra cosa, senza alcuna regola, ordine, e misura, che veder si possa con gusto.'

35 Filippo Baldinucci, *Vita del Cavaliere Gio[vanni] Lorenzo Bernino, scultore, architetto e pittore* (Florence, 1682), p.81: 'Seguitando il proprio capriccio, talvolta uscì tanto di regola, che s'accostò alla Gottica maniera.' – See also Filippo Baldinucci, *Vita des Gio. Lorenzo Bernini*, mit Übersetzung und Kommentar von Alois Riegl, aus seinem Nachlass hrsg. von Arthur Burda und Oskar Pollak (Vienna, 1912), p.247.

36 Serlio, *Regole* (1537), fol. Vr and v. – Erik Forssman, *Dorisch, jonisch, korinthisch: Studien über den Gebrauch der Säulenordnungen in der Architektur des 16.–18. Jahrhunderts* . . . (Stockholm, Gothenburg and Uppsala, 1961).

37 Vitruv[ius], *Zehn Bücher über Architektur*, übersetzt und mit Anmerkungen versehen von Curt Fensterbusch (i.e. annotated bilingual edition), (Darmstadt, 1964), pp.144 and 146 (= Book III, Chap. III). – 'L'opera rustica' in Serlio, *Regole* (1537), fol. Vv.

38 Vitruv, *Zehn Bücher* (1964), pp.166, 168, 170, 172, and 174 (= Book IV, Chap. I).

39 Andrea Palladio, *I Quattro libri dell'architettura* . . . (Venice, 1570; facsimile editions Milan, 1945 and 1951), Book I, p.44.

40 Guarino Guarini, *Architettura civile: opera postuma dedicata a Sua Sacra Reale Maestà* [edited by Bernardo Vittone] (Turin, 1737), p.83. – Guarino Guarini, *Architettura civile*, introduzione di Nino Carboneri, note e appendice a cura di Bianca La Greca . . . (Milan, 1968), p.127: 'L'Architettura Romana prima spiacque ai Goti, e l'Architettura Gotica a noi stessi dispiace.' – See also Paolo Marconi, 'Guarino Guarini ed il Gotico' in *Guarino Guarini e l'internazionalità del Barocco: Atti del Convegno internazionale promosso dell'Academia delle Scienze di Torino, 30. settembre–5. ottobre 1968*, 2 vols. (Turin, 1970), I, pp.613–35.

words 'style' and 'taste', for at that time it was possible to negate the normally positive force of these expressions by the mere addition of an adjective.

The ambiguity of the word 'ordine' still created difficulties for Filippo Baldinucci (1624–96). In his *Vocabolario* of 1681 he defined the 'Ordine Gottico' in the following terms: '. . . the working method in vogue under the Goths, the German manner and a kind of proportion which has nothing in common with the five good orders of Antique architecture; on the contrary, it is a completely barbaric fashion involving excessively slender, elongated, distorted and – in every sense of the word – enervated columns, imposed one on top of the other and cluttered with small tabernacles, pyramids, projections, disruptions, little consoles, crockets, animal carvings and tendrils, all one on top of the other, with no order, no rule, no proportion and no taste.'[34]

For Baldinucci the Gothic was an order without order. True, he still used the words 'ordine' and 'maniera' synonymously, but in his day the Gothic was commonly regarded in Italy as the epitome of bad architecture. This was why Baldinucci was able to say of Francesco Borromini: 'In indulging his whims he sometimes departed from the rules to such an extent that he came close to the Gothic manner.'[35]

Not only Serlio, but all those who subscribed to Vitruvius's architectural theory in the period up to 1800, regarded the Antique orders as generic styles which could be used only in certain clearly defined spheres.[36] In actual fact, most of these disciples subscribed to Vitruvius's doctrine in a somewhat condensed form, for they dispensed with his intercolumniation ratios – the *pycnostyle*, *systyle*, *diastyle*, etc. – and compensated for these by introducing rusticated columns.[37] Vitruvius looked upon the Doric, Ionic and Corinthian orders as 'discoveries' made by the Dorians, Ionians and Corinthians, respectively, in different historical periods. In other words, he regarded them as both regional and historical styles.[38] Vitruvius also described the Tuscan order, whilst his disciples elaborated on the Composite or Latin order,[39] a Roman combination of elements from the Ionic and Corinthian orders, which they were able to observe in Antique monuments. Vitruvius considered that structures *evolved* on a regional or historical basis were part of the architect's stock in trade: they were *available* to him and he used them as and when appropriate. His disciples regarded German or Gothic structures in much the same light: they used them because they were obliged to do so in order to complete Gothic churches in a conformist style. The reasons why the architectural theorists of the Renaissance insisted on 'conformità' need not concern us.

To the extent to which the authoritative architectural theory of the Renaissance developed into an aesthetic based on taste, the decline of Gothic architecture posed a problem, which was expressed in the following aphorism by Guarino Guarini (1624–83) in his *Architettura civile*, which was published posthumously in 1737: 'First the Goths disliked Roman architecture, now we dislike Gothic architecture.'[40]

But Guarini did not let matters rest there. On the contrary, he made

a determined attempt to understand Gothic architecture, which appears to have fascinated him, and devoted one entire chapter of his book – 'Dell'Ordine Gotico, e sue proporzioni' – to this subject:
'Although proud of their military prowess and, as a nation, born to destroy rather than build, the Goths gradually grew accustomed to the milder climes of Italy, Spain and France and eventually, not only turned Christian, but also became spiritual and pious, changing from destroyers of temples into liberal and highly gifted builders of churches . . . And yet, to the best of my knowledge, no regulations or proportions have ever been laid down for this architecture; and as we know from old portraits that the people of those times were remarkably elegant, slim and short of stature, they quite naturally found it pleasing to build churches that were very tall in comparison to their width; and that was why they made such very slender pillars, and when they had to be made thicker in order to support an unusually heavy weight, they joined several shafts together in a cluster, so as not to lose the lightness which they loved, and made a sort of compound structure . . . , in which each pillar supported the base of the four sections which make up a rib vault, a type of vault that was much to their liking . . . But to return to the Gothic order, it should be mentioned that there are three kinds of pillars, one of twenty . . . , one of eighteen and one of fifteen modules. The capitals do not normally exceed one module in height and have no volutes, being joined to the circular or octagonal shaft by a chamfer.'[41]

Guarini distinguished between the Goths living at the time of the migration of peoples and the Gothic architects of a later age. He also recognized the common style shared by Gothic sculpture and Gothic architecture, but mistakenly derived the proportions on which this was based from the physical stature of the people living in the Middle Ages. This is not altogether surprising since, as a disciple of Vitruvius, he naturally regarded the proportions of the human form as the true basis of the architectural orders and, for that matter, of the whole of architecture. He then tried to describe these proportions on the basis of the modular principle and correctly assumed that the number of shafts in the clustered piers was determined by the number of sections and ribs in the vaults.

For our present purpose – the development of the concept of 'style' – it is significant that Guarini spoke of 'ordine' when he was dealing exclusively with architecture, but changed to 'style' when he discussed architecture within the framework of the other plastic arts. His view that architecture 'follows the style of other things' presupposes the concept of 'arte del disegno', which appeared almost contemporaneously on the title page of Baldinucci's *Vocabolario*.[42]

In the course of the eighteenth century France assumed the undisputed leadership in the field of architectural theory. Because of their common Latin background the French and Italians embarked on a lively debate, which produced extremely subtle undertones and shifts of meaning in the architectural vocabulary of the times. For this reason I now propose to pursue the development of the concept of 'style'

41 Guarini, *Architettura civile* (1737), pp.133–4 (and 1968 edition, pp.207–10): 'I Goti benchè fierissimi, e gente nata piuttosto a distruggere, che ad edificare, assuefacendosi a poco a poco alle arie più dolci dell'Italia, e della Spagna, e Francia, finalmente divennero non solamente Christiani, ma Religiosi, e pij, e di destruttori de' Tempj si fecero alla fine non solamente liberali, ma anche ingegnosi edificatori . . . Or di quest'Architettura, che si sappia, non sono stati mai dati precetti o assegnate le proporzioni . . . ; e perchè gli uomini di quel tempo avevano per singolare leggiadra il comparire svelti, e minuti, come si vede negli antichi ritratti, così a loro piacque conseguente-mente nelle loro Chiese, che fecero proporzionamente alla larghezza molto elevate; onde seguendo lo stile nelle altre cose fecero eziando le Colonne di somma sveltezza, e quando la necessità portò pel peso eccessivo di farle più grosse per non perdere la loro amata sottilezza n'unirono molte insieme, e ne fecero come un composto . . . , ciascuna delle quali portava un piede de' quattro, che formano la volta a crocciera, della qual maniera di volte molto si dilettarono . . . Ma per ritornare all'ordine Gottico vi sono colonne di tre sorte, alcune sono di 20 moduli . . . , altre di 18, altre di 15. I Capitelli ordinariamente non eccedevano un modulo, ne avevano volute; ma dal quadro con uno smusso discendevano nel tondo, ò ottangolare.'

42 Paul Oskar Kristeller, 'The Modern System of the Arts: a Study in the History of Aesthetics' in *Journal of the History of Ideas*, XII (1951), pp.496–527; XIII (1952), pp.17–46; reprinted in *Ideas in Cultural Perspective*, edited by P[hilip] P[aul] Wiener and A[aron] Noland (New Brunswick [N.J], 1962), pp.145–206. – See also Tigler, *Die Architekturtheorie des Filarete* (1963), pp. 144–6, on 'disegno'.

and of other alternative expressions within the framework of French architectural theory.

3 The Word 'Style' in French

France possesses a cathedral whose development was in many respects similar to that of the Church of San Petronio in Bologna. I refer to the Cathedral of Sainte-Croix in Orleans.

Work on this cathedral began in 1287, but progress was slow. Then, in 1568, the early Romanesque structure and the newer Gothic structure were destroyed by the Huguenots.[43] In 1601, in the presence of Henri IV, the first stone was laid for the reconstruction of the cathedral.[44] A report drawn up in 1611 recommended that the choir pillars should be designed to 'match the architecture of the newly made pillars only on the altar side whilst on the sides facing the aisles they should be made in the same type of architecture as the old pillars which have survived'.[45] Thus, the expert who submitted this report, distinguished between thirteenth- and sixteenth-century Gothic and, like the majority of the experts who reported on San Petronio, he opted for conformity.

Vitruvianism quickly took root in France, where it not only influenced French architecture but also affected French architectural terminology. Recording his impressions of the Cathedral of Sainte-Croix in 1645 the chronicler François Le Maire said that the western sections were 'in the Tuscan fashion and rusticated, quite plain and bare with very few ornaments'.[46] In Orleans, as in Bologna, the Gothic was conceived in terms of the Corinthian order and consequently the pillars of the ambulatory vaults received Corinthian capitals. The vaults themselves were designed by Salomon de Brosse (1571–1626).[47] When they were ready to proceed with the transept the church authorities initiated discussions and asked various architects to submit designs. Those taking part in the competition included the Jesuit architect Etienne Martellange (1569–1641); Théodore Lefebvre the Younger (d.1654); Salomon de Brosse; de Brosse's assistants Jean Androuet du Cerceau the Elder (c.1590–c.1650), Paul de Brosse (c.1592–post 1644) and Charles du Ry (documented 1611–36), who submitted a joint design; Claude Johannet the Younger and Jacques(?) Le Mercier (c.1585–1654). Lefebvre and the four Huguenot architects based their designs on the façades of Saint-Gervais and Saint-Protais in Paris (1616).[48] But the commission went to Martellange.[49] An entry in the official records dated 21 July 1626 stated:
'Father Martellange appeared before the building committee and undertook to produce a design in the Gothic manner for the transept of Ste-Croix.'[50]

In the following year it was reported that Martellange's design conformed 'in every respect to the order of the said church'.[51] The Jesuit himself referred to his project as an 'ouvrage à la moderne' in

43 Georges Chenesseau, *Sainte-Croix d'Orléans, histoire d'une cathédrale gothique réédifiée par les Bourbons, 1599–1829*, I: *L'œuvre artistique*, II: *L'œuvre administrative*, III: *Album* (thèse lettres Paris; Paris, 1921), I, pp. V–VI.

44 *Ibid.*, pp.9–10.

45 *Ibid.*, p.35: 'conformément à l'architecture de ceulx qui sont faict de nouveau, du costé de l'auttel seulement, et du costé des ailles les faire de mesme architecture que les antiens qui sont demourez.'

46 *Ibid.*, pp. VIII and 70.

47 *Ibid.*, pp.62–3. – Collapsed 1904.

48 *Ibid.*, pp.78–83; III, figs.60–4.

49 *Ibid.*, I, pp.74–5.

50 *Ibid.*, p.83: 'Le père Martellange s'est présenté au bureau et a promis de faire ung desseing à la Gotique pour la croisée de Ste-Croix.'

51 *Ibid.*, p.84: 'entièrement l'ordre de lad[ite] Eglise.'

3

52 *Ibid.*, p.88.

53 *Ibid.*, p.95: 'Touchant la grandeur de la grand Rose, laquelle doibt estre à ce que j'ay remarqué en d'aultres Eglises basties à la Moderne et d'ordre gotique, de toutte la hauteur des grands vitraux de la nef, aultant que le diamètre du pignon le permettra.'

54 *Ibid.*, p.128.

55 *Ibid.*, I, pp.128–9; III, fig.74.

56 *Ibid.*, I, p.130.

57 *Ibid.*, pp.234 and 236.

58 *Ibid.*, pp.237 and 241.

59 *Ibid.*, p.343: 'Le peu d'usage que l'on a du gothique demande aussi une singulière application à bien commencer un ouvrage pour le bien finir.'

60 Michael Petzet, *Soufflots Sainte-Geneviève und der französische Kirchenbau des 18. Jahrhunderts* . . . (Berlin, 1961), p.83: 'Sur la réunion du gotique et de l'entique, vostre bonté a bien daigné approuver avec estime l'ouvrage que jé fait pour le portail et tours de l'église d'Orléans.'

61 J[ules] Corblet, 'L'architecture du moyen-âge jugée par les écrivains des deux derniers siècles' in *Revue de l'art chrétien*, III (1859), pp.68–74, 97–103, 201–6, 298–308, 398–405, and 540–4. – E[smond] S[amuel] de Beer, 'Gothic: Origin and Diffusion of the Term; the Idea of Style in Architecture' in *Journal of the Warburg and Courtauld Institutes*, XI (1948), pp.143–62. – R[obin] D. Middleton, 'The Abbé de Cordemoy and the Graeco-Gothic Ideal: a Prelude to Romantic Classicism' in *Journal of the Warburg and Courtauld Institutes*, XXV (1962), pp.278–320; XVI (1963), pp.90–123. – Marie E. Lein, 'Persistance et renouveau du gothique en France avant Chateaubriand' in *Modern Philology*, LVI (1968), pp.121–35; my attention was drawn to this article by Alfred Anderau. – Fritz Nies, 'Die semantische Aufwertung von französisch *gothique* vor Chateaubriand' in *Zeitschrift für romanische Philologie*, LXXXIV (1968), pp.67–88; my attention was drawn to this article by Professor Claude Pichois and Peter Zürrer. – Enrico Castelnuovo, 'Alpi gotiche' in *Rivista storica italiana*, LXXIX (1967), pp.182–94.

62 V. S., *Histoire de l'auguste et vénérable église de Chartres* . . . (Chartres, 1671), p.23; quotation taken from Corblet, 'L'architecture du moyen-âge' (1859), p.404.

order to distinguish its Gothic style from the Classical style of Antiquity and the Classical revival of the Renaissance.[52] When asked to change certain aspects of his rose window in 1630, Martellange replied: 'As far as the size of the great rose window is concerned, judging by what I have seen in other churches built in the modern Gothic order, it should be as high as the clerestory windows in the nave, provided the gable is wide enough to allow this.'[53]

The transepts are symmetrical. The northern one was completed first, followed by the southern one in 1662.[54]

Since the Crown had granted large subsidies for the work on the cathedral ever since the reign of Henri IV, Colbert – who was appointed Surintendant des Arts et Bâtiments in 1664 – held an audit of the building accounts, and as a result of this official intervention François Le Vau (1613?–76), the brother of the more celebrated Louis Le Vau, was asked to submit a design for a contemporary façade.[55] But a memorandum drafted in the following year recommended that 'l'ancien dessin gothique' should be employed.[56]

Then, in 1705, new plans were ratified which provided for a façade 'd'une façon moderne' and not of the 'ordre gothique'. However, in 1707 Louis XIV reversed this decision and opted for the 'ordre gothique'. This alone, he felt, would be 'convenable',[57] and he commanded Robert de Cotte (1656–1735) to produce a series of designs for a Gothic façade.[58] Cotte then entered into correspondence with the architect and builder Guillaume Hénault (d.1725?), and in c.1708 Hénault suggested that a model should be constructed from his plans: 'Since we have so little experience of the Gothic we have to make quite certain that we start the work properly, if we want to finish it properly.'[59]

Hénault and Cotte evidently wanted to introduce certain elements of the contemporary Classical style into the Gothic design for the principal façade of Sainte-Croix. This is quite clear from the letter which Hénault wrote to Cotte in 1718 when he was working on the designs for Notre-Dame-de-Bonne-Nouvelle in Orleans: 'With regard to the integration of the Gothic and the Antique, you have been so kind as to approve the design that I have produced for the façade and towers of the church in Orleans.'[60]

It is now time to review the terminology used by the architects and officials concerned with the reconstruction of the Cathedral of Sainte-Croix in Orleans.

No mention at all is made in the records of the word 'style'. In 1626 we find 'à la Gotique', in 1627 'l'ordre de ladite Eglise', in 1630 as a hendiadys 'à la Moderne et d'ordre gotique', in 1668 'l'ancien dessin gautique', in 1705 'façon moderne' (used to denote seventeenth-century Classical architecture as opposed to the 'ordre gotique'), and in 1708 'le gotique' as a substantive. In 1718 the French contrasted 'le gotique' with 'l'entique' where today they would contrast it with 'l'antiquité'.

From the examples cited in works on the history of semantics it is obvious that the phrase 'ordre gothique' was in common use in the late

63 Charles Perrault, *Mémoire de ma vie*; Claude Perrault, *Voyage à Bordeaux* (*1669*), publié avec une introduction, des notes et un index par Paul Bonnefon (Paris, 1909), p.155; quotation taken from Middleton, 'The Abbé de Cordemoy', I (1962), p.298.

64 C. P., *Les dix livres d'architecture de Vitruve* (Paris, 1684), p.79.

65 J.-F. F., *Les plans et les descriptions de deux des plus belles maisons de campagne de Plinie le consul, avec . . . une Dissertation touchant l'architecture antique & l'architecture gothique* (Paris, 1699), pp. 169–89. – (Later editions Amsterdam, 1706, and London, 1707).

66 Nies, 'Semantische Aufwertung von französisch *gothique* (1968), p.73, note 25.

67 In his *Die Kunstliteratur: ein Handbuch zur Quellenkunde der neueren Kunstgeschichte* (Vienna, 1924) Julius Schlosser Magnino confused the Abbé with Louis Géraud de Cordemoy. This work was subsequently translated into Italian: J. S. M., *La Letteratura artistica, manuale delle fonti della storia dell'arte moderna*, traduzione di Filippo Rossi, terza edizione aggiornata da Otto Kurz . . . (Florence and Vienna, 1964; reprinted 1967); it is this edition that I have used; see *ibid.*, p.652. – [J.-L.] de Cordemoy, *Nouveau traité de toute l'architecture ou L'art de bastir . . .* (Paris, 1706; 2nd ed. Paris, 1714; facsimile edition of the 1714 edition Farnborough, 1966).

68 *Ibid.* (2nd ed.), p.83.

69 *Ibid.*, p.67: 'Je ne parleray point icy des Colonnes à bossages: cela est si gotique, que je ne présume pas qu'on y doive jamais donner.'

70 *Ibid.*, pp.109–10.

71 *Ibid.*, p.110: 'Je veux dire le dégagement & l'apreté des Entrecolonnemens, qui nous plaisent si fort. Par exemple, est-ce que les Eglises de Royaumont, de Longpont & de Sainte Croix d'Orléans ne seroient pas de la derniere beauté, si elles avoient les ornemens de l'ancienne Architecture? Y peut-on entrer, toutes Gothiques qu'elles soient, sans être saisi d'admiration, & sentir en soy-même une secrete joye mêlée de vénération & d'estime, qui nous oblige à leur accorder une entière approbation?'

72 *Ibid.*, p.121: 'qui n'ont nul raport avec l'Ordre Gothique ou Arabesque, qui y régne ou qui la compose.'

seventeenth century. A number of alternative words are also mentioned in these works.[61]

A further source of information is provided by the writings of contemporary authors. Thus, in 1671 Vincent Sablon referred to the 'ordre gothique' which graced the Cathedral of Chartres[62] whilst in 1669 Claude Perrault (1613-88) published an account of a journey to Bordeaux, in which he described rib vaults as one of the characteristic features of the 'ordre gothique'.[63] In his defence of his Louvre Colonnade in 1684 he used the substantive form 'le Gothique'; he also described the Gothic style as a 'genre d'architecture' and the Gothic architects as 'les Gothiques'.[64] In 1699 Jean-François Félibien (1658–1733) published a *Dissertation touchant l'architecture antique et l'architecture gothique*,[65] in which he used the word 'architecture' as an alternative term to the word 'ordre'. During this period the expression 'le goût gothique' was frequently used in the pejorative sense of a barbaric taste.[66]

The state of affairs obtaining at the beginning of the eighteenth century was revealed by the Abbé J.-L. de Cordemoy, who was a great admirer of the technical refinements of Gothic churches, in a treatise which was first published in 1706 and went into a second edition in 1714.[67] At first, like everyone else, Cordemoy used the word 'gothic' in a pejorative sense:[68]
'I do not intend to discuss rusticated columns in this treatise: they are so Gothic that, in my opinion, they should never be employed.'[69]

But he went on to express his admiration for the great height of the buildings in 'Architecture Gothique' and regretted that Michelangelo had not retained 'ce qu'il y a de bon dans le Gotique' when he came to complete St Peter's:[70]
'What I have in mind', he continued, 'is the openness and severity of the intercolumniation, which we find so pleasing. For example, would not the churches of Royaumont [Seine-et-Oise], Longpont [Aisne or Seine-et-Oise] and Sainte-Croix in Orleans be infinitely beautiful if they had the embellishments of Antique architecture? Although they are entirely Gothic, is it possible to enter them without being seized by a sense of admiration and feeling a secret joy mingled with veneration and respect, which leaves us no option but to accord them our full approval?'[71]

The substantive form 'Gotique' denotes the mediaeval style of architecture. The predicate adjective, on the other hand, is used in a pejorative sense at the beginning of the sentence before being finally transformed into a straightforward technical term. Cordemoy regretted that the choir pillars of Notre-Dame in Paris were enclosed by columns which 'bear no relationship to the Gothic or Arabian order which dominates or constitutes the building'.[72]

The use of 'Arabesque' (Arabian) as a synonym for 'Gothique' need not concern us for the present. It will be considered later, in connexion with the theories evolved to explain the origin of the word 'Gothic'. But what does concern us within the present context is the fact that Cordemoy clearly regarded the 'Ordre Gothique' not simply as an arrangement of columns, but as a comprehensive system of architectural forms 'which dominates or constitutes the building'.

Like other theorists Cordemoy used the expression 'le goût Gothique' in a pejorative sense. The architects of the sixteenth and seventeenth centuries, he said, were happy to abandon the 'Gothic taste' and to revert to a style of architecture based on columns.[73] He described mediaeval architects, as did Claude Perrault, as 'les Architectes Gothiques'.[74]

In the appendix to the second edition of his treatise Cordemoy provided a glossary of terms which casts further light on contemporary usage, for glossaries are naturally far more precise than written texts. Unlike Baldinucci, Cordemoy listed the various orders under their names:
'GOTHIC. *Gothic order*: the order in accordance with which our old churches were built . . .'[75]

The Gothic order is not mentioned in the entry on 'Ordres d'Architectures', nor is there an entry for 'Style'.[76]

The modern meaning of 'style' as 'a mode of building, a form of art peculiar to a particular district', did not appear in the *Encyclopédie*. As far as the fine arts were concerned, d'Alembert and Diderot restricted the use of this word to painting, where – by direct analogy with rhetorical style – it denoted a conscious attempt on the part of the painter to give a particular character to his work. We still speak of an 'heroic style' in landscape painting.[77] Jacques-François Blondel (1705–74) then applied the word 'style' in this specialized sense to architecture.[78] He was attracted by a certain analogy 'which must exist between the style of sculptures and the character of architectural orders',[79] and suggested that a building could be given a 'sublime, noble and elevated style' or a 'naïve, simple and true character':[80]
'In a word: the style which we are discussing and which resembles rhetorical style is able to express, in architecture, the sacred genre, the heroic genre or the pastoral genre.'[81]

The interest evinced by Blondel and his contemporaries in architectural theory was prompted almost entirely by comparisons with the other fine arts. But more of this later. Suffice it to say for the present that François-René de Chateaubriand (1768–1848) in his *Génie du Christianisme* of 1802 and Aubin-Louis Millin (1759–1818) in his *Dictionnaire des Beaux-Arts* of 1806 must have been among the first to use the word style to describe the buildings of a particular period. Their stylistic boldness can be judged by the fact that they eschewed the composite phrase 'style gothique'.[82] But it was not until 1821, in a chapter of *Mémoires d'Outre-Tombe* written in that year, that we find the modern distinction between 'ordre' and 'style'. Under Francis I, Chateaubriand observed, 'les ordres grecs se vinrent mêler au style gothique'.[83]

The examples cited above could, of course, be multiplied many times over. But I have purposely avoided reproducing too many paradigms so as not to lose track of the main theme: *Gothic Revival in Europe and*

73 *Ibid.*, p.141.

74 *Ibid.*, p.166.

75 *Ibid.*, p.241: 'GOTHIQUE. *Ordre Gothique*, est cet Ordre, selon lequel nos anciennes Eglises d'à présent, sont bâties . . .'

76 *Ibid.*, pp.254 and 264.

77 *Encyclopédie ou Dictionnaire raisonné des sciences, des arts et des métiers . . .*, publié par . . . [Denis] Diderot et . . . [Jean Le Rond] d'Alembert, XV: *SEU-TCH* (Neuchâtel, 1765), p.556.

78 J[acques]-F[rançois] Blondel, *Cours d'architecture ou Traité de la décoration, distribution & construction des bâtiments, contenant les leçons données en 1750, & les années suivantes, dans son Ecole des Arts . . .*, 6 vols. of text and 3 vols. of plates (Paris 1771–7). – The lectures were rewritten for publication.

79 *Ibid.*, I (1771), p.205: 'qui doit se trouver entre le style de la Sculpture et le caractere de l'ordre.'

80 *Ibid.*, p.373: 'style sublime, noble, élevé' or a 'caractere naïf, simple, vrai.'

81 *Ibid.*, IV (1773), p.lv: 'En un mot, le style dont nous parlons, semblable à celui de l'éloquence, peut parvenir à faire peindre à l'Architecte le genre sacré, le genre héroïque, le genre pastoral.'

82 [François-René de] Chateaubriand, *Œuvres complètes, nouvelle édition . . . , précédée d'une étude littéraire sur Chateaubriand par M. Sainte-Beuve*, II: *Génie du Christianisme* (Paris, 1861), p.290. – A[ubin] L[ouis] Millin, *Dictionnaire des Beaux-Arts*, 3 vols. (Paris, 1806), I, p.71.

83 Quotation taken from the Pléiade edition: [François-René de] Chateaubriand, *Mémoires d'Outre-Tombe*, édition nouvelle établie d'après l'édition originale et les deux dernières copies du texte, avec une introduction, des variantes, des notes, un appendice et des index par Maurice Levaillant et Georges Mouliner . . . , 2 vols. (Paris, 1946; 3rd impression 1957; reprinted 1962), p.182 (= Book V, Chap. 14).

Britain: Sources, Influences and Ideas. It is quite possible, that by adopting this course, I may have failed, in some instances, to quote the earliest examples. Absolute certainty on this point is scarcely possible. But then neither is it really necessary for, from the evidence I have produced, it is quite obvious that in French and Italian the word used to denote both Vitruvian and mediaeval architecture in the seventeenth century was 'order' ('ordre', 'ordine'). Then, in the eighteenth century, due to the decline of Vitruvianism, a reappraisal of architectural terminology was instituted.[84]

In the fourth volume of his *Parallèle des Anciens et des Modernes*, which was published in 1697, Charles Perrault (1628–1703) described a proposal mooted by Minister Colbert:
'He suggested that, once the Louvre had been completed, a recommendation should be submitted to His Majesty to the effect that, instead of having all of the many rooms which it contained decorated in the French fashion, he should have them decorated in the fashions favoured by the different nations of the world – Italian, German, Turkish, Persian, Mongolian, Chinese – and, in doing so, should not only order exact copies of the ornaments with which these nations embellish the interiors of their palaces, but should also discover by painstaking enquiry all the different kinds of furniture and conveniences favoured by each nation, so that visitors to our capital would have the pleasure of finding both their own country, so to speak, and all the splendours of the world contained within a single palace.'[85]

This cosmopolitan proposal for the interior of the Louvre – which has also been ascribed to Perrault's brother, Claude[86] – could be dismissed as an idle fantasy were it not for the fact that it so faithfully reflects the French view of architecture at the end of the seventeenth century. Charles Perrault was one of the leading protagonists in the *Querelle des Anciens et des Modernes*, an academic dispute as to the merits of contemporary and Antique architecture, in which the 'Modernes' tried to establish specific spheres in which their own period – the period of the Sun King – was superior to Antiquity. As a result of this dispute people acquired a greater awareness of the essentially relative nature of critical assessments and a keener eye for the imperfections of Antique art: 'When all is said and done, there is a difference between the concept of perfection and the most beautiful works of the Ancients.'[87] According to Vitruvian theory the proportions of the various Antique orders had been based on the proportions of the human body. Thus, the Doric order had been derived from a male body, the Ionic order from a female body and the Corinthian order from the body of a young virgin. It was this relationship that had given them their absolute validity. But once the relationship was questioned, as it was by the modernist faction under Louis XIV, the Antique orders no longer enjoyed their absolute status:
'The diversity of the proportions used for each order shows quite clearly that they are arbitrary and that their beauty is based on convention and habit.'[88]

84 Forssman, *Dorisch, jonisch, korinthisch* (1961), pp.112–25.

85 [Charles] Perrault, *Parallèle des Anciens et des Modernes en ce qui regarde les arts et les sciences . . .*, 4 vols. (Paris, 1688–97; facsimile edition in 1 vol. [with an introduction by H. R. Jauss and art-historical commentaries by M. Indahl] . . ., Munich, 1964) pp.440–1 (= IV, pp.273–4): 'C'étoit de proposer à sa Majesté, en cas que l'on eût achevé le Louvre, de ne point faire à la françoise tout le grand nombre d'appartemens qu'il doit contenir, mais en faire à la mode de toutes les Nations du Monde: à l'Italienne, à l'Espagnolle, à l'Allemande, à la Turque, à la Persienne, à la maniere du Mogol, à la maniere de la Chine, non seulement par une exacte imitation de tous les ornemens dont ces Nations embellissent differemment les dedans de leurs Palais; mais aussi par une recherche exacte de tous les meubles & de toutes les commoditez qui leur sont particulieres, en sorte que tous les Etrangers eussent le plaisir de retrouver chez Nous en quelque sorte leur propre Pays, & toute la magnificence du Monde renfermée dans un seul Palais.'

86 Louis Hautecœur, *Histoire de l'architecture classique en France*, 7 (really 10) vols. Paris, 1943–57; 2nd ed. 1963 ff.), II: *Le règne de Louis XIV* (1948), 1st half vol., p.452; see also the section entitled 'L'exotisme', *ibid.*, pp.361–3.

87 Perrault, *Parallèle*, I (1688), p.11 (and 1964 edition, p.103): 'Il y a encore quelque distance entre l'idée de la perfection & les plus beaux ouvrages des Anciens'.

88 *Ibid.*, p.138 (and 1964 edition, p.165): 'Cette diversité de proportions assignée à chaque ordre marque bien qu'elle sont arbitraires, & que leur beauté n'est fondée que sur la convention des hommes & sur l'accoustumance.'

21

89 Antonio Hernandez, *Grundzüge einer Ideengeschichte der französischen Architekturtheorie von 1560–1800* (typewritten thesis; Basle, 1965), pp.55–6.

90 Philibert de l'Orme, *Le premier tome de l'architecture de Philibert de l'Orme . . .* (Paris, 1567; 2nd ed. 1568; 3rd ed. 1576; 4th ed. 1626, 5th ed. 1648; reprints of the 1648 edition Paris, 1894, and Farnborough 1964); quotation taken from *ibid.* (1648 edition), fol. 218v.: 'qui empeschera que nous François n'en inuentions quelques-vnes, & les appelions Françoises . . . ?' – See also Erik Forssman, *Säule und Ornament: Studien zum Problem des Manierismus in den nordischen Säulen-büchern und Vorlageblättern des 16. und 17. Jahrhunderts . . .* (Stockholm and Cologne, 1956), p.82.

91 Hautecœur, *Histoire de l'architecture classique*, II (1948), 1st half vol., pp.351–4 and 451.

92 Séb[astien] Le Clerc, *Traité d'architecture . . .*, 2 vols. (text and plates), (Paris, 1714), I, pp.22 and 193 ff. – Le Clerc's work has been translated into English (1723–4), German (1759; 2nd ed. 1797) and Dutch (n.d.).

93 For an inventory of these styles see Christian Ludwig Stieglitz, *Encyclopädie der bürgerlichen Baukunst . . .*, 5 vols. (Leipzig, 1792–8), IV: *N-SCHE* (1797), pp.123–4. – See also Léonce Lex, 'De la recherche d'un sixième ordre d'architecture' in *Annales de l'Académie de Mâcon*, 3rd Series, IX (1904), pp.159–200.

94 Henry Emlyn, *A Proposition for a New Order in Architecture, with Rules for Drawing the Several Parts* (London, 1781; 2nd ed. 1784; 3rd ed. 1797). – Emlyn refers to his French precursors: *ibid.* (2nd ed.), p. IV.

95 Vitruv, *Zehn Bücher* (1964), pp.38 and 40 (= Book I, Chap. II).

96 [Germain] Boffrand, *Livre d'architecture . . .* (French and Latin; Paris, 1745; facsimile edition Farnborough, 1966).

This attack on the proportions of the Antique orders, which was recorded by Charles Perrault but was actually launched by his brother Claude, preceded the *Querelle des Anciens et des Modernes* and anticipated many of the arguments advanced by the modernists.[89]

The decline of Vitruvianism was also heralded by the emergence of a whole series of 'invented' orders. In 1567 Philibert de l'Orme (1510?–70) wrote:
'Who can stop us in France from inventing some [orders] and calling them French?'
He then went on to suggest that they should build columns with shaft rings and call them the 'French order'.[90] In 1671 Colbert staged a competition to promote the creation of a new French order.[91] Sébastien Le Clerc (1637–1714) designed a second Tuscan, a Spanish and a French order.[92] From then until the end of the nineteenth century repeated attempts were made throughout Europe to extend the architectural repertoire by the creation of new national styles. The first of these were derived from the Corinthian order, but later they were conceived within the context of the Gothic Revival.[93] Although these 'invented' orders were seldom used by practising architects, it would seem that they played a not insignificant part in the field of architectural theory, for they invariably appeared in volumes with *de luxe* bindings, many of which ran to several editions. The *Proposition for a New Order in Architecture* by Henry Emlyn (1729–1816) is a case in point: after first appearing in 1781, this book was reprinted in 1784 and again in 1797.[94]

But the rejection of Vitruvian proportions and the extension of the Greek and Roman orders by the creation of national orders were not the only new development. There was also a growing insistence on the need to create special architectural genres for different types of buildings and to accord to each of these genres a specific style or 'character'. This projected development was, of course, essentially the same as the one that had already taken place in the spheres of rhetoric and poetry. There were also precedents within the architectural sphere itself. After all, Vitruvius had stipulated that different orders and different kinds of temples should be used for different gods and heroes: Doric temples for Minerva, Mars and Hercules, Corinthian temples for Venus, Flora, Proserpine and the Nymphs, Ionic temples for Juno, Diana and Bacchus.[95] And then the Renaissance extended the architectural repertoire by the introduction of rusticated masonry. But it was not until the eighteenth century, when Germain Boffrand (1667–1754) published his *Livre d'architecture*, that a really comprehensive system emerged. Boffrand evolved a complete theory of architectural 'character' by analogy with the principles laid down in Horace's *Poetics*:[96] 'Although architecture appears to be concerned only with the application of inanimate matter, in actual fact it also incorporates a whole variety of genres, which animate its component spheres, so to speak, by means of the different kinds of character that it expresses. Just as a dramatic composition in a theatre expresses the pastoral or tragic nature of a particular scene, so the composition of an architectural

97 *Ibid.*, pp.16–17: 'L'Architecture, quoiqu'il semble que son objet ne soit que l'emploi de ce qui est materiel, est susceptible de differens genres qui rendent ses parties, pour ainsi dire, animées par les différents caracteres qu'elle fait sentir. Un Edifice par sa composition exprime comme sur un Théatre, que la scene est Pastorale ou Tragique, que c'est un Temple ou un Palais, un Edifice public destiné à certain usage, ou une maison particuliere. Ces differents Edifices par leur disposition, par leur structure, par la maniere dont ils sont décorés, doivent annoncer au spectateur leur destination; et s'il ne le font pas, ils pechent contre l'expression, et ne sont pas ce qu'ils doivent être.
'Il en est de même de la Poësie: il y en a de différents genres, et le stile de l'un ne convient pas à l'autre: Horace en a donné d'excellents principes dans son Art Poëtique; et quoi qu'il n'ait jamais pensé à l'Architecture, il m'a paru qu'ils y avoient tant de rapport, que j'ai crû qu'on pouvoit les y joindre, et en faire une très-juste application à ceux qui nous ont été donnés pour l'Architecture par les Anciens et par les Modernes, et qu'ils pourroient encore les enricher d'un caractere plus sublime.'

98 Boffrand, *Livre d'architecture* (1745), pp.25–6.

99 *Ibid.*, p.27: 'Si l'on veut faire un mausolée, il faut que l'édifice soit traité par la matiere, et par un genre d'Architecture et de décoration qui soit sérieux et triste; car la nature forme notre cœur susceptible de ces differentes impressions, et il est toujours remué par l'unison.'

100 Adolf Max Vogt, *Boulées Newton-Denkmal; Sakralbau und Kugelidee . . .* (Basle and Stuttgart, 1969). – For an analysis of the theory of character see Emil Kaufmann, 'Three Revolutionary Architects: Boullée, Ledoux, and Lequeu' in *Transactions of the American Philosophical Society*, New Series, XLII, Part 3 (1952), pp.429–564, and Hernandez, *Grundzüge* (typescript, 1965), pp.72–3, 90–5 and 98–101.

101 See also Note 81 above.

structure expresses the nature of that structure; namely, that it is a temple or a palace, a public building designed for a particular function, or a private house. These different structures have to inform the observer, by means of their functional and constructional design, of the use for which they are intended; and if they fail to do so, then they are sinning against architectural expression and are not what they are supposed to be.

'We find the same state of affairs in poetry: there are different genres, and the style of one genre does not suit another. Horace has laid down excellent principles in his *Poetics*; and although he gave no thought to architecture, it seemed to me that his principles had so much bearing on this activity that it would be permissible to link them with it, and also entirely reasonable to apply them to the principles laid down for architecture by both the Ancients and the Moderns, and that they would make these even more productive and would give them a more noble character.'[97]

Boffrand argued that, to acquire character, buildings did not need columns, they simply needed to be well proportioned; and he considered that those who failed to give their buildings the sort of character demanded by their function and nature did not deserve to be called architects.[98] The extent to which Boffrand replaced the authoritative standpoint of traditional aesthetics by a more sensualist approach is demonstrated by the following excerpt:

'If one wishes to build a mausoleum the structure must be executed in suitable materials and in an architectural and decorative style that is both serious and solemn; for nature has made the human heart susceptible to diverse impressions, and it is always moved by harmony.'[99]

The next generation of French architects, which continued to apply Boffrand's 'character' theory, was virtually obsessed with the architectural genre represented by the mausoleum.[100]

Jacques-François Blondel used the words 'genre' and 'style' (the latter, as we have seen, by analogy with rhetoric) in addition to, and virtually as synonymous with, 'caractère'.[101] The new collective concept of the 'fine arts', which embraced both the terminology and the theoretical premises of poetry, rhetoric, music, painting, sculpture, landscape gardening and architecture, the growing interest in impressions and expression, in feeling and sensibility, created the necessary setting for the development of the multiple styles that were to be the hallmark of nineteenth-century France, and paved the way for the incorporation of the word 'style' into architectural theory. But from Colbert's cosmopolitan proposal for the interior design of the Louvre to the actual emergence of stylistic pluralism was a major step. How that step came to be taken is explained by the developments in English art.

4 The Word 'Style' in English

When he was asked to complete Westminster Abbey, Sir Christopher Wren (1632–1723) found himself faced with the same sort of problem as that posed by the Church of San Petronio in Bologna and the Cathedral of Sainte-Croix in Orleans.

His proposals for the restoration and completion of the Abbey were prefaced by a résumé of the development of mediaeval architecture, which illustrates the use of such words as 'mode', 'manner', 'fashion', 'style' and 'form' in England in the year 1713.[102] The Abbey Church, Wren tells us, was restored by King Edgar in the tenth century after the Danish incursions:
'This, it is probable, was a strong good Building, after the Mode of that Age, not much altered from the *Roman*. We have some Examples of this ancient *Saxon* Manner, which was with Peers or round Pillars, much stronger than *Tuscan*, round headed Arches, and Windows; such was *Winchester* cathedral of old.'[103]

The first stone of the present Abbey was laid in 1220 and the first part of the new structure was built:
'according to the Mode, which came into Fashion after the Holy War. 'This we now call the *Gothic* Manner of Architecture (so the Italians called what was not after the *Roman* Style) tho' the *Goths* were rather Destroyers than Builders; I think it should with more Reason be called the *Saracen* Style.'[104]

Wren wanted pinnacles on the corners of the façade of the northern transept 'conformable to the old style, to make the whole of a Piece'.[105] For structural reasons he also wanted a crossing tower:
'I have made a Design, which will not be very expensive but light and still in the *Gothic* Form, and of a Style with the rest of the Structure, which I would strictly adhere to, throughout the whole Intention: to deviate from the old Form, would be to run into a disagreeable Mixture, which no Person of a good Taste could relish.'[106]

Wren adopted a similar approach to the reconstruction of a number of parish churches after the Fire of London. There too he was forced to 'deviate from a better Style'.[107]

A fragment from Wren's literary estate, in which the architect commented on the orders, is very much in line with the thinking of Johann Bernhard Fischer von Erlach (1656–1723):
'Architecture aims at Eternity; and therefore the only Thing incapable of Modes and Fashions in its Principals, the *Orders*. 'The Orders are not only *Roman* and *Greek*, but *Phoenician*, *Hebrew*, and *Assyrian*.'[108]

In his diary John Evelyn (1620–1706) frequently used the phrase 'Gothic manner'.[109] There are also two references to the phrase 'Gothic Ordonance'[110] and one to the substantive form 'Gotick'.[111] Apart from this, Evelyn used the expressions 'design', 'architecture', 'fabric', 'building', 'structure', 'work' and 'à la gotic'.[112]

Occasionally we also encounter the phrase 'Gothic order' in English.

102 [Christopher Wren the Younger,] *Parentelia, or Memoirs of the Family of the Wrens, viz. of Mathew, Bishop of Ely, Christopher, Dean of Windsor, &c, but Chiefly of Sir Christopher Wren . . .*, compiled by his son Christopher, now published by his grandson Stephen Wren . . . (London, 1750; facsimile reprint from the 'heirloom' copy of the R.I.B.A. Farnborough, 1965).

103 *Ibid.*, p.296.

104 *Ibid.*, p.297.

105 *Ibid.*, p.302.

106 *Ibid.*

107 *Ibid.*

108 *Ibid.*, p.351.

109 John Evelyn, *The Diary of J.E.*, edited by E. S. de Beer, 6 vols. (Oxford, 1955), II, pp.64, 99, 126, and 319. – The spelling of 'gothic' varies.

110 *Ibid.*, pp.266 and 271. – Note the French spelling of 'gothic'.

111 *Ibid.*, I, p.30.

112 For 'design' see *ibid.*, II, pp.50 and 494. – For 'architecture' see *ibid.*, II, p.85; III, pp.129 and 323. – For 'fabric' see *ibid.*, II, pp.95 and 246; III, p.427. – For 'building' see *ibid.*, II, p.144; III, p.556. – For 'structure' see *ibid.*, IV, p.131. – For 'work' see *ibid.*, III, pp.113 and 121. – For 'à la gotic' see *ibid.*, II, p.153.

For example, the design produced by the architect Daniel Hague (d.1816) for the Church of St Paul, Portland Square in Bristol in 1787, which was an early example of the Gothic Revival, was described as a 'plan of the Gothic Order, drawn by Mr Hague, an eminent mason'.[113] Towards the end of the eighteenth century the word 'order' regained its original significance. In 1789 Thomas Pownall published his 'Observations on the Origin and Progress of Gothic Architecture, and on the Corporation of Free Masons Supposed to be the Establishers of it as a Regular Order'[114] in *Archaeologia*. Quoting from the writings of mediaeval authors, who had recorded the history of wooden churches, Pownall traced the Gothic back to the work of the mediaeval carpenters, thus establishing the same derivation for this style of architecture as for Greek Temple architecture. He argued that the freemasons were the first architects, 'who reduced it [the Gothic] to, and introduced it as, a regular order'.[115] Pownall was one of a group of antiquarians who paved the way for modern research into Gothic architecture by systematically examining existing buildings in the light of literary sources.

But in the generation before Pownall's, numerous small buildings – which between them represented every national style and every historical period – had been erected in the English landscape gardens, where they served to create or reinforce a particular mood. In Kew Gardens (Surrey) alone, twenty-one such buildings were erected in the five-year period from 1757 to 1762;[116] and these included the mock 'Gothic Cathedral' designed by Johann Heinrich Müntz in *c*.1758.[117]

In 1742 Batty Langley (1696–1751) and Thomas Langley published a series of engravings of country houses and garden buildings (or *fabriques*), which is usually referred to under the title given to the second and third editions (1747 and *c*.1790): *Gothic Architecture, Improved by Rules and Proportions, in Many Grand Designs of Columns, Doors, Windows, Chimney-Pieces, Arcades, Colonades, Porticos, Umbrellos, Temples, and Pavillions &c., with Plans, Elevations and Profiles, Geometrically Explained*.[118] In the preface to this second edition Batty Langley wrote: 'The Rules by which the ancient Buildings of this Kingdom were erected and adorned, having been entirely lost for many centuries; I have, therefore, for upwards of twenty years, in order to restore and publish them for the good of posterity, assiduously employed myself, as opportunities have happened, in making researches into many of the most ancient buildings now standing in this kingdom: and from thence have extracted rules for forming such designs and ornaments in the ancient mode, which will be exceedingly beautiful in all parts of private buildings . . . By this unhappy devastation [Danish invasion] posterity was deprived not only of the Saxon modes or Orders of Architecture, but also of the geometrical rules by which their buildings in general were designed, set out, erected, and adorned.'[119]

To understand this passage of Langley's and to assess the validity of his assertions we must briefly consider his engravings and the captions which he used for them. By way of an introduction to the illustrations,

22–4

6

5

113 Walter Ison, *The Georgian Buildings of Bristol* (London, 1952), p.77.

114 Thomas Pownall, 'Observations . . .' in *Archaeologia or Miscellaneous Tracts Relating to Antiquity*, published by the Society of Antiquaries of London, IX (1798), pp.110–26.

115 *Ibid.*, p.122.

116 H. F. Clark, 'Eighteenth-Century Elysium: the Rôle of "Associations" in the Landscape Movement' in *Journal of the Warburg and Courtauld Institutes*, VI (1943), pp.165–89, esp. p.181, note 2.

117 William Chambers, *Plans, Elevations, Sections, and Perspective Views of the Gardens and Buildings at Kew (Surrey)* . . . (London, 1763), p.6 and plate 29.

118 Facsimile of the 1747 edition (Farnborough, 1967). I do not know any copy of the original with the introduction.

119 Quotation taken from the edition of *c*.1790, pp.1–2.

the following notice appeared immediately above the first plate:
'NB. *We shall first exhibit* five new Orders *of* Columns, *Plain & Enrich'd, and then shew their Use in the Forming of Designs for Frontispieces, to* Doors, Windows, Chimney-Pieces, Insides *of* Rooms *&c. in the* Gothick manner.'[120]

4 These new orders in the Gothic manner incorporated all the elements of the Classical orders: plinth, base, shaft, capital, architrave, frieze and cornice. The shaft rings, the cylindrical plinths, the pointed arches and the open or blind tracery create a Gothic impression; some of the shafts are octagonal or quatrefoil in section, others are compound piers or 'piliers cantonnés'. Only one of the illustrations features an arcade, which was a common motif in Gothic architecture. The last two plates are representations of the choir and nave of Westminster Abbey.

We see, therefore, that despite their theoretical insistence on the need to revive the original Gothic mode, in actual fact the Langleys were more concerned with the introduction of viable 'new' orders. True, they did not actually set out to 'invent' new orders. But of all their engravings only the last two genuinely supported their theoretical objectives and reflected a serious interest in the Gothic architecture of the Middle Ages, an interest which, moreover, was entirely restricted to the Gothic 'orders'. On the other hand, it must have appeared to eighteenth-century observers that the only possible way of reviving the Gothic mode was by 'translating' it into Vitruvian terms. And, in this connexion, it was of course no accident that the Langleys presented their five Gothic orders in conjunction with the five Vitruvian orders: Tuscan, Doric, Ionic, Corinthian, and Composite.

When he visited Ghent in 1773 the architect James Essex (1722–84), who was an authority on Gothic architecture, made a diary entry in which he described the pillars of the Beguine Church as 'Corinthian Gothic'. He also referred to the capitals of the Church of Notre-Dame in Ghent, which has since been destroyed, as 'Corinthian Gothic',[121] by which he meant that they were leaf capitals. The sketches which Essex provided show quite clearly what he had in mind and also indicate that, like the Langleys, he was interested primarily in columns and capitals. These sketches depict tracery (1), ground-plans of two churches (1 each), sections of pillars (3), secular buildings (4), church bays (4), details of church buildings (5) and capitals (7). In another diary entry, written when he was in Bruges, Essex remarked: 'Most of the Churches and Houses in this City are built with bricks, and we find here every Style of Gothic Architecture in that material.' Shortly before he had been speaking of the 'antient' style and the 'richest' style, from which it would follow that, in referring to 'every Style of Gothic Architecture', Essex meant to embrace both genre styles, which are concurrent, and historical styles, which are consecutive.[122] Normally, of course, the word 'style' refers to the style of a whole period, and to subsequent imitations. Essex commented on this conception in his notes for a history of the Gothic style: 'The general practice of composing from fragments rather than from well established principles is one reason

120 The plates are the same in all editions.

121 James Essex, *Journal of a Tour through Part of Flandres and France in August [and September], 1773*, edited by W. M. Fawcett . . . (Cambridge, 1888), pp.29 and 33.

122 *Ibid.*, p.21; see also p.18.

hy so little progress has hitherto been made in that style.'[123]

Although necessarily brief and based on somewhat random evidence, this synopsis of English usage none the less illustrates the following features:

In England the process whereby the word 'style' began to compete with the neutral expression 'manner' set in at an earlier stage than the corresponding process in France and Italy. In England the word 'style' was frequently used to denote the modes of building available to the architect, especially those conforming to older monuments. The English word 'order' was less neutral than the corresponding French and Italian words and was often employed by those who, with the help of further Vitruvian concepts, tried to represent Gothic architecture as a system of structures. Using Gothic elements, Batty and Thomas Langley produced five 'new' orders, thus increasing the number of available structures. Their designs have often been ridiculed. But, to do them justice, they would really have to be considered in the light of Guillaume Hénault's experiments in Orleans or Germain Boffrand's theory of architectural 'character'.

As for German architectural theory in the eighteenth century, this was very much under the influence of French and English writers, as is apparent from the incredible number of translations published at that time. But French influence was opposed by the emerging spirit of German patriotism, which reached its peak in the War of Liberation (from 1813 onwards) and led to a determined attempt to purge the German language of all words of foreign origin. Until late in the nineteenth century the word 'Bauart', whose success could never be explained by semantic analysis alone, continued to vie with the word 'Stil'. The German word 'Art' has never acquired the frivolous connotation of French and English 'mode'; it corresponds to Italian 'modo', not 'moda'.

This survey of the historical development of architectural concepts in Europe was designed to show how a genre style was evolved from an historical style. Consequently, we have been concerned up to now primarily with the concept of style. But we must now turn our attention to the concept of the Gothic and the associations to which this gave rise.

5 The Gothic and the Doctrine of Mimesis

Although mimesis – here understood as the imitation of nature – played only a subsidiary part in Vitruvius's treatise, his sixteenth-, seventeenth- and eighteenth-century disciples constantly referred to those parts of the *De Architectura* in which it appeared. In the first **11** chapter of the second book Vitruvius described the primitive hut which, in the eighteenth century, came to be regarded as the natural model for all columniform architecture. In the first chapter of the third book he derived units of measure, such as the foot and the ell, and the modules employed in Antique temples from the human body. In the

123 Donald R. Stewart, 'James Essex' in *Architectural Review*, CVIII (1950), pp.317–21, esp. p.320.

first chapter of the fourth book he demonstrated the supposed relationship between the Doric column and naked male beauty, between the Ionic column and female grace and symmetry, and between the Corinthian column and virginal tenderness. (The Corinthian capital, he said, was invented by the sculptor Callimachus who represented a basket overgrown with acanthus and covered by a slate, which he had found on the grave of a Corinthian girl.) Finally, in the second chapter of the fourth book he described the derivation of Greek architecture from carpentry.

When Count Castiglione died, a memorandum addressed to Pope Julius II and dating from the year 1510 was found among his papers and was eventually published under his name in 1733. But this memorandum, which called for the protection of architectural monuments with 'pietà verso i parenti, e la patria', has also been attributed to Raphael and Bramante, of whom the latter seems the most likely author. According to Bramante – for I shall assume his authorship – the Romans were exemplary architects and had:

'the most beautiful cornices, beautiful friezes and architraves, and columns with excellent decorative capitals and bases calculated in accordance with the proportions of the male and female bodies. But the only form of decoration used by the Germans (whose manner is still in vogue in many parts) are small, squat, badly executed figures, which they place beneath the beams of their buildings in the form of corbels, and strange animals, figures and coarsely executed ornamental foliage, which they employ without rhyme or reason. Incidentally, their architecture is said to have originated in the following way: from unfelled trees, whose branches, when bent and bound together, produced their pointed arches. And, although this derivation is not to be despised in every respect, such architecture is none the less weak. With their pillars, ridge timbers and roofs the huts made from tree trunks which Vitruvius has identified as the origin of the Doric order are far more powerful than the pointed arches with their twin centres.'[124]

Thus, according to Bramante, Roman columns were based on the proportions of the male and female figure whilst the general model for Roman buildings was the log hut; and, although they also had their origins in nature, the pointed arches of Gothic architecture were not so powerful as the round arches of Roman architecture. We must remember, however, that this memorandum was drafted in 1510, at a time when Late Gothic ornamentation with its leafless branches had reached its peak; and it could well be that Bramante was thinking of this late style when he gave his 'naturalistic' derivation of Gothic architecture. Certainly, Philibert de l'Orme, who grew up in the stone-mason tradition, had this in mind when he wrote the first volume of his *Architecture*:

'And would it not be agreeable to find branches above these columns joining up to form haunches and a sort of vault?'[125]

In his *Dissertation* of 1699 Jean-François Félibien (1658–1733)

124 The whole memorandum has been reproduced in Otto H[elmut] Förster, *Bramante* (Vienna and Munich, 1956), pp.284–7; quotation taken from *ibid.*, p.285: 'bellissimi cornici, belli fregi, architravi, colonne ornatissime di capitelli, e basi, e misurate con la proporzione dell'uomo, e della donna: e li Tedeschi (la maniera de' quali in molti luoghi ancor dura) per ornamento spesso ponevano solamente un qualche figurino rannicchiato, e mal fatto, per mensola a sostenere un trave; e animali strani, e figure, e fogliami goffi, e fuori d'ogni ragione naturale. Pur'ebbe la loro Architettura questa origine, che nacque dagli arbori non ancor tagliati, li quali, piegati li rami, e rilegati insieme, fanno li loro terzi acuti. E benchè questa origine non sia in tutto da sprezzare; pure è debole; perchè molto più reggerebbono le capanne fatte di travi incatenate, e poste a uso di colonne, con li culmi, e coprimenti, come descrive Vitruvio della origine dell'opera Dorica, che gli terzi acuti, li quali hanno due centri.'

125 L'Orme, *Le premier tome de l'architecture* (1648), fol. 220r.: 'D'auantage ne seroit-il pas aysé de trouuer au dessus des dites colonnes des branches qui se lient l'vne à l'autre, et facent une forme de voûte & d'arceau?' – See also Margot Braun (-Reichenbacher), *Das Ast- und Laubwerk, Entwicklung, Merkmale und Bedeutung einer spätgotischen Ornamentform* . . . (Nuremberg, 1966). – The forest metaphors have also been treated in Jurgis Baltrušaitis, 'Le roman de l'architecture gothique' in J. B., *Aberrations: quatre essais sur la légende des formes* . . . (n.p. [Paris], 1957), pp.73–96.

compared the clustered piers, ribs and tracery of Gothic buildings with the 'branches and trunks of trees'.[126] In 1724 William Stukeley (1687–1765) praised the Gothic architects for having imitated nature, and recommended that this style should be used for the interior design of galleries and libraries. His admiration was prompted by the sight of Gloucester Cathedral, which he found quite overwhelming:

'Nothing could have made me so much in love with Gothic Architecture (so-called), and I judge for a gallery, library, or the like, 'tis the best manner of building, because the idea of it is taken from a walk of trees, whose touching heads are curiously imitated by the roof.'[127]

Stukeley was the first man to 'fall in love' with Gothic architecture, and he was also the first to advocate imitation. But the comparison which he drew with tree-lined walks was by no means new. On the contrary, it was typical of the general preference evinced during the Baroque period for *enfilades* or perspective views. When Wren was working on St Paul's he wrote:

'The excessive Length of Buildings is not otherwise commendable, but because it yields a pleasing Perspective by the continu'd optical Diminution of the Columns; and if this be cut off by Columns ranging within their Fellows, the Grace that would be acquir'd by the Length is totally lost.'[128]

Although this statement (like the whole of Wren's account of the St Paul's design) raises some problems, it leaves us in no doubt about Wren's predilection for long, regular rows of columns.[129] But his liking for tree-lined walks was even greater: 'A Walk of Trees is more beautiful than the most artificial Portico.'[130]

Both Bramante and Félibien compared individual trees with architectural columns. Wren, on the other hand, was concerned with the comparison between tree-lined walks and colonnades. This progression, which reflected the new approach to nature adopted in the eighteenth century, is also evident in the writings of Johann Georg Sulzer (1720–77). In diary entries made in 1775/6, when he was travelling in Europe, he compared a Greek peristyle with an avenue of poplars, then a colonnade with a row of topped willows and, finally, a Gothic church with a forest. Sulzer – a learned gentleman – tried to make out that this last comparison was a completely original idea which had occurred to him on the 'romantic journey to Bellinzona':

'Here, in more than one locality, I witnessed scenes which gave me a most unusual idea. In certain places, where the ground was quite level and tall forest trees were growing, I felt as if I were in a large Gothic church. [In all of these places] two rows of tall trees, spaced fairly far apart, joined together at a considerable height from the ground to form a pointed vault, just like the Gothic vaults in our large churches, and the wide expanse between these trees seemed to me like the nave of the church; two further rows of trees to the right and left constituted the aisles whilst, to my mind, the dark end of these walks, which abutted on to a mountain side, formed the chancel.

'The similarity was most striking, and I found myself quite unable to

126 Félibien, *Les plans et descriptions . . . , avec une Dissertation* (1699), p.173.

127 W. S., *Itinerarium curiosum: or an Account of the Antiquitys and Remarkable Curiositys in Nature thro' Great Britain . . .* (London, 1724; 2nd ed. 1776); quotation taken from Arthur O[ncken] Lovejoy, *Essays in the History of Ideas . . .* (Baltimore, 1948), p.153.

128 Wren, *Parentelia* (1750), p.276.

129 For an account of the St Paul's design see also Victor Fürst, *The Architecture of Sir Christopher Wren* (London, 1956), pp.24 ff.

130 Wren, *Parentelia* (1750), p.353.

131 Johann Georg Sulzer, *Tagebuch einer von Berlin nach den mittäglichen Ländern von Europa in den Jahren 1775 und 1776 gethanen Reise und Rückreise* (Lcipzig, 1780), pp.290 and 292; quotation taken from *ibid.*, p.353: 'Hier sah ich an mehr als einem Orte Scenen, die mich auf einen sonderbaren Gedanken geführt haben. Mir kam es bisweilen an ganz ebenen, mit hohen und sehr waldigen Bäumen besetzten Plätzen vor, als wenn ich mich in einer sehr grossen gothischen Kirche befände. Zwey weit aus einander stehende Reihen solcher Bäume schlossen in einer beträchtlichen Höhe ein spitzig zulaufendes Gewölbe, gerade wie die gothischen Gewölber grosser Kirchen sind, und der weite Raum zwischen diesen Bäumen schien mir das Schiff der Kirche; wieder zwey andre, weiter rechter und linker Hand entfernt stehende Reihen eben solcher Bäume bildeten die beyden Abseiten einer solchen Kirche, und das hintere gegen einen Berg stossende insgemein dunkele Ende dieser Alleen bildete, nach meiner Vorstellung, den Chor der Kirche vor.
'Ich konnte mich nicht enthalten, mich selbst zu überreden, dass entweder dieses die Originalmuster seyn müssten, daher die gothischen Baumeister die Ideen zu ihren grossen Kirchen genommen, oder dass die, welche diese Bäume gepflanzt, diese Plätze nach der Form der Kirchen eingerichtet haben; so offenbar schien mir die Ähnlichkeit beyder Gegenstände. Das erstere ist mir wahrscheinlicher; denn es erklärte mir nicht nur den Ursprung der zugespitzten Gewölber, sondern auch die Verzierungen sowohl dieser Gewölber, als der ebenfalls zugespitzten Bogen über die Hauptportale solcher Kirchen. Diese Bogen bestehen meistentheils aus einer Menge erhobener runder Glieder, die mit den von beyden Seiten zusammenstossenden schlanken Ästen der Bäume grosse Ähnlichkeit haben. Hiebei fiel mir auch noch ein, wie so viel alte Völker dergleichen dunkle und zu feierlich andächtigen Empfindungen einladende Haine, nicht ohne einen natürlichen Wink, zum Orte ihrer gottesdienstlichen Gebräuche gewählt haben.' – My attention was drawn to these obscure passages by Hanspeter Rebsamen.

132 [Francis Hutcheson,] *An Enquiry into the Original of Our Ideas of Beauty and Virtue . . .* (London, 1725), Part IV, p.76; quotation taken from Josef Haslag, '*Gothic' im 17. und 18. Jahrhundert, eine wortgeschichtliche Untersuchung . . .* (Cologne and Graz, 1963), p.118. – Francis Hutcheson the Elder's work appeared in numerous editions, and was translated into French in 1749 and German in 1762.

133 H.L., *Architecture des églises anciennes et nouvelles* (Paris, 1733), p.14.

resist the notion that, either these places were the original model from which the Gothic architects had taken the idea for their great churches, or else that the people who had planted the trees had modelled these places on churches. The first explanation seemed the more likely; for it established the origin, not only of the pointed vaults, but also of the ornamentation found both on the vaults and on the pointed arches above the main entrance of these churches. For the most part such arches are composed of a cluster of raised, circular members, which bear a strong resemblance to the thin lateral branches of trees. It also occurred to me in this connexion that many early tribes – taking their lead from nature, so to speak – had used dark groves of this kind, which are conducive to religious feelings, for their devotional rites.'[131]

None of these ideas was in any way new. In 1725 Francis Hutcheson (1694–1746) had pointed to the parallel between dark forest groves and Gothic churches, but had rejected the idea that they both created the same religious atmosphere as a false analogy.[132] Moreover, the argument advanced by Sulzer to the effect that the Gothic architects had tried to evoke the Celtic twilight of forest groves in their churches had already been expounded by the Frenchman H. Le Blanc in a book on church architecture in 1733.[133] And when Germain Boffrand (1667–1754) traced Gothic architecture back to the Druids' temples in 1745, he too no doubt will have had such places of worship in mind.[134] Finally, William Warburton (1698–1779), Bishop of Gloucester, had also defended Gothic architecture on the grounds that it imitated nature and, in doing so, inspired religious feelings:
'For could the *Arches* be otherwise than *pointed* when the Workman was to imitate that curve which branches make by their intersection with one another? Or could the *Columns* be otherwise than split into distinct shafts, when they were to represent the Stems of a group of Trees? On the same principle was formed the spreading ramification of the stone-work in the windows, and the stained glass in the interstices; the one being to represent the branches, and the other the leaves of an opening Grove; and both concurring to preserve that gloomy light inspiring religious horror. Lastly, we see the reason of their studied aversion to *apparent* solidity in these stupendous masses, deemed so absurd by men accustomed to the *apparent* as well as *real* strength of Grecian Architecture.'[135]

In April 1797 Sir James Hall (1761–1832), one of the leading geologists of his day, gave a lecture in Edinburgh, in which he argued that Gothic architecture had been evolved from wicker huts.[136] As a scientist Sir James subjected his theory to experiment. In 1792/3 he had a miniature cathedral built in his garden from willow rods, which was modelled on the cloisters of Westminster Abbey and the tower of St Nicholas's, Newcastle upon Tyne.[137] In 1796 he was able to observe how the bark of the willow peeled away from the rods in the tracery of his cathedral, and from this he argued that the cusps in Gothic tracery were an imitation in stone of this deformation of an original willow prototype.[138] Other factors were explained on constructional grounds:

14

for example, the sections of the bars in the tracery (which were said to be calculated on the basis of wind pressure) and, of course, the flying buttresses (to which Sir James took exception).[139] Although he was well aware that the use of decorative branches was a feature of the Late Gothic, Sir James none the less represented this development as 'direct proof' of his theory in the chapter entitled 'Literal Imitations of the Prototype'.[140] After adopting a strictly scientific approach up to this point, Sir James turned to historical methods. On the basis of pictorial evidence – which was far from comprehensive – he argued that the churches built by the English missions in the first century must have been of wicker construction. Later, at the time of the Crusades, when relics were very much in vogue and the Church was consequently preoccupied with the early years of Christianity, these wicker churches would have been reproduced in stone.[141] This positively modernistic thesis was supplemented by a defence of the Gothic based on a philosophical view in which nature was represented as the source of all beauty. Then, with his argument firmly entrenched in the principle of mimesis, Sir James concluded that it was perfectly admissible to revive any style that suited the purposes of contemporary architecture or – like Callimachus – even to invent such a style.[142] Although this theory seems utterly absurd today, it was cited by architectural historians until late in the nineteenth century. Whether it inspired other garden structures apart from Sir James's own 'wicker fabric' or 'willow cathedral' is a question that could only be answered by an authority on the English landscape garden. There is a hut made of branches and incorporating pointed arches in the park designed by Humphrey Repton (1752–1818) for Blaise Castle in Henbury (Bristol). But that is more reminiscent of other 'primitive huts', which were popular with landscape gardeners at that time.

Many new ideas, which were tested in the parks and gardens of the British Isles, were subsequently taken over by Continental architects, who used them for interior designs. We have already seen that Colbert's proposal for decorating the apartments in the Louvre in a variety of national styles was followed by the appearance of temples, mosques, pyramids, and pagodas in English gardens. Now, during the last thirty years of the eighteenth century, it was England's turn to influence the Continent; and in that period many Continental designers used an early form of panoramic painting in order to create the illusion of a garden scene in their interiors.[143] In c.1780 Johann Bergl (1718–89) decorated a whole suite of rooms in the Castle of Schönbrunn near Vienna in this style. In 1765 the Abbé Marc-Antoine Laugier (1713–69), who was the most ardent adherent of the 'primitive hut' theory of Greek architecture in his day, described a fantasy design for a church, in which the ribs of the vaults sprouted from the columns like the leaves in an avenue of palms. This idea was subsequently taken up by Francesco Milizia (1725–98), who held similar views on the derivation of Gothic architecture (for which he coined the phrase 'imitazione de' boschi', i.e., imitation of a forest), and by Johann Friedrich Dauthe, who

134 Boffrand, *Livre d'architecture* (1745), pp.6–7.

135 Alexander Pope, *The Works, in Nine Volumes Complete* . . . , together with the commentaries and notes of Mr [William] Warburton (London, 1751), III, p.268.

136 James Hall, 'Essay on the Origin and Principles of Gothic Architecture', read April 6, 1797, (offprint) from the *Transactions of the Royal Society of Edinburgh*, IV (1798); later Hall expanded his essay, adding an historical section and a series of quite splendid engravings, some of them executed by Le Keux from drawings by the architect Edward Blore; this revised and enlarged edition was then published as J.H., *Essay on the Origin, History, and Principles of Gothic Architecture* (London and Edinburgh, 1813).

137 For dating see *ibid*. (1798 edition), p.25. – See also *ibid*. (1813 edition), p.27. [Cf. fig. 15 in this book]

138 *Ibid*. (1813 edition), p.32.

139 *Ibid*., p.73.

140 *Ibid*., pp.85–8.

141 *Ibid*., pp.114–25.

142 *Ibid*., pp.132 and 148.

143 Hella Müller, *Natur-Illusion in der Innenraumkunst des späteren 18. Jahrhunderts* (thesis Göttingen University 1957; n.p., 1961).

144 [Marc-Antoine] Laugier, *Observations sur l'architecture* (The Hague, 1769; facsimile edition Farnborough, 1966), p.117. – [Francesco Milizia,] *Principj di architettura civile*, 3 vols. (Finale, 1781); 2nd ed. (Bassano, 1785), I, pp.26 and 201–2; II, pp.422–6. – Wolfgang Herrmann, *Laugier and Eighteenth-Century French Theory* ... (London, 1962), esp. pp.186–7. – Eva Brües, 'Die Schriften des Francesco Milizia (1725–1798)' in *Jahrbuch für Ästhetik und allgemeine Kunstwissenschaft*, VI (1961), pp.69–113, esp. p.104. – Hella Müller, *Natur-Illusion* (1961), pp.156–68. – A general work which throws new light on the use of iconographic motifs: Eva Börsch (-Supan), *Garten-, Landschafts- und Paradiesmotive im Innenraum, eine ikonographische Untersuchung* ... (Berlin, 1967), pp.176–85. – See also W[illiam] D[ouglas] Robson-Scott, *The Literary Background of the Gothic Revival in Germany, a Chapter in the History of Taste* (Oxford, 1965), pp.49–54. John Maass, '"Sylvan Temples", Dead Ends in the Gothic Forest' in *Landscape Architecture*, October 1970.

145 Hella Müller, *Natur-Illusion* (1961), p.186.

146 *Ibid.*, pp.173–80.

147 *William Lovell*, Book V, Chap. 6; quoted from Ludwig Tieck, *Werke in vier Bänden* ..., hrsg. von Marianne Thalmann (Munich, n.d. [1963–5]), I: *Frühe Erzählungen und Romane*, p.464: 'dunkle Alleen mit hohen Bäumen, die sich oben wie das Dach einer Kirche wölben ...'

148 *Aus dem Leben eines Taugenichts*, Chap. 1; quotation taken from Joseph von Eichendorff, *Ausgewählte Werke*, hrsg. von Paul Stapf ... (Berlin and Darmstadt, 1955), p.736: 'Und in den hohen Buchenalleen, da war es noch so still, kühl und andächtig wie in einer Kirche, nur die Vögel flatterten und pickten auf dem Sande.'

149 Milizia, *Principj* (1785), I, p.26: 'L'Architettura è un'Arte d'Imitazione, a un di presso come la Pittura, la Scultura, l'Eloquenza, la Poesia, la Musica.'

150 Wittkower, *Grundlagen der Architektur* (1969), pp.20–1; figs. on plates 1–11.

151 James [Cavanah] Murphy, *Plans, Elevations, Sections, and Views of the Church of Batalha in the Province of Estremadura in Portugal* ... (London, [1792–]1795; 2nd ed. 1836); quotation taken from 1795 edition, p.17. – German translation, 1813.

152 *Ibid.* (1795 edition), pp.14–16.

rebuilt the Gothic Church of St Nicholas, Leipzig in 1784 in accordance with the principle evolved by Laugier. Thus, the Vitruvian derivation of Gothic architecture, the eighteenth-century attitude to nature, and iconographic motifs combined to introduce an element of garden design into church architecture.[144] Even in Schinkel's design for a mausoleum for Queen Luise of Prussia, which dates from 1810, the ribs of the vaults were still shaped like palm leaves.[145]

In the Romantic period the aetiological approach to the relationship between churches and forests was superseded by an associative approach.[146] In his *William Lovell*, which first appeared in 1795/6, Ludwig Tieck (1773–1853) referred to 'dark avenues with lofty trees which join together up above to form a vault like the roof of a church'[147] whilst in his novel *Aus dem Leben eines Taugenichts*, which was first published in 1826, Joseph von Eichendorff (1788–1857) made a similar comparison:
'And in the lofty avenues of beeches it was still as quiet, cool and devotional as in a church; only the birds fluttered and pecked in the sand.'[148]

The Vitruvians tried to explain the Gothic in terms of mimesis. But subsequently their idea of mimesis underwent a transformation when it was influenced by the ideas prevailing in the other branches of art. And so, as in the early stages of Boffrand's theory of 'character', we find architectural theory levelling out in favour of the theories underlying the fine arts. Milizia, who often summarized the intellectual currents of the eighteenth century, made the following observation in his *Principj*: 'Architecture is an imitative art, almost like painting, sculpture, rhetoric, poetry and music.'[149]

Another aspect of Vitruvian doctrine, which was described by Vitruvius at the beginning of the third book of the *De Architectura*, involved a sign consisting of a human figure drawn inside a square or circle. This feature was far less important for the understanding or interpretation of the Gothic than the 'primitive hut' theory, which linked this style of architecture with forest groves. But it was important to the artists of the Renaissance, since it appeared to demonstrate that the proportions of the human body were of the same order as a group of simple geometrical figures, and consequently it was thought to symbolize a certain mathematical affinity between the microcosm and the macrocosm.[150]

It was not until 1789 that this symbol was incorporated into a Gothic building. In that year James Cavanagh Murphy (1760–1814) made detailed drawings of the monastery chapel of Batalha in Portugal based on accurate measurements, thus providing the first reproduction of a Gothic building comparable with the splendid and precise reproductions of Antique temples made some forty years before; and in one of his diagrams – a cross-section and not, as would have been the case with a Renaissance architect, a ground-plan – Murphy drew a human figure.[151] He also drew an isosceles triangle in this cross-section, after the manner of Cesariano, in order to establish the proportions. According to

153 *Ibid.*, p.2.

154 A[lois] Hirt, *Die Baukunst nach den Grundsätzen der Alten* (Berlin, 1809), p.13: 'Man kann jedes architektonische Werk als ein organisches Ganzes betrachten, das aus Haupt-, Unter- und Nebentheilen besteht, welche zu einander ein bestimmtes Grössenmass haben. Bey den organischen Körpern hat die Natur die Verhältnisse der Theile zu einander nach individuellen Zwecken angeordnet. Bey den Bauwerken ist der Anordner der Mensch selbst. Will man z.B. bey dem menschlichen Körper die Verhältnisse der Theile und Glieder unter einander und zum Ganzen bestimmen; so nimmt man irgend einen Theil dieses Körpers selbst zum Massstab, als den Ellbogen, den Fuss, die Spanne, die Querhand, die Fingerbreite, die Kopf- oder Gesichtslänge. Auf eine ähnliche Weise verfährt man bey den Bauwerken, indem man irgend einem Theil an dem auszuführenden Gebäude zum Massstab machet, nach welchem dann alle übrigen bestimmt werden. Gewöhnlich nimmt man hiezu den untern Durchmesser der Säule, oder die Hälfte desselben. Daher der in der architektonischen Sprache angenommene Ausdruck *Modul* (Massstab).' – This early use of the concept appears to have been overlooked by authors such as: Agnes [Eleanor] Addison, *Romanticism and the Gothic Revival* . . . (New York, 1938), p.120. – Peter Collins, 'Biological Analogy' in *Architectural Review*, CXXVI (1959), pp.303–6. – Peter Collins, *Changing Ideals in Modern Architecture: 1750–1950* (London, 1965), pp.149–58. – Edward Robert De Zurko, *Origins of Functionalist Theory* . . . (New York, 1957), p.190; De Zurko was the first author to find the correct approach. – James Early, *Romanticism and American Architecture* (New York and London, 1965), pp.84–111. – Donald Drew Egbert, 'The Idea of Organic Expression and American Architecture' in *Evolutionary Thought in America*, edited by Stow Persons (New Haven etc., 1950), pp.336–96. – Katharine [Everett] Gilbert, 'Clean and Organic: a Study in Architectural Semantics' in *Journal of the Society of Architectural Historians*, X (1951), pp.3–7. – Lovejoy, *Essays in the History of Ideas* (1948), pp.69–77. – Hella Müller, *Natur-Illusion* (1961), pp.174–5. – Goerd Peschken, 'Technologische Ästhetik in Schinkels Architektur' in *Zeitschrift des Deutschen Vereins für Kunstwissenschaft*, XXII (1968), pp.45–81; Peschken was the first to recognize Hirt's importance for the development of nineteenth-century architectural theory, although he failed to perceive his contribution to architectural terminology. – Ch[arles] Robin, 'Recherches historiques sur l'origine et le sens des termes *organisme* et *organisation*' in *Journal de l'anatomie et de la physiologie*

Murphy, the mediaeval architects had adopted the pyramid as a funereal symbol from the Ancient Egyptians and incorporated it into their churches, since these were situated in graveyards. He then argued that the 'visual pyramids' were also pyramids and that consequently all pyramidal forms were natural forms. This, he maintained, was axiomatic, irrespective of whether Ancient Egyptian and mediaeval artists had thought in these terms.[152] Clearly, Murphy's ideas had been influenced by contemporary mausoleum design. But what matters to us is the fact that, unlike the majority of eighteenth-century architectural writers, he was not a country gentleman, a prelate or a courtier with artistic leanings, but a practising architect who was better acquainted with the history of architectural theory than with recent developments in aesthetics. The virtues which Murphy attributed to the Gothic architects were all traditional:

'Their works discover signs of mathematical knowledge, of philosophical penetration, and of religious sentiments, which future generations may perhaps seek for in vain, in the productions of the Architecture of this enlightened age.'[153]

But the concepts of 'nature' and the 'imitation of nature' became so diffuse during the Age of the Enlightenment that by 1800 they were quite meaningless. The almost mythical explanations of the Antique Greek orders and colonnades and the equally mythical interpretations of Gothic architecture were simply brushed aside by the antiquarians and historians of that period.

Meanwhile, the word 'natural' disappeared from the scene and was replaced in the early nineteenth century by the word 'organic'. As far as architectural theory is concerned, this change took place in the course of the theoretical discussion of the Greek temple.

Alois Hirt (1759–1839), Goethe's companion on his walks through the Antique districts of Rome and subsequently director of the Berlin Museum, seems to have been the first to have used the word 'organic' as a basic concept of architectural theory. He did so in 1809:

'Every work of architecture may be considered as an organic whole made up of primary, secondary and contingent parts which stand in a specific volumetric relationship to one another. Where organic structures are concerned, this relationship is determined by nature itself in such a way as to meet the particular functional needs of individual structures. In respect of architectural structures it is determined by man. Thus, if we wish to establish the relationship between the different parts of the human body, we take one of those parts – e.g. the elbow, the foot or instep, the span of a hand, the width of a finger or the length of the head or face – as a standard. And we proceed in a similar manner with buildings, selecting one specific part as a standard and determining all other parts according to that standard, which is usually the diameter, or half the diameter, of a column at its base and is referred to in architectonic terminology as a *module*.'[154]

Hirt's 'organic whole' appears to be synonymous with Vitruvius's 'symmetria'. In fact, this whole passage is little more than a paraphrase

normales et pathologiques de l'homme et des animaux, XVI (1880), pp.1–55; Robin's study is important for the early period of zoology. – Lore Termehr, Romanische Baukunst: Beitrag zur Geistesgeschichte des Stilbegriffs (typewritten thesis; Bonn, 1950), pp.70–3.

155 Hirt, Baukunst (1809), p.14: 'Die richtigen Verhältnisse sind das Produkt mehrerer Rücksichten, die in die Wesenheit der Baukunst eingreifen. Das Grössenmass der Theile zu einander und zum Ganzen wird theils durch das Erforderniss der Festigkeit, theils durch die zur Bequemlichkeit erforderliche Anlage, theils durch die Wirkung, welche man bey einem Baue beabsichtigt, begründet. Demnach müssen erstlich die Verhältnisse dem Mechanismus einer festen Construction entsprechen. Dieser kann aber nach dem Material, nach der Constructionsweise und nach der Grösse des Baues bedeutende Modificationen erleiden. Andere Verhältnisse erlaubt der Bau in Holz, andere erfordert der Steinbau, u.s.w. Zweytens müssen sich die Verhältnisse nach der individuellen Bestimmung eines Baues richten ... Klima, Gebräuche und Sitten können indessen manches bey den Raumverhält-nissen modificiren. Wärmere Himmelsstriche erfordern höhere und geräumigere Abtheilungen, und grössere Luftöffnungen; in kältern hingegen sind kleinere, und im Verhältniss niedrigere und mehr geschlossene Abtheilungen dem Bedürfnis mehr angemessen u.s.w. Drittens behaupten auch die Gesetze der sinnlichen Anschauung einen wesentlichen Antheil an den Modificationen des Verhältnissmasses. Jeder Bau machet einen in seiner Art eigenen Eindruck auf das Sehorgan. Das Starke und Massive erwecket Ernst, das Leichte und Schlanke giebt Heiterkeit, das Geräumige mit gehöriger Höhe machet frey, das Niedrige beklommen, u.s.w.'

156 Ibid., p.27: 'Die Architektur ist keine nachahmende Kunst, wie die Bildhauerey oder Mahlerey. Ihr Wesen beruht auf den Gesetzen einer richtigen Mechanik, wovon die Natur kein Modell zur Nachahmung aufgestellt hat. Sie ist das Werk der Erfahrungen und Erfindungen von vielen Menschen, Zeitaltern und Völkern. Man sammelte diese Erfahrungen und Entdeckungen und zog davon Lehren, Gesetze und Regeln ab. Hiedurch erhielt die Construction allmählig jene Erweite-rung, Dauerhaftigkeit und Vereinfachung, dass ein Bau sich gleichsam zur Vollkommenheit eines naturorganischen Körpers erhob. Erst dann, als die Kunst auf diesem Punkt angelangt war, entstand eine Art von allgemeinem Vorbilde, wozu hauptsächlich die Zimmerkunst die Grundlage gab.'

of the first chapter of the third book of the De Architectura. The only novel feature is the concept of 'purpose', which Hirt unobtrusively interspersed and which was quite un-Vitruvian. Thus, according to Hirt, the proportions of organic bodies are functionally determined. Consequently – and this Hirt went on to state in quite specific terms – the component members of architectural systems should also be functionally determined.

'The true relationships are determined by a number of factors which go to the very root of architecture. The proportional relationships between the various parts, and between each individual part and the whole, is determined partly by considerations of stability, partly by the need for comfort and partly by the architect's desire to create a particular impression. In the first place, therefore, the relationships must conform to the technical requirements of a solid structure, whose form may vary considerably, depending on the size of the projected building and on the building method and type of material used in its construction. The proportions of a wooden structure, for example, will be different from those found in a stone structure, and so on. In the second place, the relationships must take account of the purpose for which each particular building has been designed ... Spatial relationships are, of course, subject to variation, depending on local usage, customs and climate. Thus, warmer climes call for loftier and more spacious compartments, and larger apertures for ventilation; in colder climes, on the other hand, lower and more enclosed compartments are more appropriate, and so on. In the third place, these proportions are frequently modified by perceptual factors. Different kinds of buildings create different impressions: strong, massive structures arouse feelings of gravity; light, slender structures an impression of gaiety; tall, spacious structures a sense of freedom; low structures a sense of oppression; and so on.'[155]

From this it follows that the proportions of every individual building would be determined by its construction, function, and appearance. At the same time, however, they would also have to comply with a module based on the proportions of the human body in order to ensure the creation of an 'organic whole'. Hirt was well aware that he was reinterpreting the mimesis theory or, to be more precise, the analogy with nature expounded by his predecessors:

'Architecture is not an imitative art, like sculpture or painting. It is based on technical laws, for which nature has provided no model. It is a product of the experiences and inventions of numerous individuals, eras, and races. People recorded these experiences and inventions, and from them derived doctrines, rules, and laws. Thus, the art of construction was expanded, and codified, and gradually acquired a kind of permanence, so that buildings were elevated, so to speak, to the level of organic or natural phenomena. And it was only when the art of construction reached this stage of development that it provided a kind of universal model, which was derived primarily from carpentry.'[156]

In this particular respect Hirt followed Vitruvius much more closely than the earlier Vitruvians, who had invariably based their arguments on Vitruvius's primitive hut despite the fact that there is only a passing reference to this in the *De Architectura*. On the other hand, Hirt rejected Vitruvius's legendary accounts of the derivation of the Classical orders: 'By measuring the human body, sculptors discovered the relationship between its component parts, and between those parts and the whole, and so were able to form a clear conception of the organic perfection and beauty of the human figure. Architects, many of whom (to wit Polycletes and Scopas) were also sculptors, were very sensitive to the coarseness and heaviness of early buildings, and became more and more aware of the need for more pleasing, diverse, and delicate proportions. True, the human form could never really be used as a model for a column. But since no other form is able to give such a clear impression of the general concept of proportion, the application of this concept to buildings was by no means unprofitable. It gave architecture a higher standing (without subjecting it to ridicule by engaging in meaningless allegory).'[157]

But although Hirt was not prepared to accept the historical validity of Vitruvius's explanations, he none the less considered them to be valuable since they had established the principle of analogy with nature.

For the German Romantics the word 'organic' was the magic key to every nook and cranny of the mind and to every secret retreat in the whole of nature. Consequently, we will find that Hirt's cautious synthesis of the old and the new is more readily understandable in the light of their observations on this concept, which was applied to the sphere of architecture by the philosopher August Wilhelm Schlegel (1767–1845). In 1801 Schlegel began a series of 'Lectures on Literature and Art' in Berlin, which were eventually published in book form in 1884. He too was interested in the relationship between nature and architecture:

'Since architectural works would appear to manifest none of the great and eternal ideas which nature instils into its creations, it follows that they must be governed by a human idea: in other words, they must serve a purpose. This effectively deals with the demand that architecture should be utilitarian, for it is apparent that this demand can no longer be rejected on the grounds that the [alternative] demand for beauty is all important, since in this case beauty can clearly coexist with utility.'[158]

It should perhaps be mentioned in passing that this rather cumbersome explanation corresponds to the idea of 'fitness', which was one of the theoretical concepts of English art theory in the eighteenth century.[159] After making this point Schlegel went on to say:
'In architecture the human mind does not create reproductions of natural objects, it executes its own designs. And yet it can never entirely dissociate itself from nature . . .
'Architecture imitates nature in its general method, but not in the way it deals with individual objects. Since it is concerned with inanimate materials, it must proceed in the first instance in a *geometrical* and *mechanical* manner; that is the basis of good architecture. Only when he

157 *Ibid.*, p.46: 'Die plastischen Künstler hatten durch Ausmessen des menschlichen Körpers die Verhältnisse der einzelnen Theile und Glieder desselben zu einander und zum Ganzen kennen gelernt, und sich dadurch einen deutlichen Begriff von der organischen Vollkommenheit und Schönheit der menschlichen Gestalt überhaupt verschafft. Die Baukünstler, von denen mehr als einer zugleich Plastiker war (man erinnere sich des Polyklet und des Skopas), fühlten das Rohe und Schwerfällige des Mechanismus älterer Bauwerke. Das Streben nach gefälligern, mannigfaltigern und nach zierlichen Verhältnissen ward in ihnen immer reger. Zwar konnte die menschliche Gestalt im eigentlichen Sinne nie Vorbild der Säule seyn. Aber da keine Gestalt den allgemeinen Begriff von Verhältniss so anschaulich machen kann, wie die menschliche; so ward durch die Übertragung dieses Begriffs auf die Baukörper nicht wenig gewonnen. Die Baukunst hatte sich dadurch (doch ohne je in ein lächerliches Allegorisieren zu verfallen) einen höhern Standpunkt gesetzt.'

158 August Wilhelm Schlegel, *Kritische Schriften und Briefe*, hrsg. von Edgar Lohner, II: *Die Kunstlehre* (Stuttgart, 1963), p.140: 'Da ihre Werke demnach keinen von den grossen ewigen Gedanken, welche die Natur ihren Schöpfungen eindrückt, sichtbar machen, so muss ein menschlicher Gedanke sie bestimmen: d.h. sie müssen auf einen Zweck gerichtet sein. Hiermit ist zugleich die Forderung der Nützlichkeit, welche an die Architektur gemacht wird, abgeleitet, und zwar auf solche Weise, dass wir sehen, sie könne nie der des Schönen weichen, da dieses hier unter der Bedingung der Zweckmässigkeit existieren kann.'

159 See J[ohannes] Dobai, 'William Hogarth and Antoine Parent' in *Journal of the Warburg and Courtauld Institutes*, XXXI (1968), pp.336–82, esp. pp.337–9 and 364–5. – See also works listed under Note 154 above.

has satisfied this requirement is the architect at liberty to consider the decorative aspect of his work, which allows a greater degree of freedom and which must therefore inevitably involve some direct or indirect allusion to the *organic world*.'[160]

Thus, according to Schlegel, man created in the image of God had been replaced as exemplar by the whole of the organic world, in which function and beauty were synonymous.

But the organic world, like the individual organism, presupposed development; and this aspect was also dealt with in the eighteenth century. In 1769, Charles Bonnet, the Swiss philosopher and naturalist (1720–93), published a work entitled *La Palingénésie philosophique*, which seems to have been widely read and which was based on the idea that all animate beings develop in accordance with an innate design and are capable of constant regeneration in accordance with that design.[161] Bonnet summarized his findings in the following passage: 'And now from all this I have drawn a general conclusion, which I consider to be philosophical; namely, that all organic wholes are *preformed* and that those of the same species are confined, one inside the other, in order that they may develop, one from the other; the small from the large, the invisible from the visible . . .
'Although it may seem extremely simple, a *fibre* is none the less an *organic whole*, which nourishes itself, grows and sends forth shoots. If I cut off one end, it quickly reproduces another part similar to the one that I have cut off.'[162]

This is probably the origin of the phrase 'an organic whole', which is still in common use today. In the sphere of aesthetics this phrase means:

– functional beauty
– natural beauty
– intrinsic unity.

Alois Hirt was opposed to Gothic architecture. But the magic word 'organic', which he had introduced into architectural theory, was soon adopted by the members of the Gothic camp, who used it as a battle cry in their war on the Classicists. As recently as 1939 Frank Lloyd Wright (1869–1959) made the following pronouncement:
'The Gothic cathedrals in the Middle Ages had much in them that was organic in character, and they became influential and beautiful in so far as that quality lived in them which was *organic*, as did all other architectures possessing it. Greek architecture knew it – not at all! It was the supreme search for the elegant solution.'[163]

It was a long time before the Vitruvians developed their tree analogies and their module theory from the original analogies advanced by Vitruvius himself and, because it is so much closer to our own day, the subsequent development from Hirt to Wright seems equally protracted. But although I would not go so far as to say that the concept of organic growth in recent architectural theory is specifically Vitruvian, it seems to me that, in the light of the evidence cited above,

160 A. W. Schlegel, *Kritische Schriften und Breife*, II (1963), pp.141 and 144: 'Der menschliche Geist stellt in der Architektur nicht Nachbilder von Naturgegenständen auf, sondern Ausführungen eigener Entwürfe. Doch kann er dabei niemals ganz aus der Natur herausgehen.
'Die Architektur ahmt nicht in einzelnen Gegenständen die Natur nach, sondern in ihrer allgemeinen Methode. Da sie es mit toten Materien zu tun hat, so muss sie zuvörderst *geometrisch* und *mechanisch* bauen, darin besteht die architektonische Richtigkeit. Erst wann dieser Genüge geleistet ist, darf an eine freiere Ausschmückung gedacht werden, die eben deswegen unfehlbar eine nähere oder entferntere, aber immer unverkennbare Anspielung auf das *Organische* sein wird.'

161 Ch[arles] Bonnet, *La palingénésie philosophique, ou Idées sur l'état passé et sur l'état futur des êtres vivans; ouvrage destiné à servir de supplément aux derniers écrits de l'auteur, et qui contient principalement le précis de ces recherches sur le Christianisme*, 2 vols. (Geneva, 1769). – German translation by Johann Caspar Lavater (Zurich, 1770).

162 Bonnet, *Palingénésie* (1769), I, pp.356 and 363: 'J'ai donc tiré de tout ceci une Conclusion générale, que j'ai jugée philosophique; c'est que les Touts Organiques ont été originairement *préformés*, et que ceux d'une même Espèce ont été renfermés les uns dans les autres, pour se développer les uns par les autres; le petit, par le grand; l'invisible, par le visible . . .
'Une *Fibre*, toute simple qu'elle peut paroître, est neanmoins un *Tout organique*, qui se nourrit, croît, végète. Je retranche une de ses extrémités, et en peu de temps elle reproduit une Partie égale et semblable à celle que j'ai retranchée.'

163 Frank Lloyd Wright, *An Organic Architecture: the Architecture of Democracy* . . . (London, 1939; reprinted in 1941 and 1970), p.11. – Wright's conception of the Gothic as an organic style has been rightly linked with John Ruskin; see Roger B[reed] Stein, *John Ruskin and Aesthetic Thought in America, 1840–1900* (Cambridge [Mass.], 1967), p.208.

it must be regarded as a descendant of the Vitruvian theory of mimesis. On a later page I hope to show how it was employed and elaborated by the theorists of the Gothic Revival.

6 The Concept of Historical Development

Vitruvius's theory concerning the origin of the Classical orders formed the basis of the theory of architectural 'character' or genre styles and for the theory of mimesis or analogy with nature. Over and above this, however, it paved the way for the emergence of the concept of historical development, for Vitruvius maintained that the orders were developed, or invented, one after the other.[164] He also provided later generations with an inventory of names, which had originally denoted the place of origin of the different orders, with the result that when the Renaissance architects came to describe the innovations made in the Middle Ages, they did so in Vitruvian terms. But, despite this incongruity, the concept of historical development none the less undermined the rigid structures prescribed by the Vitruvians, just as the concept of organic growth undermined belief in the analogy with nature.

At this point I would like to return to the line of enquiry pursued in Chapter 2 and reconsider the phrase 'Gothic style', concentrating this time on the semantics of the word 'Gothic'. Exhaustive research has been carried out into the historical evolution of this concept within the various European languages, although we still lack a general synopsis covering its international development.[165] In this present context I myself will be dealing only with the particular line of development leading up to the establishment of nineteenth-century art-historical terminology.[166]

This terminology was important for the Gothic Revival in so far as it reflected the growing differentiation that was made in the nineteenth century between historical and regional styles. As a result of this development those who wished to copy mediaeval buildings without mixing different phases of the Gothic were obliged to select their models from a diminishing group of monuments or else abandon any attempt to reproduce Gothic detail and concentrate instead on general principles. At first, the concept of 'style', which was taken over from the sphere of rhetoric and became firmly established in architectural *theory* in the eighteenth century, had been applied both to the original Gothic models and to the Neo-Gothic copies. But this concept was progressively threatened as the architectural *historians* showed more and more clearly that the original models had formed part of a continuous development.

Although Vasari did not actually establish the word 'Gothic' as an historical concept, because he was such a widely read author he influenced academic discussion of the Goths and the Gothic for a full 200 years. The first edition of his *Lives* appeared in Florence in 1550.[167] For philological purposes it is fairly immaterial which monuments Vasari was actually dealing with, since there were no illustrations in the early editions of his book and, consequently, foreign readers were at

164 Vitruv, *Zehn Bücher* (1964), pp.168–73 (= Book IV, Chap. I).

165 For the Italian and French development see Note 61 above, for the English development see the splendid work by Haslag, '*Gothic*' (1963). – In Germany this development has been traced primarily in encyclopaedias and dictionaries; see G[erhard] Lüdtke, '"Gothisch" im 18. und 19. Jahrhundert' in *Zeitschrift für deutsche Wortforschung*, IV (1903), pp.133–52 (this is Lüdtke's Heidelberg thesis and has been published as such under a slightly different title in Strasbourg, 1903). Recent German research has also been noted and evaluated by Robson-Scott, *The Literary Background of the Gothic Revival in Germany* (1965).

166 Frankl, *The Gothic* (1960). – Termehr, *Romanische Baukunst* (typescript, 1950).

167 Giorgio Vasari, *Le Vite de piu eccellenti architetti, pittori, et scultori italiani, da Cimabue insino a' tempi nostri* . . ., in three parts (Florence, 1550); quotation taken from G. V., *Le Vite de' più eccellenti pittori, scultori e architettori, nelle redazioni del 1550 e 1568*, testo a cura di Rosanna Bettarini, commento secolare a cura di Paola Barocchi, 3 vols. to date (Florence, 1966 ff.).

liberty to apply his observations to their native monuments. The crucial passage in his work, as far as we are concerned, appears at the end of the second chapter of the section in which he introduces the reader to the history of architecture:

'There are works of another sort that are called German, which differ greatly in ornament and proportion from the antique and the modern. Today they are not employed by distinguished architects but are avoided by them as monstrous and barbarous, since they ignore every familiar idea or order; which one can rather call confusion and disorder, for in their buildings, of which there are so many that they have contaminated the whole world, they made portals adorned with thin columns twisted in corkscrew fashion (vine tendrils), which do not have the strength to support a burden, however light. And so, above all their façades and their other decorative parts, they built one cursed tabernacle on top of the other, with so many pyramids (pinnacles) and points and leaves that they do not stand, as it appears, not to mention their being able to hold themselves up, and they have more the quality of seeming to have been made from paper, than of stone or marble. And in these works they made so many projections, openings, little consoles, and twining vines that they threw the works that they built out of proportion; and often they reached such a height, by placing one thing on top of another, that the end of a door touched its roof. This manner was invented by the Goths, who, after the destruction of the ancient buildings and the dying out of architects because of the wars, afterwards built – those who survived – edifices in this manner: those men fashioned the vaults with pointed arches of quarter circles, and filled all Italy with these damnable buildings, so that their whole method has been given up, in order not to let any more be built.'[168]

Although he was not favourably disposed towards it, Vasari was quite perceptive on the subject of Gothic architecture. Like most writers of his day he referred to it as 'German', but he actually traced it back to the Goths, whom he blamed for the destruction of the architectural monuments of Ancient Rome. And like Vitruvius, who spoke of the *invention* ('inventio') of the Corinthian order, Vasari considered that the Gothic manner 'was *invented* by the Goths'. Moreover, although the Gothic buildings described by Vasari dated from the thirteenth to sixteenth centuries, he referred to the whole of mediaeval architecture as 'Gothic' or, to be precise, as having been 'invented by the Goths'. The earliest reference to mediaeval architecture as 'Gothic' rather than 'German' is thought to date from 1610. In that year the Jesuit Carolus Scribanius described the Antwerp Bourse, which had been built in 1531, as an 'opus Goticum'.[169]

The fact that this early reference stemmed from a Belgian Jesuit is interesting, for the Belgian Jesuits have always revealed a marked preference for Gothic forms. But although we now know of many subsequent references to the 'Gothic' in the period immediately following 1621, this is hardly a sufficient ground for regarding these two developments as a case of cause and effect.[170]

168 *Ibid.*, I, 1st half vol., pp.67–8: 'Eccì un'altra specie di lavori che si chiamano tedeschi, i quali sono di ornamenti e di proporzione molto differenti dagli antichi e da' moderni; né oggi s'usano per gli eccellenti, ma son fuggiti da loro come mostruosi e barbari, dimenticando ogni lor cosa di ordine – che più tosto confusione o disordine si può chiamare –, avendo fatto nelle lor fabbriche, che son tante ch'anno ammorbato il mondo, le porte ornate di colonne sottili e attorte a uso di vite, le quali non possono aver forza a reggere il peso di che leggerezza si sia. E così per tutte le facce et altri loro ornamenti facevano una maledizzione di tabernacoli l'un sopra l'altro, con tante piramidi e punte e foglie, che, non ch'elle possano stare, pare impossibile ch'elle possino reggere, et hanno più il modo da **parer** fatte di carta che di pietro o di marmi. Et in queste opere facevano tanti **risalti**, rotture, mensoline e viticci che sproporzio-navano quelle opere che facevano, **e** spesso con mettere cosa sopra cosa andavano in tanta altezza che la fine d'una porta toccava loro il tetto. Questa maniera fu trovata dai Goti che, per aver ruinate le fabriche antiche e morti gli architetti per le guerre, fecero dopo, chi rimase, le fabriche di questa maniera (a) le quali girarono le volte con quarti acuti, e riempirono tutta Italia di questa maledizzione di fabriche, che, per non averne a far più, s'è dismesso ogni modo loro.' Translation taken from Frankl, *The Gothic* (1960), p.290.

169 C[arolus] Scribanius, *Antverpia* (Antwerp, 1610), p.51; quotation taken from de Beer, 'Gothic: Origin and Diffusion of the Term' (1948), p.150. – Later de Beer found an additional source: Evelyn, *The Diary* (1955), VI, p.4.

170 This de Beer does. See 'Gothic: Origin and Diffusion of the Term' (1948), p.149.

171 See Note 34 above. – See also
Giovanni Baglione, *Le Vite de' pittori,
scultori ed architetti . . .* (Rome, 1642), p.175
('Vita di Giovanni Fiammingo,
Architettore').

172 J.-F. F., *Recueil historique de la vie et
des ouvrages des plus célèbres architectes*
(Paris, 1687); quotation taken from
Middleton, 'The Abbé de Cordemoy', I
(1962), pp.299–300.

173 *Encyclopédie*, VII: *FO-GYT* (Paris,
1757), p.749.

174 Corblet, 'L'architecture du moyen-
âge' (1859), pp.399–400. – There were
occasions, however, when Lebeuf was more
than a hundred years out in his
assessments.

175 J. L., *L'histoire de la prise d'Auxerre
. . .* (Auxerre, 1723), p.52, note 6;
quotation taken from Middleton, 'The
Abbé de Cordemoy', I (1962), p.316. – Dr
Johannes Dobai has drawn my attention
to the amazing critical powers of the
architect Nicholas Hawksmoor in the
mid-1730's; see Kerry Downes,
Hawksmoor . . . (London, 1959), pp.255–8
(= letter 147).

176 Pope, *The Works*, edited by
Warburton (1751), III, p.266, note.

177 T. W., *Observations on the Fairy
Queen of Spenser*, 2nd ed. (London, 1762),
pp.184 ff.; quotation taken from *Essays on
Gothic Architecture by T[homas] Warton,
J[ames] Bentham, [Francis] Grose, and
J[ohn] Milner, with a Letter to the Publisher
[John Taylor] . . .* (London, 1800; 2nd ed.
1802; 3rd ed. 1808), 2nd ed., p.8. – In this
anthology Warton's essay reached a wide
public; it was mentioned by C[arl]
F[riedrich] von Rumohr, *Italienische
Forschungen*, 3 vols. (Berlin and Stettin,
1827–31), III, p.224, note.

178 T. G., *Correspondence of Thomas Gray*,
edited by . . . Paget Toynbee and Leonard
Whibley, 3 vols. (with consecutive page
numbers), (Oxford, 1935), II, p.862;
quotation taken from Haslag, 'Gothic'
(1963), p.76.

179 *Encyclopaedia Britannica*, 3rd ed.
(London, 1797), II, p.221; quotation taken
from *A New English Dictionary on
Historical Principles (The Oxford English
Dictionary)*, edited by James A[ugustinus]
H[enry] Murray . . ., VIII, 2nd half vol.:
S-SH (Oxford, 1914), p.149.

180 L'Orme, *Le premier tome de l'architecture* (1648), fol. 110v.; see also fols. 107r.
and 112r. for similar descriptions.

181 See Note 50 above.

Incidentally, the conception of the Gothic as an 'order without order', which I discussed in Chapter 2 in connexion with Baldinucci, also stemmed in the first instance from Vasari, as is quite clear from the passage quoted above.[171]

As historical knowledge increased, it became possible to identify two separate stages of mediaeval architecture. In the preface to his *Recueil historique* of 1687 Jean-François Félibien distinguished between 'gothique ancien' and 'gothique moderne'; and from his description of these two periods it is apparent that he placed the line of demarcation between them at *c.*1200.[172] This distinction of Félibien was subsequently popularized by the *Encyclopédie*.[173] Jean Lebeuf (1687–1760), an antiquarian who studied under Bernard de Montfaucon and who was able to date the various parts of mediaeval buildings to within twenty years,[174] proposed further subdivisions – 'mérovingiaque', 'carlovingiaque', 'gothique', and 'enriciastique' – in his *Histoire de la prise d'Auxerre* of 1723. But despite his undoubted ability, Lebeuf's proposals elicited no immediate response.[175]

This attempt to establish architectural periods corresponding to the successive French dynasties was followed by a similar attempt in England. In 1751 William Warburton (1698–1779) distinguished between two types of mediaeval church: 'the one built in the Saxon times; the other during our Norman race of Kings'.[176]

It was not until the eighteenth century that the different stages of mediaeval architecture were defined in architectural terms; and – significantly – this classification was effected not by an antiquarian, but by a man of letters. In the second edition of his *Observations on the Fairy Queen of Spenser*, which appeared in 1762, Thomas Warton (1728–90) distinguished between 'the Gothic Saxon' (Salisbury Cathedral), 'the Absolute Gothic' (Winchester Cathedral), 'the Ornamental Gothic' (King's College Chapel, Cambridge), and 'the Florid Gothic' (Henry VII's Chapel, Westminster).[177] Thus, Warton freed the word 'Gothic' not only from the pejorative sense of 'barbaric', but also from the false origins which had been ascribed to it. But three years later, in 1765, Thomas Gray (1716–71) wrote a letter to James Bentham (1708–94), in which, like Warburton, he recommended that Gothic architecture should be described as 'Saxon' and 'Norman' architecture.[178] These alternative terms appeared in the third edition of the *Encyclopaedia Britannica* in 1797 and so reached a wide public.[179]

Until the Italian theory of art – whose adherents despised the architectural forms of the Middle Ages and ascribed them to the Goths – became pre-eminent in Europe, the northern countries evidently regarded the Gothic as a vernacular style. In his architectural treatise of 1567 Philibert de l'Orme unhesitatingly described rib vaults with projecting keystones as vaults 'à la mode françoise'.[180] But we have already seen that only two generations later, when work started on the completion of the Cathedral of Orleans, French architects were already speaking of a 'desseing à la Gothique'.[181] By then even the structures of Gothic buildings appear to have become alien to the

French, for the vault above the choir (which was built in 1617 but collapsed in 1904) was to be modelled on an existing Gothic vault, namely that of Notre-Dame in nearby Cléry.[182]

No sooner had mediaeval architecture been broken down into two distinct modes of building than people began to look for an 'inventor' for the second of the two modes. In 1699 the sculptor and painter Florent le Comte (d.1712) described the style of St Mark's in Venice as a mixture of the 'goût Antique' and the 'goût Arabesque', and the Spanish style of building as 'la manière de bâtir des Sarazins ou Arabes'.[183] A theory was then evolved, in which it was argued that Gothic architecture must either have been taken over from the Spanish Arabs or else have been introduced into Europe from the Middle East during the Crusades.[184] This theory, which seems to have originated among the members of John Evelyn's and Christopher Wren's circle, might be dismissed as a mere curiosity but for the fact that it was repeated throughout the eighteenth century. Due partly to the unbelievable ignorance of the eighteenth-century public about historic monuments and partly to the disproportionate significance which it attached to the synonymic use of words such as 'Gothic', 'Arabian' and 'Saracenic', there was a tendency to introduce exotic elements during the early period of the Gothic Revival.

The young Goethe also seems to have been strangely confused over terminology. When he saw Strasbourg Cathedral and was so overcome by its west façade, he described the Gothic as 'German Architecture' ('deutsche Baukunst'), attacked the Italians – to whom he was indebted for this expression – for their lack of understanding, and voiced his strong disapproval of the term 'Gothic', which was then a common classification and to which, at that time, he ascribed 'all the synonymic misunderstandings [that have arisen]'.[185]

The way in which the English antiquarians of the late eighteenth century abandoned traditional enquiries into the origins of the Gothic in order to concentrate on the origins of what they regarded as its principal characteristic – namely, the pointed arch – may be regarded as a final resurgence of Vitruvianism. Just as the styles of Antique architecture had been identified by reference to different kinds of capital, so the styles of mediaeval architecture were identified by reference to different kinds of arch. And the more people came to prefer the Greek before Roman architecture and to regard the former as a trabeated style, the more they tended to regard mediaeval architecture as an arched style. The antiquarians of the eighteenth century even tried to establish architectural classifications based on such terms: 'Pointed Style' in England, 'style ogival' in France, and 'Rundbogenstil' and 'Spitzbogenstil' in Germany.

Describing the 'Saxon style' in 1762 Warton said that it consisted of 'round arches, round-headed windows, and round massy pillars', and was in fact no more than 'an adulteration or a rude imitation of the genuine Grecian or Roman manner'. He claimed that, although the buildings erected by the Normans in England after the Conquest were

182 Chenesseau, *Sainte-Croix d'Orléans* (1921), I, pp.49–50; II, figs.45–7. – The choice of model – but not the copyism – appears to have been determined by iconological considerations: King Louis XI founded the Church of Notre-Dame, and is also buried there.

183 Florent Le Comte, *Cabinet des singularitez d'architecture, peinture, sculpture et gravure . . .*, 3 vols. (Paris, 1699–1700), I, p. iii.

184 Frankl, *The Gothic* (1960), p.137. – Haslag, 'Gothic' (1963), pp.71–4. – Lovejoy, *Essays in the History of Ideas* (1948), p.137. – Wren: see Note 104 above.

185 Ernst Beutler, *Von deutscher Baukunst: Goethes Hymnus auf Erwin von Steinbach, seine Entstehung und Wirkung . . .* (Munich, 1943), pp.8 and 12. – Beutler's study contains the text of the the first impression: [Johann Wolfgang Goethe,] *Von deutscher Baukunst, D[ivis] M[anibus] Ervini a Steinbach* (n.p., 1773 [actually 1772]). – For information about recent English translations and commentaries see Robson-Scott, *The Literary Background of the Gothic Revival in Germany* (1965), p.80.

bigger than those found on the Continent of Europe, in all other respects they were the same.[186] Later, he said, they acquired something of the 'Saracen fashion' and, with the advent of the Crusades, began to feature pointed arches.[187]

In the monograph which he published on the Cathedral of Ely in 1771 James Bentham (1708–94) presented elements of art historiography in mediaeval texts, from which he concluded that the customary mediaeval classification for the style of the early Middle Ages had been 'the Roman manner'.[188] Like Warton, Bentham began his account by listing the various characteristics of Norman architecture: 'the circular arch, round-headed doors and windows, massive pillars . . .'[189] In 1771 the 'Norman style' had not yet been precisely defined, and consequently Bentham was still able to speak of 'the Saxon or Norman style' and of 'this early Norman style (I mean with round arches and large pillars)'.[190] In his day the epithet 'Gothic' was normally reserved for buildings with pointed arches,[191] and Bentham observed in this connexion that the pointed arch may conceivably have been derived from the interlacing arcading found in Norman buildings.[192] This derivation had already been suggested by Thomas Gray in 1754 (although the treatise in which the suggestion appeared was not published until 1814).[193] In Bentham's case we find that the theory formed part of a general conception of historical development: 'The transition from one style to another is usually effected by degrees, and therefore not very remarkable at first, but it becomes so at some distance of time; towards the latter part indeed of his [Henry II's] reign, and in that of Edward II we begin to discover a manifest change of the mode as well in the vaulting and make of the columns as the formation of the windows.'[194]

Horace Walpole (1717–97) formulated a more conventional theory, in which he argued that Gothic architecture had come about as a result of the debasement of earlier architectural forms. Like Bentham's theory of progressive development, this departed from the Vitruvian concept of an 'invented' style, and it had a considerable bearing on the later concept of the 'Romanesque style'. Moreover, Walpole was probably the first antiquarian to compare mediaeval architecture with the 'Roman language':
'When men enquire, "Who invented Gothic buildings?" they might as well ask, "Who invented bad Latin?". The former was a corruption of the Roman Architecture, as the latter was of the Roman language. Both were debased in barbarous ages; both were refined, as the age polished itself; but neither was restored to the original standard.'[195]

In 1769 Walpole made contact with the Reverend William Cole, the Reverend Michael Tyson and the architect James Essex (1722–84) with a view to publishing a joint work on Gothic architecture. As it happens, most of the notes and designs which he made for this project were never published, but it seems probable that Essex's ideas will have been propagated by word of mouth.[196] In the same year he began to work for Walpole in an architectural capacity.[197] According to Thomas Kerrich,

186 *Essays on Gothic Architecture* (1802), p.4.

187 *Ibid.*, pp.4 and 6.

188 *Ibid.*, p.43. – First impression: James Bentham, *The History and Antiquities of the Conventual and Cathedral Church of Ely; from the Foundation of the Monastery, A.D. 673 to the year 1771* (Cambridge, 1771), p.25.

189 *Essays on Gothic Architecture* (1802), p.67.

190 *Ibid.*, pp.69–71.

191 *Ibid.*, p.75.

192 *Ibid.*, p.76.

193 Thomas Gray, *Architectura Gothica* (1814); Frankl, *The Gothic* (1960), p.403, quotes from T.G., *The Works of Gray*, edited by J[ohn] Mitford, v (London, 1843), p.327.

194 *Essays on Gothic Architecture* (1802), p.83.

195 Horace Walpole, *Anecdotes of Painting in England . . .*, edited by Ralph N[icholson] Wornum (London, 1888), I, p.116, note 1.

196 Stewart, 'James Essex' (1950). – James Essex, 'Some Observations on Lincoln Cathedral', read at the Society of Antiquaries, March 16, 1775, (printed) in *Archaeologia or Miscellaneous Tracts Relating to Antiquity*, published by the Society of Antiquaries of London, IV (1777), pp.149–59. – J. E. 'Remarks on the Antiquity and the Different Modes of Brick and Stone Buildings of England', read at the Society of Antiquaries, Dec. 8 etc., 1774, (printed) *ibid.*, pp.73–109. – For the *Journal* see Notes 121–2 above. – T[homas] Kerrich also refers to Essex: see T.K., 'Some Observations on the Gothic Buildings Abroad, Particularly those of Italy, and on Gothic Architecture in General', read 11th and 18th May, and 1st June 1809 at the Society of Antiquaries, (printed) in *Archaeologia . . .*, XVI (1812), pp.292–325; see esp. pp.306–10, note 1.

197 Stewart, 'James Essex' (1950), pp. 319–20.

Essex discovered practical advantages in the pointed arch, since it could be built to the same height with varying spans, and the same centreing could be used in all cases.[198]

In 1798 John Milner (1752–1826), the Catholic Bishop of Castabala, published a book on Winchester, in which he said that the pointed arch was not only a characteristic of the Gothic, but the very principle on which it was based.[199] He was the first critic to refer to:
'that beautiful style of architecture properly called the *pointed*, and abusively the *Gothic*, order.'[200]

Milner's new term – 'the pointed style' – was publicized by John Taylor, the London publisher, in a collection of essays on Gothic architecture. A letter, in which Milner explained to Taylor why he had found it necessary to introduce this expression, was also printed.[201] One of these two men evidently thought out the terminological implications of the new expression, for in his preface Taylor spoke of the 'difference of character and effect of the circular and of the pointed styles of ancient English architecture'.[202] Incidentally, it is quite apparent from this statement that the expression 'circular style' is of earlier provenance than the equivalent expression 'Rundbogenstil', which is frequently used nowadays in English- as well as German-speaking countries and has come to mean something akin to the Romanesque Revival. Apart from appearing in Taylor's preface, the expression 'the Saxon or circular style of architecture' featured in the captions for the illustrations.[203] However, Taylor also suggested an alternative expression:
'This style of architecture may properly be called English architecture, for if it had not its origin in this country, it certainly arrived at maturity here; under the Saxon dynasty this style of building was introduced, and under the Norman dynasty it received its ultimate degree of beauty and perfection.'[204]

Neither the English landscape gardeners nor the architects who designed country houses were interested in terminology that reflected the historical development of Gothic architecture. What they wanted were expressions which would enable them to differentiate between the various genre styles. Accordingly, Humphrey Repton (1752–1818), the influential landscape gardener who collaborated with the architect John Nash for a number of years, distinguished between 'Castle Gothic', 'Church Gothic', and 'House Gothic' in 1803.[205] It is quite possible that these distinctions were already generally accepted at that time, for the architect Richard Elsam also differentiated between secular and ecclesiastical architecture in 1803:[206]
'It would evidently be extremely absurd to employ the same sort of window for a house as in a church.'[207]

Like Elsam, Robert Lugar (1773–1855) regarded the Gothic as a specifically English style which was particularly suitable for houses in rural settings, such as vicarages:
'A taste for the Gothic style of architecture having of late become very prevalent, I am induced to make some observations on the true style or

198 *Archaeologia* . . . , pp.310–16. – See also the manuscripts reproduced in Stewart, 'James Essex' (1950), p.320.

199 John Milner, *The History, Civil and Ecclesiastical, & Survey of the Antiquities of Winchester* (Winchester, 1798), esp. II, pp.148–9; see also Frankl, *The Gothic* (1960), p.445. – Part of Milner's study was reproduced in *Essays on Gothic Architecture* (1st ed. 1800 etc.).

200 *Ibid.*, pp.126–7. – The precise German equivalent of 'pointed' is 'spitz'; but in the nineteenth century 'Pointed style' was normally translated as 'Spitzbogenstyl'.

201 *Ibid.*, p. xiii.

202 *Ibid.*, p. iv (Roman pagination in the first section.)

203 *Ibid.*, pp.135 ff.

204 *Ibid.*, p. iv.

205 Humphrey Repton, *Observations on the Theory and Practice of Landscape Gardening* . . . (London, 1803), p.190.

206 R.E., *An Essay on Rural Architecture* . . . (London, 1803), p.16.

207 *Ibid.*, p.16.

character applicable to houses of this description, which may properly be called the *ancient English style of building*, and commonly called Gothic.'[208]

The antiquarians were better informed. The following observations were made by the Reverend James Dallaway (1763–1834) in 1806: 'Our own Gothick was not brought us from Spain, but from Normandy and France . . . Whether this early Gothick originated in Palestine, or was borrowed from the Moors in Spain, has given rise to conjecture; but a more bold deviation from the established style could have been scarcely made . . . It will be contended by the French antiquaries, that this new mode was not exclusively our own, but that it appeared, if not earlier, at least in the same century, in the magnificent cathedrals I have noticed, as then recently erected in France.'[209]

We do not know where Dallaway gained his insight into French architecture. He may have been acquainted with George Downing Whittington, who made a tour of France prior to 1806 but did not publish an account of his journey until 1809; he may have consorted with French emigrants; or he may have visited France himself. At all events, he seems to have been extremely well informed, for he referred to Suger, Abbot of St Denis, a sure sign of knowledge.[210] Dallaway preferred the new expression 'pointed style'[211] to the traditional expressions which it had replaced, and used it to describe the transition from the Romanesque to the Gothic: 'The pointed style was frequently mixed with the round.'[212]

Incidentally, this also shows that the expression 'round style' was used at an early date in English.

By 1809 Thomas Kerrich was already complaining about the confusion created by the new terminology.[213] He pointed out that, far from being the sole constituent of Gothic architecture, the pointed arch invariably appeared in combination with slender columns and shafts, elegant crockets, tracery, vaulting, and so on. From this he argued that to refer to Gothic architecture as 'the pointed style' was a misnomer, and that it would be better to classify it in terms of centuries for, although the Gothic style had been subject to constant change, the principal stages in its development did in fact correspond, more or less, to the successive centuries.[214] This suggestion of Kerrich's met with a favourable response and his system of classification has remained in force right down to the present day.

A second system, which has also stood the test of time, was subsequently evolved by Thomas Rickman (1776–1841), who, like James Essex, combined the practical skills of the architect with the scholarship and dedication of the antiquarian. Among other things, his *Attempt to Discriminate the Styles of English Architecture* was intended to provide a manual for ecclesiastical administrators and to 'render them more capable of deciding on the various designs for churches in imitation of the English styles'.[215] Rickman described the Gothic as the 'English style' because he believed that it had originated in England.[216] He distinguished between:

208 R[obert] Lugar, *Architectural Sketches for Cottages, Rural Dwellings, and Villas in the Grecian, Gothic and Fancy Styles . . .* (London, 1805), p.12.

209 James Dallaway, *Observations on English Architecture, Military, Ecclesiastical, and Civil . . .* (London, 1806), pp.14, 22, and 23.

210 *Ibid.*, p.210. – Frankl, *The Gothic* (1960), pp.498–9, refers only to Whittington; Dallaway appears to have escaped his attention.

211 Dallaway, *Observations on English Architecture* (1806), pp.2, 19, etc.

212 *Ibid.*, p.28.

213 Kerrich, 'Some Observations' (1812), p.293 (based on a lecture given in 1809).

214 *Ibid.*, pp.296–7.

215 Thomas Rickman, *An Attempt to Discriminate the Styles of English Architecture, from the Conquest to the Reformation; Preceded by a Sketch of the Grecian and Roman Orders, with Notices of Nearly Five Hundred Buildings* (London, n.d. [1817]), p. iii. – Rickman's study was first printed in J. Smith, *The Panorama of Science and Art*, 2 vols. (Liverpool, 1815).

216 Rickman, *An Attempt to Discriminate the Styles of English Architecture* (1817), p.38.

the 'Norman style' (from *c*.1066),
the 'Early English style' (from 1189),
the 'Decorated English style' (from 1307),
and the 'Perpendicular style' (from 1377 or later to 1630–40).[217]

But Rickman also helped to ensure that the alternative expressions to the word 'style' received a new lease of life both in England and, subsequently, in other countries as well. He was very much in favour of the word 'order', provided it was used in its rightful context:
'In dividing the Grecian and Roman architecture, the word *order* is used, and much more properly than *style*; the English styles regard not a few parts, but the conception of the whole building, but a Grecian building is denominated Doric or Ionic merely from its ornaments; and the number of columns, windows, &c. may be the same in any order, only varied in their proportion.'[218]

In Rickman's view, therefore, the word 'order' is in its rightful place in an historical setting. His attitude to the word, 'character', however, was quite different. Speaking of St Albans Abbey in Hertfordshire (now a cathedral) Rickman said that it was 'of a very bold plain character'.[219]

Two years after the publication of Rickman's manual a new generic concept was formulated which embraced both the 'Saxon style' and the 'Norman style', and which was to endure for generations. This concept was 'the Romanesque style' or, in its abbreviated form, 'the Romanesque'. With the discovery of numerous mediaeval texts, in which frequent reference was made to the 'opus Romanum', and with the growing realization that the earliest architectural monuments were, as Rickman put it, like the 'Roman mode debased', a concept of this kind was very much in the air.[220]

In his *Inquiry into the Origin and Influence of Gothic Architecture*, which was published in 1819[221] but which, according to the author, was actually completed in 1813, William Gunn (1750–1841) maintained that the crucial factor in the development of mediaeval architecture had been the Late Roman preference for arches supported by columns rather than arches framed by columns plus entablatures.[222] From the reign of Constantine the Great, Gunn continued,
'it became their prevailing character, and which, as expression of the architecture from which it is a vitious deviation, I shall denominate ROMANESQUE. From the utter inability to adopt a term sufficiently expressive, I feel myself under the necessity of modifying one for my purpose. The Italian termination *esco*, the English and French *esque*, is occasionally allowable; thus we may say *pittoresco*, *picturesque* and *pictoresque*, as partaking of the quality to which it refers. A modern Roman, for instance, of whatever degree, calls himself *Romano*, a distinction he disallows to *an inhabitant* of his native city, whom, though long domiciled, yet from dubious origin, foreign extraction or alliance, he stigmatizes by the term ROMANESCO. I consider the architecture under discussion in the same point of view.'[223]

Gunn drew a parallel between 'the deterioration of letters' and the decline of architecture.[224] Why it was that the Englishman Gunn settled

217 *Ibid.*, pp.39 and 44.

218 *Ibid.*, p.8.

219 *Ibid.*, p.127.

220 *Ibid.*, p.4.

221 William Gunn, *An Inquiry into the Origin and Influence of Gothic Architecture* (London, 1819), p. iv.

222 *Ibid.*, p.4.

223 *Ibid.*, p.6.

224 *Ibid.*, p.37.

225 Frankl, *The Gothic* (1960), whose account of terminological developments is the weakest part of his book, overlooks the lexicographic difficulties posed by English terminology; see *ibid.*, p.507.

226 First published in F[erdinand] Gidon, 'L'invention du terme "architecture romane" par Gerville (1818) d'après quelques lettres de Gerville à Le Prévost' in *Bulletin de la Société des Antiquaires de Normandie*, XLII (1935), pp.268–88; quotation taken from *ibid.*, p.285: 'Je vous ai quelquefois parlé d'architecture romane. C'est un mot de ma façon qui me paraît heureusement inventé pour remplacer les mots insignifiants de *saxone* et de *normande*. Tout le monde convient que cette architecture lourde et grossière est l'*opus romanum* dénaturé ou successivement dégradé par nos rudes ancêtres. Alors aussi, de la langue latine, également estropiée, se faisait cette langue romane dont l'origine et la dégradation ont tant d'analogie avec l'origine et les progrès de l'architecture. Dites-moi donc, je vous prie, que mon nom *romane* est heureusement trouvé.'

227 [Charles-Alexis-Adrien Duhérissier] de Gerville, 'Lettre adressée à M. de Vanssay, préfect du département de la Manche, en janvier 1820, contenant des recherches sur l'architecture des églises de ce département' in *Mémoires de la Société des Antiquaires de la Normandie*, 1824, 1ère partie (published in 1825), pp.78–105, note 1; Gerville refers to an earlier letter in connexion with the new concept of 'architecture romane'.

228 *Ibid.*, p.78. – See *ibid.*, p.91, for the substantive form of 'roman', and p.99, for 'le genre roman'.

229 [Arcisse] de Caumont, 'Essai sur l'architecture religieuse du moyen âge, particulièrement en Normandie', communiqué à la Société d'Emulation de Caen, en décembre 1823, lu à la Société des Antiquaires de la Normandie, le 8 mai 1824, in *Mémoires de la Société des Antiquaires de la Normandie*, 1824, 2e partie (published in 1825), pp.535–677.

230 *Ibid.*, p.538, note 2, and p.550. – Caumont knew Dallaway; see *ibid.*, p.607.

on the expression 'Romanesque' (which he used both in the substantive and the adjectival sense) whilst French scholars chose 'roman' and the Germans 'romanisch' is far too complex a problem to be analysed here.[225] All that matters for our purposes is the fact that this concept provided a connecting link between Roman and mediaeval architecture and, subsequently, between Classicism and the Gothic Revival.

In France, too, the concept of historical development and the emergence of the new terminology were closely related. But in France the crucial advance was not made until the nineteenth century, after French emigrants like Charles-Alexis-Adrien Duhérissier de Gerville (1769–1853) had made contact with the English antiquarians. It was Gerville who coined the expression 'architecture romane'; and since, as we have already seen, the idea of a modern derivative from the Latin *romanus* was very much in the air at that time, it is quite possible that he will have arrived at this formulation independently of Gunn. On 18 December 1818 Gerville wrote to Auguste Le Prévost (1787–1859): 'I have spoken to you before about "architecture romane". It is a phrase which I coined myself and which seems to me to be a fortunate discovery with which to replace the rather meaningless expressions 'Norman' and 'Saxon'. Everybody is agreed that this cumbersome and coarse architecture is a latterday version of the *opus romanum* that has been debased or degraded by successive generations of our uncouth forebears. The post-Latin language, whose origin and subsequent degradation reveal so many analogies with the origin and subsequent development of architecture, emerged in exactly the same way from the Latin language, after it too had been mutilated. So please tell me that my name *romane* is a fortunate discovery.'[226]

Although this letter was not published until 1935 and a similar letter may well have been lost, Gerville wrote a third letter on this subject which was published in 1825.[227] In it he repeated his arguments in favour of 'architecture romane', and fixed its duration from the Carolingian period to the twelfth century. He also referred without comment to 'architecture à ogives' (instead of 'architecture gothique'), which would suggest that this concept was then already well established among the antiquarians (or *archéologues*) of the Normandy region.[228] In the first thirty years of the nineteenth century 'ogive' often meant 'pointed arch'.

Of the Norman antiquarians by far the most gifted organizer was Arcisse de Caumont (1801–73), who publicized the new terminology in his *Essai sur l'architecture religieuse*, which he wrote in 1822 and which was published in 1825.[229] In this work Caumont acknowledged himself to be a disciple of Gerville, and expressed his gratitude to Gerville for having introduced him to the works of Bentham, Grose, Warton, and Whittington.[230]
'Prior to the twelfth century nearly all the buildings in our province had semicircular arcades, in which we are able to recognize a debased form of Roman architecture, and which I propose to call the *Romanesque genre*.

231 *Ibid.*, p.540: 'Avant le XIIᵉ siècle, presque tous les édifices de notre province ont des arcades semi-circulaires; on y reconnaît l'architecture romaine dégénérée: c'est ce que j'appelle le genre *roman*.
'Depuis le XIIᵉ jusqu'au XVIᵉ siècle, on trouve des arches aigües ou ogives, c'est ce que j'appelle le *genre gothique*, pour me conformer à l'expression reçue, quoiqu'impropre; mais il est facile d'arriver à plus de précision et de suivre l'architecture, pour ainsi dire, siècle par siècle. Afin de mettre quelque ordre dans les caractères qu'elle présente successivement, j'ai cru devoir subdiviser de la manière suivante les deux genres principaux que je viens d'établir:

Roman { Primordial, depuis l'expulsion des Romains de la Gaule jusqu'au Xᵉ siècle. Secondaire. Fin du Xᵉ et XIᵉ siècle.

Transition { Fin du XIᵉ et première moitié du XIIᵉ siècle.

Gothique { Primordial. Fin du XIIᵉ et première moitié du XIIIᵉ siècle. Secondaire. Fin du XIIIᵉ siècle et XIVᵉ. Tertiaire. XVᵉ et XVIᵉ siècles.'

232 *Ibid.*, pp.607 and 614 ff.

233 *Ibid.*, pp.566 and 597.

234 *Ibid.*, p.603.

235 *Ibid.*, p.603: 'Moi-même j'avais balancé à lui donner le nom de romantique, par opposition à l'architecture romane qui offre encore quelque chose de classique, puisque ses principaux caractères sont tirés de l'antique.' – It is possible that this concept went from Germany to England, and from England to France; in this connexion see J[ean]-B[aptiste]-L[ouis]-G[eorges] Séroux d'Agincourt, *Histoire de l'art par les monuments depuis sa décadence au IVᵉ siècle jusqu'à son renouvellement au XVIᵉ*, 3 vols. of text and 3 vols. of plates (Paris [1811–]1823) I, Section entitled 'Histoire de l'art par les monumens', p.81 (my own pagination). – For 'romantico' in an Italian publication of 1828 cf. Enrico Castelnuovo, 'Una disputa ottocentesca sull' "Architettura Simbolica" ' in *Essays in the History of Architecture Presented to Rudolf Wittkower* ... (n.p. [London], 1967), pp.219–27.

236 Jean Mallion, *Victor Hugo et l'art architectural* ..., 2 editions (Paris and Grenoble, 1962), see esp. pp.62 ff.

237 Victor Hugo, *Œuvres poétiques*; préface par Gaëtan Picon, édition établie et annotée par Pierre Albouy ..., 2 vols.

'From the twelfth to the sixteenth century we find pointed arches or ogives, which I propose to call the *Gothic genre* in order to conform to the traditional, albeit inaccurate, classification. It is, however, quite a simple matter to achieve greater precision, and to follow the development of architecture from century to century, as it were. In order to represent the different characters which it has revealed in successive periods in a rather more orderly fashion, I felt it necessary to subdivide my two principal genres in the following way:

Romanesque { First stage: from the departure of the Romans from Gaul to the 10th century. Second stage: end of the 10th and the first part of the 11th centuries.

Transitional { End of the 11th and the first half of the 12th centuries.

Gothic { First stage: end of the 12th and the first half of the 13th centuries. Second stage: end of the 13th and the whole of the 14th centuries. Third stage: 15th and 16th centuries.'[231]

But Caumont was also attracted by Le Prévost's classification of the Gothic into 'gothique à lancettes', 'gothique rayonnant' and 'gothique flamboyant'; and so he also produced a composite system embracing both his own and Le Prévost's categories.[232] On the other hand – and despite the fact that, on one occasion at least, he employed the phrase 'architecture à ogive ou gothique'[233] – Caumont was fundamentally opposed to expressions such as 'architecture à ogive', 'genre oriental' and 'genre sarrasin', which had been put forward as alternatives to the older expressions 'architecture gothique' and 'style gothique'.[234] But there was one new concept of German origin to which Caumont gave serious consideration:
'For my part, I had debated whether to give it [the Gothic] the name Romantic in order to distinguish it from Romanesque architecture, which has retained a certain Classical quality because its principal characteristics are drawn from the Antique.'[235]

An indication of the speed with which Caumont's terminology was disseminated is provided by Victor Hugo (1802–70). Hugo actively supported the movement for the conservation of artistic monuments in France, and was quite prepared to introduce technical terms into his poems, dramas, and novels, which often produced a bizarre effect.[236] The third section of his ode *Le Voyage*, which dates from 1825, ends with the following quatrain:

'He often spoke about the Gothic arch, referring
To its eastern origin, whilst sitting there with you;
He also told us of the Romanesque, of spires lost from view
Amidst the clouds, their shingled faces like a living carving.'[237]

(Paris, 1964–7), I: *Avant l'exil*, p.478:
'Il nous a dit souvent, assis à vos côtés,
L'ogive chez les goths de l'Orient venue,
Et la flèche romane aiguisant dans la nue
Ses huit angles de pierre en écailles sculptés.'

238 Victor Hugo, *Notre-Dame de Paris
1482*; introduction, notes et choix de
variantes par Marius-François Guyard
(Paris, 1961); 'gothique' (adj.): *ibid.*, pp.3,
13 (twice), 17, 18, 71, 82, 128, 129, 130
(twice), 132 (twice), 133, 134, 135, 143,
146, 147, 148, 149, 155, 158, 162, 216, 220,
222, 264, 276, and 307; 'ogival': *ibid.*,
p.134; 'ogive' (adj.): *ibid.*, pp.15, 149, 229,
237, 305, and 351; 'ogive' (subst.): *ibid.*,
pp.17, 113, 126, 127, 130, 131, 133, 213,
227, 257, 307, 399, 400, 402, 414, 470, and
485; 'roman' (adj.): *ibid.*, pp.130, 131
(twice), 132, 133, 134, 143, 147, 158, 177,
213 (three times), 214, 216 (twice), 223,
237, 241, and 403.

239 Hugo, *Notre-Dame* (1961 edition),
p.133, note 2: 'C'est la même qui s'appelle
aussi, selon les lieux, les climats et les
espèces, lombarde, saxonne et byzantine.
Ce sont quatre architectures sœurs et
parallèles, ayant chacune leur caractère
particulier, mais dérivant du même
principe, le plein cintre.'

240 Hugo, *Notre-Dame* (1961 edition);
'saxon': *ibid.*, pp.131, 132, 150 (twice),
and 180; 'byzantin': *ibid.*, p.147.

241 For a general account and for further
details see Robson-Scott, *The Literary
Background of the Gothic Revival in
Germany* (1965).

242 See Note 185 above.

243 A[lois] Hirt, 'Historisch-
architektonische Beobachtungen über die
christlichen Kirchen; an H[errn] v[on]
G[oethe] in W[eimar]' in *Italien und
Deutschland, eine Zeitschrift*, hrsg. von
K[arl] P[hilipp] Moritz und A[lois] Hirt, I,
1. Stück (1789), pp.33–74.

244 *Ibid.*, p.51: 'Die Baukunst der
mittleren Zeit, die aus dem gänzlichen
Verfall der Griechischrömischen entstand,
nemlich die Arabische, und die sogenannte
Gothische, das Kind der Arabischen,
verlohr den Plan der Basilik nie ganz aus
dem Gesichte.'

245 *Ibid.*, p.53: 'Arabischgothische
Baukunst.'

246 *Ibid.*, p.55: 'gothischen Plan,
gothische Verhältnisse mit altrömischen
Ordnungen, und altrömischer Art zu
construiren.'

247 *Ibid.*, figs.1–3.

Hugo's highly successful novel, *Notre-Dame de Paris*, was published in 1831–2, and the long descriptive passages in this work provided the French public, which had had little or no previous knowledge of mediaeval architecture, with a basic vocabulary of antiquarian terms. In this novel I discovered thirty instances of the adjective 'gothique', one instance of the adjective 'ogival' (which appears to have been little used at that time), six instances of the adjective and seventeen of the substantive 'ogive', and twenty instances of the adjective 'roman'.[238] In a footnote Hugo defined Romanesque architecture as follows: 'In other places with other climates and categories this architecture is called Lombardic, Saxon or Byzantine. These are four parallel sister-architectures, which all have their own special character but which are all derived from the same principle, the round arch.'[239]

In actual fact, however, Hugo normally used the word 'Saxon' as if it were synonymous with 'Romanesque'.[240] As for the expressions 'Lombardic' and 'Byzantine', which originated in Italy and Germany, the precise date when these were adopted by French antiquarians has yet to be established.

The most extravagant words and phrases were coined by German antiquarians concerned with the origins and development of the Gothic. For reasons of space I can reproduce only a small selection of their ideas.[241]

Goethe's proposal that the Gothic should be renamed as 'deutsche Baukunst', which he put forward in 1772, was not adopted until after 1800.[242] Initially, German antiquarian enquiries were conducted along much the same lines as those in France and England, the only difference being that the Germans tended to pay rather more attention to Italian developments. In an article, which he dedicated to Goethe, Alois Hirt (1759–1839) investigated the early Christian basilicas and (like the Abbé de Cordemoy, but with rather more emphasis on the typological and evolutionary aspects of the subject) traced the development of this form of architecture right down to modern times:[243] 'The architecture of the Middle Ages, which came into being as a result of the total decline of Greco-Roman architecture, in other words Arabian architecture and its offspring which is known as Gothic architecture, never quite lost sight of basilica design.'[244]

Hirt then went on to subject 'Arabian-Gothic' architecture to every conceivable criticism and compared it with the kind of scholastic theology evolved by Averroes and Thomas Aquinas.[245] But Hirt was no less critical of more recent church buildings which, he maintained, combined 'a Gothic design and Gothic conditions with Roman orders and Roman methods of construction'.[246] His own solution was a basilica with a gallery after the manner of Sant'Agnese fuori le mura in Rome but with a portico incorporated into the main façade.[247]

The development of the terminology used by Johann Dominik Fiorillo (1748–1821) in his *Geschichte der zeichnenden Künste*, a work in five volumes which appeared over a period of ten years, is quite remarkable. The text of all five volumes, which were widely read by the

248 J[ohann] D[ominik] Fiorillo, *Geschichte der zeichnenden Künste von ihrer Wiederauflebung bis auf die neuesten Zeiten*, 5 vols. (Göttingen, 1798–1808), I (1798), p. XX.

249 *Ibid.*, p.39: 'In den folgenden Zeiten wurden die Araber in verschiedenen Ländern Mitbürger der Europäer, und als ausser den Kriegen allmählig auch ein anderweitiger Verkehr mit ihnen gestiftet ward, so verbreitete sich in Europa der sogenannte Arabische Geschmack in der Baukunst. Es ist ein gewöhnlicher Missbrauch alle die fremden Arten zu bauen unter dem Nahmen Gothischer Architektur mit einander zu vermischen.'

250 *Ibid.*, II (1801), pp.379–80.

251 *Ibid.*, III (1805), p.15: 'Sehr wahrscheinlich ist es nun, dass Karl, der dem Reiche der Langobarden ein Ende machte, viele Künstler, die ehedem am Hofe des Desiderius lebten, mit sich nach Frankreich nahm, und auf diese Weise den Longobardischen Styl dahin verpflanzte.'

252 *Ibid.*: 'Karl, der für ihre Schönheit empfänglich war, bemühte sich, die Christliche Baukunst mit ihr in Verbindung zu setzen, und gab in seinen Gebäuden zu Aachen die erste Probe einer gemischten, Römisch-Gothischen, Lombardischen und Arabischen Architectur, woraus in der Folge die so genannte neuere Gothische entstanden ist, die, wie wir an einem andern Orte umständlich zeigen werden, von den Deutschen Künstlern zur höchsten Vollkommenheit gebracht wurde.' – Fiorillo may well be drawing a parallel here between German art and the German (i.e. Holy Roman) Empire. In this connexion see Robson-Scott, *The Literary Background of the Gothic Revival in Germany* (1965), p.239.

253 Fiorillo, *Geschichte der zeichnenden Künste*, III (1805), p.22, note.

254 *Ibid.*, IV (1806), p.16: 'Die Gothen . . . bauten in dem damals allgemein herrschenden verdorbenen Geschmack, der, wie wir oft bemerkt, in den neuern Zeiten fälschlich der *Gothische* genannt wurde, und seinen Ursprung den Teutschen und Arabern verdankt.'

Romantics, was revised from the point of view of style by August Wilhelm Schlegel.[248] Fiorillo became a professor at Göttingen University, where he held the first chair in the History of Art. In the first volume of his work, which was published in 1798, he described the way in which European architecture developed following the migration of peoples: 'In the following periods Arabs lived side by side with Europeans in various countries, and as military confrontation gradually gave way to other forms of contact, the so-called Arabian taste in architecture spread throughout Europe. It is a common fallacy to subsume all foreign modes of building under the generic name of Gothic architecture.'[249]

In his second volume, which appeared in 1801, Fiorello introduced the word 'German' ('Teutsch') as a replacement for 'Gothic'. But although his 'German architecture', 'German style', and 'German taste' embraced the whole of Romanesque art, he regarded the fourteenth century as the high point of this development.[250]

In 1805 he published his third volume, in which he set out his Lombardic theory: 'It seems highly probable that, when Charlemagne conquered the kingdom of Langobardy, he will have taken many of the artists who had been living at the Court of Desiderius back to France with him, thus transplanting the Lombardic style.'[251]

But Fiorillo still had to incorporate Arabian architecture into his theory: 'Charlemagne, who was receptive to its [Arabian architecture's] beauty, tried to amalgamate Christian and Arabian architecture, and in the new buildings in Aix-la-Chapelle he provided the first examples of a composite architecture incorporating Roman-Gothic, Lombardic, and Arabian features; from this composite architecture the so-called new Gothic architecture emerged which, as I shall demonstrate in detail on a later page, was carried to its highest peak of perfection by German artists.'[252]

Thus, Fiorillo would seem to have denoted the 'Romanesque' style by 'Lombardic'. On an earlier page in the same volume he also described the Abbey of Cluny as Lombardic.[253]

But in the fourth volume, which was published in 1806, a Classicist reaction set in. The Goths in Spain, Fiorillo said, 'built in the corrupt taste prevailing at that time, which, as I have frequently observed, has been wrongly called the Gothic taste of more recent times and which owed its inception to the Germans and Arabs.'[254] Fiorillo even went so far as to reject the word 'Gothic' as a designation for the architecture of the Visigoths.

In the autumn of 1803 Friedrich Schlegel (1772–1829), the brother of August Wilhelm Schlegel, whom we have already encountered twice in the course of this book, met the Brothers Sulpiz Boisserée (1783–1854) and Melchior Boisserée (1786–1851) in Paris, and in 1804 he accompanied these young but extremely knowledgeable antiquarians to Cologne, where he remained until 1806. It was during this period that

255 F. S., *Kritische Friedrich-Schlegel-Ausgabe*, 1. Abteilung, IV: *Ansichten und Ideen von der christlichen Kunst*, hrsg. und eingeleitet von Hans Eichner (Paderborn, Munich and Vienna, 1959), pp.153–204.

256 *Ibid.*, p.161: 'Gewiss würden mich die ältesten Denkmale der griechischen Kunst zu Athen, Girgenti und Paestum mit Ehrfurcht erfüllen.'

257 *Ibid.*: 'Keine Art soll die andere verdrängen in der Kunst.'

258 *Iibd.*, pp.161–3: 'romantische Bauart' ('Romantic architecture'), 'altsächsisch' ('Ancient Saxon'), 'normännisch' ('Norman'), 'neugriechisch' ('Neo-Greek'), 'neurömisch' (Neo-Roman'), 'altchristlich' ('Early Christian').

259 *Ibid.*, p.63: 'Fantasie', 'Naturgefühl'.

260 *Ibid.*, pp.176 and 180: 'christlich griechisch', 'gräzisierende Baukunst'.

261 Pierre Moisy, *Les séjours en France de Sulpice Boisserée (1820–1825): contribution à l'étude des relations intellectuelles franco-allemandes* . . . (Lyons and Paris, 1956).

262 Sulpiz Boisserée, *Geschichte und Beschreibung des Doms von Köln, nebst Untersuchungen über die alte Kirchen-baukunst, als Text zu den Ansichten, Rissen und einzelnen Theilen des Doms von Köln* (Stuttgart, 1823 [–1832]), main text pp.30 and 41; captions p.37. – The title of the volume of text, which appeared in German and French (Paris), incorporated the title of the volume of plates, which had appeared two years before, in 1821. When the Munich 'Volksausgabe' appeared in 1842, this composite title was dropped. – Boisserée's terms were 'Rundbogenstyl' and 'Spitzbogenstyl'.

263 Sulpiz Boisserée, 'Über die Beschreibung des Tempels des heiligen Grales in dem Heldengedicht: Titurel Kap. III' in *Abhandlungen der Philosophisch-philologischen Classe der Königlich Bayerischen Akademie der Wissenschaften*, I (1835), pp.307–92; quotation taken from *ibid.*, pp.330–1: 'altdeutsch'.

264 Boisserée, *Geschichte und Beschreibung des Doms von Köln* (1823–32), main text, p.41: 'Die Kunst aber, wenn sie bei einem Volke sich eigenthümlich entwickelt, wird auch immer den ursprünglichen Lebensgeist des Volkes athmen, und dies ist gerade bei der Baukunst ganz vorzüglich der Fall.'

he wrote his *Briefe auf einer Reise*, which he subsequently revised for inclusion in his Collected Works (published 1823) under the title *Grundzüge der gotischen Baukunst*. A comparison of the two versions is highly enlightening.[255] Schlegel was not an antiquarian himself, and consequently it is not surprising to find that he tended to think in antithetical and not evolutionary terms. He acknowledged a 'marked preference for Gothic architecture', but was none the less convinced that, if he ever had the good fortune to see them, 'the earliest monuments of Greek art in Athens, Agrigentum and Paestum would fill him with awe',[256] for 'no one genre should supplant another in art'.[257] Elsewhere, in using the epithet 'German' instead of 'Gothic' he appealed, not to Goethe, but to Fiorillo, as his authority. In the 1823 version, i.e. the *Grundzüge*, he assessed the new expressions coined meanwhile. He said that he preferred 'Romantic architecture' to 'Gothic architecture' but felt it was too late to effect a change in this respect since the word 'Gothic' was too well established. He also rejected 'German' because it was not comprehensive enough, 'Germanic' because it did not reflect the political conditions obtaining in the Middle Ages, and 'Ancient Saxon' and 'Norman' because they were applicable only to England. Instead of 'Neo-Greek' and 'Neo-Roman' he proposed that 'Early Christian' should be used as a designation for the circular style.[258] He also claimed that the essential characteristics of 'Romantic architecture' were imagination and a feeling for nature.[259] In the 1804/5 version of the *Briefe* the circular style was referred to as 'Greco-Christian' or 'Graecizing' architecture.[260]

Expressions such as 'Neo-Greek', 'Greco-Christian', 'Graecizing' and 'Byzantine' were prompted by the early Italian view of history rather than by a knowledge of architectural monuments. But meanwhile Sulpiz Boisserée (1783–1854), whose major work began to appear in the same year as Friedrich Schlegel's *Grundzüge*, was trying to extend contemporary knowledge of such monuments. During the 1820's Boisserée made several protracted visits to France with a view to obtaining subscriptions for his folio publication on Cologne Cathedral and in the hope of finding a printer.[261] Whilst there, he made contact with French antiquarians and became conversant with the new terminology which they had evolved. In the text of his *Domwerk*, which was published in 1823, he spoke of the 'early Byzantine and Romanesque style of architecture' and of the 'heavy Romanesque or Byzantine style of architecture with circular arches'. But in the captions for the illustrations, which were not published until 1832, we find the expressions 'circular style' and 'pointed style'.[262] Boisserée vacillated for a long time between these alternative terms. In his later article on 'The Temple of the Holy Grail' he used the expression 'Ancient German', which reflected his thinking best of all:[263]
'But when the art of a nation develops in a particular way, it is always inspired by the original character of that nation; and this is especially the case with architecture.'[264]

But Boisserée's evolutionary view of architecture was overlaid by the

265 *Ibid.*, p.42: 'Es musste nur ein solcher Meister erscheinen, der das Zusammen-treffen der geometrischen Gliederung mit der vegetabilischen Bildung erkannte, um wie durch den Hauch des Frühlings die dürren Äste und Zweige zu beleben, und das Ganze in *ein* harmonisches *Bild* zu vollenden.' – For further details see Herbert Rode, 'Der Kölner Dom in der Anschauung Sulpiz Boisserées' in *Jahrbuch des Kölnischen Geschichtsvereins*, XXIX/XXX (1954/5), pp.260–90.

266 Arnold Wolff, 'Chronologie der ersten Bauzeit des Kölner Domes' in *Kölner Domblatt, Jahrbuch des Zentral-Dombau-vereins*, XXVIII/XXIX (1968), pp.7–230 (this is Wolff's Aachen thesis).

267 Rumohr, *Italienische Forschungen* (1827–31).

268 In a footnote he speaks of the 'affinity between the *beau idéal* of the Italian Mannerists and that of modern aesthetes' ('Stammverwandtschaft der Idealbegriffe italienischer Manieristen und moderner Ästhetiker'); quotation taken from *ibid.*, I (1827), p.53.

269 *Ibid.*, p.178: 'altchristlich'.

270 *Ibid.*, p.179: 'eigentümlich Neugriechisches'.

271 *Ibid.*, p.209: 'die römischchristliche Kunstart in sein Gebiet wiedereinzu-führen.'

272 *Ibid.*, p.213: 'lauter römische Elemente.' – Lorsch is situated in Hessen, West Germany.

273 *Ibid.*, p.259: 'vorgotisch'.

274 *Ibid.*, p.322.

275 *Ibid.*, p.317: 'deutsch-byzantinische Schule.'

276 *Ibid.*, pp.348 and 351: 'Pracht byzantinischer Baukunst . . . Dennoch erscheinen während der dunkleren Jahrhunderte des Mittelalters nur abgerissene Spuren eines vorübergehenden erfolglosen Einflusses der Byzantiner . . .; in der Baukunst aber war die römische Schule, wie ich in nachstehender Abhandlung zeigen werde, nie so gänzlich unterbrochen worden, war das Fremde, welches in dieser Kunstart während des zwölften und dreizehnten Jahrhunderts sich eingedrängt hatte, nicht etwa bloss ein byzantinisches oder anderes, sondern gar viel und mancherlei.'

277 *Ibid.*, III (1831), p.164: 'gotisch', 'langobardisch', 'byzantinisch', 'arabisch'; 'das Vorwaltende aber ist das Zeitliche.'

51

belief that all that was needed to 'perfect the whole [discipline, and transform it] into a *single* harmonious *system*' was the appearance of 'just such a master' as the Master of Cologne Cathedral.[265] Boisserée's Master Gerhard had more in common with Vitruvius's Callimachus, the inventor of the Corinthian capital, than with Arnold Wolff's Master Gerhard.[266]

Boisserée, who was acclaimed as one of the leading European antiquarians after the publication of his *Domwerk*, had restricted his investigations to a single building. By contrast, Carl Friedrich von Rumohr (1785–1842), who had studied under Fiorillo, pursued a more general line of enquiry, working mainly from archives. His most interesting work from our point of view is his *Italienische Forschungen* because it provides the first documented commentary on what subsequently came to be known as the 'Byzantine question'.[267] Rumohr had an incomparable grasp of the philosophical aspects of contemporary aesthetic theory;[268] and he was a completely impartial observer.

Rumohr used the expression 'Early Christian' because it was not possible to distinguish between the works of the Greeks, the Romans and the Barbarians during the period of the migration of peoples.[269] He showed that the first specifically modern Greek elements that could be identified as such dated from the seventh century,[270] and he pointed out that it was Charlemagne who 'reintroduced Roman-Christian art into his territory'.[271] Rumohr recognized the existence of a 'Carolingian Renaissance', and on the entrance gateway of the convent at Lorsch he identified 'exclusively Roman elements'.[272] Rumohr described twelfth-century Italian architecture as 'pre-Gothic'.[273] He analysed the works of Italian authors, maintaining that they had underestimated Byzantine influence despite the fact that, as far back as 1400, Cennino Cennini had said of Giotto: 'Rimutò l'arte di Greco in Latino' (he transformed painting from a Greek into a Latin art).[274] Rumohr also referred to the 'German-Byzantine school' of craftsmen under Emperor Heinrich II.[275] But he pointed out that, notwithstanding the 'splendour of Byzantine architecture' in Constantinople, 'only desultory traces of a temporary and ultimately ineffectual influence on the part of the Byzantines [appeared] during the darker centuries of the Middle Ages'. 'The Roman school [of architecture]', Rumohr said, 'was never so completely disrupted, the exotic elements which had intruded into this branch of art during the twelfth and thirteenth centuries were not simply Byzantine elements, but many and varied.'[276] The mere fact that Rumohr used the word 'influence' shows how evolutionary his thinking was.

In the third volume of his *Italienische Forschungen*, which appeared in 1831, Rumohr made a further attempt to clarify the critical concepts in current use. He pointed to 'Gothic', 'Lombardic', 'Byzantine' and 'Arabian' as instances of geographical concepts, but insisted that the 'dominant factor is temporal':[277]

'The English antiquarians distinguish between Saxon, Norman and Gothic "modern" architecture by reference to different periods of their

278 *Ibid.*, 164, note: 'Die englischen Altertumsforscher unterscheiden sächsische, normännische und neugotische Bauart nach den Epochen ihrer eignen Geschichte. Diese Unterscheidung, deren erste wir carolingisch, die zweite, nach dem bisherigen Gebrauch, vorgotisch nennen würden, gehen nur England an, kommen daher hier nicht in Betracht.' – Rumohr may have discovered this 'Carolingian' category in the writings of the Abbé Lebeuf; see Note 175 above.

279 Rumohr, *Italienische Forschungen*, III (1831), p.170: 'germanische Architektur'.

280 *Ibid.*, pp.216 and 221: 'vorgermanische Bauart'.

281 *Ibid.*, p.219: 'Die germanische Bauart aber entwickelte sich organisch, bildete, was in ihr bloss verzierend ist, systematisch aus ihren Grundformen hervor.'

282 L[eo] von Klenze, *Anweisung zur Architectur des christlichen Cultus* (Munich, 1834), p.13: 'byzantinischer und romanischer Baustyl.' – It has been claimed that Rumohr did, in fact, use the word 'romanisch'; see Van der Grinten, *Enquiries into the History of Art-Historical Functions and Terms* (1952), pp.90 and 125 (Van der Grinten gives no precise references).

283 Klenze, *Anweisungen* (1834), pp.14 and 20: 'mittelalterlicher Basilika-Styl', 'christlich-hierarchischer Baustyl'. – Further references to the use of 'romanisch' are to be found in Georg Germann, 'Architecture romane' in *Neue Zürcher Zeitung*, January 12, 1969, pp.49–50.

284 Franz Kugler, *Handbuch der Kunstgeschichte* (Stuttgart, 1842), pp.415–17; see also p.516.

285 *Ibid.*, pp.467–8: 'classische Kunst', 'romantische Kunst', 'romanischer Styl', 'germanischer Styl'.

286 *Ibid.*, p.495: 'organisch gesetzmässige Entwicklung des künstlerischen Styles.'

287 *Ibid.*, p.535: 'Behandlung, die dem schöneren und mehr harmonischen Style der deutsch-germanischen Architektur auffallend nahesteht.'

288 *Ibid.*, p.547.

national history. These categories, the first of which we would call Carolingian and the second, in accordance with present usage, pre-Gothic, are applicable only to England and consequently are unacceptable.'[278]

By the same token, Rumohr argued, the Gothic should not be called 'German', because there were also a French and an English Gothic; it could, however, be accurately described as 'Germanic architecture'.[279] Having suggested this definition, Rumohr quite logically referred not only to 'Germanic', but also to 'pre-Germanic', architecture in his subsequent writings.[280]

In the *Italienische Forschungen* Rumohr distinguished between Arabian and Byzantine architecture on the one hand and Germanic architecture on the other; for, whereas the former had merely been 'derived' from Late Roman architecture, the latter was an organic development, in which even the purely decorative elements had resulted from the systematic evolution of certain basic forms.[281]

While Rumohr seems to have avoided the word 'Romanesque' – perhaps because he realized that the origins of mediaeval architecture were infinitely complex – practising architects such as Leo von Klenze (1784–1864) used it without any hesitation whatsoever.[282] But then the proposals which von Klenze put forward in 1834 were not designed to clarify the historical development of architectural terminology but merely to provide a working vocabulary. For the Romanesque and the Gothic he suggested 'Mediaeval Basilica style' and 'Christian-hierarchical style'.[283]

It was not until Franz Kugler (1808–58), the Berlin art historian, published his *Handbuch der Kunstgeschichte* in 1842 that the word 'romanisch' – as conceived by the French *archéologues* – was able to make real headway in Germany.[284] In his manual, which was highly successful and ran to five editions by 1872, Kugler distinguished between 'Classical art' and 'Romantic art'. Under Romantic art he included both the 'Romanesque style' and the 'Germanic style'. Since the entrance gateway at Lorsch did not fit in with his scheme of things, Kugler blithely updated it to the second half of the twelfth century;[285] for he was a firm believer in the 'organic and systematic development of artistic style'.[286] Although he was well acquainted with the early Gothic buildings in France, he regarded the German Gothic of the thirteenth and fourteenth centuries as the peak of this development. Kugler's strange assertion that the Sainte-Chapelle in Paris revealed a method of 'treatment remarkably similar to the more beautiful and more harmonious style of German-Germanic architecture'[287] is directly attributable to this basic attitude. Kugler was well aware that the system of Gothic architecture taken over by the Germans had already been largely perfected. And yet in this case he clearly implied that the style had been perfected in Germany and had subsequently influenced the design of the Sainte-Chapelle.[288]

If we consider that the art historians of the mid-nineteenth century were constantly providing the architects of the period with new material, it is easy to understand why those architects should have found it necessary to concentrate on one particular historical phase and, therefore, easier to excuse the terminological consequences to which this gave rise.

As long as the nineteenth-century architects and their patrons were able to think of the different historical styles as constants, they were able to employ them as specific genres, i.e. as completely self-contained styles with their own particular 'characters'. But once the art historians began to depict the emergence of these different historical styles as an evolutionary process and the styles themselves as the artistic expression of a general historical situation, the architects and their patrons were obliged to ask themselves why it was that their generation had been unable to produce a style of its own in the nineteenth century. With this the babel of styles became a problem.

II Early Theories of the Gothic Revival

1 From the Landscape Garden to Pugin's Churches

1 This has been pointed out, above all, by Nikolaus Pevsner; see Reyner Banham, 'Revenge of the Picturesque: English Architectural Polemics, 1945–1965' in *Concerning Architecture, Essays on Architectural Writers and Writing Presented to Nikolaus Pevsner*, edited by John Summerson (London, 1968), pp.265–73. – See also John Barr, 'A Selected Bibliography of the Publications of Nikolaus Pevsner', *ibid.*, pp.275–85, and the same author's complete Pevsner bibliography (Charlottesville [Virginia], 1970).

2 Christopher Hussey, *The Picturesque: Studies in a Point of View* (London and New York, 1927; reprinted London, 1967), esp. pp.186 ff.: 'Architecture'. – H. F. Clark, 'Eighteenth-Century Elysium' (1943). – Lovejoy, *Essays in the History of Ideas* (1948), esp. pp.99 ff.: 'The Chinese Origin of Romanticism', and pp.136 ff.: 'The First Gothic Revival and the Return to Nature'. – S[usanne] Lang and N[ikolaus] Pevsner, 'Sir William Temple and Sharawaggi' in *Architectural Review*, cvi (1949), pp.391–3; reprinted in Nikolaus Pevsner, *Studies in Architecture and Design*, 2 vols. (London, 1968), i, pp.103–7; German version in N. P., *Architektur und Design von der Romantik zur Sachlichkeit* ... (Munich, 1971), pp.41–7.

3 Jacob Burckhardt, *Gesamtausgabe*, vi: *Die Kunst der Renaissance in Italien*, hrsg. von Heinrich Wölfflin (Basle, 1932), pp.161–2 (= § 125); first printed in 1867 under the title *Die Renaissance in Italien* in the series *Geschichte der Baukunst*.

4 Erich Bachmann, 'Anfänge des Landschaftsgartens in Deutschland' in *Zeitschrift für Kunstwissenschaft*, v (1951), pp.203–28, esp. pp.207–8.

5 S[usanne] Lang, 'Principles of the Gothic Revival in England' in *Journal of the Society of Architectural Historians*, xxv (1966), pp.240–67, esp. p.250.

The eighteenth-century English garden has influenced architectural theory in three important respects. Our view of the relationship between architecture and nature, our assessment of symmetrical and asymmetrical design and our attitude to historical and exotic architecture are still determined to a considerable extent by this development.[1] The artists of the Continental Rococo also had a predilection for asymmetrical design and exotic features, and yet their influence has not been anywhere near as great or as enduring.

The first English gardens go back to *c*.1720. The extent to which this new fashion was inspired by Chinese gardens, which had been described by English missionaries returning from the Far East, by the accounts provided by Pliny the Younger of his villas, and by the terms 'Sharawaggi' and 'Elysium', have been dealt with at length by others.[2]

The first indication of the Gothic Revival in English landscape design came with the introduction of artificial ruins, which were used as means of heightening the atmosphere in certain parts of the gardens. Artificial ruins as such were, of course, by no means new. We know from Vasari's account of the life of Gerolamo Genga that they were a feature of Renaissance gardens, where they served as reminders of the splendour of ancient Rome.[3] Many other components of the eighteenth-century English garden had already been in existence in the sixteenth and seventeenth centuries. The *selvaggio*, which was found in virtually every large Italian garden in the Renaissance, was introduced into England in the seventeenth century and was known as 'the wilderness'. In 1717 in Neuwald, near Kukus in Bohemia, a park was laid out with two hermitages, each with its own hermit, and with recumbent, kneeling and standing statues of saints set out among the trees. But although in its original condition this park was no doubt intended to testify to Baroque piety, it soon became a precursor of the sentimental garden, for within a very short space of time the two living hermits were replaced by two additional statues.[4]

From this Bohemian natural park it was only a short step to the Gothic Temple of Flora erected by William Stukeley (1687–1765). Stukeley, who was such a great admirer of Gloucester Cathedral, had old stained-glass windows fitted in his temple, which he visited every morning to ring the bell.[5] The fact that Stukeley dedicated his Gothic Temple to Flora was presumably due to his naturalistic conception of the Gothic.

13

In 1750, when Horace Walpole (1717–97) initiated a series of alterations in the Gothic style in his country house – Strawberry Hill, near Twickenham, on the Thames – he took the frivolous ideas evolved by contemporary landscape designers and transformed them into a new style of domestic architecture. The son of a prime minister, a brilliant conversationalist and letterwriter, the author of the first Gothic novel and of a history of English art, Walpole was ideally suited for this undertaking.[6] From the eighteenth century onwards Strawberry Hill has always been regarded as the prototype of the *Gothic Revival*, and although we now know that there were in fact many earlier works in this mode, Walpole's villa remains far and away the most significant and influential. For this villa really was Walpole's creation. True, he employed architects, but he changed them so often that the over-all responsibility for the design of the villa can only be ascribed to him.[7] Walpole's observations on the Gothic, and on his villa, are scattered throughout his writings, where they testify to his adaptable taste but can hardly be said to constitute a consistent doctrine.[8] In his younger years Walpole applied to the Gothic the kind of epithets which he used to describe the Rococo. Thus, in 1748 he called it 'the charming venerable Gothic'.[9] Various observations which he made in a letter dated 25 February 1750 help to explain why he chose this style for Strawberry Hill:

'The Grecian is only proper for magnificent and public buildings. Columns and all their beautiful ornaments look ridiculous when crowded into a closet or cheesecake-house.'[10]

For Walpole, the Grecian – by which he meant the Antique – was simply a genre style, and not a universally valid norm. The grandeur and solemnity of Antique columniform architecture were at variance with his own villa-oriented conception; for we are told in the same letter: 'The variety is little, and admits no charming irregularities.' Multiplicity and irregularity (or asymmetry) constituted the *leitmotif* of the new landscape design, which Walpole now proposed to reproduce in his villa on the grounds that this formed the focal point of its own particular landscape. He called this *leitmotif* by the pseudo-Chinese name 'Sharawaggi' and – still in the same letter – he wrote:

'I am almost as fond of the Sharawaggi, or Chinese want of symmetry, in buildings, as in grounds or gardens.'

Richard Bentley (1708–82), a man of unreliable character but a gifted designer, was the first artist Walpole engaged for the conversion of his villa. Commenting on Bentley's abilities, Walpole said that he was the only man he knew who was capable of combining 'the grace of Grecian architecture and the irregular lightness and solemnity of Gothic'.[11] This would indicate that, at that time, Walpole's conception of 'Grecian architecture' was based not on the Doric order exemplified by the Temples of Paestum, but on the Palladian revival of Roman architecture. He identified the principal characteristics of Gothic architecture as irregularity, lightness, and solemnity, the solemnity being inspired partly by religious and partly by historical associations. In actual fact,

6 See the splendid biography by the American Walpole collector and expert: Wilmarth Sheldon Lewis, *Horace Walpole* ... (Washington and London, 1961).

7 Horace Walpole, *The Letters of H. W.* ..., edited by ... Paget Toynbee, 16 vols. (Oxford, 1903–5); 3 supplementary vols. (1918–25). – [Horace Walpole,] *A Description of the Villa of Mr. Horace Walpole, Youngest Son of Sir Robert Walpole Earl of Orford, at Strawberry Hill near Twickenham, Middlesex, with an Inventory of the Furniture, Pictures, Curiosities, &c.* (Strawberry Hill, 1784; with subsequent appendices; facsimile edition London, 1964).

8 A selection with commentary is to be found in Haslag, 'Gothic' (1963), pp.125–6 and 150–1. – Lang, 'Principles of the Gothic Revival' (1966), pp.251–3.

9 Letter to George Montagu of July 25, 1748, in Walpole, *The Letters*, ii (1903), p.325, No.276. – See also [Nikolaus Pevsner,] 'Rococo Gothic: Walpole and Strawberry Hill' in *Architectural Review*, xcviii (1945), pp.151–4.

10 Letter to Horace Mann in Walpole, *The Letters*, ii (1903), p.433, No.308.

11 Letter to Horace Mann of October 24, 1758, in Walpole, *The Letters*, iv (1903), p.212, No.600. – See also Lewis, *Horace Walpole* (1961), p.56.

one room at Strawberry Hill, which was called the 'Cabinet', was so solemn that when the Duc de Nivernois visited the villa, he mistook this room for a chapel, and upon entering it removed his hat.[12] As for the historical associations, it was these that prompted Walpole to refer to Gothic architecture as 'our architecture'.[13] And it was high praise on his part when, in 1758, he said of the artificial ruin created by Sanderson Miller (1717–80) in Hagley (Worcestershire; 1747–9): 'It has the true rust of the Barons' Wars.'[14] In other words, the right patina: a new problem for associative architecture!

Although Walpole sometimes referred to his villa as the 'Castle', and although its 'fantastic fabric' provided the inspiration for his novel *The Castle of Otranto* (1765), most of the individual conversions which he carried out at Strawberry Hill were based on ecclesiastical and not secular models.[15] It seems that it was only when he met the architect James Essex that Walpole came to realize that different genre styles had already been used in the Middle Ages. According to Walpole, the New Offices designed by Essex and built after his death by James Wyatt were in a 'collegiate style'.[16] Throughout his life Walpole retained an open and enquiring mind, and during his later years he was well aware that, in their knowledge of Gothic architecture, the younger generation of antiquarians far outstripped him, just as he had outstripped Batty and Thomas Langley in his early period. In 1794 he made the following comment about the rooms at Strawberry Hill in a letter to Mary Berry: 'Every true Goth must perceive that they are more the works of fancy than of imitation.'[17]

If proof is needed of Walpole's intellectual qualities, it is surely to be found in the fact that he was able to recognize the quality of men such as the architect Essex, the architect, painter and student of encaustic processes Johann Heinrich Müntz and the architect, engraver and antiquarian John Carter.

John Carter (1748–1817) was probably the first writer to hazard an explanation as to why the Gothic style should have proved so suitable for church architecture. Between 1774 and 1778 he edited – first in conjunction with a number of other architects and later, it seems, alone – a publication entitled *The Builder's Magazine*, which purported to be a 'Monthly Companion' but was really an architectural dictionary issued in instalments.[18] This publication appeared in conjunction with a series of designs, which we must now consider. As a genre style the Gothic had, of course, not yet been restricted to churches. Consequently we find a design for a 'Gothic Observatory', which in many respects anticipated the monument erected to Sir Walter Scott in Edinburgh in 1844. Like all eighteenth-century observatories, it was shaped like a tower, which may well have been the reason why its designer chose the Gothic style.[19] There was also a design for a circular Gothic temple for use in a landscape garden, a type of design that had been popularized by the Langleys and had been virtually *de rigueur* ever since.[20] There were two designs by Carter himself dating from 1775. One of these was for a Gothic dovecot;[21] the other – which brings out the relationship

12 Letter to Horace Mann of April 30, 1763, in Walpole, *The Letters*, v (1904), p.314, No.876. – See also Kenneth [Mackenzie] Clark, *The Gothic Revival: an Essay in the History of Taste* (London, 1928); the reference is to the Penguin edition (Harmondsworth, 1964), p.50.

13 Quotation taken from Lang, 'Principles of the Gothic Revival' (1966), p.251.

14 Letter to Richard Bentley of September 1753 in Walpole, *The Letters*, III (1903), p.186, No.376. – See also Clark, *The Gothic Revival* (1964), p.37.

15 Walpole, *A Description of the Villa* (1784), pp. iv, 1–2, 6, 33, 42–3, 53, 55, 72, and 80–2.

16 Letter to William Cole of June 1, 1776, in Walpole, *The Letters*, IX (1904), p.372, No.1702.

17 Letter to Mary Berry of October 17, 1794, *ibid.*, xv (1905), p.327, No.2951.

18 *The Builder's Magazine: or Monthly Companion for Architects, Carpenters, Masons, Bricklayers, &c., as well as for Every Gentleman who Would Wish to Be a Competent Judge of the Elegant and Necessary Art of Building; Consisting of Designs in Architecture, in Every Stile and Taste . . .*, by a Society of Architects, each having undertaken the department in which they particularly excels (London, 1774–8); the captions are numbered separately.

19 *Ibid.*, pl. XXXVIII.

20 *Ibid.*, pl. XVI.

21 *Ibid.*, pl. LI.

between house and garden – was entitled: 'The Plan and Elevation of a Design for a Gothic Mansion to be erected on an Eminence that commands an extensive Prospect' (1775).[22] Other designs by Carter include: a Gothic Seat of Retirement (1776), a Gothic Pulpit (1776), a Market Cross (1776), a Gothic Pavilion (1778) and a Gothic Charnel-house (1778). During the last two years of publication a series of designs appeared, which showed details of a Gothic church and various interior fittings.[23] The accompanying texts which Carter composed for these designs were remarkable. So too was the fact that the most detailed of these appeared beneath a cross-section of the proposed church:

'The Gothic architecture has, for these few years past, fallen greatly under the censure of the immoderate admirers of Grecian architecture, yet if we candidly consider we find both styles have their separate beauties and use. The Grecian taste certainly best suits those public buildings; such as palaces, courts of justice, exchanges, hospitals, music-rooms, banqueting-rooms, mansions, &c., but for religious structures Gothic undoubtedly ought to be preferred: the difference is easily to be decided: by spending a few hours in St Paul's and St Peter's Westminster, we may easily and seriously tell which has the greatest effect on the mind; which pile of buildings conveys the more devote ideas; which fills the senses with the greatest attention of the heaven above us; which leads us more to contemplate on the life to come?'[24]

This caption is so full of pathos that it precluded all possibility of reverting to the fancy Gothic of earlier years, which is probably what Carter intended. He left the reader to make his own comparison between St Paul's and Westminster Abbey, for he knew that the educated public of his day would be predisposed by the numerous publications which had appeared throughout the eighteenth century and in which Gothic architecture had been represented as a catalyst for religious feelings. In the closing sentences of *The Builder's Magazine* Carter referred to the nature of those feelings:

'I must confess myself a zealous admirer of Gothic architecture – affirming with confidence, nothing can be more in character, and better adapted to a place of worship, than that awful style of building, and that Grecian and Roman architecture should be confined to mansions and other structures of ease and pleasure.'[25]

It was because the Gothic inspired feelings of awe that Carter approved of the Gothic style for churches. His line of argument is strangely reminiscent of the requirements laid down by Leon Battista Alberti for church architecture:

'The windows in churches should be placed high up near the roof, so that all that can be seen through them is the sky, and neither the celebrants nor the supplicants are distracted from their devotion to the deity. The sense of awe aroused by the darkness strengthens the spirit in its reverence; thus gravity is linked to a high degree with glory.'[26]

A hundred years later Michel de Montaigne (1533–92) praised the 'vastité sombre de nos églises';[27] and some forty years after Montaigne, Henry Wotton (1568–1639) wrote in his *Elements of Architecture*:

22 *Ibid.*, pl. LXII; Supplement Plate LXV of 1776.

23 *Ibid.*, pls. CX, CXIII, CXVI, CXIX, CXXVI, CXXX, CLXIII, and CLVIII.

24 *Ibid.*, Caption for Plate CXIX.

25 *Ibid.*, Caption for Plate CLXXXV.

26 Alberti, *L'Architettura (De re aedificatoria)* (1966), II, p.617 (= Book VII, Chap. XII): 'Apertiones fenestrarum in templis esse oportet modicas et sublimes, unde nihil praeter caelum spectes, unde et qui sacrum faciunt quive supplicant, nequicquem a re divina mentibus distrahantur. Horror, qui ex umbra excitatur, natura sui auget in animis venerationem; et coniuncta quidem multa ex parte maiestati est austeritas.'

27 Michel de Montaigne, *Essais*, 4 vols. (Paris, 1802), II, p.363 (1st ed. 1580).

28 Henry Wotton, *The Elements of Architecture, Collected by Henry Wotton Knight from the Best Authors and Examples* (London, 1624; commented facsimile edition Charlottesville [Virginia], 1968), p.55.

29 From Vanbrugh's unpublished 'Proposal for Building ye new Churches' (1711); quotation taken from S[usanne] Lang, 'Vanbrugh's Theory and Hawksmoor's Buildings' in *Journal of the Society of Architectural Historians*, XXIV (1965), p.130.

30 Eleven further assessments, five of them English, are to be found in Séroux d'Agincourt, *Histoire de l'art* (1823), Section entitled 'Histoire', pp.68–9, note b.

31 Walter John Hipple, Jr., *The Beautiful, the Sublime, & the Picturesque in Eighteenth-Century British Aesthetic Theory* (Carbondale [Ill.], 1957), esp. pp.21–2.

32 Alexander Gerard, *An Essay on Taste* (n.p. [Edinburgh], 1759; 2nd ed. 1764, 3rd ed. 1780; American edition 1804; translated into French in 1766); quotation taken from the facsimile reproduction of the 3rd ed. (1780), with an introduction by Walter J[ohn] Hipple, Jr. (Gainesville [Florida], 1963), Part I, sect. II, p.16.

33 [Edmund Burke,] *A Philosophical Enquiry into the Origin of Our Ideas of the Sublime and Beautiful* [London, 1757]; quotations taken from the edition with introduction and notes by J. T. Boulton (London, 1958), which is based on the 1759 edition, pp. 73 and 81.

34 H[oward] M[ontagu] Colvin, *A Biographical Dictionary of English Architects, 1660–1840* (London, 1954), pp.125–7.

35 *The Builder's Magazine* (1774–8), Caption for Plate CLXXXV.

'And indeed, I must confess that a Franke Light, can misbecome noe Aedifice whatsoever, *Temples* only excepted; which were anciently darke, as they are likewise at this day in some Proportion. *Devotion more requiring collected than defused Spirits.*'[28]

In his 'Proposal' for the fifty new churches commissioned under Queen Anne in 1711 John Vanbrugh (1664–1726) said that a church needed 'the most Solemn and Awfull Appearances both without and within, that is possible.'[29]

From then onwards assessments of this kind proliferated.[30] With the emergence of sensualism and the new science of aesthetics the phenomenon of terror was analysed in considerable detail. For the most part a high evaluation was placed on 'terror'; it was considered to be the principal effect of the 'sublime', which stood on a par with 'beauty'.[31]

Alexander Gerard (1728–95) commented on this phenomenon in his *Essay on Taste* (1759):
'Objects exciting terror are . . . in general sublime; for terror always implies astonishment, occupies the whole soul, and suspends all its motions.'[32]

So too did Edmund Burke (1730–92) who, although he made only a passing reference to Gothic architecture, none the less provided the next two generations with all the key concepts needed for its interpretation: 'Another source of the sublime is *infinity* . . . Infinity has a tendency to fill the mind with that sort of delightful horror, which is the most genuine effect, and truest test of the sublime . . .
'As the management of light is a matter of importance in architecture, it is worth enquiring how far this remark is applicable to building. I think then, that all edifices calculated to produce an idea of the sublime ought to be dark and gloomy.'[33]

Carter can hardly be regarded as the founder of the Romantic genre within the Gothic Revival; for although his designs for a Gothic church and a Gothic charnel-house and, more especially, the explanatory texts which he composed for these designs were early examples of this genre, they made relatively little impression on his contemporaries. His attacks on James Wyatt's restorations and his major work *The Ancient Architecture of England* (1795–1814) had a far greater impact. But even if he was not the original founder, he was certainly one of the early workers in this field. The same holds true in respect of the 'archaeological' movement within the Gothic Revival. There too – in his theoretical writings at least – Carter was active from the very beginning.[34] It was because of his archaeological interest in mediaeval Gothic that he was so averse to mixed styles:
'The student is to observe, that as all churches should be built in the Gothic taste, as being more suitable to such structures than the Grecian taste, so likewise every part appertaining to it must be in the same style . . . For true it is, nothing can be more absurd than mixing one taste with the other, as is too commonly the case, for instance, the towers of Westminster Abbey, what a medley of Grecian and Gothic architecture is there!'[35]

57

Once Gothic architecture was taken seriously, the idea of amalgamating it with specific elements of Antique architecture, as conceived by Walpole and many of his contemporaries, was soon dismissed.[36]

When William Kent converted Esher Place (Surrey) in this mixed style Walpole reacted with the delighted exclamation 'Kentissime!' However, Thomas Gray (1716–71), who had accompanied Walpole on the *grand tour* but who was by no means prepared to condone all of his foibles, wrote the following lines to Thomas Warton in 1754: 'Mr Kent supplied the rest, but I think with you, that he had not read the Gothic Classicks with taste or attention. He introduced a mix'd Style, which now goes by the name of the "Battey Langley Manner".'[37]

Until well into the second half of the nineteenth century each new generation of critics accused its predecessors of having failed to understand the Gothic. John Carter belonged to the second of these generations; and it was he who published the first reproductions of Gothic buildings, with the express purpose of promoting a Gothic renaissance.[38] Later on, during the Napoleonic Wars, Carter shifted his emphasis from ecclesiastical architecture, which he referred to as 'that awful style of building', to 'our National Architecture', which he described as 'the native growth of the Pointed Arch style amongst us'.[39] He consciously modelled his new work on the publications in which Antique monuments had been reproduced in scale drawings; and in the captions to his illustrations he used the word 'order' for 'style', possibly in order to draw a parallel between Antique and mediaeval architecture for propaganda purposes.

But the Antique and the Gothic were not the only forms of architecture vying for supremacy at that time. A whole host of different styles was readily available; and these styles were applied quite indiscriminately, with no consideration for functional requirements. This confused state of affairs was described by James Malton (d.1803) in the year 1798: 'There is no discrimination in the present stile of Architecture as practised in England: every kind of Structure meets with similar treatment. Churches in towns are scarcely distinguishable from warehouses; or from stables, by their still greater resemblance, on account of their belfries. Country houses on the common, are reared like town houses in the streets of London. The peculiars of every nation form a mongrel species in England; the rude ornaments of Indostan supersede those of Greece; and the returned Nabob, heated in his pursuit of wealth, imagines he imports the *chaleur* of the East with its riches; and we behold the stretched awning to form the cool shade, in the moist clime of Britain; the new fashioned windows of Italy, opening to the floor, with lengthened balcony, originally intended to survey the lawns, the vistas, and the groves of *Claude*, in their summer attire, or the canals of Venice; are now to be seen in every confined street of London, that a clear survey may be enjoyed of muddy streets, and to inhale the full fragrance of the effluvia, or dust of scavengers, from below.'[40]

36 See Note 11 for Part II above. – For further advocates of the mixed style see S[usanne] Lang, 'Richard Payne Knight and the Idea of Modernity' in *Concerning Architecture, Essays on Architectural Writers and Writing Presented to Nikolaus Pevsner*, edited by John Summerson (London, 1968), pp.85–97. – See also Addison, *Romanticism* (1938), p.53.

37 J. W. Lindus Forge, 'Kentissime' in *Architectural Review*, CVI (1949), pp.187–8. – Gray, *Correspondence* (1935), I, p.404.

38 John Carter, *The Ancient Architecture of England*, Part I: *The Orders of Architecture during the British, Roman, Saxon, and Norman Æras* (London, 1795 [–1806]); Part II: *The Orders of Architecture during the Reigns of Henry III, Edward III, Richard II, Henry VI, Henry VII, and Henry VIII* (London, 1808[–1814]), verso of the dedication page of 1806.

39 *Ibid.*

40 James Malton, *An Essay on British Cottage Architecture: Being an Attempt to Perpetuate on Principle that Peculiar Mode of Building, which Was Originally the Effect of Chance . . .* (London, 1798), p.10.

Malton was not an inveterate 'Goth', like Carter. On the contrary, we have seen that he was prepared to work 'to any particular style desired'.[41] In fact, he belonged to a small group of architects and dilettante scholars, who had received no antiquarian training and who tried, in the period around 1800, to promote 'picturesque' country houses and cottages of every kind.[42] But, like the 'sublime', the 'picturesque' also provided a key to the interpretation of the Gothic and a possible means of bringing about a Gothic Revival. In the closing years of the eighteenth century a debate was conducted, chiefly by those interested in the theoretical aspects of landscape gardening, in an attempt to establish the precise meaning of the word 'picturesque'. Malton also joined in this debate, but in his capacity as an architect: 'A well chosen irregularity is most pleasing; but it does not of consequence follow, that all irregularity must necessarily be picturesque. To combine irregularity into picturesque, is the excellence of Cottage construction.'[43]

Malton was, of course, aware of the great advantages of an irregular and picturesque ground-plan for the interior design of cottages.[44] But he still vacillated between the functional and the artistic facets of the picturesque: 'One point, however, is principally to be regarded by those, who are desirous to build picturesque rural dwellings; which is, never to *aim* at regularity, but to let the outward figure conform only to the internal conveniency; and rather to overcharge projecting parts than in any wise to curtail them; for on a judicious contrast of light and shade, does the picturesque in great measure depend.'[45]

The concept of the 'picturesque' opened Malton's eyes to the character of the English mediaeval country churches and prompted a proposal which we would not really have expected to find until *c*.1840: 'The durability and picturesque beauty of our old country churches, must, and do, strike every person of taste in rustic scenery. Could not the best of them be easily singled out, and others raised on the same model, if the builder have not invention to construct a design equally pleasing?'[46]

Here Malton was recommending that English architects should copy not the component elements of mediaeval buildings, but the buildings themselves. Although a similar trend was taking place in Neo-Classical architecture at that time, as far as the Gothic Revival was concerned this was a completely new development.[47]

Malton was anything but a systematic thinker, and his writings tend to be distinctly anecdotal. In fact, it is almost as if he were carrying on a conversation with other architects and landscape designers. In his *Collection of Designs for Rural Retreats, as Villas*, which appeared in 1802, he advocated a multiplicity and even a mixture of styles. Consequently, like so many of his contemporaries, he was a great admirer of the style evolved by Sir John Vanbrugh (1664–1726),[48] which he included among the 'intermediate or mixed styles of architecture'.[49] One of the designs in his 'Villa Book', which is reminiscent of the

41 See Note 1 for Part I above.

42 An inventory with commentaries is provided in Hussey, *The Picturesque* (1927), pp.219–28.

43 Malton, *An Essay on British Cottage Architecture* (1798), p.19.

44 *Ibid.*, p.26.

45 *Ibid.*, p.27.

46 *Ibid.*, p.12.

47 Early, *Romanticism and American Architecture* (1965), pp.13–21 (Capitol in Richmond, Virginia, and Maison Carrée in Nîmes). – Carroll L[ouis] V[anderslice] Meeks, *Italian Architecture, 1750–1914* (New Haven and London, 1966), pp.166–90: 'The Pantheon as a Paradigm'.

48 Malton, *A Collection of Designs for Rural Retreats, as Villas* (1802) p.7. – Lang, 'Vanbrugh's Theory' (1965). – It would in fact be true to say that the picturesque aesthetic was invented in 1709 by Vanbrugh; in this connexion see David Watkin, *Thomas Hope, 1769–1831, and the Neo-Classical Idea* (London, 1968), p.125.

49 Malton, *A Collection of Designs for Rural Retreats, as Villas* (1802), p.31.

buildings of Sir John Soane (1753–1837), he described as 'modern British'.[50] The first of these villa designs was presented with four alternative elevations: two Classical, one in castellated Gothic and one in the Gothic church style. The thirteenth design is 'in the castle style of architecture; presenting an appearance, I think, picturesque, and corresponding thereto' whilst the sixteenth 'might be denominated a mean between gothic and castle construction'.

Although Malton regarded himself as an architect, he was essentially a dilettante. This was not the case with Robert Lugar (c.1773–1855). He really was an architect, with numerous works to his name and an 'ample portion of practical knowledge'.[51] Lugar argued that if an architect wanted to produce picturesque effects, he must in many cases approach his task with the eye of a painter:

'. . . but it must however be observed, that the varied or broken line should arise from apparent wants, from the necessity of the case, and not for the sake of merely destroying a continued line'.[52]

He also insisted that the three types of Gothic – 'Castle Gothic', 'Church Gothic', and 'House Gothic' – should be used only in their proper setting.[53] This was also the first time that historical precision had been called for:

'The elevations in this style in the subsequent part of this work are of a mixed style in point of dates; but in selecting the parts, care has been taken to keep in view a consistency of character. The flat-headed window, with a moulding over it, the porch and the buttress are the chief requisites which constitute the true house gothic: these are in opposition to the newborn gothic, and pointed windows, which we so frequently see adopted in modern Cottages and dwelling houses; but we may easily trace the source of such misapplications to the village carpenter, who, for lack of better skill, and for the sake of novelty invades propriety, and gives us three, four, or five pointed openings as windows, battlements of inch deal, etc. exhibiting such an air of littleness, spruceness, and affectation, as the eye of taste and discrimination revolts at.'[54]

Although Lugar did not actually refer to Malton by name in this passage, he could hardly have condemned his designs more roundly. And yet he himself was not averse to proposing a house 'of a fancy, broken or varied character'.[55] But perhaps the most striking thing of all about Lugar's book were the grounds on which he recommended his 'Castle style' not only to the reader, but also to prospective clients. He spoke of its 'bold, broken and massive outlines', of 'broad light and shadow, giving to the whole an awful gloominess productive of grand, majestic and sublime ideas':

'The various accommodations on the plan are calculated for a family of the first rank, while the exterior invites to the hospitality of some renowned ancestor.'[56]

This description was calculated to appeal both to the wistful 'epigone' and to the status-hungry *nouveau riche*.

As villa designers, Lugar and Malton were conscious of the need to

50 *Ibid.*

51 Lugar, *Architectural Sketches for Cottages* (1805), p.3.

52 *Ibid.*, p.13.

53 *Ibid.*

54 *Ibid.*

55 *Ibid.*, p.24.

56 *Ibid.* p.26.

design their houses and gardens in such a way that they would harmonize with one another, and would be integrated into the surrounding landscape. In the main they took their lead from Humphrey Repton (1752–1818):

'It is not necessary that the house and grounds should correspond with each other in point of size, but the characters of each should be in strict harmony.'[57]

Repton, a landscape gardener, was not concerned with the niceties of stylistic classification:

'I venture to deliver it as my opinion that there are only two characters of buildings: the one may be called perpendicular, and the other horizontal. Under the first I class all buildings erected in England before and during the early part of Queen Elizabeth's reign, whether deemed Saracenic, Saxon, Norman, or the Gothic of the thirteenth and fourteenth centuries; and even that peculiar kind called Queen Elizabeth's Gothic, in which turrets prevailed, though battlements were discarded and Grecian columns occasionally introduced. Under the horizontal character I include all edifices built since the introduction of a more regular architecture, whether it copies the remains of Grecian or Roman models.'[58]

Given such a simplistic view, it is not surprising that Repton should have wanted to contrast Grecian buildings with coniferous trees and Gothic buildings with deciduous trees.[59]

Faced with the problems posed by such outbuildings, which were an essential facet of the eighteenth-century country house but which had been quite unknown in mediaeval England, Repton adopted a traditionalist view:

'Under such circumstances it is perhaps better to apply old expedients than to invent a new and absurd style of Gothic or Grecian architecture.'[60]

16 Accordingly, Repton proposed a greenhouse with a cast-iron frame based on the octagonal structures of traditional chapter-houses. Although he frequently ridiculed the antiquarians for their pedantry, he none the less wanted to see the three Gothic styles – 'the Castle, the **17** Abbey, and the House-Gothic' – properly applied; and when he asked, 'Shall we imitate the thing and forget its application?', his question was purely rhetorical.[61]

What concerned Repton was that his work should be authentic; and this insistence on authenticity naturally affected his choice of building materials. But although he was well aware that the introduction of papier mâché had frequently led to excessive and tasteless ornamentation, he none the less defended the use of cheap materials. He argued that they were perfectly natural, and drew a comparison between such materials and the dust on the wings of butterflies, the sepals of flowers, and so on.[62]

Later, some of Repton's theories were contested by John Claudius Loudon (1783–1843), a man interested in both the botanical and the architectural aspects of country estates. His first major work – *A Treatise*

57 Humphrey Repton, *Sketches and Hints on Landscape Gardening* . . . (London, n.d. [1794]); quotation taken from H.R., *The Art of Landscape Gardening, Including His 'Sketches and Hints on Landscape Gardening' and '[Observations on the] Theory and Practice of Landscape Gardening'*, edited by John Nolen (Boston and New York, 1907), pp.14–15.

58 *Ibid.*, p.18.

59 *Ibid.*, p.20. – Repton's views were often disputed.

60 Repton, *Observations* (1803); quotation taken from Repton, *The Art of Landscape Gardening* (1907), p.147.

61 *Ibid.*, pp.198 and 212.

62 *Ibid.*, p.185.

on Forming, Improving, and Managing Country Residences – appeared in two volumes in 1806[63] and contained over 700 pages; it was a comprehensive and remarkably advanced manual. In the chapter entitled 'Truth, or Nature' Loudon set out his theoretical premise: 'The first thing perceived by the mind in any object, on its being presented, is its truth or falsehood, or in other words its congeniality. We instantly perceive this in the general form and parts of animal; and when we find the leaf of a tree, or the ear of a horse, not similar to those of its kind, we instantly pronounce it to be false or monstrous. The same thing applies to all the qualities of the matter.'[64]

In this passage Loudon came very close to the concept of the 'organic whole', which Alois Hirt was to introduce into architectural theory three years later.[65] He also compared architecture with machinery, although not under the same auspices as those obtaining during subsequent decades:
'Utility is best perceived when accompanied with simplicity; as in the spade or plough; and least perceived when joined with complexity, which requires the assistance of reason, as in spinning or cotton machinery. An object with no other quality or property to recommend it than its use is still pleasing to those who are interested in it; but destroy that property, and it only excites our contempt.'[66]

Loudon also interpreted the concepts of 'fitness' and 'proportion' in anatomical terms:
'FITNESS, or PROPORTION, is nearly allied with utility, and always supposes that we are acquainted with the end or purpose for which the animal or object is intended.'[67]

Loudon wanted architectural forms to look convincing. He expected columns not only to be loadbearing, but to look as if they were loadbearing; and he insisted on rectilinear window lintels in multi-storeyed buildings because he found the combination of arched windows and beamed ceilings incongruous.[68]

This kind of attitude was typical of the eighteenth century.[69] So too was the idea, which was also advanced by Loudon, that by giving a building or a landscape a particular character, it was possible to trigger mental associations, which would then produce an emotional response. But although the idea was not original, Loudon's analysis of it is extremely informative, for it listed a considerable number of different characters:
'Sublimity; Beauty; Deformity; Picturesque Beauty; Sculpturesque Beauty; Antique Beauty; Romantic Beauty; Wildness; Tranquillity; Melancholy; Age and Ruin; Elegance; Gaiety; Novelty; Ridicule.'[70]

Loudon defined 'character' as the effect produced by a building or garden, and 'style' as the method used by its designer:
'This different way or manner of producing the same effect, is what is called STYLE in architecture. There may, therefore, be many different styles; and it is natural to think, that every country would originally produce one of its own, according to the materials with which it most abounded. Be that as it may, there are now two styles which in Europe

63 John [Claudius] Loudon, *A Treatise on Forming, Improving and Managing Country Residences: and on the Choice of Situations Appropriate to Every Class of Purchasers . . .* , 2 vols. (with consecutive page numbers), (London, 1806; facsimile edition Farnborough, 1971).

64 *Ibid.*, p.29.

65 See Notes 154–7 for Part I above.

66 Loudon, *A Treatise* (1806), I, pp.29–30.

67 *Ibid.*, p.30. – See also the 'functionalist' statement in Alberti, *L'Architettura (De re aedificatoria)* (1966), II, p.455 (= Book VI, Chap. III).

68 Loudon, *A Treatise* (1806), I, p.73.

69 See Emil Kaufmann, 'Piranesi, Algarotti and Lodoli: a Controversy in XVIII Century Venice' in *Gazette des Beaux-Arts*, 6th Series, XLVI (1955, 2), pp.21–8.

70 Loudon, *A Treatise* (1806), I, pp.37 ff. – Loudon also explains the nature of each character.

prevail over all others, and which are well known under the names of Grecian and Gothic.'[71]

In 1806, when he wrote his *Treatise*, Loudon was convinced that, before long, the Grecian style would have been completely superseded by the Gothic, a development which he welcomed, since, in his view, the Gothic was more 'congenial' than any other style to the English climate and to the functional requirements of English architecture.[72]

After suggesting a derivation for Gothic architecture essentially the same as that furnished by Sir James Hall (without giving any acknowledgement) Loudon embarked on the following eulogy:
'I shall not quit this style, however, without mentioning that it is the most perfect which exists in Europe. The beauty of fitness is so prevalent, that no one part appears superfluous. All the parts of the columns as they spread seem to cooperate with each other in supporting the roof; and all the mullions, or divisions of the windows, seem to unite in dividing it into partitions of agreeable shape and conveniency. Externally, the buttresses appear to assist, and really do assist, in supporting the wall and the roof. By an examination into the mechanical principles which pervade the whole, this fitness is no less apparent than real or necessary; so much so, indeed, that not one single buttress, and in some cases (as in the ribs of open crowns on the tops of spires) not one single pinnacle, could be taken away without injuring that part of the fabric. Whether we regard the variety in the columns, and the intricacy of the roof from the tracery, the leaves, and other ornaments, or consider the noble perspectives of the middle and side aisles, we must be constrained to say, that the general effect of a cathedral of this style far surpasses that of any Grecian building in producing that exhilarating sublimity which is so analogous to the purpose for which they are erected. This may be *felt* by comparing the effect of Westminster Abbey, or York Cathedral, with St Paul's.'[73]

Loudon may well have been the first architectural theorist to look upon the Gothic as a universal style that was suitable for all kinds of buildings, although it should be pointed out in this connexion that in his conception of the Gothic he also included the circular style.

He distinguished between 'Saxon Gothic' and the 'pointed style' as follows:
'I proceed to make some observations on the common style formed upon these, and used for mansions. The compounds which may be formed from these two styles are applicable to all kinds of public and private edifices, and are capable of supplying every internal convenience, luxury, or ornament. In towns or cities they may be raised of any height, and made perfectly symmetrical. In the country they may spread out in every direction, and be made either high or low, uniform or varied, at pleasure. It is suited to produce every expression, whether of elegance, grandeur, melancholy, or picturesque beauty, and is equally applicable to the palace and the cottage. With respect to the internal arrangement, it is equally advantageous. The symmetry and regularity of the Grecian style often occasions much loss of space, confines the size, and renders

71 *Ibid.*, p.80.

72 *Ibid.*, p.14.

73 *Ibid.*, pp.101–2.

it difficult to give sufficient light to the appartments. If any error of that kind be produced in this style, the fault is entirely in the architect.'[74]

Clearly, Loudon was not given to half measures. But, in actual fact, he had little choice in the matter, for any nineteenth-century architect who regarded the Gothic as a universal style and wanted to see it applied in urban as well as rural design was obliged to argue that the picturesque principles underlying landscape gardening were equally valid for town-planning purposes.[75] Consequently, Loudon advocated that roads should follow the line of the terrain, thus creating natural curves, and on any straight sections of road the houses should project over the pavements in order to disrupt the rectilinear pattern. These irregular façades were to be modelled on existing mediaeval streets, such as High Holborn in London and the High Street in Edinburgh.[76]

Let me now try to summarize Loudon's theories.

He insisted that all buildings must look convincing and must be functionally efficient, like animate beings, tools or machines. Consequently, he advocated the Gothic style of architecture, for since it had originated in England, it suited the climate and the available building materials, and consequently fulfilled these requirements to a very high degree; it could also be used for all kinds of buildings, both rural and urban, and was able to express any desired character. Moreover, since it leant itself to both regular and irregular designs, it would facilitate town planning. Finally, where urban roads were built in accordance with picturesque principles, the resulting roadscapes would be far more attractive.

Although a number of Loudon's theses were doubtless taken over from other writers, his achievement was none the less remarkable, for he succeeded in constructing a complete architectural system while still in his early twenties; and although he may not have been one of the really great architectural theorists, he was certainly one of the most influential. This was especially true from 1834 onwards, when he published *The Architectural Magazine*, the first of its kind in Europe.[77]

Another influential author of this period was John Papworth (1775–1847), whose local reputation was so great that he was given the sobriquet 'Buonarotti' by his well-intentioned but over-zealous friends.

Papworth's mouthpiece was Rudolph Ackermann's *Repository of Arts, Literature, Fashions, Manufactures, &c.*[78] But, unlike Loudon, Papworth began his architectural career at a practical level. Acting on the advice of William Chambers and influenced, no doubt, by his father, who was one of the leading stucco-workers of the day, he apprenticed himself to a builder. Later he created designs for virtually everything, from pocket handkerchiefs to Thames steamers, from cast-iron roofs to castle grounds; he also painted water-colours and wrote plays for the theatre.

Although he was not such an ardent adherent of the Gothic as Loudon, Papworth none the less deserves a place in the history of the Gothic Revival, for he was the first nineteenth-century writer to broach two important questions: the development of a national style and the

74 *Ibid.*, pp.105–6.

75 *Ibid.*, pp.147–51.

76 For small towns Alberti also recommended winding roads because they provide alternating vistas; see Alberti, *L'Architettura (De re aedificatoria)* (1966), I, p.307 (= Book IV, Chap. V). – Sir Joshua Reynolds made the same point at the end of his Thirteenth Discourse in the Royal Academy; see J. R., *Fifteen Discourses, Delivered in the Royal Academy* (London, 1769–91).

77 Frank Jenkins, 'Nineteenth-Century Architectural Periodicals' in *Concerning Architecture, Essays on Architectural Writers and Writing Presented to Nikolaus Pevsner*, edited by John Summerson (London, 1968), pp.153–60. – John Gloag, *Mr Loudon's England: the Life and Work of John Claudius Loudon, and His Influence on Architectural and Furniture Design* (Newcastle upon Tyne, 1970).

78 Wyatt Papworth, *John B. Papworth, Architect to the King of Wurtemburg: a Brief Record of His Life and Works, Being a Contribution to the History of Art and of Architecture during the Period 1775–1847* (London, 1879). – Colvin, *A Biographical Dictionary* (1954), pp.436–43. – Edward T. Joy, 'A Versatile Victorian Designer: J. B. Papworth' in *Country Life*, CXLVII (1970), pp.130–1.

future role of arts and crafts. He also commented on the conflict between speculative building and town planning.

Inevitably, Papworth's first book was an architectural treatise on *Rural Residences*[79] which appeared in 1818 when England was still celebrating the victorious outcome of the Napoleonic Wars. In this book Papworth defended the artist-architect against the speculative builder. After describing architecture as 'a fine art, subject to laws of fitness, and founded on a combination of brilliant fancy and sound judgement',[80] he went on to argue that it was the mother of the fine arts. This theme had, of course, been under discussion ever since the Renaissance. But Papworth's approach was distinctly novel:
'When building is encouraged, painting, sculpture, gardening, and all the other decorative arts flourish of course, and these have an influence on manufactures, even on the minutest mechanic productions; for design is of universal advantage, and stamps a value on the most trifling performances; the consequences of which to a trading people, are too obvious to require illustration.'[81]

Although Papworth's comment on the cottages which he designed for agricultural workers still reflects the patriarchal opinions of the eighteenth-century philanthropists and physiocrats it none the less seems to mark a new departure:
'The ornaments which fancy in her playful mood may suggest, ill associate with the modest and moderate claims of this respectable and useful class of society.'[82]

The decorated cottage, or cottage orné, was a new type of building, whose properties Papworth defined in his *Rural Residences*:
'The cottage orné is a new species of building in the economy of domestic architecture and subject to its own laws of fitness and propriety. It is not the habitation of the laborious, but of the affluent, of the man of study, of science, or of leisure . . . Perhaps it is essential that this building . . . should combine properly with the surrounding objects, and appear to be native to the spot, and not one of those crude rule-and-square excrescences of the environs of London, the illegitimate family of town and country.'[83]

The accompanying plate shows an irregular house in the Neo-Gothic manner set in a park, with a gardener working in the foreground.

In choosing the 'right kind' of Gothic for different purposes Papworth was guided partly by his own historical sense, partly by the 'Gothic' genre styles, and partly by Repton's theory of contrast. For 'romantic scenery' he recommended a combination of Church and Castle Gothic, and claimed that this mixed style was to be found in buildings dating from the reigns of the first three Edwards (1272–1377).[84] However, he considered that the Decorative style evolved in the fourteenth century constituted the major achievement of the Gothic period, and maintained that it was not until the reign of Henry VII (1488–1509) that the Gothic went into a decline.[85] The trouble was that, like so many of his contemporaries, Papworth was obliged to seek the models for his secular buildings in the Late Gothic; moreover, since his outlook was

79 John B[uonarotti] Papworth, *Rural Residences, Consisting of a Series of Designs for Cottages, Decorated Cottages, Small Villas, and Other Ornamental Buildings* . . . (London, 1818; facsimile edition Farnborough, 1971). – A shorter version appeared as 'Architectural Hints . . .' in *Repository of Arts* . . . in 1816/17.

80 Papworth, *Rural Residences* (1818), p. v.

81 *Ibid.*, p. vii. – The first school of industrial design in England was founded in 1760.

82 *Ibid.*, p.9.

83 *Ibid.*, p.25.

84 *Ibid.*, pp.33–4.

85 *Ibid.*, pp.48; see also *ibid.*, p.26.

19

not sufficiently antiquarian, he failed to perceive his dilemma, and so was unable to resolve it.

Papworth advocated the use of the Gothic style in three principal areas: firstly, for low-cost buildings designed to produce a picturesque effect, because with the irregular ground-plan of Gothic structures 'the convenience of arrangement is made to govern the design'; secondly, for vicarages, because it provides a 'visible link of connexion between the church itself and the pastor who is devoted to its duties; and also leads the spectator very naturally from contemplating the dwelling, to regard the pious character of its inhabitants'; and thirdly, for 'romantic scenery'.[86] But Papworth's *Rural Residences* also contains a design for an irregular Renaissance villa, which was supposed to evoke the paintings of Claude Lorrain and Nicolas Poussin, and which was introduced as an example of 'the painter's style of building'.[87] Thus, for Papworth, the Gothic was no longer the epitome of the picturesque style.

In 1806, when Richard Payne Knight (1750–1824) suggested a new mixed style composed of Grecian and Gothic elements as a basis for further development, he was concerned not with its national character, but with its future potential.[88] But in 1822, when John Buonarotti Papworth discussed the question of a new style in Ackermann's magazine, he called his article 'On a National Style of Architecture'.[89] The conception which he outlined in that article was also distinctly progressive:

'With us, a fine national style of architecture can only result from works designed with British feeling by men of genius, well grounded in the principles on which the ancient architects executed the finest specimens of art. A suitable adaptation of the works to the climate, to the purpose required, and to the habits of the people, will necessarily give to the style a peculiar character, differing perhaps as much from the Roman, as the Roman from the Greek . . . By a national style is meant, that character which architecture assumes, identifying itself with the country in which it originates; because of its peculiar suitableness to the place, its climate, its government, its religion, the manners of the people, the local circumstances of nature, and the materials for building which the country affords. Suitableness to all these is the foundation of a national style of architecture, and it must eventually exist in all countries where national wealth permits the operations of art, and where genius is encouraged to create, rather than to copy and adapt . . . Why should a mere copy in architecture be more tolerated or esteemed than a mere copy of a picture in painting? Yet it is so, and originality is wholly disregarded.'[90]

Papworth's conception of a national style becomes clearer if we consider it in the light of his reaction to the national monument, which it was proposed to erect at Calton Hill, near Edinburgh. The monument chosen for this purpose was to be a copy of the Parthenon, and Papworth was duly incensed. He did not by any means consider that the Mediterranean nations would always be superior to the

18

48

86 *Ibid.*, p.53 (first area), p.45 (second) and p.33 (third).

87 *Ibid.*, p.69.

88 R. P. K., *An Analytical Inquiry into the Principles of Taste* (London, 1805, 2nd ed. 1805, 3rd ed. 1806, 4th ed. 1808); quotation taken from Lang, 'Richard Payne Knight' (1968), pp.90–1; the reference is to the 1806 edition, pp.223 ff.

89 This was the title Papworth used in the Table of Contents and Index; his essay was printed as an explanatory text for a series entitled 'Select Views of London' and was based on Sir John Soane's buildings in Regent Street, which have since been demolished. – See John B[uonarotti] Papworth, 'On a National Style of Architecture' in *Repository of Arts, Literature, Fashions, Manufactures, &c.*, 2nd Series, XIV (1822), pp.311–14.

90 *Ibid.*, pp.312–13.

91 See Note 2 for Part I above.

92 John B[uonarotti] Papworth, 'On the Benefits Resulting to the Manufactures of a Country, from a well Directed Cultivation of Architecture, and of the Art of Ornamental Design', read at the Ordinary Meeting held Monday the 27th of July, 1835, in *Transactions of the Institute of British Architects of London,* Sessions 1835–6, Vol. I, Part I, 2nd ed. (1837), pp.111–14. – In this connexion see Utz Haltern, *Die Londoner Weltausstellung von 1851: ein Beitrag zur Geschichte der bürgerlich-industriellen Gesellschaft im 19. Jahrhundert* ... (Münster [Westfalen], 1971) esp. pp.35–42.

93 Alf Bøe, *From Gothic Revival to Functional Form: a Study in Victorian Theory of Design* ... (Oslo and Oxford, 1957), pp.40–56.

94 Charles L[ocke] Eastlake, *A History of the Gothic Revival: an Attempt to Show how the Taste for Mediaeval Architecture which Lingered in England during the Two Last Centuries Has since Been Encouraged and Developed* (London, 1872), p.169. – In the Victorian Library edition by J. Mordaunt Crook, Eastlake's narrative text has been reproduced in facsimile, but the appendix 'Selected Examples of Gothic Buildings ...' has been corrected and expanded, there are additional illustrations, a modern bibliography and a splendid index (Leicester and New York, 1970). – Clark, *The Gothic Revival* (1964), p.93. – Henry-Russell Hitchcock, *Early Victorian Architecture in Britain* ... , 2 vols. (text and plates), (London and New Haven, 1954), I, pp.43–6. – Mark Girouard, 'Attitudes to Elizabethan Architecture, 1600–1900' in *Concerning Architecture, Essays on Architectural Writers and Writing Presented to Nikolaus Pevsner,* edited by John Summerson (London, 1968), pp.13–27, see esp. p.22.

95 Phoebe B. Stanton, 'Pugin: Principles of Design versus Revivalism' in *Journal of the Society of Architectural Historians,* XIII (1954), pp.20–5; quotation taken from *ibid.,* p.22.

English, despite their more favourable climate. But neither did he share the widely held view that the Gothic constituted a national style. He was quite prepared to allow an architect of the calibre of Sir John Soane to indulge 'the dreams and visions of his fancy', but he flatly rejected the notion that these provided the basis for a national style. Like all the architectural theorists of his generation, Papworth tried to reconcile the concept of an invented style with the antithetical concept of an organic style'[91] The optimistic view of the future held by so many of his contemporaries was clouded for Papworth by his fear of a loss of national identity; and he was convinced that this threat could only be dispelled by a national architecture that would really reflect the country in which it had been conceived. It was not 'copies' that were needed, but 'feeling'.

Papworth was Vice-President of the Institute of British Architects, and at a meeting of the Institute in 1835 he gave a lecture on the promotion of the arts and crafts, in which he enlarged on the ideas first formulated in his *Rural Residences* in 1818.[92]

After pointing out that English industrial art had a bad reputation, he suggested that the only way of changing this unsatisfactory state of affairs was for the architects themselves to take matters in hand and exercise effective control over every aspect of the work programme. He also insisted that all designs must be executed by first-class artists, who were prepared to follow Grecian, Roman and Italian prototypes, for otherwise they would never succeed in suppressing the Louis XIV and Louis XV styles that were then in vogue. Papworth called for state protection in the form of a patent law, so as to ensure that the designs produced by such artists could be made to pay. A second demand made by Papworth in this lecture – for a state school of arts and crafts – was granted shortly afterwards, for in 1837 The Government School of Design was founded. It was the first of its kind in England, and Papworth was its first director.[93]

On 16 October 1834 the seat of the English Parliament in Westminster was burnt down. In June 1835 the parliamentary committee responsible for the reconstruction of the Houses of Parliament announced a competition for a new building to be erected on the site of the Old Palace in either a Gothic or an Elizabethan style.[94] Charles Barry (1795–1860) won the first prize with a Late Gothic design, which verged on the Elizabethan. Both the conditions imposed on the competitors and the decisions reached by the jury were determined to a large extent by considerations of conformity – conformity with nearby Westminster Abbey, conformity with Westminster Hall, which had survived the fire, and conformity with St Stephen's Chapel, which was to be preserved. However, this was not the official version of events. The reason given by the committee for its choice of a Gothic building was quite different:
'The peculiar charm of Gothic architecture is in its associations; these are delightful because they are historical, patriotic, local and intimately blended with early reminiscences.'[95]

30–2

Because of the lengthy construction period – the first stone was not laid until 1840 and the work continued for a full twenty years – Barry's building exerted little direct influence on contemporary architecture: it was out of date before it was completed. None the less, the Houses of Parliament were the greatest public building of the century, and they occupied a site in the very heart of London. Consequently, they were extremely important; they fulfilled the requirements laid down by Loudon, and established the Gothic Revival as the principal style of the century.

Not surprisingly, the 'Greeks' and the 'Goths' engaged in a fierce battle before the foundation stone was laid.[96] Countless pamphlets were published, in which the issue was debated at great length. One of these was penned by James Savage (1779–1852), the church architect and bridge builder who, it will be remembered, designed the first stone vault for a Neo-Gothic church.[97] Savage was even more implacable in his opposition to imitative architecture than Papworth:[98]

'The imitation of styles is a valuable discipline for a pupil, but it is a confession of incapacity in a professor . . . It is the usual fate of imitators to transmit an exaggeration of some prominent peculiarity, rather than the intrinsic excellence of the models. Simplicity becomes baldness; what is rustic becomes coarse; and other excellencies degenerate into the vices which ape them. All imitation is essentially affectation – the shew of a quality not really felt. If attempted seriously, it is puerile.'[99]

According to Savage, this malpractice was initiated in the Renaissance:

'The imitation of the Greek has perverted the whole taste of modern Europe on the subject of architectural composition. It gives a style independent of ideas, and is setting manner above matter. It is the nonsense verses of the schoolboy.'[100]

Commenting on the axiom formulated by Georges-Louis Leclerc de Buffon in 1753 to the effect that style is identical with man ('Le style est l'homme même'), Savage pointed out that, just as literary style reflects the character of the writers who create it, so the architectural style of a particular epoch should reflect the character of that epoch.[101] As for the appreciation of architectural style, Savage insisted that this could not be acquired at school:

'We may here observe, that the great works of architecture, as well as other *high art*, require a preparation of mind before they can be enjoyed. Not the preparation of the schools, or the technical knowledge of the professor, but that cultivated sensibility which allows the mental sympathy to be excited.'[102]

This was an early and surprisingly violent attack on the English schools of art.[103]

Next the bridge-builder in Savage came to the fore with a new conception of 'fitness' involving an anatomical view of architecture:

'A correct knowledge of the principles of construction is as necessary to the architect as anatomy to the painter and sculptor. Construction is,

28, 29

96 Clark, *The Gothic Revival* (1964), pp.93–105 (=Chap.6). – Michael Trappes-Lomax, *Pugin, a Mediaeval Victorian* (London, 1932), pp.78 f.

97 See Note 3 for Part I above.

98 See Note 90 for Part II above.

99 Savage, *Observations on Style* (1836), pp.23–4.

100 *Ibid.*, p.27.

101 There are various versions of Buffon's original statement, which Savage merely paraphrased; see *ibid.*, p.29.

102 *Ibid.*, p.32.

103 Nikolaus Pevsner, *Academies of Art, Past and Present* (Cambridge, 1940).

in fact, the anatomy of architecture, and the very base upon which design in that art must be founded. This latter branch of architecture, viz. design or composition, may be said to consist in the production of visible beauty; but this beauty requires, for one of its elements, an apparent, as well as real strength and stability.'[104]

But if, at this point, we were to expect Savage to propose the Gothic cathedrals of the Middle Ages as models of 'constructive beauty', we would be disappointed. Although he genuinely admired these buildings and considered that they were the perfect embodiment of the Christian mysteries, he was fundamentally opposed to all forms of imitation, and so refused to accord undue prominence to either of the two major styles.

This was not the case with Pugin.

Augustus Welby Northmore Pugin (1812–52) was the son of a French émigré who had settled in London in 1792, where he acquired a considerable reputation, both as a draughtsman and as an editor of illustrated books on Gothic architecture. During his early years Pugin helped his father with these publications. Subsequently, he lived a restless life, which led him to an early grave. At the age of 15 he designed furniture for Windsor Castle and stage sets for a London theatre; at 18 he was captain of his own schooner, which was wrecked off the Firth of Forth; at 19 he became director of a firm of stonemasons, which was facing bankruptcy; at 23 he helped Barry with his competition design for the Houses of Parliament, and was converted to the Catholic faith, which was making great inroads in England at that time, due to the large-scale immigration of Irish Catholics; at 29 he reached the peak of his architectural career, which was virtually confined to a five-year period; at 32 he again collaborated with Barry, on the details of the façades and the fitments for the Houses of Parliament, and also began to produce designs for goldsmith's articles, stained-glass windows, ceramic dishes – in short, for virtually everything used in the way of fitments for Catholic and Anglican churches. He was married three times and had eight children; he was Professor of Antiquities at St Mary's College at Oscott, near Birmingham; and he wrote, and illustrated, books on architectural theory and the liturgy of the mass, mostly in a polemical vein. As an architectural theorist he was quite as influential as Schinkel and Viollet-le-Duc. He himself considered that his contribution to English architecture was principally theoretical.[105] In 1851, the year before his death, he remarked:
'My writings, much more than what I have been able to do, have revolutionized the taste of England.'[106]

And in 1857, five years after Pugin's death, George Gilbert Scott recalled the influence exerted by Pugin on a whole generation of English architects:
'About the time I am referring to, an immense impulse was given to the reformation of architecture by the earlier publications of Pugin.'[107]

Much of Pugin's architectural theory was quite obviously evolved from the native ideas which I have outlined above, but certain aspects of his thinking seem to have been based on Continental concepts, such as

104 Savage, *Observations on Style* (1836), p.6.

105 Benjamin Ferrey, *Recollections of A. N. Welby Pugin* and *His Father Augustus Pugin: with Notices of Their Works; with an Appendix by E[dmund] Sheridan Purcell* (London, 1861). – Trappes-Lomax, *Pugin, a Mediaeval Victorian* (1932). – N[ikolaus] Pevsner, 'A Short Pugin Florilegium' in *Architectural Review*, XCIV (1943), pp.31–4. – Denis [Rollestone] Gwynn, *Lord Shrewsbury, Pugin and the Catholic Revival* (London, 1946). – Phoebe [B.] Stanton, *Pugin*, Preface by Nikolaus Pevsner (London, 1971).

106 Phoebe B. Stanton, 'Some Comments on the Life and Work of Augustus Welby Northmore Pugin', read before the R.I.B.A. Library Group on 18 November 1952, in *Journal of the Royal Institute of British Architects*, 3rd Series, LX (1953), pp.47–54; quotation taken from *ibid.*, p.53, and from Stanton, *Pugin* (1971), p.194. – A similar statement is attributed to Pugin in Ferrey, *Recollections* (1861), p.248.

107 George Gilbert Scott, 'On the Present Position and Future Prospects of the Revival of Gothic Architecture', read at the meeting of the Yorkshire and Lincoln Architectural Societies at Doncaster, September 23, 1857, in *Associated Architectural Societies: Reports and Papers*, IV (1858), pp.69–83; quotation taken from *ibid.*, p.73.

30–40

the antithesis between the Gothic or Christian and the Antique or Pagan.[108]

Although Pugin sometimes ridiculed his own zeal for the Gothic, it is apparent from his correspondence that he was quite obsessed by it. In 1833 or 1834 he wrote to his friend William Osmond, thanking him for an enormous Cheddar cheese 'which although not strictly Gothic in its present shape may be daily rendered more so by cutting it into 4, which will make it a quatrefoil'; later in the same letter he referred to Osmond and himself as 'real Gothic men'.[109] And in another letter to Osmond dating from 1834 he discussed the relationship between architecture and religion:

'I can assure you that, after a most close and impartial investigation, I feel perfectly convinced the Roman Catholic Church is the only true one, and the only one in which the grand and sublime style of architecture can ever be restored.'[110]

The restoration of the sublime style of architecture was, of course, Pugin's principal aim in life. Even in the 1830's, during the public debate on the style to be adopted for the new Houses of Parliament, he defended the Gothic on the grounds that it is 'suited to our country and climate',[111] and rejected the notion that Gothic architecture was incompatible with painting and sculpture.[112] But the two representatives of mediaeval painting and sculpture whom Pugin cited in support of his thesis were Albrecht Dürer and Adam Krafft, whose major works date from the sixteenth century.[113] We have, of course, already seen that this predilection for the Late Gothic was typical of the 1830's in England.

When Pugin published his second pamphlet in 1836, it became apparent that he was interested, not only in the revival of a particular style of architecture, but also in the restoration of the Christian world order in which that style had been grounded. In this pamphlet Pugin took a number of buildings dating from the fifteenth century and contrasted them with similar types of buildings erected in his own day. Then, having demonstrated the functional differences between the architectural practices of these two centuries, he engaged in a Christian-based form of social criticism by presenting 'Contrasted Residences for the Poor'.[114] In this section of his tract he described the daily lives of the poor in great detail. Thus, we are told that in the fifteenth century the daily diet of the inmates of a typical poorhouse consisted of 'BEEF MVTTON BACON/ALE AND CIDER/MILK PORRIDGE/WHEAT BREAD/CHEESE', and in the nineteenth century '2 OZ OF BREAD I PINT OF GRUEL/2 OZ OF BREAD I PINT OF GRUEL I OZ OF BREAD I/2 PINT OF GRUEL/OATMEAL POTATOES'. But drastic though the contrast in diet was, it could not compare with the contrast in funeral arrangements. These Pugin illustrated by two drawings, one showing a group of coffins labelled 'FOR DISSECTION', the other a priest conducting a funeral service above an open grave, accompanied by deacons bearing the cross and candles. Pugin wanted nothing less than 'a restoration of the ancient feelings and sentiments'.[115]

38

108 Frankl, *The Gothic* (1960), p.555. – See also the following chapter.

109 Ferrey, *Recollections* (1861), pp.76 and 78.

110 *Ibid.*, p.88.

111 A[ugustus] Welby [Northmore] Pugin, *A Letter to A.W. Hakewill, Architect, in Answer to His 'Reflections on the Style for Rebuilding the Houses of Parliament'* (Salisbury, 1835), p.13.

112 *Ibid.*, p.9.

113 *Ibid.*, pp.9 and 12.

114 A[ugustus] Welby [Northmore] Pugin, *Contrasts, or, A Parallel between the Noble Edifices of the Fourteenth and Fifteenth Centuries, and Similar Buildings of the Present Day; Shewing the Present Decay of Taste* (London, 1836; 2nd ed. 1841); facsimile edition of the 2nd ed. in the Victorian Library with an introduction by H.R. Hitchcock (Leicester and New York, 1969). The reference on this page is to the 2nd ed. (1841). The date in the caption to fig.38 on p.208 should therefore read: 1841.

115 Pugin, *Contrasts* (1836), p.22.

There were three reasons why Pugin advocated the imitation of the Gothic:

1. The fitness of Gothic architecture was both real and readily apparent; this was not the case with any other style of architecture.
2. Gothic architecture was a Christian architecture.
3. Gothic architecture was a national architecture.

35, 36 By the 1840's Pugin's particular preference was for the English parish churches of the fourteenth century:

'An old English parish church, as originally used for the ancient worship, was one of the most beautiful and appropriate buildings that the mind of man could conceive; every portion of it answered both a useful and mystical purpose.'[116]

His conception of the national attributes of the Gothic was not so clearly defined:

'Another objection to Italian architecture is this, – We are not Italians, we are Englishmen. God in his wisdom has implanted a love of nation and country in every man, and we should always cultivate this feeling; – we ought to view the habits and manners of other nations without prejudice, derive improvement from all we observe admirable, but we should never forget our own land.'[117]

Pugin was opposed to the retention of architectural forms which no longer served any useful function. Thus, he objected to the castellated style in modern castles since these were no longer required to fulfil a defensive role; he also objected to the abbey style in houses such as

15 Fonthill Abbey (built by James Wyatt for William Beckford from 1796 onwards); but he objected most of all to the 'nondescript modern style' which was inundating the towns and cities of England.[118] For Pugin the Gothic was 'the only correct expression of the faith, wants, and climate of our country'.[119] He regarded it as the perfect style, because it was the embodiment of Christianity,[120] and he rejected the contention that the Christians would hardly have waited 1200 years before developing a Christian style of architecture, arguing that it had taken even longer before the Jews had been able to build their Temple in Jerusalem.[121] Pugin believed that the Christian style should be used in every sphere of life, and in order to demonstrate his thesis he designed two railway bridges 'on the antient principles'.[122]

Ever since the early years of the eighteenth century the word 'principles' had been one of the catch phrases of architectural theory.

Continuing in the tradition established by the 'villa architects', Pugin described the Scylla and Charybdis which every architect was obliged to negotiate:

'In the first place, many architects apply the details and minor features of the pointed style to classic *masses* and arrangements; they adhere scrupulously to the regularity and symmetry of the latter, while they attempt to disguise it by the mouldings and accessories of the former.'[123]

37 This was the first danger to which he drew attention in his *True Principles*. But those who managed to avoid it still had to contend with a second:

116 A[ugustus] Welby [Northmore] Pugin, *The True Principles of Pointed or Christian Architecture; Set forth in Two Lectures Delivered at St. Marie's Oscott* (London, 1841; 2nd ed. 1853); facsimile edition of the 2nd ed. (Oxford, 1969). – The French edition *Les vrais principes de l'architecture ogivale ou chrétienne* appeared with different title-pages, each with a different place of publication (Bruges, 1850; Brussels, 1850; Brussels and Leipzig, 1850); in this connexion see [Paul Breman,] *The Gothic of Gothick* (= Weinreb Catalogue, XIV), (London, 1966), No.227. – Quotation taken from the 1841 edition, p.49.

117 Pugin, *The True Principles* (1841), p.56.

118 *Ibid.*, pp.56–60.

119 A[ugustus] Welby [Northmore] Pugin, *An Apology for the Revival of Christian Architecture in England* (London, 1843); facsimile edition (Oxford, 1969), p.4.

120 *Ibid.*, p.4.

121 *Ibid.*, pp.6–7.

122 *Ibid.*, pl. III (facing p.10).

123 Pugin, *The True Principles* (1841), p.62.

'The picturesque effect of the ancient buildings results from the ingenious methods by which the older builders overcame local and constructive difficulties. An edifice which is arranged with the principle view of looking picturesque is sure to resemble an artificial waterfall or a made-up rock, which are generally so unnaturally natural as to appear ridiculous.'[124]

But Pugin did not let matters rest there; having identified the dangers, he went on to outline the correct method of procedure. Picturesque effects, he suggested, would arise quite spontaneously, provided the architect based his design on a suitable ground-plan. In his view, the fundamental weakness of Classical design was the fact that it started, not from a suitable ground-plan, but from an impressive elevation. And yet, although the Classical architects had attached major importance to their elevations, Pugin none the less considered that Gothic elevations were superior; because the Gothic architects had used standard components – either singly or, in the case of larger structures, in multiples – their buildings looked as big as they actually were.

Like Savage, Pugin was opposed to the imitation of earlier architectural styles. But he was not opposed to the imitation or, rather, the adoption of the principles underlying such styles. Consequently, Pugin rejected both the suspect originality displayed by his eighteenth-century predecessors and the copyism of his own day, and called for architects who had absorbed the spirit of the Gothic and grasped the principles on which it was based.[125] He even rejected the word 'style' as inappropriate in this context:

'We do not want to revive a facsimile of the works or style of any particular individual, or even period; but it is the devotion, majesty, and repose of Christian art, for which we are contending; – it is not a *style*, but a principle.'[126]

Pugin regarded the reign of Edward I (1272–1307) as the apogee of the Gothic period.[127] He loved the crossing towers which were a feature of late thirteenth-century architecture, and revealed a general preference for asymmetrical structures composed of inter-relating cubes.[128] The fact that he defended the use of rood lofts and chancel screens, even though they clashed with his liturgical ideas, was probably due to this general preference.[129] He liked natural stone, but hated large squared stones.[130] He spoke highly of the spaciousness and brightness of French churches, but made no reference to the fact that, unlike English churches, they usually had vaulted roofs.[131] He attached absolute importance to the vertical principle and was quite convinced that, prior to 1400, no church towers were built in England without spires.[132] He also insisted that church architects must use authentic materials, since they alone were capable of expressing the spirit of Christiantity.[133] Finally, after carrying out a large number of structural and archaeological investigations (a practice initiated in England by James Essex), Pugin was able to declare:

'The architects of the middle ages were the first who turned the natural

33, 34

39, 40

124 *Ibid.*, pp.62–3.

125 A[ugustus] Welby [Northmore] Pugin, *The Present State of Ecclesiastical Architecture in England* (London, 1843); first printed in *Dublin Review*, XX (1841) and XIII (1842); facsimile edition of the 1843 edition with an index (Oxford, 1969), p.108, note.

126 Pugin, *An Apology* (1843), p.22.

127 Pugin, *The Present State* (1843), p.30.

128 Pugin, *An Apology* (1843), p.20. – Pugin, *The Present State* (1843), p.61.

129 *Ibid.*, pp.25–33 and 69–74. – A[ugustus] Welby [Northmore] Pugin, *A Treatise on Chancel Screens and Rood Lofts: Their Antiquity, Use, and Symbolic Signification* (London, 1851).

130 Pugin, *An Apology* (1843), p.20. – Pugin, *The Present State* (1843), p.7. – Pugin, *The True Principles* (1841), p.18.

131 *Ibid.*, p.66.

132 *Ibid.*, pp.7 and 10. – Pugin, *The Present State* (1843), pp.17–18.

133 *Ibid.*, pp.79, 88 and 99. – Pugin, *An Apology* (1843), p.21. – Pugin, *The True Principles* (1841), p.44.

properties of the various materials to their full account, and made their mechanism a vehicle for their art . . . A pointed church is the masterpiece of masonry.'[134]

Because he matured at an early age, Pugin became the spokesman for his generation; and because of his skill as a writer and draughtsman, and his profound scholarship, he acquired a reputation that has outlived the memory of his brilliant personality. His belief that truth, utility and beauty must necessarily coincide in good architecture was shared by the pioneers of the modern movement, who propounded it with the same moral fervour. But the men of Pugin's generation were equally convinced that the only occasion on which truth, utility and beauty actually coincided was in fourteenth-century architecture.[135]

Where did the moral fervour of the nineteenth-century architectural theorists come from? Clearly, this is not a question that can be dealt with in detail in an enquiry into the theoretical premises of the Gothic Revival. But what is immediately apparent is that concepts such as 'expression' and 'character', which were introduced into art theory in the mid-eighteenth century, and Buffon's reappraisal of the concept of 'style', established a new connexion and new analogies between works of art, on the one hand, and the artists, or artistic periods, responsible for their creation, on the other. It was only a small step from 'bienséance' to 'caractère', from the apparent reality of coloured imitation marble to the authenticity of highly polished Purbeck stone; but it was a step that had far-reaching repercussions.

2 Soufflot, Chateaubriand and Hugo

In the preceding chapter we saw that, in the early phase of the Gothic Revival in England, the English theorists tended to concentrate on the sentimental aspects of the Gothic. In the corresponding phase in France, which I shall be dealing with in this chapter, the main emphasis was on the constructive properties of the Gothic.

In 1780 the architect Maximilien de Brébion (1716–96?) commented on the church of Sainte-Geneviève (now the Panthéon) in Paris: 'M. Soufflot's principal aim in building his church was to combine, in an extremely beautiful design, the lightweight construction of Gothic edifices with the purity and splendour of Greek architecture.'[136]

This one sentence would serve as a general heading for all French church architecture in the second half of the eighteenth century. For despite their Antique appearance, the colonnade churches of this period mark the beginning of the Gothic Revival in France. As early as 1673 Charles Perrault (1613–88) defended the Louvre Colonnade with its pairs of slender columns by pointing to the Gothic-like lightness of the design; and although Perrault's defence met with opposition,[137] from then onwards this new elegant style found numerous advocates among the French architectural theorists, most of whom were attracted by the

41

42

134 *Ibid.*, pp.1–2. – A synopsis of the structural and archaeological investigations carried out into the Gothic is provided in John Britton, *A Chronological History and Graphic Illustration of Christian Architecture in England* . . . (London, 1827), Chap. I.

135 See e.g. George Gilbert Scott, *Remarks on Secular and Domestic Architecture, Present and Future* (London, 1857), pp.117 and 237.

136 Manuscript; quotation taken from Petzet, *Soufflots Sainte-Geneviève* (1961), p.73: 'Le principal objet de M. Soufflot en bâtissant son église a été de réunir sous une des plus belles formes la légèreté de la construction des édifices gothiques avec la pureté et la magnificence de l'architecture grecque.'

137 See Herrmann, *Laugier* (1962), pp.76–7. – See also Middleton, 'The Abbé de Cordemoy', I (1962), p.299.

138 Cordemoy, *Nouveau traité d'architecture* (1714), esp. pp.166–7. – Middleton, 'The Abbé de Cordemoy' (1962–3).

139 [Amédée-François] Frézier, *La théorie et la pratique de la coupe des pierres et des bois, pour la construction des voûtes et autres parties des bâtimens civils et militaires, ou Traité de stéréotomie à l'usage de l'architecture*, 3 vols. (Strasbourg and Paris, 1737–9; 2nd ed. 1754–69); quotation taken from 1st ed., I (1737), p. xij: 'Les Architectes de ces tems faisoient leurs Ceintres par deux arcs de cercles égaux, mais de differens centres, dans le dessein d'en tenir les pentes plus rapides, et par ce moyen diminuer cet effort en les rendant aussi plus minces et plus légeres: ils les traversoient encore par d'autres parties et voutes, qui formoient quantité d'angles saillans dont les arêtes étoient cachées et fortifiées per *des Nervures d'Ogives*, des *Arcs doubleaux*, des *Tiercerons*, et des *Formerets*, dont ils formoient une infinité de compartimens, aboutissans souvent à des culs de lampes suspendus en l'air. Toutes ces naissances entrelassées, et les intersections des Moulures demandoient une grande intelligence dans l'Art de la Coupe des Pierres; d'où je conjecture que c'est à l'Architecture *Gotique* que nous devons rapporter l'Origine, ou du moins l'Adolescence de ce Art.'

140 *Ibid.*, III (1739), p.362: 'Si l'on vouloit construire une Voute composée de boules infiniment petits et parfaitement polies, qui se soutînssent d'elles-mêmes en équilibre, il faudroit que la courbe qui passeroit par les centres de toutes ces boules eût la figure d'une chainette renversée.'

141 Hans Straub, *Die Geschichte der Bauingenieurkunst, ein Überblick von der Antike bis in die Neuzeit* (Basle and Stuttgart, 1949); reference to 2nd ed. (1964), pp. 179–86. – English editions appeared in 1952, 1960 and 1964.

142 J[ean]-B[aptiste]-A[ntoine] Lassus, 'Considérations sur la renaissance de l'art français au XIXe siècle' in Villard de Honnecourt, *Villard de Honnecourt, architecte du XIIIe siècle, manuscrit publié en fac-simile . . . par J.-B.-A. Lassus . . .* (Paris, 1858), pp.1–41; quotation taken from *ibid.*, p.30. – I do not know whether the facsimile edition (Paris, 1968) contains Lassus's 'Considérations'.

idea of a colonnade church. This they regarded as an ideal solution.[138] The churches of their own day, in which the nave was separated from the aisles by heavy pillars and arches, seemed to them far too cumbersome, and they considered that the detached columns and entablatures of Greek and Early Christian architecture looked far more elegant when they appeared in the form of colonnades. At the same time they recognized that, no matter how irregular they were, Gothic churches invariably created an impression of lightness, a quality which they found highly desirable. They also pointed to the vast size and great age of these churches as proof that the Gothic style leant itself to bold structural designs.

In the 1730s Amadée-François Frézier (1682–1733) tried to evolve a scientific, i.e. a stereometrically based and mechanically operated, method of stone-cutting. In the process he analysed the structure of Gothic arches and vaults with an expertise unequalled in his day. It seems that not even Sir Christopher Wren could compete with him in this field.

At the very beginning of his manual of stone-cutting (*stéréotomie*) Frézier considered the structural properties of Gothic architecture: 'The architects of those days formed their arches from the segments of two circles with equal radii but different centres, a procedure which enabled them to produce steeper haunches, and so reduce the thrust by making their voussoirs smaller and lighter; they also introduced transverse vaults, thus producing a large number of groins, which were concealed and strengthened by diagonal ribs, transverse ribs, tiercerons and formerets; with these they formed an intricate network, whose knots consisted of pendants. With their complex springers and their intersecting mouldings, these vaults called for great skill in the art of stone-cutting; and from this I conclude that it is in Gothic architecture that we must seek the origin, or at least the adolescence, of this art.'[139]

Although he did not actually say so, it would seem that Frézier considered the pointed or equilateral arch to be closely related to the catenary: 'If one wished to construct a vault from infinitely small and completely smooth balls, which would remain in a state of equilibrium of their own accord, then the curve passing through the centres of these balls would have to describe the arc of an inverted chain.'[140] (A catenary is the curve formed by a uniform chain hanging freely from two points.)

It was through Frézier that the French architects of the second half of the eighteenth and early nineteenth centuries became acquainted with the calculations and hypotheses produced by the mathematicians and physicists of his own and earlier generations. This was Frézier's principal contribution to statics and consequently to the development of structural design.[141] He was still being quoted as late as 1858 (in a posthumously published work), by Jean-Baptiste-Antoine Lassus (1807–57).[142]

Meanwhile, French architects gradually came to appreciate the great technical skill of the mediaeval masons who had built the Gothic cathedrals. In the end, they came to regard these cathedrals as technical miracles.

This was an important development because it helped to dispel the idea, one which had been widespread in the seventeenth and eighteenth centuries, that Gothic buildings were acts of folly or temerity.[143]

Jacques-Germain Soufflot (1713–80) undoubtedly exerted a greater influence on French architecture by building the Panthéon than by the lecture which he gave to the Académie des Sciences in Lyon in 1741 (and which was not published in full until the second half of the twentieth century).[144] But this lecture remains an important contemporary source, for Soufflot was probably the first French architect to make drawings of Gothic churches on a significant scale, and consequently his opinions have to be taken seriously.[145] He was still only 28 years old when he delivered his 'Mémoire sur l'architecture gothique' to the academicians of Lyon, and his powers of observation were extremely acute:

'Some of these piers are thick, others are thin, but they are all diagonally aligned, with the result that they all stand edge-on to the nave. They are built up from a number of circular shafts; some of these are thick, and serve as vaulting or arcade shafts; others are slender, and are situated between the thicker shafts, often accompanying them to the very top of the pier.'[146]

But Soufflot's interest was not confined to structural design as such. In addition, he drew attention to the impression of lightness created by Gothic architecture, and identified the ribs in the vaulting, the shape of the buttresses and the absence of an entablature above the arcades as the principal sources of this visual illusion.[147] He also attached importance to the height–width ratio:

'When we enter a Gothic church our eyes, deceived by its proportions, afford us a pleasure which at first takes us unawares, and leaves us quite astonished, but which then prompts us to remark, as we admire the building, on the prodigious length and height of the nave.[148]

Soufflot's attitude to Gothic buildings was essentially the same as his attitude to the Temples of Paestum, which he recorded in a series of scale drawings in 1750. In both cases he stressed the links with traditional types and forms. The formal or associative appeal of the unusual elements in these buildings seemed to him less important.[149]

It would appear that, with certain exceptions,[150] the atmospheric quality of the Gothic cathedrals, which the English found so attractive, had no appeal for the French architectural theorists. Even Etienne-Louis Boullée (1728–99), who set such great store by lighting effects, considered the Gothic from a purely structural viewpoint. In c.1780 Boullée conceived an idea for a church, whose structural members would be completely masked from the inside:

'It follows from what I have said that the buttresses in my temple will be faced so that, like the Gothic churches, it will seem to stand as if by a a miracle: and, moreover, that it will be decorated after the Grecian mode with the richest architectural ornaments ... It will be possible to

143 For sources see Herrmann, *Laugier* (1962), pp.235–9.

144 First complete publication in Petzet, *Soufflots Sainte-Geneviève* (1961), pp.135–42.

145 Murphy, *Plans, Elevations ... of the Church of Batalha* (1795), p.12.

146 Quotation taken from Petzet, *Soufflots Sainte-Geneviève* (1961), p.137: 'Ces piliers sont plus ou moins gros mais toujours posés diagonalement de manière qu'ils présentent un de leurs angles à la grande nef. Ils sont composés de quantité de colonnes cilindriques; les uns sont grosses et portent les retombés des voûtes et des arcades; les autres petites et placées entre les grosses qu'elles accompagnent souvent jusqu'en haut.'

147 *Ibid.*, pp.138 and 142.

148 *Ibid.*, p.141: 'Si nous entrons dans une église gothique, nos yeux, trompés par ses proportions, procurent à notre âme un plaisir qui la surprend et l'étonne d'abord, et nous fait dire en l'admirant: voilà un vaisseau d'une longueur et d'une hauteur prodigieuses.'

149 For Soufflot's attitude to Paestum see Dora Wiebenson, *Sources of Greek Revival Architecture ...* (London, 1969), pp.44–5, 66, 72, and 120–3. – See also Petzet, *Soufflots Sainte-Geneviève* (1961), pp.100–1.

150 See Note 27 for Part II and Note 133 for Part I above. – The best known statement by a French author advocating the 'atmospheric' view is to be found in Blondel, *Cours d'architecture*, I (1771), p.378: 'Le genre sublime dont nous voulons parler, devroit être par exemple, le propre de l'Architecture de nos Temples; en effet, tout y doit avoir un caractère sacré qui rappelle l'homme à Dieu, à la Religion, à lui même. Qu'on y prenne garde, certaines Eglises gothiques modernes, portent cette empreinte: une grande hauteur de voûte qui n'a rien de vulgaire, des nefs et des bas-côtés spacieux, une lumière modérée et analogue aux mystères, des façades élevées et pyramidales, une symétrie intérieure dans les côtés respectifs.'

151 Etienne-Louis Boullée, *Boullée's Treatise on Architecture: a Complete Presentation of the 'Architecture, Essai sur l'art', which Forms Part of the Boullée Papers (Ms. 9153) in the Bibliothèque Nationale, Paris*, edited by Helen Rosenau (London, 1953). – Quotation taken from the French edition: Etienne-Louis Boullée, *Architecture, Essai sur l'art*, textes réunis et présentés par Jean-Marie Pérouse de Montclos . . . (Paris, 1968), pp.92–3 (= fol. 95r. and v.): 'De cette disposition, il résulte qu'à l'instar des Goths les forces résistantes de mon temple sont masquées et qu'il paraîtra aussi se soutenir comme par miracle, et que d'ailleurs, à l'imitation des Grecs, il sera décoré par les plus grandes richesses de l'architecture. Les colonnes occupent le premier plan, elles facilitent les moyens d'introduire le jour d'une manière mystérieuse, en ce que leur saillie ne laisserait pas apercevoir comment la lumière pénètre dans le temple.' – For the dating of this quotation see Vogt, *Boullées Newton-Denkmal* (1969), pp.183 and 186.

152 Blondel, *Cours d'architecture*, I (1771), pp.458–9: 'Ce n'est pas que les Goths s'ils eussent montré plus de choix dans leurs ordonnances, et sur-tout plus de goût dans leurs ornements, n'eussent mérité d'être imité par leurs successeurs: mais leurs productions sont presque toujours une sorte d'enigme pour l'œil qui les examine; en sorte que le spectateur se trouve embarassé pour en démêler les beautés; défaut qui certainement ne se rencontre pas dans l'Architecture des Grecs et des Romains.'

153 Boullée, *Architecture* (1968), p.89 (= fols. 92v. and 93): 'Quoique les Goths aient bâti dans des temps où les arts étaient peu avancés, quoiqu'ils semblent n'avoir pas eu les connaissances de la belle architecture, cependant ils ont trouvé l'art de donner à leurs temples un grand caractère. Ils les ont rendu étonnants en les portant à une élévation si extra-ordinaire qu'ils semblent s'élancer dans les nues. Ils ont introduit la magie de l'art en voilant toutes les forces résistantes de leurs temples, en sorte qu'ils paraissent soutenus par une puissance surnaturelle.' – Commenting on the façade tower of Strasbourg Cathedral in 1457 Enea Silvio Piccolomini, who later became Pope Pius II, said: 'Caput inter nubila condit' (It hides its head in the clouds); this famous formulation of Vergil's (*Aeneid*, IV, 177), which was based on a line of Homer's (*Iliad*, IV, 443), was frequently discussed by the eighteenth-century rhetoricians; but whether Boullée was introduced to it by writers such as Boileau or Charles Perrault, or whether he discovered it in one of the guidebooks published on Strasbourg Cathedral, I do not know; in

introduce the daylight in a mysterious manner, for the rows of columns projecting into the nave will prevent anyone from seeing how the light enters the temple.'[151]

It was not the lighting effects themselves that the French architects took over from their Gothic predecessors but merely the technique for transferring thrust from the vaults to outer supports. The fact that this technique facilitated such lighting effects was purely incidental. Nor was there any mention during this period of stained-glass windows. The whole emphasis was on construction, and we find that Gothic structural design underwent a complete reappraisal within the framework of the new aesthetic that was evolved in France during the late eighteenth and early nineteenth centuries. The following comment by Jacques-François Blondel (1705–74), Boullée's mentor, dates from 1771: 'If the Goths had been more selective in their composition and, above all, had shown more taste in their ornamentation, they would have deserved to be imitated by their successors: but their works almost invariably pose an enigma for the observer, who finds himself at a loss as to how he should unravel their beauties. This is a defect which is certainly not encountered in Greek and Roman architecture.'[152]

Some fifteen years later Boullée wrote on the same subject in a much more positive vein: 'Although the Goths built at a time when little progress had been made in the arts, and although they seem to have known little about beautiful architecture, they none the less discovered how to lend great character to their temples. They made them wonderful by building them so extraordinarily high that they seem to tower up into the clouds. They introduced the magic of art by masking all the buttresses in their temples in such a way that these seem to be supported by a supernatural power.'[153]

Instead of referring to the 'technical miracle' of Gothic architecture, Boullée spoke of the 'magic of art'[154] in 'wonderful' Gothic temples. This kind of approach presupposed no technical knowledge, and was therefore calculated to appeal to a public versed in literature.[155]

The first French appreciation of Gothic churches that was completely in line with the English view was probably that penned by the historian Claude Villaret (1715–66). In his *Histoire de France*, which was not published until after his death, he wrote: 'The antique majesty of these sacred naves inspires a kind of religious *horror*, which seems to proclaim, and instil in our minds, the sanctity of the mysteries which are celebrated there.'[156]

Perhaps it was a profane post-Revolutionary form of this 'horror' that prompted an anonymous Grand Prix competitor to submit a design for a state prison with pointed arches in 1795.[157]

In the closing decade of the eighteenth century France seemed to be paralysed, and it was not until the émigrés began to return that a new conception of Gothic architecture was able to take root. Germany played a part in this respect, but England played a bigger one;[158] and the most important mediator between England and France during this

this connexion see Frankl, *The Gothic* (1960), p.246.

154 'Le merveilleux' was not connected with Gothic architecture until 1800, as a result of a translation from the German; see Lein, 'Persistence et renouveau du gothique' (1968), p.125; unfortunately, this author does not distinguish between original French passages and translations into the French.

155 See *ibid.* and Nies, 'Die semantische Aufwertung von französisch *gothique*' (1968).

156 Claude Villaret, *Histoire de France* ..., XI (Paris, 1783), p.141: 'L'antique majesté de ces vaisseaux sacrés inspire une certaine *horreur* religieuse qui semble nous avertir et nous pénétrer de la sainteté des mysteres qu'on y célebre.'

157 Helen Rosenau, 'The Engravings of the *Grand Prix* of the French Academy of Architecture' in *Architectural History*, III (1960), pp.15–180; pl.117; commentary p.166: 'The austere façade and the functional introduction of the Gothic arch in this design is in advance of its time.'

158 Fernand Baldensperger, *Le mouvement des idées dans l'émigration française (1789–1815)*, I: *Les expériences du présent* (Paris, 1924), esp. pp.70–3.

159 Paul Léon, *La vie des monuments français: destruction, restauration* (Paris, 1951), p.75.

160 Chateaubriand, *Œuvres complètes*, II (1861), p.290: 'Au moyen du *dôme*, inconnu des anciens, la religion a fait un heureux mélange de ce que l'ordre gothique a de hardi et de ce que les ordres grecs ont de simple et de gracieux. 'Ce *dôme*, qui se change en *clocher*, dans la plupart de nos églises, donne à nos hameaux et à nos villes un caractère moral que ne pouvaient avoir les cités antiques. ... Un paysage paraît-il nu, triste, désert, placez-y un clocher champêtre: à l'instant tout va s'animer; les douces idées de *pasteur* et de *troupeau*, d'asile pour le voyageur, d'aumône pour le pélerin, d'hospitalité et de fraternité chrétienne, vont naître de toutes parts.' – See also Alice Poirier, *Les idées artistiques de Chateaubriand: les sources* ... (Paris, 1930), esp. p.319.

161 Chateaubriand, *Œuvres complètes*, II (1861), p.292.

162 *Ibid.*, p.293. – See also Note 144 for Part I above.

163 Chateaubriand, *Œuvres complètes*, II (1861), pp.293–4: 'On ne pouvait entrer

period was François-René de Chateaubriand (1768–1848). His *Génie du Christianisme* was published four days before Napoleon concluded his concordat with the Curia; and just as Napoleon's agreement marked a turning-point in the political life, so Chateaubriand's book marked a turning-point in the intellectual life, of the country.[159] One of the best-known passages in this book reflects the fusion of the French and English views of the Gothic:

'Thanks to these *domes*, religion has created a happy combination of all that is bold in the Gothic order and all that is simple and graceful in the Greek orders.

'These *domes*, which have assumed the form of bell-towers in the majority of our churches, give to our villages and towns a moral character that was denied to the cities of antiquity ... Take a bare, dismal and deserted landscape, place in it a rural bell-tower, and it comes to life at once, evoking sweet thoughts of *shepherds* and their *flocks*, of shelter for the traveller, of alms for the pilgrim, of Christian hospitality and fraternity.'[160]

Chateaubriand projected his ideal conception of a dome church – such as the Panthéon – backwards into the past, and on the basis of this projection he concluded that bell towers had been derived from domes. Consequently – always assuming that he thought in typological and evolutionary terms – he must also have envisaged the development of crossing towers. Why, he asked himself, did the poets and writers of the eighteenth century introduce Gothic castles and churches into their works? The answer was obvious. For what could be more natural than to revert to the customs of one's ancestors, since both the religion and the history of the motherland were imbued with such sweet memories?[161]

Chateaubriand was acquainted with various theories concerning the origin of the Gothic; namely, the Arabian, the Egyptian and the so-called 'natural' theory. Moreover, since he referred to the 'colonne palmiste' in this connexion, he also appears to have read Laugier's *Observations* (1765) or a work by one of Laugier's many plagiarizers.[162] But, above all, Chateaubriand knew, and used, the themes evolved by the Romantics:

'It was impossible to enter a Gothic church without feeling a sort of chilling sensation and receiving a vague presentiment of the deity ... Ancient France seemed to live again ... The more remote those times were, the more magical they seemed to us, the more they inspired in us the kind of thoughts which invariably end in reflections on the insignificance of man and the brevity of human life ... Everything in Gothic churches recalls labyrinthine forests, everything evokes religious awe, the mysteries and the deity. The lofty twin towers ... set against the azure blue of the sky, create a *picturesque* effect.'[163]

Apart from the closing sentence, which is purely conventional, this passage reveals no appreciation whatsoever of the formal properties of Gothic architecture. Chateaubriand was quite as blind in this respect as the Classicist architectural theorists of earlier generations. For him Gothic churches were the pantheons of a better world that had long since disappeared. This was why he revealed such a marked preference for the abbey churches of St Denis and Westminster.[164] In his *Mémoires d'Outre-Tombe* Chateaubriand claimed to have been imprisoned in Westminster Abbey from closing time until midnight, and it is significant that, whether we believe his story or not, it makes no difference whatsoever to our assessment of his art.[165] It is also characteristic of his attitude to Gothic monuments that he should have acquired his first impression of Rheims Cathedral in Berlin, where he was French envoy from 1821 to 1822 and saw a production of Schiller's *Jungfrau von Orleans* with stage sets by Schinkel.[166]

50

Commenting on the impact of his *Génie du Christianisme* in 1837, Chateaubriand wrote:

'It is from this work that the present day taste for mediaeval buildings derives: it was due to my prompting that the people of this present century first came to admire these old churches . . . But if they are now bored to death with the endless discussions of the Gothic, that is not my fault.'[167]

Chateaubriand's ambivalent attitude to architecture was perfectly illustrated by his country house in the Vallée-aux-Loups, near Sceaux. He owned this house from 1807 to 1817, and during this period carried out a Gothic conversion similar to that undertaken by Walpole at Strawberry Hill, albeit on a far more modest scale. On the garden side he added a portico with two black columns and two white marble caryatids. But on the other side of the house both the entrance door and the windows received pointed arches while the garden wall was crenellated. 'In this way', Chateaubriand wrote in 1839, 'I anticipated the mediaeval mania by which we are now besotted.'[168] In fact, his house is precisely what we would have expected; it reminds us of the kind of designs produced by French students of architecture for their examinations (*Maisons des Cosmopolites*), especially those in which each of the four façades is executed in the style of one of the four old continents.[169] Chateaubriand's converted house did not exert any noteworthy influence on the development of French architecture.

Although modern research into the Gothic Revival in France is still in its infancy, it is already apparent that this movement set in later there than in England, and that far fewer people were inclined to recommend its adoption as a universal style. None the less, it had its supporters, the most distinguished being Alexandre de Laborde (1761–1839), who is well known for his early attempts to preserve France's historical monuments. Laborde openly advocated the adoption of the Gothic as a universal style:

'It ought to be quite simple to evolve a Gothic style that would be more in keeping than Greek architecture with our customs, the type of dwellings we prefer, and the small amount of money that we devote to their upkeep: more convenient corridors and stairs (*dégagements*), more varied windows, perpendicular forms intersecting the horizon.'[170]

By his use of the word 'dégagement' Laborde revealed his indebtedness to Claude Perrault. But where Perrault reacted against

dans une église gothique sans éprouver une sorte de frissonnement et un sentiment vague de la Divinité . . . L'ancienne France semblait revivre . . . Plus ces temps étaient éloignés de nous, plus ils nous paraissaient magiques, plus ils nous remplissaient de ces pensées qui finissent toujours par une réflexion sur le néant de l'homme et la rapidité de la vie . . . Tout retrace les labyrinthes des bois dans l'église gothique, tout en fait sentir la religieuse horreur, les mystères et la divinité. Les deux tours hautaines . . . font un effet *pittoresque* sur l'azur du ciel.'

164 Chateaubriand, *Mémoires d'Outre-Tombe* (1962–4); according to the index of this edition Chateaubriand refers to Saint-Denis 25 times and to Westminster Abbey 10 times.

165 *Ibid.*, I, pp.355–6.

166 *Ibid.*, II, p.45. – [Karl Friedrich] Schinkel, *Sammlung von Theater-Decorationen* (Potsdam, 1819; further editions up to 1874); reference to the 2nd ed. (Berlin, [1847–]1849), pls. 8–9 (probably from 1817).

167 Chateaubriand, *Mémoires d'Outre-Tombe* (1962–4), I, p.465: 'C'est encore à cet ouvrage que se rattache le goût actuel pour les édifices du moyen âge: c'est moi qui ai rappelé le jeune siècle à l'admiration des vieux temples . . . Si à force d'entendre rabâcher du gothique on en meurt d'ennui, ce n'est pas ma faute.'

168 Hautecœur, *Histoire de l'architecture classique*, v (1953), figs.189 and 216. – Chateaubriand, *Mémoires d'Outre-Tombe* (1962–4), I, p.632: 'Je précédais ainsi la manie du moyen âge, qui nous hébète à présent.'

169 The Zentralbibliothek in Lucerne possesses an early nineteenth-century design of this kind.

170 Quotation taken from Léon, *La vie des monuments* (1951), pp.78–9; no source is given by this author: 'Il semble qu'il serait facile de composer un style gothique qui conviendrait mieux que l'architecture grecque à nos mœurs, au genre de nos habitations, au peu de dépense que l'on est à même d'y consacrer: dégagements plus commodes, jours plus multiples, formes perpendiculaires coupant l'horizon.'

the heaviness of Baroque architecture, Laborde opposed the archaeological excesses of the Greek Revival; the blind walls and pycnostyle order of Greek temples really were not calculated to provide the bright living areas to which people had grown accustomed and which they found so desirable. Incidentally, although Laborde decried the use of Gothic 'fabriques' in landscape gardens, as one of the earliest protagonists of the Gothic Revival in France he not unnaturally wrote a book on landscape gardening.[171] In this book we are able to follow his development up to the point where he came to advocate the adoption of the Gothic as a universal style. He spoke highly of the Park of Raincy near Paris because, instead of being purely decorative, the buildings erected there could be used for either residential or agricultural purposes.[172] Thus, without wishing to question the validity of scenic effects, Laborde insisted that all buildings must serve some practical purpose.

Like Chateaubriand, Montalembert (1810–70) spent part of his youth in England, and later became a writer and politician with strong Catholic sympathies. In view of these sympathies it is hardly surprising that he should have regarded mediaeval art as 'the most important manifestation of the Church'.[173] In an article entitled 'Du Vandalisme en France', which appeared in 1833, he called for the preservation and imitation of mediaeval architectural monuments.[174] In a broad synopsis of the contemporary scene he introduced his compatriots to the architectural developments that had been taking place abroad. He was particularly interested in English Church architecture, which he considered to have been remarkably successful:
'If these copies, several of which are quite remarkable, lack the vitality imparted by an original inspiration, they none the less have the great merit of being completely in accord, and harmonizing, with the ideas which they represent; the Gothic reaction has now passed from religious architecture to secular architecture; wealthy estate owners are having castles built, which are exact reproductions of the kinds of castle found in the different feudal periods, whilst private individuals, corporations, diocesan districts, and committees are making enormous sacrifices in order to conserve in, or restore to, their original condition any monuments that have survived from these periods.'[175]

Montalembert considered that artistic taste had been 'false, ridiculous and pagan'[176] ever since the Renaissance. He placed his hope in the clergy, for he was convinced that there could be 'no art without faith.'[177]

Politically, Montalembert was a Catholic Liberal:
'In Germany the peoples seek out the rubble of the old castles to hold their liberal assemblies, as if they wanted to place their newly emerging liberty under the protection of past times.'[178]

The need to exploit Gothic architecture for purposes of political propaganda led to a remarkable reassessment of this style in France. In 1831 Ludovic Vitet (1802–73), the historian and politician, provided the following definition of the Gothic:
'Its underlying principle is the emancipation of liberty, of the sense of

43, 44

171 Alexandre[-Louis-Joseph] de Laborde, *Description des nouveaux jardins de la France* . . . (French, German and English), (Paris, 1808); facsimile edition (Hildesheim and New York, 1971).

172 *Ibid.*, p.135.

173 [Charles-René Forbes] de Montalembert, *Œuvres*, VI: *Mélanges d'art et de littérature* (Paris, 1861), p.8.

174 *Ibid.*, pp.7–75.

175 *Ibid.*, pp.10–11: 'Si ces copies, dont plusieurs sont très-remarquables, manquent de la vie que donne l'inspiration originale, elles ont le grand mérite de la convenance et de l'harmonie avec les idées qu'elles représentent; de l'architecture religieuse, la réaction gothique a passé dans l'architecture civile; les riches propriétaires se font bâtir des châteaux qui reproduisent exactement les types des différents âges de la féodalité, tandis que les particuliers, les corporations, les diocèses, les comités, s'imposent les plus grands sacrifices pour conserver dans leur intégrité tous les monuments originaux de ces âges, et pour leur rendre leur aspect primitif.'

176 Montalembert, *Œuvres*, VI (1861), p.42.

177 *Ibid.*, p.75.

178 *Ibid.*, p.14: 'En Allemagne les populations choisissent les décombres des vieux châteaux pour tenir leurs assemblées liberales, comme pour mettre leur liberté renaissante sous la protection des anciens jours.'

association and community expressed in our indigenous and national feelings. It is bourgeois; and, over and above this, it is French, English, Teutonic.'[179]

Vitet's formulation, which was essentially an attempt to secularize the Gothic, was taken up subsequently by Viollet-le-Duc, who evolved a whole new historical theory on this basis:

'We must not forget that French architecture was first established in the midst of the conquered people and in the face of its conquerors; it drew its inspiration from the bosom of this indigenous group, the largest group in the nation; immediately following its initial attempts to free itself, it fell into the hands of the laity; it was neither theocratic nor feudal.'[180]

As an introduction to Gothic architecture, Victor Hugo's *Notre-Dame de Paris*[181] was no less influential than Montalembert's 'Du Vandalisme', the first edition of which, incidentally, took the form of a letter to Hugo.

According to Louis Hautecœur, '. . . for Victor Hugo the soul of Notre-Dame is the hunchback Quasimodo'.[182] In point of fact, it seems far more likely that Hugo was inspired by the gargoyles than by the architecture of the cathedral. None the less, and despite the fact that Hugo employed a wide range of architectural terms to describe Notre-Dame, there can be no doubt that, on occasions, he was also overwhelmed by the dark and inscrutable forces in the cathedral, which he described as

'the sombre and powerful cathedral which, according to the chroniclers, inspires terror.'[183]

And yet, in another passage, he spoke of Notre-Dame as a logical and well-proportioned building.[184] In general, however, Hugo's interpretation of particular aspects of the Gothic is less important than his declared intention of instilling a sense of respect for France's architectural monuments:

'If it is possible, let us inspire in the nation a love of our national architecture. This, the author declares, is one of the principal aims of his book; it is one of the principal aims of his life.'[185]

Chateaubriand, Hugo, Montalembert: these writers spoke up in defence of Gothic architecture until well into the 1830's, and their voices commanded attention. Like Arcisse de Caumont and the many other highly gifted antiquarians who joined them in their campaign, they were more interested in the conservation of mediaeval monuments, many of which had suffered grievously in the French Revolution, than in a Gothic Revival. It was not until the 1840's that the French architects entered the scene, and – like their eighteenth-century counterparts – they tended at first to regard the Gothic cathedrals as technical miracles.

179 Quotation taken from Hautecœur, *Histoire de l'architecture classique*, VI (1955), p.285: 'Son principe est l'émancipation de la liberté, de l'esprit d'association et de commune dans les sentiments tout indigènes et nationaux. Elle est bourgeoise et, de plus, elle est française, anglaise, teutonique.'

180 [Eugène-Emmanuel] Viollet-le-Duc, *Dictionnaire raisonné de l'architecture française du XIe au XVIe siècle*, 10 vols. (Paris, 1854–68; reprinted up to 1924), I (1854), p.153: 'On ne doit pas oublier que l'architecture française s'était constituée au milieu du peuple conquis en face de ses conquérants, elle prenait ses inspirations dans le sein de cette fraction indigène, la plus nombreuse de la nation; elle était tombée au mains des laïques sitôt après les premières tentatives d'émancipation, elle n'était ni théocratique ni féodale.'

181 See Notes 238–40 for Part I above.

182 Hautecœur, *Histoire de l'architecture classique*, VI (1955), p.282.

183 Hugo, *Notre-Dame* (1961), p.126: 'la grave et puissante cathédrale, qui terrifie, au dire des chroniqueurs.'

184 *Ibid.*

185 *Ibid.*, p.7: 'Inspirons, s'il est possible, à la nation l'amour de l'architecture nationale. C'est là, l'auteur le déclare, un des buts principaux de ce livre; c'est là un des buts principaux de sa vie.' – Of course, Hugo also regarded the Gothic as 'progressive et populaire' and as 'l'enfantement du peuple en travail': *ibid.*, pp.131–2; for a similar statement see *ibid.*, pp.213 ff.

186 Hans Tietze, 'Wiener Gotik im XVIII. Jahrhundert' in *Kunstgeschichtliches Jahrbuch der k.k. Zentral-Kommission für Erforschung und Erhaltung der Kunst- und historischen Denkmale*, III (1909), pp.162–86. – Alfred Neumeyer, 'Die Erweckung der Gotik in der deutschen Kunst des späten 18. Jahrhunderts: ein Beitrag zur Vorgeschichte der Romantik' in *Repertorium für Kunstwissenschaft*, XLI (1928), pp.75–123 and 159–85. – [Robert Hugo] Arndt Schreiber, *Frühklassizistische Kritik an der Gotik, 1759–1789* (Würzburg, 1938; as a Berlin thesis published in Berlin, 1937). – Alfred Kamphausen, *Gotik ohne Gott, ein Beitrag zur Deutung der Neugotik und des 19. Jahrhunderts* (Tübingen, 1952). – Robson-Scott, *The Literary Background of the Gothic Revival* (1965); with a comprehensive bibliography arranged in chapters.

187 Klaus Merten, *Der Bayreuther Hofarchitekt Joseph Saint-Pierre, 1708/9–1754* (Bayreuth, 1964), pp.23–41.– This study is an offprint from *Archiv für die Geschichte von Oberfranken*, XLIV, pp. 5–160.

188 C[hristian] C[ay] L[aurenz] Hirschfeld, *Theorie der Gartenkunst*, 5 vols. (Leipzig, 1779–85), I (1779), p.73: 'Und was kann uns bereden, Nationalanlagen mit einem fremden Namen zu belegen, der sie für blosse Nachahmung ausgiebt? Ist es etwa mehr Empfehlung, wenn der *deutsche* Fürst einen *ausländischen*, als wenn er einen *deutschen* Garten hat? Lässt sich nicht eine Manier denken und einführen, die *deutsch* genug ist, um diesen Namen anzunehmen?' – This emphasis on national achievements did not prevent Hirschfeld from publishing a French edition of his work (Leipzig, 1779–85).

189 See e.g. Immanuel Kant, *Critik der Urtheilskraft* (Berlin and Libau, 1790), pp.41, 70, 206–7 and 212 ff.

190 Hirschfeld, *Theorie der Gartenkunst*, I (1779), p.138: 'Der Architekt will auf einmal das Auge befriedigen, es auf einmal die ganze harmonische Einrichtung seines Werks unfassen lassen; der Gartenkünstler will nach und nach mit einer allmähligen Fortschreitung unterhalten.'

191 *Ibid.*, pp.139–41.

192 For the history of the concept 'Romantic' see Richard Ullmann, 'Der Begriff "romantisch"' in *Begriffsbestimmungen der Romantik*, hrsg. von Helmut Prang ... (Darmstadt, 1968), pp.145–58; this paper was first printed in 1928.

3 The German National Monument

In a book dealing with the theories underlying the Gothic Revival it is inevitable that literary sources should be quoted which are not referred to in publications dealing with other aspects of this movement (such as the early buildings executed in this style, the emergence of the modern interest in Gothic architecture or the culturally pessimistic conception of the 'Gothic without God'), and *vice versa*.[186]

I now propose to pursue the development leading up to the greatest project carried out during the Gothic Revival in Germany: the continuation of Cologne Cathedral.

The first Gothic buildings installed in German landscape gardens were designed at such an early date that they will almost certainly have been indigenous creations. Subsequently, however, the English influence became all powerful,[187] and by 1779 Christian Cay Laurenz Hirschfeld (1742–92), the professor of philosophy and garden theorist, was complaining bitterly, albeit fruitlessly, on this account:
'And what could have persuaded us to call our national achievements [i.e. gardens] by a foreign name, which brands them as a mere imitation? Is it a greater recommendation for a *German* prince to own an *English* rather than a *German* garden? Are we incapable of conceiving and introducing a manner that would be sufficiently German to warrant this name?'[188]

Hirschfeld was the most widely read German theorist writing on garden design at a time when this discipline was generally regarded as one of the fine arts.[189] His significance for the history of ideas lies in the fact that he was the first German scholar to combine English landscape theory with the French theory of architectural character. True, this did not prevent him from contrasting the tasks facing the architect with those facing the landscape gardener. But then it was customary in his day to draw contrasts between the various artistic disciplines. Lessing's *Laocoon*, which appeared in 1766, leaves us in no doubt about this practice. Hirschfeld himself made the following distinction:
'The architect wants to satisfy the viewer all at once, he wants him to be able to grasp the harmonious disposition of his work at a glance; the landscape gardener, on the other hand, wants to engage his attention gradually, as he wanders slowly through his garden.'[190]

Where architectural theory was concerned Hirschfeld was a French Classicist, but when it came to landscape theory he was an English pre-Romantic. That was why he insisted that buildings must be symmetrical and gardens asymmetrical (although he was prepared to allow symmetrical installations in the immediate vicinity of houses and palaces, and for public walks).[191]

He also advocated the use of Gothic buildings as a means of heightening the atmosphere of Romantic landscapes:[192]
'We see how nature forms districts with different characters and effects. But such natural characters can be reinforced in diverse ways through human agency. Thus, a cheerful district can be effectively enhanced by a

193 Hirschfeld, *Theorie der Gartenkunst*, I (1779), p.227: 'Wir sehen, wie die Natur Gegenden von verschiedenen Charakteren und Einwirkungen bildet. Allein diese natürlichen Charaktere können noch auf eine mannigfaltige Weise durch die Hand des Menschen verstärkt werden. So kann eine muntere Gegend durch eine Schäferhütte oder ein Landhaus, eine melancholische durch ein Kloster oder eine Urne, eine romantische durch gothische Ruinen, eine feyerliche durch Tempel, oder wie wir bey Montserrat gesehen, durch eine Menge von Einsiedeleyen, sehr viel an Einwirkung gewinnen.'

194 *Ibid.*, III (1780), p.111: 'So erwecken die Ruinen eines Bergschlosses, eines Klosters, eines alten Landsitzes sehr abgeänderte Bewegungen, besonders abgeändert durch die Betrachtung der Zeit- und anderer Umstände, die an sich so vielfältig unterschieden seyn können. Man kehrt in Zeiten zurück, die nicht mehr sind. Man lebt auf einige Augenblicke wieder in den Jahrhunderten der Barbarey und der Fehde, aber auch der Stärke und der Tapferkeit; in den Jahrhunderten des Aberglaubens, aber auch der eingezogenen Andacht; in den Jahrhunderten der Wildheit und der Jagdbegier, aber auch der Gastfreundschaft.'

195 *Ibid.*, pp.114–15: '. . . eine Wahrscheinlichkeit'.

196 *Ibid.*, IV (1785), p.105: 'Man geht hier nach der Burg. Dies ist ein alter halb verfallener gothischer Thurm, in einem wahren täuschenden Styl, nach der Zeichnung des Prinzen vortrefflich gebaut.' – The ruin was built in 1779–80 from plans drawn up by Crown Prince Wilhelm IX of Hesse.

197 *Ibid.*, III (1780), p.61: 'Dieser würde, nach seinem besondern Character betrachtet, sich besser in den Park eines Königs schicken, noch besser auf einen schönen Platz in der Residenz, als ein öffentliches Nationalgebäude.'

198 *Ibid.*, pp.81–2: 'Übrigens ist es wohl ohne Beweise klar, dass bey der Nachahmung fremder Bauarten die griechische einen grossen Vorzug verdient. Es ist wahr, dass sie in gewissem Verstand für uns fremde ist. Allein sie ist seit Jahrhunderten in dem Besitz des Beyfalls der Kenner; ihre Schönheiten sind unzweifelhaft und entschieden; sie gefallen allen Nationen, sobald sich bey ihnen die Gefühle für das Edle und Grosse entwickeln . . . Doch versteht es sich, dass die Nachahmung in keine sclavische Nachfolge übergehen und nichts mehr aufnehmen darf, als was nach unserm Klima, nach unserer veränderten Lebensart, und nach

shepherd's hut or a cottage, a melancholy district by a monastery or an urn, a romantic district by Gothic ruins, a solemn district by temples or, as we have seen in Montserrat, by a collection of hermitages.'[193]

Hirschfeld himself was interested primarily in Gothic ruins: 'Thus, the ruins of a lofty castle, a monastery or an old country house produce highly diverse stimuli, chiefly as a result of our awareness of temporal and other factors, which are themselves extremely diverse. We are transported into times long past. For a few brief moments we find ourselves living in the centuries of barbarity and feudal warfare, but also of strength and courage; in the centuries of superstition, but also of inward piety; in the centuries of savagery and rapacity, but also of hospitality.'[194]

After providing this detailed inventory of associations, Hirschfeld made a comparison between Greek and Gothic ruins, from which he concluded that the Gothic ruins 'possess a *vraisemblance* that is lacking in the Greek'. From this concept of *vraisemblance*, which he took from the sphere of dramaturgy, Hirschfeld was able to proceed to a concept of reality and truth, which persuaded him that genuine ruins were preferable to artificial ruins.[195] In his assessment of Wilhelmsbad near Hanau these two concepts combine in a quite remarkable synthesis: 'Here people go to the castle. This is an old, half derelict Gothic tower, which was extremely well built, from a drawing made by the prince, in a true, illusionist style.'[196]

Hirschfeld was also interested in the question of national monuments, although his observations on this subject have yet to be fully evaluated. In his description of the Temple of Concordia at Stowe in Buckinghamshire, a peripteral structure with Ionic columns, he wrote: 'In view of its special character this would be more suitable for a royal park or – better still – for a beautiful square in a royal residence than a . . . national building.'[197]

Hirschfeld did not elaborate on this notion so that we have no means of knowing whether he considered that a 'national building' of this kind should simply be endowed with a monumental character or whether it should also serve some practical purpose. But what is quite apparent from this section of Hirschfeld's book is the extensive role which he ascribed to Greek architecture: 'It is, of course, quite evident that, as far as the imitation of foreign styles of architecture is concerned, the Greek style enjoys a great advantage. In a certain sense, it is true, this style is alien to us. But for centuries it has received the approbation of connoisseurs; its beauties are unquestionable and quite specific; they appeal to every nation that has developed a sense for the noble and sublime . . . It goes without saying that imitation must never become completely stereotype, and should embrace nothing that cannot be put to some useful purpose within the context of our different climate, our different customs, and our different needs.'[198]

In Hirschfeld's view, there was nothing contradictory in the adoption of a Greek temple design for the construction of a German national monument. This view was shared by Hans Christian Genelli (1763–1823), who submitted a design based on a Doric temple for a monument to Frederick the Great in 1786, and by Friedrich Gilly (1771–1800), who adopted a similar approach when faced with the same task in 1797; it was also shared by Ludwig I of Bavaria and his architect Leo von Klenze in 1830, when they started work on the Walhalla near Regensburg. Although neither of these buildings was actually called a national monument, that is what they both were.[199]

46, 47

We have already seen that Hirschfeld objected to the use of Greek temples for purposes of scenic display in landscape gardens. From the following excerpt it is clear that he raised the same objection when chapels were degraded in this way:

'These buildings seem almost too important to be used simply as models for reproductions; and yet, in a number of British parks Gothic churches have been built, which were far too costly to have been erected as superfluous monuments to an outmoded style of architecture . . . In the case of large estates a chapel of this kind can be used as the normal place of worship for the estate owner and his staff, thus replacing the local church, which may be situated at some considerable distance.'[200]

Both from this and from other passages in Hirschfeld's book it is clear that he was opposed to follies. It was not that he wanted all fanciful structures to be suppressed. On the contrary, he wanted to see them removed from landscape gardens so that they could be developed into monumental buildings. In this he was not alone.

In 1788 a book entitled *Untersuchungen über den Charakter der Gebäude* (Treatise on the Character of Buildings) was published in Leipzig. But although it did not appear until 1788 this anonymous work was actually written prior to that year, for the preface is dated January 1784. And from this treatise it is apparent that the theory of associations evolved by the German landscape gardeners was very different from Boffrand's theory of architectural character and was not readily applicable to monumental architecture.[201] This we see from the following excerpt: 'The architect always conceives the spirit of his building first, and then allows this to radiate from its body; because he knows that this spirit cannot be breathed into the building, either by emblems or by inscriptions.'[202]

The anonymous author devoted a great deal of space to a description of the 'Romantic character', and defined its principal features as disorder, carelessness, asymmetry and unexpectedness. But he also held that the 'combination of many different kinds of architecture . . . was not the noblest form of Romanticism'.[203] And he went on to say: 'But how are we to express the special character of a building save by an unexpected combination of its component parts? Admittedly, the type of composition used is bound to be a major factor in this respect, and it is equally certain that architects would be extremely restricted in the application of this [Romantic] character but for the fortunate circumstance that they are also able to draw on another source. This

unsern verschiedenen Bedürfnissen einer Anwendung fähig ist.'

199 Thomas Nipperdey, 'Nationalidee und Nationaldenkmal in Deutschland im 19. Jahrhundert' in *Historische Zeitschrift*, CCVI (1968), pp.529–85.

200 Hirschfeld, *Theorie der Gartenkunst*, III (1780), pp.108–9: 'Diese Werke scheinen fast zu wichtig, um blos Werke zur Nachahmung zu seyn; so wie man in einigen brittischen Parks gothische Kirchen errichtet hat, die zu viel Kosten erforderten, als dass man sie blos als überflüssige Denkmäler einer überlebten Baukunst hätte wiederaufstellen sollen. . . . Bey grossen Landsitzen kann eine solche Capelle der gewöhnliche Ort des Gottesdienstes für den Gutsbesitzer und seine Hofhaltung werden, und die Abgelegenheit einer Kirche ersetzen.'

201 *Untersuchungen über den Charakter der Gebäude; über die Verbindung der Baukunst mit den schönen Künsten, und über die Wirkungen, welche durch dieselbe hervorgebracht werden sollen* (Leipzig, 1788).

202 *Ibid.*, p.12: 'Überhaupt denkt sich der Baukünstler allezeit den Geist des Gebäudes zuerst, und lässt ihn aus dem Körper desselben athmen; fest überzeugt, dass er ihm weder durch Embleme, noch durch Inschriften eingehaucht werden könne.'

203 *Ibid.*, pp.157–8: '. . . würde wenigstens nicht die edelste Art des Romantischen seyn.'

204 *Ibid.*, pp.158–9: 'Wie kann man aber die ungewöhnliche Bestimmung eines Gebäudes anders, als durch eine seltsame Combination seiner Theile ausdrücken? Ich gestehe, dass die Art der Composition sehr viel dazu beytragen muss, und eben so gewiss ist es, dass die Baukunst in Anwendung dieses Characters sehr eingeschränkt seyn würde, wenn sie nicht glücklicherweise noch aus einer andern Quelle schöpfen könnte. Diese entspringt in der mittlern Zeit der Barbarey, oder, welches gleichviel ist, in der Epoche des Aberglaubens, der Zauberey, der Gespenster und irrenden Ritterschaft. Aus eben dieser Periode überliefert uns aber die gothische Kunst mancherley Formen, die wir unverändert beybehalten können, wenn wir nur den Character eines

Gebäudes jedesmal durch die Art der Composition genau bestimmen. Die Wirkung solcher Gebäude wird unfehlbar und allgemeyn seyn, da der Glaube an Zauberey, Rittergeschichten u.s.w. volksmässig ist.'

205 *Ibid.*, pp.160–3.

206 *Ibid.*, pp.107–16.

207 *Ibid.*, pp.181–2: 'Es giebt aber Fälle . . ., wo man nicht die Freyheit hat, den Gedanken auszuführen, der das Gebäude am stärksten charakterisiren würde. Ich will die Kirche zum Beyspiel aufführen. 'Wenn man sich vorstellt, dass dieses Gebäude der Sitz der Gottheit sey, so ist dieser Gedanke für die Einbildungskraft ungemein fruchtbar. Ausserdem wird er durch einige Aussprüche der heiligen Schrift so begünstigt, dass er unmöglich anstössig seyn kann. Hierzu kommt noch, dass er sich durch die Baukunst sehr stark bezeichnen lässt. Denn das Geheimnisvolle und Unbegreifliche, welches uns für die Gottheit mit Anbetung und tiefer Ehrfurcht erfüllt, kann die Baukunst durch Stille und Dunkelheit andeuten. Ein Gebäude also, welches der Gottheit geheiligt seyn soll, könnte nicht würdiger behandelt werden, als wenn man es als eine Wohnung derselben vorstellte. 'Aber die Einrichtung des christlichen Gottesdienstes gestattet eine solche Ausführung nicht. Jetzt ist die Kirche kein Tempel mehr, sondern ein gottes- dienstlicher Hörsaal, in welchem kein Baumeister so viel Licht verschaffen kann, dass man nicht noch über Dunkelheit klagt.'

208 Heinrich Lützeler, 'Der Kölner Dom in der deutschen Geistesgeschichte' in *Der Kölner Dom, Festschrift zur Siebenhundert- jahrfeier*, hrsg. vom Zentral-Dombau- Verein (Cologne, 1948), pp.195–250. – Robson-Scott, *The Literary Background of the Gothic Revival* (1965), see esp. pp.96– 107.

209 [Wilhelm Heinse,] *Ardinghello und die glückseeligen Inseln, eine Italiänische Geschichte aus dem sechszehnten Jahr- hundert*, 2 vols. (Lemgo, 1787), I, p.56: 'Ein feyerlicher gothischer Dom mit seinem freyen ungeheuren Raume, von vernünftigen Barbaren entworfen, wo die Stimme des Priesters Donner wird, und der Choral des Volks ein Meersturm, der den Vater des Weltalls preist und den kühnsten Ungläubigen erschüttert, indess der Tyrann der Musik, die Orgel, wie ein Orkan darein rast und tiefe Fluthen wälzt: wird immer das kleinliche Gemäch im Grossen, seys nach dem niedlichsten Venustempel von dem geschmackvollsten Athenienser! bey einem Manne von unverfälschtem Sinn zu Schanden machen.'

second source is the barbarous Middle Ages or – and this amounts to the same thing – the era of superstition, magic, ghosts, and knights errant. But from the Gothic art of this selfsame period we have inherited many forms which we are able to use unaltered, provided we determine the character of each and every building by using a specific type of composition. Such buildings cannot fail to produce a universal effect, since a belief in magic, stories of mediaeval knights, etc. is firmly established amongst the people.'[204]

The author then listed various kinds of 'Gothic' buildings: a hermitage, a chapel, a knight's castle, a grotto and a fairy palace.[205] But neither here nor in his description of the 'noble style' – which, he considered, was designed to produce feelings of amazement, admiration, sympathy, piety, reverence, and humility by means of simple forms and muted light – did he suggest that the house of God could be characterized in a similar manner.[206] In fact, he explained why this could not be done:

'But there are occasions . . . when we are not at liberty to express the idea that would best characterize a particular building. This is so in the case of a church.

'If we consider that such a building is the seat of the Deity, it is readily apparent that this idea is pregnant with meaning. Moreover, it is reinforced by various statements in the scriptures, and so cannot possibly give offence. And then there is the further fact that it lends itself extremely well to architectural expression. For the aura of mystery, which fills us with awe and profound reverence for the Deity, can be indicated in architecture by stillness and darkness. It would seem, therefore, that a building that is to be consecrated to the godhead could not be more worthily treated than by representing it as the house of God.

'But the arrangement of divine worship in the Christian Church does not permit such treatment. Today a church is no longer a temple but an auditorium used for divine service, and no matter how much light an architect were to provide, people would still complain that the building was too dark.'[207]

We should not be misled by the use of the word 'temple'. The author was undoubtedly a Protestant, and what he had in mind when he outlined his ideas for an ideal church was almost certainly a building of the Gothic Revival.

The 'aura of mystery' referred to here was discovered in Gothic churches by the *Sturm und Drang* generation.[208] But there were many nuances to this aura, which were illustrated by contemporary authors. In his novel *Ardinghello*, in which he dealt with many of the artistic questions of his day, Wilhelm Heinse (1749–1803) gave the following impression of a Gothic cathedral:

'With its enormous open space, a solemn Gothic cathedral designed by sensible barbarians, in which the voice of the priest turns to thunder, and the chorus of the people becomes a storming sea that praises the father of the universe and confounds the boldest disbeliever, whilst that

210 Georg Forster, *Ansichten vom Niederrhein, von Brabant, Flandern, Holland, England und Frankreich, im April, Mai und Junius 1790*, 2 parts in 2 vols. (Berlin, 1791); first printed in Schiller's *Thalia* (1790). – Quotation taken from 1791 edition, I, pp.70–3: 'So oft ich Kölln besuche, geh ich immer wieder in diesen herrlichen Tempel, um die Schauder des Erhabenen zu fühlen. Vor der Kühnheit der Meisterwerke stürzt der Geist voll Erstaunen und Bewunderung zur Erde; dann hebt er sich wieder mit stolzem Flug über das Vollbringen hinweg, das nur Eine Idee eines verwandten Geistes war . . . Die Pracht des himmelan sich wölbenden Chors hat eine majestätische Einfalt, die alle Vorstellung übertrifft. In ungeheurer Länge stehen die Gruppen schlanker Säulen da, wie die Bäume eines uralten Forstes: nur am höchsten Gipfel sind sie in eine Krone von Ästen gespalten, die sich mit ihren Nachbarn in spitzen Bogen wölbt, und dem Auge, das ihnen folgen will, fast unerreichbar ist. Lässt sich auch schon das Unermessliche des Weltalls nicht im beschränkten Raum versinnlichen, so liegt gleichwohl in diesem kühnen Empor-streben der Pfeiler und Mauern das Unaufhaltsame, welches die Einbildungs-kraft so leicht ins Gränzenlose verlängert . . . Es ist sehr zu bedauern, dass ein so prächtiges Gebäude unvollendet bleiben muss. Wenn schon der Entwurf, in Gedanken ergänzt, so mächtig erschüttern kann, wie hätte nicht die Wirklichkeit uns hingerissen! . . . Gegen das Ende unseres Aufenthalts weckte die Dunkelheit in den leeren, einsamen, von unseren Tritten wiederhallenden Gewölben, zwischen den Gräbern der Kuhrfürsten, Bischöfe und Ritter, die da in Stein gehauen liegen, manches schaurige Bild der Vorzeit in seiner [des Begleiters] Seele. In allem Ernste, mit seiner Reizbarkeit und dem in neuen Bildschöpfungen rastlos thätigen Geiste möchte ich die Nacht dort nicht einsam durchwachen.'

211 *Ibid.*, p.72; see also Note 205 for Part II above. – Landscape gardening and landscape theory had an immense influence on literature. As late as 1808 Heinrich Kleist incorporated a whole series of typical garden settings into his play *Das Kätchen von Heilbronn*: 'grotto', 'charcoal burner's hut', 'chamber in a castle', 'hermitage', 'mountainous district with waterfalls and a bridge', and a 'grotto in the Gothic style'. It goes without saying that landscape design was also influenced by stage design, and *vice versa*.

212 See Notes 146–8 for Part I above.

213 See Note 154 for Part II above.

musical tyrant, the organ, rages like a hurricane and whips up a great flood-tide, will always cause a man of unspoilt mind to reject a smaller work, even though it should be modelled on the most elegant Temple of Venus created by an Athenian of exquisite taste.'[209]

The sensuousness and extreme lyricism of this description should not blind us to its central theme – namely, the sublime feelings engendered by Gothic cathedrals – which found its principal expression in the metaphor of the storming sea.

In 1790 Georg Forster (1754–94), who had travelled widely in Asia but was still capable of enthusing over monuments nearer home, revisited Cologne Cathedral:

'Whenever I am in Cologne, I visit this splendid temple, to feel the thrill of the sublime. In the face of such bold masterpieces, the spirit prostrates itself, full of amazement and admiration; then it rises again, and soars upwards beyond these works, which were just *one* conception of a congenial spirit . . . The splendid choir, whose vault curves up towards heaven, has a majestic simplicity that no man could imagine. The groups of slender columns stretch upwards like the immensely tall trees in a primaeval forest: only at the very top do they divide into crowns, whose separate branches join with their neighbours to form pointed arches, which are almost imperceptible to the eye. Though it should be impossible to express within a confined space the infinite nature of the universe, yet there is something irresistible about these towering walls and columns, which can so easily carry the imagination over into limitless realms . . . It is greatly to be regretted that such a magnificent building must remain unfinished. If the mere design, when completed in the mind's eye, can move us so mightily, how overpowering might not the actual structure have been! . . . Towards the end of our visit the dark shadows that filled the empty, lonely vaults, in which our footsteps reverberated, and played around the graves of the Electors, Bishops and Knights, who lay there carved in stone, conjured up many a fearful image of ancient times in his [my companion's] soul. In all seriousness, if I had his sensitivity and his restless spirit, which never ceased to fashion new images, I would not like to spend the night alone in there.'[210]

True, it was not the sublime feelings inspired by the Deity, but the sublime quality of the building as a work of art that captivated Forster. But in the closing decade of the eighteenth century this distinction was far less significant than it is today. And both Heinse and Forster included a reference to the universe in their accounts. In another passage Forster remarked that Cologne Cathedral had put him in mind of 'fairy palaces', which were, of course, a favourite motif of the garden theorists.[211] He also referred to a primaeval forest; but instead of representing it as the origin of Gothic architecture, he used it for purposes of comparison.[212] The motif of the all-night vigil was also represented, and foreshadowed Chateaubriand's reference to his detention in Westminster Abbey by upwards of forty years.[213] Nor must we overlook the passage where Forster bemoaned the fact that Cologne

214 See Note 199 for Part II above.

215 Georg Friedrich Koch, 'Karl Friedrich Schinkel und die Architektur des Mittelalters: die Studien auf der ersten Italienreise und ihre Auswirkungen' in *Zeitschrift für Kunstgeschichte*, XXIX (1966), pp.177–222.

216 *Ibid.*, p.183.

217 There are versions of Schinkel's best known picture in Berlin and Munich. For assessment of this work see Rüdiger Becksmann, 'Schinkel und die Gotik: Bemerkungen zur "Komposition des viertürmigen Domes" von 1813' in *Kunstgeschichtliche Studien für Kurt Bauch zum 70. Geburtstag von seinen Schülern* (n.p. [Munich and Berlin], 1967), pp.263–76.

218 *Karl Friedrich Schinkel: Lebenswerk*, hrsg. von Paul Ortwin Rave (and, subsequently, Margarete Kühn), (Berlin and, subsequently, n.p., 1939 ff.); 13 vols. to date. – This work contains a complete inventory of the buildings with which Schinkel was associated, including those for which he merely prepared expert reports.

219 The first editor was Alfred von Wolzogen: Karl Friedrich Schinkel, *Aus Schinkel's Nachlass: Reisetagebücher, Briefe und Aphorismen*, mitgetheilt und mit einem Verzeichnis sämmtlicher Werke Schinkel's versehen von Alfred Freiherrn von Wolzogen, 4 vols. (Berlin, 1862–4).

220 Schinkel, *Briefe, Tagebücher, Gedanken* (1922), p.74: '. . . das wahre Gepräge philosophischen Kunstsinns und Charakterfülle . . . , Gegenstände von ausgezeichneter Art zu wählen, die den wahren Charakter ihres Landes und ihrer Bestimmung tragen . . .'

221 Letter to David Gilly (the father of Friedrich Gilly), *ibid.*, p.86: 'Italien enthält noch einige Werke gothischer, saracenischer oder spätmittelalterlicher Baukunst, die bisher zu wenig betrachtet und geschätzt wurden, und in denen ein Charakter liegt, der Ehrfurcht für das Zeitalter ihrer Entstehung erregt. Sie zeigen uns deutlich, dass Sorgfalt und Fleiss bei jedem Werke, verbunden mit einem unverdrängbaren Gesetz der Wahrheit, den höchsten Grad der Anwendung erhielt . . . Wenn wir

51 Cathedral had not been completed. Clearly, it was not the ancient ruins that attracted him but the finished choir, which had been built in the thirteenth-fourteenth centuries and from which he was able to form a mental picture of the whole building. Forster regarded this choir as a genuine work of art, and he accorded it the highest distinction known to eighteenth-century architectural criticism when he said that it possessed 'majestic simplicity'. He also mentioned other properties which, to the eighteenth-century mind, distinguished Gothic from Greek architecture. Thus, the vaulted roof above the choir was said to curve upwards 'towards heaven', the columns were 'immensely tall', while the internal space all but succeeded in expressing the 'infinite nature of the universe'.

During the past 500 years few, if any, architects have been as pre-eminent in their respective spheres as Schinkel was in Prussia. Karl Friedrich Schinkel (1781–1841) trained as an architect under Friedrich Gilly (who submitted a design for a Greek Doric temple which he proposed to site in the centre of a large square in Berlin, but who had also made a drawing of the Gothic Marienburg in East Prussia a few years before).[214] From 1803 to 1805 Schinkel travelled, chiefly in Italy, where he made numerous sketches of mediaeval buildings,[215] realizing no doubt that as an architect he would need a wide variety of ground-plans and sections.[216] But during the Napoleonic Wars, which brought all building to a halt in Berlin, he was obliged to earn his living as a painter.[217] Subsequently, he created many important buildings, and produced illustrated books containing designs for buildings, industrial installations and stage sets. He was also appointed head of the public works department, the highest architectural post in the kingdom, which at that time extended from East Prussia to the west bank of the Rhine.[218] Large parts of Schinkel's architectural theory remained unpublished until after his death.[219] Partly for this reason, and partly because he did not take a teaching post, his ideas on the Gothic and the Gothic Revival were known only to a small circle during his lifetime. Incidentally, Schinkel resembled both Goethe and Chateaubriand in that he started off in life as a fervent admirer of the Gothic only to become a Classicist at a later stage.

In the summer of 1804 Schinkel approached the bookseller Johann Friedrich Unger with a suggestion for a book of drawings of mediaeval Italian buildings. He urged Unger to undertake this project, since he was convinced that these buildings bore 'the genuine stamp of philosophically oriented art and were full of character'. He proposed to select 'distinctive objects, which reflected the true character of their homeland and their intrinsic function', but he reserved the right to draw them with a certain degree of freedom. In other words, he intended to produce models.[220] He was still occupied with this project in the winter of the following year, by which time he had moved from Naples to Paris. In a letter dated December 1804 he wrote:

'Italy contains a number of works in the Gothic, Saracen or Late Mediaeval style of architecture, which heretofore have received too

vergleichen, was wir selbst bei den imposantesten Werken durch Blendwerk und Übertünchung verstecken . . . , dann ist es unmöglich, dass wir bei der Betrachtung eines Werkes dieser Art ohne Hochachtung gegen den Charakter jener Zeit bleiben können, ich wenigstens muss gestehen, dass mir die Erinnerung in der Folge für die Art der Bearbeitung der mir anvertrauten Aufgaben als höchstes Muster (ich rede hier nicht vom Styl) die Werke dieser Zeit vorführen soll, die mit den Werken der Griechen (den Styl ausgenommen) alles gemein haben und in dem Umfange dieselben bei weitem übertreffen.'

222 *Ibid.*, p.85: 'Doch lässt sich für die schöne Architektur mancher Nutzen aus diesem Styl ziehn, den man gewöhnlich den Sarazenischen nennt.'

223 Johannes Krätschell, 'Karl Friedrich Schinkel in seinem Verhältnis zur gothischen Baukunst' in *Zeitschrift für Bauwesen*, XLII (1892), cols. 159–208; quotation taken from column 176, note 52: 'Ängstliche Wiederholung gewisser Anordnungen in der Architektur, die in gewisser Zeit üblich waren, können nie ein besonderes Verdienst neuer Architektur-werke sein.'

224 Schinkel's literary estate contained excerpts from Fichte, Solger, Goethe, Schiller, A. W. Schlegel, Jean Paul Richter, Tieck, Görres, Carl Gustav Carus, and Heinroth; see Karl Gotthilf Kachler, *Schinkels Kunstauffassung* . . . (Basle, 1940), p.16.

225 Schinkel, *Aus Schinkel's Nachlass*, III (1863), pp.156–8: 'Aber im Fortschritt der Wissenschaft entstand das Gewölbe, durch welches die geistige Herrschaft fortan wiederum ein neues unendliches Feld über die Materie gewann . . . Das Material war fortan kein Hindernis mehr, um den tiefsten und höchsten Anschau-ungen, deren die menschliche Natur fähig ist, in der Architektur einen entsprechen-den Ausdruck zu geben . . . Nun entstanden Ausdrucksformen für die Ideen der Erhabenheit, der Entwicklung und des Strebens nach der Höhe, der Feierlichkeit und vor allem des inneren, tiefen, geistigen, organischen Zusammen-hanges, der die Vollendung giebt. Hierdurch wird die Wirkung und der unmittelbare Einfluss eines jeden einzelnen Theils eines Werkes auf das ganze übrige Werk und umgekehrt erst sichtbar und darstellbar. Das aber war es, was den antiken Werken völlig abging, da ihnen der herrschende Zusammenhang, blos eine Zusammenstellung physischer Bedürfnisse ist, der die eigentliche geistige Verschmelzung aller Theile in das Ganze fehlt.'

little consideration or appreciation, and whose character is such as to inspire respect for the period in which they were produced. It is quite clear in every case that their creators have invested immense care and industry whilst at the same time satisfying the absolute need for truth . . . If we compare the trickery and subterfuge which we ourselves employ in order to gloss over defects in even our most important works . . . , then we cannot possibly consider works of this calibre without feeling profound respect for the character of that period; certainly, I myself have to confess that my recollections will henceforth cause me to look upon these works, which are at one in everything (save style) with the works of the Greeks, and far excel them in terms of size, as ideal models (but not in a stylistic sense) on which to base the treatment of any future tasks entrusted to me.'[221]

The new assessment of mediaeval craftsmanship made in this letter is significant. So, too, is the fact that it is linked with a new concept of truth. And yet another new factor is Schinkel's contention that large mediaeval structures provided more suitable models for nineteenth-century buildings than Greek temples, which were relatively small. For this reason, he said, 'many advantages may be derived for architecture from this style, which is usually called the Saracen style'.[222] Incidentally, it would seem that Schinkel's attitude to prototypes was already firmly established at the time this letter was written, i.e. when he was still in his early twenties:

'The fearful repetition of certain architectural arrangements, which were customary in certain periods, will never rebound to the credit of new works of architecture.'[223]

49 In 1810 Schinkel designed a mausoleum for Queen Luise of Prussia. The draft of the statement which he submitted with this design has often been quoted. It shows that he was an avid reader of books on idealistic philosophy,[224] and contains a mixture of ideas culled from architectural and philosophical history:

'But as science progressed, it produced the vault, which provided the human spirit with a new and endless sphere for the control of matter . . . From then onwards materials no longer constituted an obstacle to the expression in architectural terms of the most profound and the loftiest attitudes to which human nature can aspire . . . Then architectural forms were evolved capable of expressing the idea of the sublime, the idea of developing and striving towards the heights, the idea of solemnity, and, above all, the idea of profound, inward, mental and organic integration, which leads to perfection. It is thanks to this that the influence and immediate impact of each individual part of a work on the work as a whole (and of the work as a whole on each individual part) are rendered capable of representation and are made manifest. But it was precisely this that was lacking in the works of Antiquity, because instead of a genuine process of integration, in which all the individual parts are fused into a single whole, they simply produced a combination of different physical functions.'[225]

What Alois Hirt had claimed for Greek art – namely, that it created organic wholes – Schinkel claimed for the Gothic.[226] He did not regard the Gothic vault simply as a technical miracle but rather as the underlying principle of a system which enabled the architect to give expression if not to the 'infinite nature of the universe', then at least to the idea of the sublime. By contrast, the trabeated architecture of the Greeks must have appeared to Schinkel earthbound and stonebound, in a word 'physical'.

It is possible that in this statement Schinkel allowed himself to be carried away by the nature of the building under discussion: a mausoleum. Certainly, some of his arguments are distinctly sophistic: 'The integration used in works of art must not be the kind of integration that arises out of mere physical needs; the combination of the parts must always be used for the expression of an independent idea, and this idea must be different in each different work.
'The principal idea which I conceived during the design of the present project was this:
'To express the kind of friendly and serene view of death which Christianity, or the true religion, vouchsafes to those who are dedicated to its service . . . We cannot take Greek and Roman forms, and bend them to our purpose. And for the kind of architectural trends which we have to create the Middle Ages provide us with a few pointers.'[227]

Schinkel's description of his mausoleum design, which was never executed, is more important for the history of architectural theory than the design itself, which appeared as a water-colour:[228]
'A room with a multipartite vault, whose arches are drawn together on freestanding columns, so designed to produce an impression of a beautiful palm grove, encloses a bier raised on a dais and decorated with all manner of sprouting leaves, lilies and roses . . . The light enters through windows set in niches on three sides of the bier; the glass is of a roseate hue, with the result that the whole building, which is executed in white marble, is bathed in a soft reddish glow.'[229]

If we compare this passage with Forster's description of Cologne Cathedral, it is readily apparent that, far from trying to instil in the observer a sense of awe and a fear of death by creating a dark and ghostly setting, Schinkel wanted to introduce him to a 'friendly and serene view of death' by the use of white marble and soft lighting, and by producing an architectural arrangement with exotic and pleasing associations.

Schinkel's first published design was for a Gothic church to replace St Peter's in Berlin, which had been destroyed in a fire in 1809.[230] In his explanatory remarks he pointed out that, due to the large number of perpendicular elements, this building would give the impression of 'striving upwards'; and he added that its roof would be 'of such a kind that a continuation of the building in the perpendicular plane would appear quite inconceivable.'[231] Forster, of course, had spoken in a similar vein of Cologne Cathedral when he suggested that there was something irresistible about its towering walls and columns, 'which can so easily carry the imagination over into a limitless realm'.[232]

226 See Notes 154–7 for Part I above.

227 Schinkel, *Aus Schinkel's Nachlass*, III (1863), pp.160–1: 'Der Zusammenhang in den Kunstwerken darf nicht der Zusammenhang sein, der durch blosse physische Bedürftigkeit geboten ist; die Verbindung der Theile muss stets nur lediglich einer freien Idee dienen, die in jedem besonderen Kunstwerk eine andere sein muss.
'Die Hauptidee, welche ich bei der Entwerfung des vorliegenden Projects hatte, war die:
'Die freundliche und heitere Ansicht des Todes zu geben, welche das Christentum oder die wahre Religion den ihr Ergebenen gewährt . . . Wir können Griechisches und Römisches nicht unmittelbar anwenden, sondern müssen uns das für diesen Zweck Bedeutsame selbst schaffen. Zu dieser neuzuerschaffenden Richtung der Architektur dieser Art giebt uns das Mittelalter einigen Fingerzeig.'

228 Georg Friedrich Koch, 'Schinkels architektonische Entwürfe im gotischen Stil, 1810–1815' in *Zeitschrift für Kunstgeschichte*, XXXII (1969), pp.262–316.

229 Schinkel, *Aus Schinkel's Nachlass*, III (1863), pp.161–2: 'Ein mannigfach gewölbter Raum, dessen Bögen sich auf freistehenden Säulen zusammenziehen, so angeordnet, dass die Empfindung eines schönen Palmenhains erregt wird, umschliesst das auf Stufen mit vielen sprossenden Blättern, Lilien und Rosenkelchen sich erhebende Ruhelager. . . . Das Licht fällt durch die Fenster von drei Nischen, die das Ruhelager von drei Seiten umgeben; das Glas ist von rosenrother Farbe, wodurch über die ganze Architektur, welche in weissem Marmor ausgeführt ist, ein sanft rothes Dämmerlicht verbreitet wird.'

230 Karl Friedrich Schinkel, *Architektonischer Plan zum Wiederaufbau der eingeäscherten St. Petrikirche in Berlin* (Berlin, 1811); I have not studied this work.

231 *Ibid.*; quotation taken from Koch, 'Schinkels architektonische Entwürfe im gotischen Stil' (1969), p.270.

232 See Note 210 for Part II above.

233 Beutler, *Von deutscher Baukunst* (1943). – Robson-Scott, *The Literary Background of the Gothic Revival in Germany* (1965), pp.76–95. – Roland Recht, 'Le mythe romantique d'Erwin de Steinbach' in *L'information d'Histoire de l'art*, xv (1970), pp.38–45.

234 Walter Jackson Bate, *From Classic to Romantic: Premises of Taste in Eighteenth-Century England* (Cambridge [Mass.], 1946); reference to 2nd ed. (New York, 1961), p.155.

235 See Note 185 for Part I above.

236 Quotation taken from Beutler, *Von deutscher Baukunst* (1943), p.18: 'Hier steht sein Werk, tretet hin, und erkennt das tiefste Gefühl von Wahrheit und Schönheit der Verhältnisse, würkend aus starker, rauher, deutscher Seele, auf dem eingeschränkten düstern Pfaffenschauplatz des medii aevi.'

237 Tieck, *Werke in vier Bänden*, ɪ (1963), pp.836–7 and 850–2. – *Franz Sternbald* was first published in 1798.

238 *Ibid.*, p.852 (= Book III, Chap. 2, final section): 'Aber wahr ist es, dass diese Gebäude, die vielleicht den Deutschen angehören, den Namen des Volkes unsterblich machen müssen. Der Dom zu Wien, der unvollendete mächtige Bau in Köln, und jener in Strassburg sind die hellsten Sterne; und wie lieblich ist der kleine Dom drüben im breisgauischen Freiburg, mancher andern in Esslingen, oder Meissen, und an andern Orten nicht zu erwähnen. Vielleicht erfahren wir auch noch einmal, dass alles, was England, Spanien und Frankreich von dieser Art Herrliches besitzt, von deutschen Meistern ist gegründet worden.'

Goethe's first prose work was published anonymously in November or December 1772 under the highly significant title *Von deutscher Baukunst*.[233] When Goethe went to Strasbourg he was quite overcome by the sight of the cathedral, which he came to regard as the epitome of German artistic genius; and although his article, which was inspired by his Strasbourg experiences, had remarkably little impact on the subsequent development of architectural theory, it had a lasting effect on German attitudes towards the Gothic. Normally, *Von deutscher Baukunst* is considered against the background of the German lexicons and encyclopaedias of the times, and within this context it appears remarkably original. But if we widen the context to include eighteenth-century English art theories, its originality is far less apparent.[234] The 'national' aspect of Goethe's thesis also had wider implications. After all, the Italians had been speaking of the 'German manner' for some considerable time, a fact which would have been known to anybody who had read Vasari's *Lives*.[235] Goethe, however, made no reference to this Italian derivation for the simple reason that he was not concerned with the rehabilitation of Gothic architecture as such, but merely with the appreciation of one particular work of art, which he attributed in its entirety to Erwin von Steinbach:
'This is his work; step in front of it, and recognize the profound sense of truth and beauty in its proportions, which stems from the workings of a powerful, rugged German soul in the sombre and all-pervading papist world of the *medii aevi*.'[236]

Goethe had no sympathy with mediaeval religiosity; what interested him was the artistic achievement of Erwin von Steinbach, whom he regarded as an outstanding personality. That was why he described only the west façade of the cathedral, and why he never once referred to the building as a church, a temple, or the house of God.

Goethe's article had a quite remarkable impact on Ludwig Tieck. Although he was never in Strasbourg and had never seen the cathedral, Tieck positively enthused over this building in his novel *Franz Sternbalds Wanderungen: eine altdeutsche Geschichte*.[237] However, Tieck was not unknowledgeable on the subject of monuments:
'But it is true that these buildings, which may be peculiarly German, must immortalize the name of our nation. The cathedral in Vienna, the unfinished mighty building in Cologne, and that in Strasbourg are the brightest stars; and how elegant is the little minster in Freiburg im Breisgau, not to mention the many others, in Esslingen, or Meissen, and other places. And perhaps we shall discover one day that all the splendid buildings of this kind in England, Spain, and France were created by German masters.'[238]

Meanwhile, as in all the other European countries, nationalism made headway in Germany. Gothic architecture was German art, and the proof of this contention would not have to be provided for another forty years (when the French roots of the Gothic were discovered). Moreover, according to Tieck it was not the names of the mediaeval masters, but the name of the nation that this architecture would 'immortalize'.

And so, when the German people threw off the Napoleonic yoke and decided to erect a national monument to commemorate its victory over the French army, a Gothic cathedral seemed the natural choice. The War of Liberation was brought to a close on 18 October 1813 when Napoleon was defeated at Leipzig; and since the Germans had been dreaming of a monument for many a long year, a monument they had to have.

It seems that the expression 'Nationaldenkmal' was used for the first time in Germany in 1804 when a proposal for a monument to Luther was mooted.[239] Then, in 1806, Crown Prince Ludwig of Bavaria decided to build a pantheon to provide a final resting place for Germany's illustrious dead that could take its place alongside Westminster Abbey (parts of which, especially the south transept, had been used for this purpose ever since the eighteenth century) and the Panthéon in Paris (where the Church of Sainte-Geneviève had been secularized in 1791 to provide a suitable building).[240] Some time between 1807 and 1809 the historian Johannes von Müller suggested to Ludwig that he should call his pantheon Walhalla.[241] At this juncture designs were submitted by the architects Karl von Fischer (1782–1820) and Karl Haller von Hallerstein (1774–1817), both of whom favoured a Classical solution modelled on a Greek Doric temple.[242] In point of fact, the idea of building a national monument in the form of a temple had already been suggested by Hirschfeld. But Haller, at least, will doubtless have had his own reasons for this particular choice, for (like Schinkel) he studied under Friedrich Gilly and must have seen Gilly's Classical design for a monument to Frederick the Great in Berlin. Moreover, from 1810 onwards Haller was on friendly terms with Charles Robert Cockerell (1788–1863) who, together with William Henry Playfair (1789–1857),

48

began to build the National Monument in Edinburgh, which was modelled on the Parthenon, in 1822. In the event, the designs submitted by both Fischer and Haller were rejected, and in 1814 a competition was held, in which the participants were required to design a Walhalla in accordance with the 'renovated Antique taste'.[243] Ludwig of Bavaria justified this requirement on the grounds that it would be preferable to have a building that was a 'worthy imitation of all that was great in Antiquity rather than an original creation that was less beautiful.'[244] Schinkel simply disregarded this rule, and submitted a Gothic design.[245] The commission finally went to Leo von Klenze, who was asked to build a Doric temple on a charming rural site overlooking

46, 47

the Danube, not far from Regensburg. The first stone was laid in 1830 on the anniversary of the Battle of Leipzig; the finished temple was consecrated in 1842, also on 18 October.

Apart from building the Walhalla, Crown Prince Ludwig of Bavaria built two other national monuments: the Ruhmeshalle in Munich and the Befreiungshalle near Kelheim. Nor was that the end of his architectural activities, for the idea of completing Cologne Cathedral also seems to have stemmed from him. Here, too, he was inspired by the desire to create a national monument. On 1 August 1814 the painter

239 Nipperdey, 'Nationalidee und Nationaldenkmal' (1968), p.557.

240 For the events leading up to this decision see Leopold [David] Ettlinger, 'Denkmal und Romantik: Bemerkungen zu Leo von Klenzes Walhalla' in *Festschrift für Herbert von Einem zum 16. Februar 1965* (Berlin, 1965), pp.60–70. – For an account of the design and construction see Oswald Hederer, *Leo von Klenze, Persönlichkeit und Werk* (Munich, 1964), pp.300–14.

241 Nipperdey, 'Nationalidee und Nationaldenkmal' (1968), p.553. – John Nash also designed a 'National Valhalla'; see [Christopher] Reginald Turnor, *Nineteenth-Century Architecture in Britain* . . . (London etc., 1950), p.16.

242 Hans Kiener, 'Hallers Entwürfe zur Glyptothek und Walhalla' in *Münchner Jahrbuch der bildenden Kunst*, XIII (1923), pp.102–20. – Oswald Hederer, *Karl von Fischer, Leben und Werk* . . . (Munich, 1960), pp.97–100.

243 Ettlinger, 'Denkmal und Romantik' (1965), p.60: 'im renovirten antiken Geschmack'.

244 Wolfgang Herrmann, *Deutsche Baukunst des 19. und 20. Jahrhunderts*, I: *Von 1770 bis 1840* . . . (Breslau, 1932), p.56: '. . . als würdige Nachahmung des Grossen im Alterthume zeige, denn als minderschöne Selbsterfindung.' – No further volumes of Hermann's study were published.

245 Hederer, *Karl von Fischer* (1960), p.100.

246 August Klein, 'Die Bemühungen Kölns um die Wiedererrichtung seiner Universität (1798–1818)' in *Festschrift zur Erinnerung an die Gründung der alten Universität Köln im Jahre 1388*, hrsg. von Hubert Greven (Cologne, 1938), pp.329–83; quotation taken from p.362: 'Mit sichtbarer Freude theilte er mir den Gedanken des Kronprinzen von Bayern (welcher Ihn während einer meiner Sitzungen besuchte) mit, nehmlich die Deutschen müssten als Denkmal ihrer Befreiung den Dom von Köln ganz in seinem Styl vollenden.' – Dr Herbert Rode kindly drew my attention to this text.

247 Ettlinger, 'Denkmal und Romantik' (1965), p.68.

248 *Ibid.* – The giant column (*c.*30 feet) is a remnant of a Roman quarry in the Odenwald, near Bensheim.

249 [Wilhelm Martin Leberecht] De Wette, *Die neue Kirche oder Verstand und Glaube im Bunde* (Berlin, 1815), p.99: 'Vor allem sollte in jeder grösseren Stadt ein grosser Tempel im erhabenen Styl der deutschen Baukunst ... aufgeführt werden, zum Denkmal der wieder bey uns auferstandenen Religion und des geretteten Vaterlandes, und zum würdigen geräumigen Versammlungsort für jene gemeinsamen grossen Volksfeste.'

250 Koch, 'Schinkels architektonische Entwürfe im gotischen Stil' (1969), pp.282–300.

251 *Ibid.*, p.300: '... dieser ewig merkwürdigen Zeit ein grosses und heiliges Denkmal zu errichten, eine Kirche in dem ergreifenden Stil altdeutscher Bauart, einer Bauart, deren völlige Vollendung der kommenden Zeit aufgespart ist, nachdem ihre Entwicklung in der Blüte durch einen wunderbaren und wohltätigen Rückblick auf die Antike unterbrochen ward, wodurch, wie es scheint, die Welt geschickt werden sollte, ein dieser Kunst zur Vollendung noch fehlendes Element in ihr zu verschmelzen.' – See also Schinkel, *Aus Schinkel's Nachlass*, III (1863), pp.198–9.

252 See Notes 392–6 for Part III below.

Lützenkirchen, who was then executing a portrait of Freiherr vom Stein, wrote to the Rector of the former University of Cologne:
'He [vom Stein] informed me with obvious pleasure of the idea put forward by the Crown Prince of Bavaria (who called on him during one of his sittings) to the effect that the Germans ought to complete Cologne Cathedral in a completely homogeneous style as a monument to their liberation.'[246]

But before I deal with the implementation of this idea, let me first enumerate a number of other well-known proposals for national monuments. Ernst Moritz Arndt (1769–1860), the poet and professor, suggested that a military cemetery with a gigantic tumulus should be laid out in a grove of oak trees as a monument to the two great German victories: the Battle of the Teutoburger Wald and the Battle of Leipzig.[247] The dramatist August Kotzebue (1761–1819) recommended that the so-called Riesensäule (i.e. giant column) should be designated as a national monument to commemorate the liberation of Germany and remind the nation of the need for greater vigilance.[248] And the theologian Wilhelm Martin Leberecht De Wette (1780–1849) proposed that a whole series of national monuments should be erected. In a pamphlet published in 1815 under the title *Die neue Kirche oder Verstand und Glaube im Bunde* he wrote:
'Above all, a large temple executed in the sublime style of ancient German architecture ... should be built in every large town as a monument to the revival of our religion, and the salvation of the Fatherland, and as a worthy and spacious meeting place for those large communal and popular festivals.'[249]

But the year before De Wette's pamphlet appeared, Schinkel had already been asked to draw up plans for a memorial cathedral.[250]

In a report in which he discussed the stylistic implications of the new project Schinkel urged his compatriots:
'to erect a large sacred monument to this remarkable period in the soul-stirring style of ancient German architecture, an architecture whose ultimate perfection is to be achieved in the immediate future, since its development was broken off in its prime by a marvellous and beneficial reversion to Antiquity, with the result that the world is apparently now destined to perfect this art form by introducing an element that has been missing so far.'[251]

The same argument was advanced by a later generation of theorists, who recommended that Romanesque architecture should be adopted as the basis of a new style.[252]

In a second report Schinkel was able to disregard the question of style, for meanwhile the king had opted for the 'ancient German character'. On this occasion he focused his attention on the artistic implications of the project:
'I have treated this monument at three different levels:
1. as a religious monument;
2. as an historical monument;
3. as a living monument for the nation; in other words, a monument

whose method of construction would implant in the nation something that would grow and bear fruit . . . The old craftsmanship ethic of our forefathers, in which love, humility and a just sense of pride combined to produce works which filled their descendants with admiration, has now disappeared . . . Would not this present project acquire a character eminently suited to its purpose if it were to revive that splendid spirit in the nation by its mode of construction, and so become a living and regenerative monument? – For at least one and a half decades all the greatest artistic forces of the nation would have to be concentrated on this monument, all our leading artists would have to work on it; and during this period the excellence of the workmanship invested in the project would constitute a beneficial and a practical school that would generate a true artistic sense and lead to the creation of genuine works of art.'[253]

In this passage, in which he called for the same high standards of art and craftsmanship that he had discovered in mediaeval buildings in Italy, Schinkel hinted at the kind of artists' associations – *Bauhütten* – which had been suggested by Romantic writers, and which were subsequently formed for the completion of Cologne Cathedral and the construction of many other buildings during the Gothic Revival.[254]

Instead of erecting a new cathedral on the Leipziger Platz in Berlin, the Prussians joined with the other German states in order to complete the existing cathedral in Cologne. For several decades the main driving force behind this project was Sulpiz Boisserée, a native of Cologne, whose influence on Friedrich Schlegel I have already discussed.[255] True, the famous proclamation calling for the completion of the cathedral stemmed from Josef Görres (1776–1848), the versatile Romantic scholar; but it was from Boisserée that the project received its real impetus.[256] In 1808 he began to measure the cathedral, and had scale drawings made from his measurements; in 1810 he asked Goethe to help him with the publication of his *Domwerk*; and in 1812 he studied the organization of the masons who had worked on Strasbourg Cathedral so as to be in a position to make concrete proposals for the completion of Cologne Cathedral. Then, in 1813, he submitted the results of his survey to Crown Prince Friedrich Wilhelm in Frankfurt, who later told him: 'After seeing your drawings of the cathedral I could not sleep for three nights.'[257] In 1814 Boisserée accompanied Friedrich Wilhelm on a tour of the cathedral site, and on the following day he wrote to his brother: 'The Crown Prince wanted to start work on the completion of the cathedral there and then.'[258] At the Congress of Vienna, Cologne passed to Prussia, and from then onwards Boisserée staked everything on this one card. He persuaded Goethe to write a report on the preservation and completion of the cathedral, as a result of which Schinkel was asked to examine the structural condition of the existing building. After the restitution of the Archbishopric of Cologne, Prussia was appointed custodian of the cathedral, and in 1823 work began on the restoration of the mediaeval fabric, which had suffered from neglect during the revolutionary period. In 1833 the architect Ernst Friedrich Zwirner

253 Schinkel, *Aus Schinkel's Nachlass*, III (1863), pp.193–4: 'Dies Monument habe ich als ein Dreifaches angesehen: 1. als ein religiöses Monument; 2. als ein historisches Monument; 3. als ein lebendiges Monument in dem Volke, in dem unmittelbar durch die Art der Errichtung desselben etwas in dem Volke begründet werden soll, welches fortlebt und Früchte trägt . . . Die alten werkmeisterlichen Tugenden unserer Vorfahren sind verschwunden, wo im schönen Verein von Liebe, Demuth und gerechtem Stolz Werke entstanden, vor denen ihre späteren Nachkommen mit Bewunderung stehen . . . Sollte nicht das vorliegende Werk einem seinem Zwecke ganz vorzüglich entsprechenden Charakter zu gewinnen suchen, wenn es durch die Art seiner Entstehung jenen herrlichen Geist im Volke wieder gebären und dadurch ein lebendiges sich fortgestaltendes Monument würde.' – Durch wenigstens anderthalb Jahrzehnte hindurch müsste die Errichtung dieses Monuments der Centralpunkt aller höheren Kunstbetriebsamkeit des Landes werden, alle vorzüglichen Künstler müssten daran arbeiten, und die höchste Vollkommenheit der Ausführung würde durch den Lauf dieses Zeitraums eine so wohltätige und praktische Schule werden, dass der echte Sinn der Künstler und der Gewerke darin wiedergeboren würde.'

254 See Note 221 for Part II, and Notes 214, 219 and 423 for Part III.

255 See pp.48–9.

256 See Note 208 for Part II. – See also Eva Brües, *Karl Friedrich Schinkel: Lebenswerk*, [XII:] *Die Rheinlande (unter Verwendung des von Ehler W. Grashoff gesammelten Materials)*, (n.p. [München and Berlin], 1968), pp.304–69; and Herbert Rode and Arnold Wolff, '125 Jahre Zentral-Dombauverein: Fortbau und Erhaltung des Kölner Domes, 1841– 1966' in *Kölner Domblatt, Jahrbuch des Zentral-Dombauvereins*, XXV (1965/6), pp.9–184.

257 *Ibid.*, p.14: 'Drei Nächte habe ich über ihre Zeichnung vom Dom nicht schlafen können.'

258 *Ibid.*, p.15: 'Der Kronprinz wollte nun eben gleich den Dom ausbauen.'

(1802–61) was placed in charge of all construction work on the cathedral site. This was a fortunate appointment, for Zwirner was a capable man with the determination to carry the completion of the cathedral to a successful conclusion. He also enjoyed the confidence of both Boisserée and Schinkel.

In his *Domwerk*, which was published from 1821 onwards, Boisserée printed a series of drawings, which had been executed by leading architectural draughtsmen, such as Georg Moller (1784–1852), and which showed both the interior and the exterior of the cathedral as it would be when completed. Boisserée was convinced that Master Gerhard had produced a design for the whole building, and that those sections of the cathedral built by later architects had been executed in accordance with his plans. He and Moller managed to find a number of the mediaeval plans, which had been lost during the revolutionary period and which proved to be compatible with this thesis. Consequently, Boisserée had no difficulty in reconstructing the supposed original design on the small scale necessary for his *Domwerk*.[259] Even now that the cathedral has been completed, the splendid prints in this book have lost none of their suggestive power. And in the 1820's, when the German nation was still caught up in the full flush of victory, and individual German princes had not yet embarked on reactionary policies, their effect must have been quite overwhelming. In 1820 Christian Ludwig Stieglitz (1756–1836), the jurist, architect, engraver and editor, published a book entitled *Von altdeutscher Baukunst*, which provided the first reasonably comprehensive account of mediaeval German architecture.[260] In this book Stieglitz distinguished between mediaeval and Greek architecture:

'The Greeks consciously selected and arranged their architectural forms, and established laws which were universally binding. In the Middle Ages, on the other hand, fantasy came to the fore and, reinforced by Romanticism, led to the creation of light, free compositions which did not require a rigid framework.'

Having made this distinction, Stieglitz went on to sing the praises of the Gothic:

'No matter how beautiful a church executed in the new [Neo-Classical] style may be, it cannot possibly arouse such lofty and holy feelings as are inspired by an ancient German cathedral . . . The origin of this Romantic style of architecture may be open to dispute, but what is quite certain is that its elaboration was pursued in an exemplary fashion in Germany.'[261]

In Stieglitz's view, the mediaeval period was 'Germany's golden age'. He regretted that Cologne Cathedral had been left unfinished because to his mind this was the only building that had been 'based on a single *style* and consequently, instead of revealing stylistic traces from successive centuries, reflected the German style of architecture alone.'[262]

It seems distinctly possible that when the painter Peter von Cornelius (1783–1867) criticized the Grecian design proposed for the Walhalla in

259 Herbert Rode, 'Ernst Friedrich Zwirners Planentwicklung für den Ausbau des Kölner Domes, 1833–1844' in *Kölner Domblatt, Jahrbuch des Zentral-Dombauvereins*, xx (1961/2), pp.45–98. – Rode, 'Der Kölner Dom in der Anschauung Sulpiz Boisserées' (1954/5), p.266.

260 C[hristian] L[udwig] Stieglitz, *Von altdeutscher Baukunst*, 2 vols (text and plates), (Leipzig, 1820).

261 *Ibid.*, pp.7, 12 and 110; 'Bey den Griechen wählte und ordnete der Verstand die Formen und schrieb Gesetze vor, die nicht überschritten werden durften. Im Mittelalter erhob sich die Phantasie, schuf, durch das Romantische belebt, leichte freye Zusammensetzungen, die keine Grenzen forderten . . . Es ist nicht zu verkennen, dass keine Kirche im neueren Styl, so schön sie auch ist, so hohe, heilige Empfindungen zu erregen vermag, als ein altdeutscher Dom . . . In welchem Lande diese romantische Bauart entstanden, ist keinem Zweifel unterworfen, und es ist gewiss, dass in Deutschland die Aus-bildung derselben vorzüglich befördert wurde.'

262 *Ibid.*, p.139: 'Die Kunst verliert nicht wenig, dass dieses Werk zu jenen Zeiten . . . nicht seine Vollendung erreichte, da es das einzige ist, das, durchaus nach *einem* Style angelegt, nicht die Bauarten verschiedener Jahrhunderte zeigt, sondern allein die deutsche Baukunst aufstellt.'

November 1820, he will have been influenced by Stieglitz's ideas. In a letter to Crown Prince Ludwig, Cornelius wrote: 'Although the realization that a great and worthy monument is to be erected, at long last, to the greatness of Germany makes our hearts beat faster and, above all, reminds us, and makes us profoundly aware, of our German nationality, the proposed design none the less prompts the question as to why this great and exclusively German monument should be so completely Grecian. Are we not being inconsistent when we try to glorify our nation by the erection of a great building whilst ignoring the great and splendidly original German style of architecture?'[263]

Since Cornelius made no distinction between the mediaeval Germans and their nineteenth-century descendants, for him the new evolutionary conception of architectural style operated in favour of the Gothic Revival, not against it. In another passage in his letter he said: 'Anything that is really alive acquires its outward shape from inner conditions; it develops organically from those conditions.'[264]

Of course, Crown Prince Ludwig of Bavaria was not the only German prince to patronize the arts. The Crown Prince of Prussia, who came to be known as 'Der Romantiker auf dem Thron' (The Romantic on the Throne), and who was himself a gifted draughtsman and architectural designer, may well have excelled Ludwig in this respect.[265] But Friedrich Wilhelm did not mount the throne until 1840. Shortly afterwards the Society for the Completion of Cologne Cathedral was founded, with branches throughout Germany and even abroad. The importance of this society may be judged by the fact that the anticlerical German poet Heinrich Heine, who was then living in exile in France, became Vice-President of the Paris branch.[266] On 23 November 1840, when he authorized the setting up of the society, Friedrich Wilhelm IV granted an annual subsidy from the Prussian exchequer and asked that work should start as soon as possible on the southern transept.

But the initial impetus for the completion of the cathedral had been provided by an uneasy alliance of vastly different power groups: Prussian Protestants and Rhenish Catholics, latterday adherents of the principle of divine right and National Liberals of every hue. Not surprisingly, this alliance was shortlived.

The Romantic author Josef Görres had once said that the completion of the cathedral would become a 'symbol of the new empire that we are trying to build'; and in 1868 Wilhelm I of Prussia informed Crown Prince Umberto of Italy that he intended to have himself crowned Emperor in Cologne.[267] But between these two statements lay a long and complex development, in which serious consideration was given to the possibility of using the cathedral as a German pantheon. The idea, which may well have stemmed from Boisserée, was discussed with Friedrich Wilhelm in 1841.[268]

If we consider the historical development of popular attitudes to Gothic architecture, it soon becomes apparent that 1840 was probably the last year in which the decision to complete Cologne Cathedral could

263 Ettlinger, 'Denkmal und Romantik' (1965), p.62: 'Wenn uns bei dem Gedanken, dass nun endlich der deutschen Grösse ein grosses, würdiges Denkmal soll errichtet werden, hoch das Herz schlägt und dabei vor allen Dingen an unsere deutsche Nationalität erinnert und davon erfüllt wird, so fällt uns bei dem Entwurf gleich die Frage ein, warum soll das grösste deutsche und nur deutsche Ehrenmal so absolut griechisch sein? Geben wir uns nicht eine Demanti [sic] indem wir unsere Nationalität durch ein grosses Bauwerk verherrlichen wollen, und zugleich den grossen herrlich echt originalen deutschen Baustil ignorieren?'

264 Ibid., p.63: 'Was wahrhaftig lebt, nimmt aus inneren Bedingungen seine äussere Gestalt und wächst daraus organisch hervor.'

265 Ludwig Dehio, Friedrich Wilhelm IV. von Preussen, ein Baukünstler der Romantik ... (Munich and Berlin, 1961).

266 Eberhard Galley, 'Heine und der Kölner Dom' in Deutsche Vierteljahrsschrift für Literaturwissenschaft und Geistesgeschichte, XXXII (1958), pp.99–110.

267 Karl Hampe, Wilhelm I., Kaiserfrage und Kölner Dom: ein biographischer Beitrag zur Geschichte der deutschen Reichsgründung (Stuttgart, 1936), see esp. p.177.

268 Rode, 'Ernst Friedrich Zwirners Planentwicklung' (1961/2), p.86.

have been taken or, alternatively, the last year in which this decision would have been received with such great enthusiasm. Franz Kugler's *Handbuch der Kunstgeschichte* appeared in 1842, and was followed in 1843 by the first part of Carl Schnaase's *Geschichte der bildenden Künste*.[269] Franz Kugler (1808–58) and Carl Schnaase (1798–1875) belonged to a new generation of art historians, who pursued two quite different lines of enquiry, both of which had the effect of undermining the special position accorded to Cologne Cathedral by the German public. Kugler had realized as early as 1842 that, far from being the product of a single mind, the building had evolved gradually over a considerable period and that the original plan had been amended on successive occasions. He identified four distinct phases in the development of the cathedral: firstly, the building of the chapels, the ambulatory and the choir arcades; secondly, the building of the choir clerestory; thirdly, the building of the choir buttresses; and fourthly, the building of the west façade.[270] Moreover, Kugler had known for a number of years that the origins of the Gothic were to be found in France, not Germany.[271] And yet he regarded Cologne Cathedral as the major achievement of Gothic architecture. The all-important consideration here was the concept of 'organic' growth. According to Kugler, the French 'did not achieve a completely organic development, [i.e.] a fully integrated architectural composition.'[272] In his view, Cologne Cathedral was the key to the whole of the Gothic development, and he considered that each of its four phases marked a new departure. Thus, he said of the lower parts of the choir:
'The detailed design reveals a higher form of organic development than is found in earlier French cathedrals.'[273]

But Kugler also considered that the west façade in Cologne, which he dated to the mid-fourteenth century, was a 'much more highly developed organism' than the Strasbourg façade.[274] He was, of course, firmly convinced that only the German mediaeval architects had succeeded in producing a 'truly organic whole';[275] and when he came to review the second edition of the *Domwerk*, he suggested that Boisserée should produce a further illustrated work, one that was sufficiently detailed to enable the public 'to study, i.e. to penetrate, the organization of the architectural forms, and [so recognize] their coherence, their interdependence and interaction.'[276] The public that Kugler had in mind will no doubt have included many an architect.

Schnaase, who was ten years older than Kugler, had a more philosophical outlook. He was intent on re-establishing the clear-cut distinction which had once existed between architecture, on the one hand, and painting and sculpture, on the other, but which had become more and more blurred in the course of the eighteenth and early nineteenth centuries. Consequently, he rejected the concept of organic growth as inappropriate for purposes of architectural theory. At this, Kugler – whose whole view of architecture depended on this concept – not unnaturally took Schnaase to task. Schnaase then published a lengthy defence, from which I now propose to reproduce certain key

269 See Note 284 for Part I. – Carl Schnaase, *Geschichte der bildenden Künste*, [1st Series:] *Geschichte der bildenden Künste bei den Alten*, I: *Die Völker des Orients* (Düsseldorf, 1843).

270 Franz Kugler, 'Der Dom von Köln und seine Architektur' in F. K., *Kleine Schriften und Studien zur Kunstgeschichte*, 3 parts in 3 vols. (Stuttgart, 1853–4), II (1854), pp.123–52; first printed in 1842. – See also Notes 387–8 for Part III below.

271 Kugler, *Kleine Schriften*, I (1853), p.421. – See also Note 376 for Part III below, and Notes 287–8 for Part I above.

272 Kugler, *Kleine Schriften*, II (1854), p.128: 'Man brachte es nicht zu einer vollkommen organischen Entwicklung, zu einem innerlich bedingten Zusammenhange der Formen.'

273 *Ibid.*, p.137: 'In der Bildung der Detailformen kündigt sich das Gesetz einer höher organischen Entwicklung an, als solche bis dahin in den französischen Kathedralen gefunden wird.'

274 *Ibid.*, p.149: 'viel höherer Organismus'.

275 *Ibid.*, p.151: 'zur Herstellung eines wahrhaft organischen Ganzen'.

276 *Ibid.*, p.395: 'zum Studium, d.h. zum Eindringen in den Organismus der Formen, in deren Zusammenhang, gegenseitige Bedingung und Ausbildung'.

277 See Note 163 for Part I above.

278 C[arl] Schnaase, 'Über das Organische in der Baukunst' in *Kunstblatt*, xxv (1844), pp.245–7; quotation taken from p.245: 'Was unser wissenschaftlicher Sprachgebrauch unter dem Worte *Organismus* versteht, ist nicht streitig. Ein Ganzes, das nicht durch innere einheitliche Kraft gewachsen ist, in welchem daher die verschiedenen Theile verschiedenen Zwecken dienen, aber immer so, dass sie von dem geistigen Leben des Ganzen durchdrungen, mit andern Theilen in Wechselwirkung stehend, zugleich Mittel und Zweck sind. Mit einem Worte, eine freie Zweckmässigkeit, einen Selbstzweck. Vor allen Dingen ist daher das Leben und in höchster Instanz der *Geist* organisch, und unter den Körpern nur die, welche vom Leben durchdrungen sind. Ist daher das Schöne die vollste Einheit des Geistigen und Körperlichen, so sehr, dass selbst die Erscheinung geistigen Lebens in der Wirklichkeit dieser Anforderung noch nicht genügt, so ist es gewiss ein Organisches, und zwar in einem *eminenten Sinne*. Es liegt nicht unterhalb dieses Begriffes, vielmehr genügt ihm dieser noch nicht vollkommen.'

279 Kant, *Critik der Urtheilskraft* (1790), pp. LVI and 33–4.

280 Schnaase, 'Über das Organische' (1844), p.246: 'Das Naturelement, in welchem die Baukunst wurzelt, ist ein niedriges, der Organismus ihrer Ausbildung aber eben deshalb ein höherer, weil er freier, geistiger, zarter ist, nicht mit der groben, zwingenden sinnlichen Nothwendigkeit behaftet.
'Dies enthält den Grund, weshalb ich das Wort *Organisch* bei der allgemeinen Begründung der Baukunst nicht gebraucht habe; nicht weil ich es zu hoch für diese, sondern weil ich es für unzureichend, nicht bezeichnend genug halte. Es ist ein Lieblingswort der Zeit; solche Wörter werden dann aber leicht stereotyp oder veranlassen Irrtümer oder doch einseitige und allzu eng begränzte Urtheile.' – In France we find the term 'organique' applied to Gothic cathedrals in F[élicité Robert de] Lamenais, *Esquisse d'une philosophie*, III (Paris and Leipzig, 1840), p.176; and also to works of art in general, *ibid.*, p.458. – In England we find the statement 'Gothic architecture is an organic whole' in W[illiam] Whewell, *Architectural Notes on German Churches; with Notes Written during an Architectural Tour in Picardy and Normandy, 3rd Edition, to which are Added Notes on the Churches of the Rhine, by M. F.* [recte: *Johann Claudius*] de Lassaulx, Architectural Inspector to the King of Prussia (Cambridge and London, 1842), p.3 (preface of the 2nd ed. of 1835). – The first edition of this

passages, partly because the concept he criticized was still being used by architectural theorists as late as the 1950's, and partly because in criticizing this concept he also provided a critique of the Gothic Revival.[277] First Schnaase defined the concept:
'What scholars understand by the technical term *organism* is not in dispute. It is a whole, but not one that has been formed by the application of external pressure and external rules. On the contrary, it is a whole that has been engendered by an integrated inner force, one in which the different parts serve different purposes, but always in such a way that they are permeated by the spiritual life of the whole, enter into reciprocal relations with other parts, and constitute both a means and an end. In a word, it is a condition of independent purposiveness, an end in itself. Above all, therefore, life itself, and the human spirit, which is the highest form of life, are organic, whereas the only physical bodies to possess this property are those which are permeated by life. But if the beautiful constitutes the most perfect combination of the spiritual and the physical – a combination so perfect that even the appearance of spiritual life in reality fails to comply with its requirements – then it [the beautiful] must certainly be designated as organic, and eminently so. It is not something less than this concept. Rather, the concept fails to do complete justice to it.'[278]

Schnaase's arguments were based – far more than those advanced by Alois Hirt and Karl Friedrich Schinkel – on Immanuel Kant's concept of purposiveness, which was itself not necessarily purposive and consequently could be applied to the fine arts as an '*a priori* principle'.[279]

Subsequently, Schnaase distinguished between architecture and the other fine arts, which he considered to be more directly imitative:
'Because the natural elements in which architecture has its roots are so material, its organism, i.e. the organization of its component forms, is more sublime; it is more independent, more spiritual, more delicate, and is not subject to coarse, coercive and sensuous requirements.
'This also explains why I have not used the word *organic* in my general definition of architecture. It was not because I considered it too lofty, but because I felt it to be inadequate, and lacking in expressive power. It is a fashionable word, and fashionable words can easily become stereotyped, or give rise to errors of judgement, or assessments that are both one-sided and excessively narrow.'[280]

Schnaase was opposed to the forest metaphors, which had received a considerable boost from the concept of organic growth, because he considered that they had given rise to misinterpretations:
'These have resulted in a certain disparagement of the circular style and a corresponding over-assessment of the Gothic; and they could also lead to the emergence of a one-sided view of the history and development of [architectural] taste. For if people insist, irrespective of the circumstances, on the overriding importance of the "organic", of purpose-built structures and integrated components (and not simply in respect of the underlying conception, but also in terms of the external appearance, of buildings), and then go on from this to oppose the use of

ornaments, they will eventually find themselves adopting an impoverished view of architecture based exclusively on the concept of purposiveness. Where present-day architecture is concerned, they will find themselves veering more and more towards a monotonous architectural style, whose exponents will not dare to deviate from the established view of organic growth, whilst in respect of past architecture they will gradually lose interest in the manifold and individual achievements of other nations.'[281]

This last passage was addressed to the adherents of the Gothic Revival, whose theories, if carried to their logical conclusion, really did presuppose the elimination of all ornamental features. Schnaase had sensed that the word 'organic' was acquiring a new meaning, and that the Kantian concept of a type of 'purposiveness which was itself not necessarily purposive' was losing its force. In fact, he had sensed the advent of functionalism, which was one of the underlying aspects of the 'organic', especially in the German- and English-speaking territories.

The vehicle for this functionalism was the Gothic Revival.

work, which is an important source for the history of the subject, appeared in 1830.

281 Schnaase, 'Über das Organische' (1844), p.247: 'Eine gewisse Zurücksetzung des Rundbogenstyles, eine Überschätzung des gothischen sind daraus hervorgegangen, eine einseitige Auffassung der Geschichte und Ausbildung des Geschmackes kann daraus entstehen. Denn wenn man überall nur auf das ''Organische'', auf die Zweckbestimmung und den Zusammenhang der Glieder (nicht blos auf den innern Gedanken, sondern in äusserer Erscheinung) dringt, und in consequenter Entwicklung dieser Ansicht gegen das Ornament immer strenger wird, so wird man zuletzt von der dürftigen Auffassung der Architektur unter dem Gesichtspunkte der Zweckmässigkeit nicht weit entfernt seyn. In der Praxis wird man immer mehr in eine Monotonie gerathen, welche nicht wagt, sich von dem angenommenen Typus des Organischen zu entfernen, in der Geschichte immer spröder gegen die mannigfaltigen individuellen Gestaltungen vieler Völker werden.'

III The Gothic Revival as a Reform Movement

1 A general inventory of German-language building magazines published between 1800 and 1914 is now being prepared. See Stephan Waetzold, 'Forschungen zum 19. Jahrhundert an der Kunstbibliothek' in *Jahrbuch der Stiftung Preussischer Kulturbesitz Berlin, 1966* (Cologne and Berlin, 1967), pp.152–4. – For an inventory of English-language building magazines see Jenkins, 'Nineteenth-Century Architectural Periodicals' (1968), pp.153–60.

2 *Ibid.*, p.153. – According to the various manuals of printing, mechanical type-setting machines were not capable of this kind of output until several decades later.

3 *The Ecclesiologist*, published by the Cambridge Camden Society. – Volume I (1842; 2nd ed. – from which I have taken my quotations – Cambridge: Stevenson, 1843) consists of issues I (November, 1841) to XII/XIII (August 1842). Volume IV, which was published by John Thomas Walter (Cambridge, 1845), did not appear under the auspices of the Society, but Volume V, which was published by J. Rivington (London, 1846) did. By 1846 the Society had reverted to its original name: the Ecclesiological Society. Volumes VI to XXIX (the final volume) were published by Joseph Master (London, 1846–68). From 1850 to 1868 (Volumes XI to XXIX) the first issue of each volume was published in January. – *Annales archéologiques*, par Didron aîné, secrétaire du Comité historique des arts et monuments. – Adolphe-Napoléon Didron called himself Didron aîné to avoid confusion with his brother Victor, from whose Librairie archéologique in Paris the *Annales* were published between 1844 and 1865 (up to Volume XXV); after his brother's death, Didron aîné took over both the bookshop and the press. From 1844 to 1846 two volumes were published each year, but from 1847 onwards these were reduced to one. At the request of the subscribers a second edition of Volume I (1844) was brought out in 1854; and it is from this edition that I have taken my quotations. Volumes XXVI and XXVII (1869 and 1870) were published by Didron's nephew Edouard. The final volume (XXVIII), which appeared in 1881,

1 The Propagandists

One of our most important sources for the history of the nineteenth century is provided by contemporary periodicals and magazines.[1] In 1841, when mechanical type-setting was invented, it was possible to set six thousand characters an hour, and this led to the rapid dissemination of information and the expansion of the periodical industry.[2] As a result of this development new ideas frequently appeared in building magazines, which in those days were still virtually indistinguishable from archaeological and architectural magazines. The presentation of the material in such publications was essentially polemical, which gave these new conceptions a piquant flavour they would not otherwise have acquired.

The most important organs of the new 'Gothic movement' were *The Ecclesiologist*, the *Annales archéologiques* and the *Kölner Domblatt*, which were launched in the early 1840s.[3] Other periodicals concerned with the Gothic Revival include *The New York Ecclesiologist*, the Dutch publication *Dietsche Warende*, the Cologne *Organ für christliche Kunst*, the Leipzig *Zeitschrift für christliche Archäologie und Kunst* (a publication with Protestant leanings), and the Parisian *Revue de l'art chrétien*.

The editors and correspondents of *The Ecclesiologist*, the *Annales archéologiques* and the *Kölner Domblatt* maintained extremely close contacts. They corresponded with one another, and visited one another, with a regularity that is quite astonishing in view of the poor state of nineteenth-century communications. Both as a letter-writer and as a traveller the lawyer August Reichensperger (1808–95), who edited the *Kölner Domblatt* from 1842 to 1844 and from 1849 onwards, was quite as indefatigable as any of his fellow propagandists,[4] and as a polyglot was certainly their superior. Reichensperger visited Paris in 1833, and Belgium in 1837, and in 1839–40 travelled through France en route for Italy. In 1846 he visited England, where he saw the Roman Catholic architect Augustus Welby Northmore Pugin (1812–52), the architect of the new Houses of Parliament Charles Barry (1795–1860), and the winner of the competition for St Nicholas's in Hamburg, George Gilbert Scott (1811–78). While in England he also met Adolphe-Napoléon Didron (1806–67) who, like him, had been invited to attend the consecration of St Giles in Cheadle (Staffordshire) by John Talbot, 16th Earl of Shrewsbury (1791–1852).[5] Reichensperger seems to have met Scott

is given over to a 'Table analytique et méthodique', which was evolved by Xavier Barbier de Montault. – *Kölner Domblatt: Amtliche Mittheilungen des Central-Dombau-Vereins, mit Beiträgen historischen, kunstgeschichtlichen und technischen Inhalts*, herausgegeben vom Vorstande. – The *Kölner Domblatt* began as a weekly magazine which was distributed as a free supplement to the readers of the *Kölnische Zeitung*, a newspaper published by M. DuMont-Schauberg (Cologne). From 1845 onwards the *Domblatt* was issued as a monthly magazine; at the end of 1857 an index was published. From 1866 onwards there were frequent gaps in the series; the final issue covers the period 1885–92. For further information see Rode/Wolff, '125 Jahre Zentral-Dombauverein' (1965/6), pp.73–4; figs.11–13.

4 Ludwig Pastor, *August Reichensperger (1808–1895), sein Leben und sein Wirken auf dem Gebiet der Politik, der Kunst und der Wissenschaft, mit Benutzung seines ungedruckten Nachlasses*, 2 vols. (Freiburg im Breisgau, 1899), I, p.179.

5 *Ibid.*, pp.53 ff., 73, 89 ff., 198, and 207 ff. – *Annales archéologiques*, V (1846), pp.244–6 and 284–308; VI (1847), p.241 (note); XIII (1853), pp.16–17.

6 George Gilbert Scott, *Personal and Professional Recollections by the Late Sir George Gilbert Scott, R.A.*, edited by his son, G. Gilbert Scott . . . (London, 1879), p.147.

7 *Annales archéologiques*, X (1850), p.260. – Pastor, *Reichensperger* (1899), I, p.331.

8 *Ibid.*, p.494. – Reichensperger's assessment of the Crystal Palace was printed in *The Ecclesiologist*, XII (1851), pp.384–9. – The German version was reproduced in A. R., *Vermischte Schriften über christliche Kunst* (Leipzig, 1856), pp.432–41.

9 Pastor, *Reichensperger* (1899), I, pp.498 and 519. – *Annales archéologiques*, XIV (1854), p.384; XVI (1856), pp.111–29.

10 *The Ecclesiologist*, XVII (1856), p.382.

11 *Ibid.*, XVIII (1857), pp.18–22; XIX (1858), p.257. – *Organ für christliche Kunst*, VII (1857), pp.16 and 182; reprinted in *Kölner Domblatt*, 4 September, 1857. – See also Jochen Becker, 'Das Plastikprogramm des Kölner Doms, 1845–57' in *Kölner Domblatt, Jahrbuch des Zentral-Dombauvereins*, XXXI/XXXII (1970), pp.15–28.

12 Pastor, *Reichensperger* (1899), I, p.529.

13 *The Ecclesiologist*, XVIII (1857), p.49.

again in 1848, when he went to Frankfurt while he was a member of the Frankfurt parliament.[6] Subsequently, when the parliament moved to Erfurt, Reichensperger went to live there, and in 1850 he travelled from Erfurt to Prague and, subsequently, Vienna. Later the same year he was appointed Vice-President of the Congrès scientifique in Nancy.[7] In 1851 he revisited London for the International Exhibition, where Scott acted as his guide.[8] In 1852 Reichensperger was back in France again, and in 1854 was elected to the jury set up to judge the entries in the competition for Lille Cathedral (Département du Nord). When the jury sat in 1856, Reichensperger again encountered Didron, who was also a member.[9] The first and second prizes in this competition both went to Englishmen despite the fact that there were no English judges on the jury. Impressed by this – and, more especially, by the scholarly iconography that was such a marked feature of the prize-winning designs submitted by Henry Clutton (1819–93) and William Burges (1827–81) – Reichensperger turned to *The Ecclesiologist* for advice about the kind of windows to be used for Cologne Cathedral.[10] This advice was given in an article by Burges, which was published in *The Ecclesiologist* and was well received in Cologne.[11] In 1857 Reichensperger returned to London yet again, where he had further discussions with Scott and also met the English M.P. Alexander Beresford Hope (1820–87).[12] Beresford Hope later became President of the Ecclesiological Society, under whose auspices *The Ecclesiologist* was published and which had made Reichensperger an honorary member on 3 December 1856.[13] When he addressed the Catholic Congress in Malines in 1864, Reichensperger prefaced his speech by a brief apology, in which he alluded to the old, pejorative meaning of the word 'Gothic' and in doing so clearly gave the Congress to understand that this was his particular hobby-horse: 'I am a German and intend to remain a German; so I must ask you to excuse any Germanisms or asperities in my Gothic prose.'[14] In December 1866, thanks to the advocacy of Beresford Hope, Reichensperger was made an honorary member of the Institute of British Architects. His adversaries in Germany regarded this institute as a sort of 'Protestant academy', and in commenting on his election Reichensperger waspishly referred to their animosity, both to the Catholic Church and to the Gothic Revival: 'It should annoy those anti-Gothic anti-ultramontanes.'[15] In 1866 Reichensperger visited Lille, where he met the architect Charles Leroy (d.1879). From 1856 onwards Leroy had been in charge of the construction work on the site of the Cathedral of Notre-Dame de la Treille, which was being built from a composite design compiled from the best of the competition designs by Père Arthur Martin (1801–56)[16] and others. In 1867 Reichensperger was in England and France, and while there visited the publisher and art historian John Henry Parker (1806–84), the architect William Burges, the members of Pugin's family and Charles-René Forbes, Count of Montalembert (1810–70). (Montalembert, a member of the Chambre des Pairs and an early advocate of the Gothic Revival in France, had spent part of his youth in England.)[17] On his way back to Germany from

75

England Reichensperger stopped off in Paris to visit the International Exhibition.

Reichensperger also played the host on various occasions at both a private and a public level. In 1846 he showed the delegates to the Congrès archéologique at Metz the artistic monuments in nearby Trier.[18] In 1858 he received Didron in Cologne on the occasion of the Catholic Congress (from which Didron, who spoke neither German nor English, soon withdrew).[19] Incidentally, Reichensperger was quick to defend both himself and Didron when *The Ecclesiologist* reprinted an anonymous criticism of one of the Frenchman's archaeological assessments and wrongly attributed it to him.[20] In 1860 Reichensperger was visited in Cologne by Montalembert, with whom he had been corresponding since 1847, and later the same year he received Beresford Hope.[21] For Reichensperger, England, with its unique constitution that had developed organically over a long period, was far superior to any other European country. Commenting on what he regarded as the 'land of the Gothic Revival', he wrote: 'England for ever. England is more Germanic than Germany; it is there that I really feel myself to be in the grip of Germanic influences, and it is there that I would like to be laid to my eternal rest.'[22]

Didron was also a great traveller. But most of his journeys were undertaken in the course of scientific investigations into different aspects of European art, and not in order to establish contact with other scholars. Thus, his *Manuel d'iconographie chrétienne* of 1845 was based in part on observations made during a visit to Mount Athos in 1839. In 1843 Didron was in Nuremberg, where he measured the carved confessionals of the Liebfrauenkirche, and in 1854 visited Italy, where he amassed a considerable store of information which formed the basis of numerous articles for the *Annales archéologiques*.[23] Didron visited England twice – in 1846 and 1851 –[24] and was made an honorary member of the Ecclesiological Society and the Institute of British Architects in 1845 and 1857 respectively.[25] In both cases his election preceded that of Reichensperger. Didron also made a short visit to Amsterdam in 1855 to meet Joseph Alberdingk Tijm, the editor of *Dietsche Warende*,[26] who dedicated his publication *Over de Kompozitie in de Kunst* to him and Reichensperger. In 1856 William Burges, who created the prize-winning competition design for the Lille Cathedral project, visited Didron at his home and found him engaged on an article dealing with the iconography of the capitals of the Doge's Palace in Venice. As it happens, Burges had just come from Venice, where he had written an article on the same subject.[27] Upon discovering this, Didron generously abandoned his own article and printed the Englishman's instead, although he repeated in his introduction, footnotes and postscript the arguments concerning certain points of Burges's interpretation which he had already put to him in the course of their lively conversation.[28] This displeased *The Ecclesiologist*.[29] Burges, however, was not offended, and in 1858-9 he published another article entitled 'La Ragione de Padoue' in the *Annales archéologiques*.

14 Pastor, *Reichensperger* (1899), I, p.565. – Didron praised Reichensperger's French: *Annales archéologiques*, II (1845), p.395.

15 Pastor, *Reichensperger* (1899), I, p.574.

16 *Ibid.*, p.583. – *The Ecclesiologist*, XVIII (1857), pp.223–5.

17 Pastor, *Reichensperger* (1899), I, pp.588–91.

18 *Annales archéologiques*, V (1846), pp.38–46.

19 *Ibid.*, XVIII (1858), p.329; see also XII (1852), p.265.

20 *Ibid.*, XVIII (1858), pp.273–87 and 313–30; XIX (1859), pp.61–2. – *The Ecclesiologist*, XX (1859), pp.315–16 and 429–30.

21 Pastor, *Reichensperger* (1899), I, pp. 409 and 539.

22 *Ibid.*, II, p.307.

23 *Annales archéologiques*, I (2nd ed. 1854), p.464.

24 *Ibid.*, XI (1851), pp.292–5 and 300–16. – *Ibid.*, XXV (1865), p.388 (which shows that Didron also visited Spain in 1848).

25 *The Ecclesiologist*, V (1846), p.255. – *Annales archéologiques*, IV (1846), pp.255 and 379; XVII (1857), p.57.

26 *Ibid.*, XVI (1856), p.90.

27 *Ibid.*, XVII (1857), pp.69–70.

28 *Ibid.*, pp.69–88 and 193–216.

29 *The Ecclesiologist*, XIX (1858), pp.23–4.

Didron kept the readers of his magazine well informed about the *mouvement archéologique* in other European countries. For England he acquired the services of Beresford Hope and for Germany those of Reichensperger.[30] Other contributors included the architect Johann Claudius von Lassaulx (1781–1848) and the Canon Dr Daniel Rock (1799–1871).[31] Rock, who – like Pugin – was a protégé of Lord Shrewsbury and who held the post of chaplain at Alton Towers, Staffordshire, was a leading authority on liturgical history; Lassaulx, a native of Reichensperger's hometown of Coblenz, was on friendly terms, not only with Schinkel, but also with the Reverend William Whewell (1794–1866), a member of the Ecclesiological Society and an expert in various fields of scholarship, who translated two of his publications.[32] By contrast, the coverage of the French Gothic Revival in the *Annales archéologiques* was sparse and unenthusiastic. *The Ecclesiologist* rightly observed in this connexion that Didron was more concerned with antiquarian matters than with the contemporary scene.[33]

Didron's investigations into a wide range of mediaeval literature, on the other hand, were exhaustive and quite excellent. The Didron brothers complemented one another splendidly in this respect.

We have already seen that both Didron and Reichensperger visited England for the consecration of the Roman Catholic church of St Giles in Cheadle in 1846. In the same year the editors of *The Ecclesiologist* began to take an active interest in the development of the Gothic Revival on the Continent:

'It remains to say that we have made arrangements by which we are regularly supplied with the *Annales archéologiques*, and the *Kölner Domblatt*. We shall not fail to communicate (with due acknowledgement of our authorities) such information as they may contain of interest to the general Ecclesiological reader.'[34] The Ecclesiological Society was a liturgical extension of the Oxford Movement, which at that time was trying to bring about theological and practical reforms within the Anglican Church. The members of this movement, and of the Society, were in an extremely vulnerable position, which was reflected in their early contacts with Germany and France.

In 1843 the Reverend John Mason Neale (1818–66), who was an editor on *The Ecclesiologist* and one of the more fanatical advocates of the Ecclesiological cause, took the cure in Madeira, where he met Count Montalembert.[35] The Count's name appeared on the list of honorary members of the Ecclesiological Society from 1841.[36] But later he withdrew from the Society on the grounds that his honorary membership had not been conferred on him in a proper manner and also because he objected to the Society's use of the word *catholic* in defining its aims. This he considered to be presumptuous.[37] It is of course tempting to speculate as to whether the overzealous Neale was not responsible for Montalembert's reversion, for it was shortly after the Madeira meeting that the Count dissociated himself from the Society. But whatever the real reason may have been, *The Ecclesiologist* expressed its regret over Montalembert's decision, then proceeded to

30 *Annales archéologiques*, VI (1847), pp.65–70; IX (1849), pp.184–5 and 335–50; X (1850), pp.180–5, 283–4 and 356; XIII (1853), pp.332–5 and 338–53; XV (1855), pp.207–8; XVII (1857), pp.128–38; XVIII (1858), p.368.

31 *Ibid.*, VI (1847), p.19; XI (1851), pp. 137–47.

32 *Annales archéologiques*, V (1846), p.356: 'M. de Lassaulx est le Pugin de l'Allemagne'. – Frank Schwieger, *Johann Claudius von Lassaulx, 1781–1848, Architekt und Denkmalpfleger in Koblenz* ... (Neuss, 1968). – Nikolaus Pevsner, William Whewell and His Architectural Notes on German Churches' in *German Life and Letters, a Quarterly Review*, New Series, XXII (1969), pp.39–48.

33 *The Ecclesiologist*, V (1846), p.64.

34 *Ibid.*, pp.1–2.

35 A[rthur] G[eoffrey] Lough, *The Influence of John Mason Neale* (London, 1962), pp.109–10.

36 *Report of the Cambridge Camden Society*, 1841, p.45; 1844, p.36; 1845/6, p.20. – Cambridge Camden Society is the former name of the Ecclesiological Society.

37 Montalembert, *Œuvres*, VI (1861), pp.366–87. – Montalembert's letter was first published in Liverpool in 1844, and was reprinted by an opponent of the Society the Reverend Francis Close (1797–1882), in Cheltenham in 1845.

make political capital out of it by using his letter as a weapon against the traditionalists in the Anglican Church, who were constantly accusing the periodical of popery.[38] As it happens, their accusations were not very wide of the mark, for the pro-Catholic trend pursued by *The Ecclesiologist* undoubtedly served to conceal anti-Protestant leanings. It will be remembered that in the competition for the Church of St Nicholas in Hamburg the jury awarded George Gilbert Scott the third prize, the first and second prizes going to Gottfried Semper (1803–79) and Heinrich Strack (1805–80), and that this decision was subsequently reversed by the members of the church council who asked Ernst Friedrich Zwirner (1802–61), the architect in charge of the building works for Cologne Cathedral, to check the jury's findings. When Zwirner found in favour of Scott and he was offered the commission by the church authorities,[39] *The Ecclesiologist* was furious:

'Now this building as designed for the worship of one of the worst sections of an heretical sect (for Hamburg ministers are notorious for neology), hardly comes under our notice . . . But the question arises, how must we characterize the spirit that prostitutes Christian architecture to such a use? . . . We do earnestly trust that Mr. Scott's example will not be followed.'[40]

Scott, the son of an Anglican priest, defended the Hamburg clergy to the best of his ability. He pointed out that, in the main, the Lutheran and Anglican dogmas were easily reconciled. But it was to no avail: since the Lutherans rejected the apostolic succession, they were heretics.[41] Incidentally, Sulpiz Boisserée, the tireless champion of the Cologne Cathedral project and a practising Catholic, was quite prepared to accompany Zwirner to Hamburg to help him with his reassessment and when he was unable to do so for reasons of health, submitted a written opinion instead.[42]

But it was not long before *The Ecclesiologist* abandoned this narrow-minded attitude. In an article written in 1847 and entitled 'The New Independent Meeting House at Manchester' a contributor expressed the hope that the Calvinists would be brought back to the true faith by the Gothic Revival.[43]

Although Didron himself never had anything published in *The Ecclesiologist*, many of the contributors to the *Annales archéologiques* had dealings with the English periodical. The brothers Henri Gérente (1814–49) and Alfred Gérente (1821–68), whose mother was English, were frequent visitors to England, where they produced numerous stained-glass windows and were made honorary members of the Ecclesiological Society. Prosper Mérimée (1803–70), Inspecteur général des Monuments historiques, and his friend and protégé, the architect and restorer Eugène-Emmanuel Viollet-le-Duc (1814–79), arranged to visit Beresford Hope in London in 1850, but were obliged to postpone their journey.[44] In 1852 the architect Jean-Baptiste-Antoine Lassus (1807–57) sent *The Ecclesiologist* an account of the impressions he had formed during a visit to London, on which he had been accompanied by Emmanuel-Paul-Hilaire Durand (1806–81) and Roch-François-

38 *The Ecclesiologist*, IV (1845), p.25.

39 There were numerous reports of the competition. One such was Joseph Egle, 'Notizen über die Konkurrenz zur Lieferung eines Bauplanes für die St. Nikolai-Kirche in Hamburg' in *Allgemeine Bauzeitung*, XIII (1848), pp. 123–7; pls.171–9.

40 *The Ecclesiologist*, IV (1845), p.184.

41 *Ibid.*, pp.242–3.

42 Letter of 17 April 1845 from Boisserée to Zwirner in *Der Briefwechsel Sulpiz Boisserées mit Georg Moller, Karl Friedrich Schinkel und Ernst Friedrich Zwirner*, hrsg. von Elisabeth Christern und Herbert Rode (not yet published).

43 *The Ecclesiologist*, VII (1847), pp.171–4.

44 *Ibid.*, XI (1850), p.55. – Paul Léon, *Mérimée et son temps* (Paris, 1962), p.316.

54

Ferdinand-Marie Nolasque Baron de Guilhermy (1808–78), both of whom were connoisseurs of mediaeval art.[45] In fact, this was the second article of Lassus to appear in *The Ecclesiologist*, which had published an essay of his in 1850, in which he had described his buildings and restorations; and six years later, when one of the regular English contributors to the periodical passed what Lassus considered to be a misleading comment on the motto for his Lille design, he entered into a friendly argument over the correct interpretation of the postulate 'L'éclectisme est la plaie de l'art'.[46] Finally, Père Martin, who was primarily responsible for compiling the partially executed design for Lille Cathedral, gave a lecture in French at the annual assembly of the Ecclesiological Society in 1849.[47] He, too, was an honorary member of the Society.

As far as Germany was concerned, *The Ecclesiologist* relied on information supplied by English travellers, on the *Kölner Domblatt*, from which it regularly translated Zwirner's annual report on the progress of the Cathedral project, and on reports sent in by Reichensperger.[48] It also took note of any new ecclesiological developments in Germany, i.e. of any new publications on mediaeval liturgy, symbolism, and architecture. Almost invariably, this material was examined by Reichensperger. But there was one occasion on which *The Ecclesiologist* failed to consult him, with unfortunate results for all concerned. In an unsigned article, which had appeared in a local periodical, Didron was accused of superficiality in his assessment of the cathedral of Aix-la-Chapelle.[49] This article, which Didron believed had been written by one of the German art forgers whom he had unmasked in the *Annales archéologiques*, was reproduced in *The Ecclesiologist* and attributed to Reichensperger. The German promptly rejected the attribution and was extremely annoyed at not having been consulted. This incident occurred in 1859, the year in which the Ecclesiological Society celebrated its twentieth anniversary and was able to announce the completion of All Saints, Margaret Street, London, the first church to be built in strict accordance with ecclesiological principles. It was a year of victory and pride, in which the Gothic Revival ceased to be a reform movement.

2 'The Ecclesiologist'

The history of the Ecclesiological Society, which developed from the Cambridge Camden Society in 1846, has been recorded by numerous authors.[50] We, of course, are not concerned with the Society as such, but with the architectural theories elaborated in its periodical and with the buildings which inspired them or in which they were tested. The earliest of these buildings were the Commissioners' Churches and the colonial churches.

With the outbreak of the French Revolution, the English looked to their own defences against internal unrest, and in the early 1800's it

45 *The Ecclesiologist*, XIII (1852), pp.46–50.

46 *Ibid.*, XVII (1856), pp.86–91, 284–7, 362–4 and 414–21. – For reports by Lassus and Viollet-le-Duc on the restoration of Notre-Dame and the Sainte-Chapelle in Paris, see *ibid.*, X (1850), pp.297–301; XI (1850), pp.95–103.

47 *Ibid.*, IX (1849), pp.375 and 379.

48 *Ibid.*, XVII (1856), pp.349–52; XIX (1858), pp.88–90; XX (1859), pp.402–3.

49 See Note 20 for Part III above. – *The Ecclesiologist* wrote: 'It is no wonder that M. Didron should have very little time for editing the *Annales*; but he should not undertake more than he can do well.'

50 Edward Jacob Boyce, *A Memorial of the Cambridge Camden Society, Instituted May, 1839, and the Ecclesiological, late Cambridge Camden Society, May, 1846* (London, 1888). – Lough, *John Mason Neale* (1962), pp.6–38. – James F. White, *The Cambridge Movement, the Ecclesiologists and the Gothic Revival* (Cambridge, 1962). – Phoebe B. Stanton, *The Gothic Revival and American Church Architecture, an Episode in Taste, 1840–1856* (Baltimore, 1968), pp. xviii–29.

51 G[eorge] W[illiam] O[utram] Addleshaw and Frederick Etchells, *The Architectural Setting of Anglican Worship* . . . (London, 1948), pp.245–6.

52 M[ichael] H[arry] Port, *Six Hundred Churches: Study of the Church Building Commission, 1818–1856* . . . (London, 1961), p.39. – Dorothy Stroud, *The Architecture of Sir John Soane* . . . (London, 1961), fig.185 (drawing by Joseph Michael Gandy based on designs by Soane). – Clark, *The Gothic Revival* (1964), fig.7 (drawing by Soane).

53 Holy Trinity, 1826; see H[enry] S[tuart] Goodhart-Rendel, 'English Gothic Architecture of the Nineteenth Century' in *Journal of the Royal Institute of British Architects*, 3rd Series, XXXI (1924), pp.321–44, Conclusion. – It was Soane who introduced Barry to church building; see Marcus Whiffen, *The Architecture of Sir Charles Barry in Manchester and Neighbourhood* . . . (Manchester, 1950), pp.1–2.

54 Port, *Six Hundred Churches* (1961), pp.50, 59, 64–71, and 77.

55 *Ibid.*, pp.66–7; pl. VI.

56 *Ibid.*, pp.52–3.

57 Klenze, *Anweisung zur Architectur des christlichen Cultus* (1834). – *Entwürfe zu Kirchen, Pfarr- und Schulhäusern*, hrsg. von der Königlich preussischen Ober-Baudeputation, 6 parts (Potsdam, 1844–5); this work was unfavourably reviewed in *The Ecclesiologist*; see *ibid.*, IV (1845), pp.124–6.

seemed that one way of countering revolutionary fervour was by strengthening the Established Church. Accordingly, a 'National Society for the Education of the Poor in the Principles of the Established Church' was founded in 1811. Seven years later this Society had succeeded in persuading Parliament to pass a Church Building Act and to provide one million pounds sterling with which to build new churches. The money was entrusted to a special commission – hence the name Commissioners' Churches – which was authorized to subsidize church building in parishes with more than 4000 souls and with accommodation for less than 1000 worshippers or where the churches were too far removed from the centres of population. Alternatively, the Commission could recommend the establishment of new parishes. The new churches had to provide good auditorium facilities – a traditional feature of Protestant church architecture – at an economical price. This was the principal design requirement.[51] The Crown Architects were asked to make recommendations, and Sir John Soane (1753–1837) submitted a number of designs in different styles, together with an explanatory letter, in which he raised several interesting points. Soane suggested that economies could be made by the introduction of brickwork, and he argued that stone should only be employed where absolutely necessary, or where it was found desirable to give a particular building a characteristic appearance. He also recommended that small galleries should be supported by iron pillars, which could be clad if it was felt 'that the use of iron alone has not a sufficient character and appearance of stability'.[52] Two distinct types of church were specified by the commissioners: one costing up to £10,000, and another costing between £10,000 and £20,000. In Soane's view, the best example of the first type

25

was the church built by Charles Barry on Cloudesley Square in the Islington district of London.[53] Thomas Rickman (1776–1841) was also an advocate of iron. He had been using prefabricated iron components for the tracery and roof girders in his churches ever since 1813, and

26, 27

consequently was well equipped to produce low-cost buildings.[54] Rickman built twenty-one Commissioners' Churches, more than any other architect.[55] He also submitted designs for model churches. But the commission refused to subsidize buildings of this kind. It was not even prepared to authorize the use of standard ground-plans and standard roof systems, which was proposed by the Archdeacon of Essex, Francis John Hyde Wollaston, in 1819. In support of his proposal Wollaston pointed to its adaptability: 'And there we may have either a Greek dress for the parallelogram or a Gothic dress, and we may adapt either the one or the other.'[56] The cost of building in each of these two styles was naturally considered by the Commission, but no definitive conclusion was reached. Incidentally, similar attempts to standardize

83

church architecture in Bavaria and Prussia also failed to find approval.[57]

In 1820 and 1822 further legislation was passed, which extended the scope of the Church Building Act of 1818, and Parliament provided the Commission with additional revenue. In the thirty-eight years of its existence the Commission authorized subsidies to the value of £1,675,000. This was almost matched by the money obtained from private sources, with the result that 612 churches were built with accommodation for 600,000 worshippers.[58] During this period the population of England increased by seven millions. Even in urban areas in England it was customary for individual parishes to be divided up into smaller districts, each with its own little church. This custom was continued throughout the nineteenth century, and was seldom questioned.[59]

The Cambridge Camden Society was a student organization that was formed in the city of Cambridge in 1839 in order to further ecclesiological interests. Most of its members were students of divinity and when they left the university to go their separate ways the Society launched *The Ecclesiologist* in order to provide a rallying point for the movement.[60] What the members of the Society understood by 'ecclesiology' was: Anglican worship held in strict accordance with the established rites of the church in buildings constructed in strict accordance with the Gothic style of the fourteenth century, for they believed that both the Christian Church and the Gothic style reached their apogee in the fourteenth century. Accordingly, they paid close attention to liturgical decrees, liturgical books and the reports of visitations carried out by the bishops of the Church of England. But they also took a keen interest in church buildings and fitments, ecclesiastical garments, church music and all the symbolism of the mediaeval church, especially those forms of symbolism developed before the supposed decline of the English church in the fifteenth century. Consequently, their investigations embraced both mediaeval archaeology and the historical development of the Anglican liturgy. Church building, church restoration and liturgical reform all featured in the ecclesiological programme, which was not without its dangers for the Church of England. This soon became apparent once the Cambridge Camden Society went into print.[61] Our major source for this early period is *The Ecclesiologist*. In the first issue of this periodical, which appeared in November 1841, we are told:

'The principal design of the present periodical is to furnish such members of the Cambridge Camden Society as may reside at a distance from the University, with the informations which they have a right to expect, but at present cannot easily obtain unless at long intervals and from uncertain sources, respecting its proceedings, researches, publications, meetings, grants of money, and election of members . . . *The Ecclesiologist* is therefore, strictly speaking, a periodical report of the Society, primarily addressed to, and intended for the use of, the members of that body. But it is contemplated at the same time to conduct the publication in such a manner that its pages may convey both interesting and useful information to all connected with or in any way engaged in church-building, or the study of ecclesiastical architecture and antiquities. It is intended to give with each number among other matters pertaining to Ecclesiology in general, critical

58 Port, *Six Hundred Churches* (1961), pp.125–6.

59 William Bardwell, *Temples Ancient and Modern; or, Notes on Church Architecture* (London, 1837), p.1. – *The Ecclesiologist*, XI (1850), pp.227–33; XIV (1853), p.36; XVI (1855), pp.234–5.

60 For information about the concept of ecclesiology see *The Ecclesiologist*, I (2nd ed. 1843), p.74; IV (1845), pp.2 and 176; V (1846), pp.3–5 and 75; VII (1847), pp.7–14 and 85–8. – White, *Cambridge Movement* (1962), pp.48–53.

61 For bibliography see *ibid.*, pp.237–42.

notices of churches recently completed or in progress of building . . . , to describe accurately and impartially the restorations of ancient churches . . . , and to supply notices and reviews of any antiquarian researches, books, or essays, connected with the subject of Ecclesiology.'[62]

This issue also contained a caustic criticism of the newly built Church of St Paul in the New Town district of Cambridge. The architect was Ambrose Poynter (1796–1866):
'The church is of no particular style or shape; but it may be described as a conspicuous red brick building, of something between Elizabethan and debased perpendicular architecture. A low tower is added at the west end, in order that the rather doubtful ecclesiastical character of the edifice may not be mistaken, and for the purpose of containing, or rather displaying to advantage, three immense clock faces, which doubtless will be useful as well as ornamental appurtenances to the building. The general design of this edifice is marked by the fearless introduction of several remarkable varieties and peculiarities of arrangement, which are strictly original conceptions.'[63]

The whole article was written in this abrasive tone, which appeared excessive even to some members of the Society, with the result that a revised version of the criticism, couched in more moderate terms, had to be printed in a later issue. This was the first indication that the ambitious ecclesiological programme mapped out by the Cambridge Camden Society was likely to prove too much for a student organization. And in 1845 we find first the periodical and then the Society breaking away from the university. Shortly afterwards the Society changed its name to the Ecclesiological Society.

If we wish to understand the theories underlying the Gothic Revival in England as developed by the contributors to *The Ecclesiologist*, there are three things we must bear in mind. First: the members of the Cambridge Camden Society began to write when they were still in their early twenties, and consequently the ideas which they advanced were not put into practice until upwards of ten years later, by which time they had established themselves as clergymen or architects and so were in a position to start building on their own account. Second: the leading lights in the original Society were for the most part theologians; although they designed models for the *Instrumenta Ecclesiastica*, a collection of designs published in two volumes in 1847 and 1856, William Butterfield (1814–1900) and Richard Cromwell Carpenter (1812–55), the two architects most closely connected with *The Ecclesiologist* up to the mid 1850's, wrote no articles and gave no lectures. (George Edmund Street [1824–81],[64] on the other hand, who excelled not only as an architect and architectural historian, but also as a theoretician, certainly influenced the editors of *The Ecclesiologist*.)[65] Third: the theories evolved by the members of the Cambridge Camden Society owed less to the literary tradition of architectural theory than to the *leitmotif* furnished by the English parish churches of the Middle Ages; unlike equivalent theories on the Continent, they were derived from an ideal, not from an idea.

62 *The Ecclesiologist*, I (2nd ed. 1843), pp.1–2.

63 Quotation taken from Pugin, *The Present State* (1843), p.84.

64 When Archdeacon Thomas Thorp (1797–1877), the first President of the Society, retired in 1859 he said that 'much good had been derived in consequence of the society being connected with young and rising architects at the time of its establishment'; see *The Ecclesiologist*, XX (1859), p.273. – By 1859 Street had published six articles on the Gothic Revival and the conservation of monuments; see *The Ecclesiologist*, XI (1850), pp.227–33; XIII (1852), pp.247–62; XIV (1853), pp.70–80; XVIII (1857), pp.342–5; XIX (1858), pp.232–40 and 376–80. He also published articles on aspects of architectural history; see *ibid.*, XV (1854), pp.381 ff.; XVI (1885), pp.21 ff. and 365 ff.; XIX (1858), pp.362 ff.; XX (1859), p.332 ff. – R. J. Lambert is preparing a Street monograph.

65 The editors were the Reverend John Mason Neale (1818–66), the Reverend Benjamin Webb (1819–95) and Alexander James Beresford Hope (1820–87), Member of Parliament; see Lough, *John Mason Neale* (1962), pp.10–11. – Stanton, *Gothic Revival and American Church Architecture* (1968), p.13. – Henry William Law and Irene Law, *The Book of the Beresford Hopes* . . . (London, 1925), pp.139 and 145–6.

55–7

It is hardly surprising, therefore, that one of the first tasks undertaken by the Society was the planning of a model church.[66] True, this project was soon abandoned, but not before an article was published under the title 'A Few Words to Church Builders with an Appendix Containing Lists of Windows, Fonts, and Roodscreens, Intended to Serve as Models'.[67] The appendix to this article, which is thought to have been written by Neale, shows the kind of model church the Society had in mind. Two years later a more detailed description appeared in *The Ecclesiologist*:

'We would suggest then that instead of new designs, or "original conceptions", as they are very properly called, formed by the adaptation of a buttress from this church to a window or parapet from that, *real ancient* designs of acknowledged symmetry of proportions or beauty of detail should be selected for exact imitation in all their parts, arrangements and decorations. How often do we see a simple village church, consisting, it may be, of low and rough stone walls, surmounted, and almost overwhelmed, by an immense roof, and pierced with some two or three plain windows between as many bold irregular buttresses on each side, or having a short massive tower placed at one corner or in some seemingly accidental position, which neverthelesss every one confesses to be as picturesque and beautiful and church-like an edifice as the most critical eye or the most refined taste could wish to behold.'[68]

The vocabulary used by this writer – words such as 'bold', 'rough' and 'picturesque' – was clearly derived from the anti-urbanist themes treated by the Romantic poets and garden theorists at the turn of the century.

The church designed for the Society by the architect Anthony Salvin (1799–1881) for use in New Zealand was also derived from a particular mediaeval model: the Church of Thaon (Calvados; near Caen).[69] Incidentally, Salvin was not the first person to draw attention to the church in Thaon. This Romanesque building had already been recommended by John Shaw as a model for low-cost ecclesiastical architecture in 1839.[70] But in Salvin's case, the choice was dictated to some extent by the style of the building, which had been stipulated by the New Zealand patron, who had very few European craftsmen at his disposal:

'Norman is the style adopted; because, as the work will be chiefly done by native artists, it seems natural to teach them first that style which first prevailed in our own country; while its rudeness and massiveness, and the grotesque character of its sculpture, will probably render it easier to be understood and appreciated by them.'[71]

The Society's Committee felt that the best way of improving church architecture in the colonies was by publishing the names of suitable models from the mediaeval period in England. This decision was taken at the annual meeting of 1844:

'The Committee have to announce that they are now engaged in considering how they may best promote the improvement of church architecture in the Colonies. They propose to select such ancient

66 *Report of the Cambridge Camden Society*, 1841, p.38.

67 Published by the Cambridge Camden Society (Cambridge, 1841); quotation taken from the 2nd edition (1842).

68 'A Hint on Modern Church Architecture' in *The Ecclesiologist*, I (2nd ed. 1843), p.133.

69 *Ibid.*, pp.4 and 31.

70 John Shaw, *A Letter on Ecclesiastical Architecture as Applicable to Modern Churches: Addressed to the Right Rev. The Lord Bishop of London* (London, 1839), pp.26–7.

71 *The Ecclesiologist*, I (2nd ed. 1843), p.4.

churches as will, with the least alteration or modification, best suit the requirements of colonial church buildings, and to provide tracings from full workdrawings of the same, in answer to the numerous applications they receive from our different possessions. Some drawings for this purpose are now in progress.'[72]

The models specified in *The Ecclesiologist* were: St Mary's, Arnold, near Nottingham; All Saints, Hawton (Nottinghamshire) and St Andrew's, Heckington (Lincolnshire). All of these were examples of the Decorated style and dated from the first half of the fourteenth century.[73] It was suggested that they would be suitable for the United States of America, Australia, and New Zealand. But although at that time both the United States and Canada were in favour of imitative architecture, they were not prepared to accept the models suggested by *The Ecclesiologist* and replaced them by St John's, Shottesbrook (Berkshire) and St Mary's, Snettisham (Norfolk).[74] St John's, Shottesbrook was first brought to public notice in 1846, when it was described and illustrated by Butterfield for the Oxford Architectural Society, a somewhat less militant counterpart of the Ecclesiological Society, which also regarded itself as a 'handmaid of the Church'.[75]

As a liturgically oriented organization the Ecclesiological Society attached major importance to church fitments (both old and new) in its *Instrumenta Ecclesiastica*, and left it to other authors to provide illustrated accounts of building components. The best known work of this kind was compiled by the Brandon brothers.[76]

Where overseas projects were concerned, *The Ecclesiologist* could be quite overbearing. This tendency was clearly demonstrated in its dealings with the New York Ecclesiological Society and its architect John Wills (1822–56).[77] The question of model churches appears to have been a particularly thorny subject, for in 1850 a contributor to *The Ecclesiologist* made the following pointed comment: 'We have always, from experience, been convinced, that it is inexpedient to recommend the publication of *model* churches, as such. It would be far better for persons wishing to build churches in the colonies to send, at first at least, for designs from England.'[78]

When Salvin was asked to draw up plans for St Mark's in Alexandria, he seems to have given no thought to the exigencies of the Egyptian climate.[79] Two years later, however, Benjamin Webb read a paper at the annual assembly of the Ecclesiological Society on 'The Adaptation of Pointed Architecture to Tropical Climates'.[80] Webb argued that the reason why Gothic architecture was pre-eminently Christian was that it had been developed in Christian countries during the period when Christianity had reached its apogee. From this he concluded that although English architecture did not constitute a universal model, it was none the less desirable to preserve the essential character of Decorated Gothic in church architecture, irrespective of the geographical setting. This, however, raised the problem as to how Decorated Gothic church architecture could be adapted to meet the needs of a tropical climate. And if this problem was to be solved, Webb

72 *Ibid.*, III (1844), pp.116–17.

73 *Ibid.*, III (1844), p.134; IV (1845), p.24.

74 *Ibid.*, V (1846), pp.80–1. – St Mary's, Arnold, which was twice used as a model in the United States; see *ibid.*, VI (1846), p.193; see also IV (1845), p.135. – Stanton, *Gothic Revival and American Church Architecture* (1968).

75 *Elevations, Sections, and Details of Saint John Baptist Church at Shottesbrook, Berkshire* (Oxford, London and Cambridge, 1846). – *The Ecclesiologist*, XI (1850), p.88.

76 [John] Raphael Brandon and J[oshua] Arthur Brandon, *Analysis of Gothick Architecture: Illustrated by a Series of upwards of Seven Hundred Examples of Doorways, Windows, etc. etc., and Accompanied with Remarks on the Several Details of an Ecclesiastical Edifice*, 2 vols. (London, 1847[–1852]).

77 Stanton, *Gothic Revival and American Church Architecture* (1968).

78 *The Ecclesiologist*, XI (1850), p.212.

79 *Ibid.*, II (1843), pp.74–5; VI (1846), pp.165–9.

80 *Ibid.*, IV (1845), p.73. Printed as: Benjamin Webb, 'On the Adaptation of Pointed Architecture to Tropical Climates', a paper read before the Cambridge Camden Society, on Thursday, February 13th, 1845, in *Transactions of the Cambridge Camden Society* . . . (Cambridge, 1845), pp.199–218; from 1841 onwards the pages of the *Transactions* were numbered consecutively.

suggested, then three factors would have to be taken into consideration:

(1) the building techniques used in countries with tropical climates;

(2) the theory of architectural style;

(3) the Gothic churches of Northern Italy.

From his study of South American churches Webb had drawn the following conclusions:

'Increased area, increased height, increased solidity of walls, and increased internal gloom, may be inferred, I believe, from these cases alone, to be necessary to a tropical church.'[81]

He had also observed similar features in Northern Italy, where he had found churches with lofty auditoriums and windows set high up on the walls, whose large bare surfaces lent themselves admirably to frescoes. He wondered whether churches might not be insulated against the heat by external ambulatories built on the cloister principle. Then, after severely criticizing the designs produced by Salvin for Alexandria and John Macduff Derick (d.1861) for Colabah, Bombay (under the auspices of the Oxford Architectural Society), Webb passed a final comment on his own proposals:

'At last, if the result be unlike an English church, what will that matter provided we have a building correct in plan and detail, and accurately suited to the particular climate.'[82]

Webb's idea for an 'external ambulatory' was later taken up by Carpenter, when he was asked to design a church for Point-le-Galle in Ceylon. The original impetus for this new conception was, of course, given by the eighteenth-century architectural theorists, who held that Palladian colonnades were quite unsuitable for the English climate because they had been invented for the specific purpose of insulating buildings against the hot Mediterranean sun.[83]

But the Reverend William Scott (1813-72) who, like Webb, served as honorary secretary to the Ecclesiological Society, advanced a different theory, which was based on observations made in subtropical climates and which he called the 'speluncar theory'.[84] Scott's case depended primarily on the evidence furnished by the Cathedral of Las Palmas, the capital of the Canary Islands, which was built from 1500 onwards and from which the subtropical heat was excluded by a combination of thick walls and small windows. As it happens, the columns in this cathedral bear a certain similarity to palm-trees, and Scott did not hesitate to attribute to the architect, Diego Alfonso Motaude (or Montaude), the kind of motivations which led to the 'invention' of national orders in the eighteenth and nineteenth centuries:

'This form, that of the palm-tree, was not only in itself beautiful, and susceptible of constructive truth, but was *the* character of the city, in which he was building . . . Had tropical Pointed work followed this glorious hint, there is no saying to what it might not even in the sixteenth century have ripened.'[85]

Scott recommended that the decoration of capitals should be based on native flora. Thus, like his namesake George Gilbert Scott, and like

81 *Ibid.*, p.204.

82 *Ibid.*, p.215.

83 *The Ecclesiologist*, XI (1850), p.55; XII (1851), p.22–3.

84 William Scott, 'Some Notes on the Cathedral of Las Palmas with a Few Thoughts on Tropical Architecture' in *The Ecclesiologist*, XII (1851), pp.29–45. – For a similar view see J[ohn] F[rederick] Bourne, 'On Tropical Architecture', *ibid.*, pp.169–72.

85 Scott, 'Some Notes', *ibid.*, p.37.

Pugin, he advocated naturalistic capitals, where Street favoured 'conventional' foliage.[86] The conflict between these two opposing viewpoints proved extremely fertile for both fresco and stained-glass design.

In 1856, when the competition for the Crimean Memorial Church in Istanbul was announced, the national characteristics which the English architectural community expected to find in a project of this kind were rather different from those incorporated into colonial churches.[87] Two of the competitors, William Burges (1827–81) and George Frederick Bodley (1827–1907) both chose the same model: Sant'Andrea in Vercelli (1219–37; Piedmont). Street, on the other hand, produced a design that was more suitable for an Embassy chapel than a memorial church. It is understandable that Burges and Bodley should have opted for the thirteenth-century church of Sant'Andrea because, as Burges pointed out, it had been financed with English money and built by English workmen in circumstances closely resembling those obtaining in the case of the memorial church.[88] In the event, the first prize was awarded to Burges, the second to Street, and the third to Bodley. All three of these men were members of the Ecclesiological Society while Beresford Hope, who sat on the jury, was chairman of the Society's Committee. But despite this, *The Ecclesiologist* came out in favour of Street's design:

'For us it seems that Mr Street has here realized, more happily than Mr Burges, the conception of a grand Architectural Monument, the impressive exterior of which, with its distinctive national characteristics (only so far modified as to suit the locality), would be an unmistakable English Memorial in Constantinople of the Crimean dead.'[89]

As far as *The Ecclesiologist* was concerned, therefore, national components and climatic components were quite separate entities. Just how sensitive the editors of the periodical were to non-English characteristics is shown by the objections raised to Street's design, whose external elevations were said to resemble the Cathedral of Albi in France and which was also thought to be rather Teutonic.[90] Work started on Burges's church, but came to a halt once the foundations had been laid. The building that was eventually erected in Istanbul was based on a design by Street, which means that, in the end, *The Ecclesiologist* had its way.

Although the periodical was inexorable about the kind of style that was to be adopted for colonial architecture, it was generous in its attitude to building materials. Of course, its correspondents in the colonies had left it in no doubt about the local difficulties that had to be contended with.

In April 1845 the Oxford Architectural Society recommended that in those colonies in which the staple building material was wood, the stave churches of Norway should be taken as a model.[91] The Ecclesiological Society took a different view. The designs for timber churches which Butterfield, the first of its two regular architects, was asked to produce

86 Georg Germann and Herbert Rode, 'Neugotische Blattkapitelle' in *Kölner Domblatt, Jahrbuch des Zentral-Dombauvereins*, XXXIII/XXXIV (1971), pp.225–36.

87 *The Ecclesiologist*, XVIII (1857), pp.98–116. – Henry-Russell Hitchcock, 'G. E. Street in the 1850's' in *Journal of the Society of Architectural Historians*, XIX (1960), pp.145–71, esp. pp.158–9.

88 *The Ecclesiologist*, XVIII (1857), p.99. – This design was published in 1887; see William Burges, *The Architectural Designs*, edited by Richard Popplewell Pullan, 2 vols. (London, 1883–7), II, pls.1–7.

89 *The Ecclesiologist*, XVIII (1857), p.104.

90 *Ibid.*, pp.102 and 105.

91 *The Ecclesiologist* did not comment on this recommendation; see *ibid.*, IV (1845), p.174.

for the Bishop of Fredericton (New Brunswick, Canada) were probably derived from small English stone churches.[92] And for all its simplicity, the timber church designed by Carpenter, the Society's second regular architect, was undoubtedly based on an English stone model.[93] As a result of its involvement with these timber churches the Society went back on its undertaking not to publish designs of models:

'The design for a wooden church, by Mr Carpenter, intended for the island of Tristan d'Acunha (where a missionary has just been appointed) were so much approved that the Committee determined to publish them in the next number of their *Instrumenta Ecclesiastica*.'[94]

But the most surprising thing of all was the decision to publish a design for an iron church in the *Instrumenta*, for there could be no

61 mediaeval 'authority' for buildings made of cast-iron. On the other hand, the component parts for such buildings could be prefabricated in England, which removed the need for European trained craftsmen and also solved the problem of procuring special building materials. The English had been constructing dwelling houses from prefabricated iron components ever since the 1840's, and English architects had begun to dream of a revolutionary style of architecture, which would depend for its effect on the properties of this new material.[95] But even in 1851, when the Crystal Palace was opened to the public, the majority of contributors to *The Ecclesiologist* were still opposed to this new

60 development.[96] Reviewing the Crystal Palace, the periodical's chief correspondent referred to 'an apparent truthfulness and reality of construction beyond all praise'. But he went on to say: 'Still, the conviction has grown upon us, that it is not architecture: it is engineering – of the highest merit and excellence – but not architecture. *Form* is wholly wanting: and the idea of stability, or solidity is wanting ... Again: the infinite multiplication of the same component parts – a necessity in such a structure – appears to us to be destructive of its claim to high architectural merit.' And so he concluded that the Crystal Palace was not 'a complete "poem", an organic whole, so to say'.[97]

This view was shared by critics everywhere. Prosper Merimée, whose conception of art was equally restricted, wrote in 1854:

'In terms of art and taste it is utterly ridiculous, but it is imaginative and there is something so great and so simple about the execution that the only way of forming an impression of it is by going to England. With every step you take in this building you sense the immense power of the English. It is a toy which cost twenty-five million, and a toy in which several churches could do a waltz.'[98]

Leo von Klenze (1784–1864) also passed judgement on Joseph Paxton's Crystal Palace design in 1854:

'Paxton conceived his task as a gardener and so created a large open space with light entering on all sides. Paxton was doubtless surprised to find that he, as a gardener, had been preferred to so many architects; but it was because his design provided the greatest area of unencumbered space that it was chosen for this industrial exhibition, all other considerations being disregarded; and the technique which

92 *Ibid.*, IX (1849), p.49.

93 *Instrumenta Ecclesiastica*, II (1856), pls. XIX–XXVI.

94 *The Ecclesiologist*, XI (1850), pp.248–9. – Now Tristan da Cunha (South Atlantic).

95 Collins, *Changing Ideals* (1965), pp. 128–46. – Erich Schild, *Zwischen Glaspalast und Palais des Illusions: Form und Konstruktion im 19. Jahrhundert ...* (Berlin, Frankfurt am Main and Vienna, 1967), pp.43–7. – William Vose Pickett, *New System of Architecture, Founded on the Forms of Nature and Developing the Properties of Metals ...* (London, 1845). – Karl Bötticher, 'Das Princip der hellenischen und germanischen Bauweise hinsichtlich der Übertragung in die Bauweise unserer Tage', Rede an der Geburtstagsfeier Schinkels am 13. März 1846 im Kreise der Festversammlung, in *Allgemeine Bauzeitung*, XI (1846), pp.111–25, esp. pp.119–20.

96 *The Ecclesiologist*, XII (1851), pp.269–70, 271–3 and 384–9 (Reichensperger); XVI (1855), pp.161–2 (William White).

97 *Ibid.*, pp.268–9.

98 Léon, *Mérimée* (1962), p.318: 'Sous le rapport de l'art et du goût, cela est parfaitement ridicule, mais il y a de l'invention et dans l'execution quelque chose de si grand et de si simple qu'il faut aller en Angleterre pour s'en faire une idée. On y sent à chaque pas qu'on y fait l'énormité de la puissance anglaise. C'est un joujou qui coûte vingt-cinq millions et un joujou où plusieurs églises pourraient valser.'

99 Hederer, *Leo von Klenze* (1964), p.379: 'Paxton hat seine Aufgabe als Gärtner aufgefasst, mit dem Resultat eines grossen freien Raumes mit Licht von allen Seiten. Paxton war sicherlich selber erstaunt, vor so vielen Architekten den Preis als Gärtner bekommen zu haben, deshalb wählte man auch zu dieser Industrieausstellung den Entwurf, der den freiesten Raum enthielt, ohne auf andere Punkte Rücksicht zu nehmen, und nun ist aus Paxtons Praxis in Treibhaus- und Mistbeetbau, die Gewohnheit in Eisen und Glas zu bauen, schon so tief verwurzelt, dass er hier gar nicht anders konnte.' – For other assessments see: Hilda Lietzmann, *Bibliographie zur Kunstgeschichte des 19. Jahrhunderts, Publikationen der Jahre 1940–1966 . . .* (Munich, 1968), Nos.409–19, 886, 984, and 986. – Gerhard Schlitt, *Die Betrachtung und Würdigung einzelner Bauwerke in deutschen Zeitungen und Zeitschriften . . .* (Hanover, 1965), pp.89–101. – Nikolaus Pevsner, 'High Victorian Design' in N.P., *Studies in Art, Architecture and Design*, 2 vols. (London, 1968), II, pp.39–95 (1st ed. 1951; for German version see Note 2 for Part II above).

100 *The Ecclesiologist*, XII (1851), p.272.

101 *Ibid.*, I (2nd ed. 1843), p.11.

102 *Ibid.*, p.134.

103 *Ibid.*, pp.137 and 211 (wood and iron).

104 *Ibid.*, III (1844), pp.86–7; IX (1849), pp.137–8; XII (1851), p.179. – Hitchcock, *Early Victorian Architecture* (1954), I, pp.122–4, 136 and 155; II, pl. IV, fig.22.– Robert Jolley, 'Edmund Sharp and the "Pot" Churches', in *Architectural Review*, CXLVI (1969), pp.427–31. – At the Annual Meeting of the Cambridge Camden Society in 1842 Sharp read an extremely well-documented paper entitled 'The Early History of Christian Architecture', a condensed version of which appeared in *The Ecclesiologist*, I (2nd ed. 1843), pp. 120–2.

105 *Ibid.*, IX (1849), p.137; see also *ibid.*, XIX (1858), p.19.

106 *The Ecclesiologist*, X (1850), pp.64–5 and 432–4; XI (1850), p.54; XIII (1852), pp.260–1; XV (1854), p.432; XVI (1855), p.292; XX (1859), pp.184–9, 262 and 390.

107 *Ibid.*, I (2nd ed. 1843), pp.133–4.

108 'On Masonry', *ibid.*, VI (1846), pp. 41–5.

Paxton had developed for his greenhouse and hotbed structures, his practice of building in iron and glass, had become so deeply ingrained that he was unable to approach this task in any other way.'[99]

And yet, as early as 1851, even *The Ecclesiologist* was referring to the 'iron style'.[100]

If we consider all the statements – including passing references – made in *The Ecclesiologist* on different building materials and the way in which they were to be treated, we are able to observe a gradual but profound change of attitude. The only constant was the insistence on 'reality'. In the very first issue we are told:
'Stucco, and paint, and composition, and graining, are not out of place in the theatre or the ball-room; but in GOD's House every thing should be *real*.'[101]

Initially, *The Ecclesiologist* took a firm stand against cast-iron, not least because cast-iron pillars were used as supports for galleries, which were regarded with particular loathing in the ecclesiological camp.[102] In defence of this attitude it was pointed out that, in casting and pressing processes, it was extremely difficult to produce cavettoes and other hollowed mouldings.[103] When Edmund Sharp (1809–77) used terra-cotta for the Church of St Stephen and All Martyrs, Lever Bridge, Bolton-le-Moors (Lancashire) the practice was roundly condemned.[104] But Sharp built three churches in terra-cotta (between 1842 and 1844), and it is significant that when it came to criticize the second of these – Holy Trinity, Platt, Manchester – *The Ecclesiologist* was much more restrained:
'We are sorry to see the question of building in brick (for terra-cotta is but a sort of brick) prejudiced by so unsatisfactory an experiment.'[105]

58, 59

The important thing to note here is the date. This second criticism was written in 1849, the year in which Butterfield began work on the polychromatic brick church of All Saints, Margaret Street, St Marylebone, London, a project of major concern to the Ecclesiological Society and one to which Beresford Hope, who was then Chairman of the Society's Committee, devoted part of his private fortune.[106]

Originally, the Camdenians had been completely opposed to the use of brick. Their ideal – 'rough stone walls' and the 'rude hammer-dressed ashlar or rubble work of the ancient mode' – still reflected the mediaeval parish church.[107] After visiting a quarry near Caen, one of the *The Ecclesiologist*'s correspondents wrote an article, in which he claimed that the Late Romanesque masonry in Normandy 'suits the style . . . You admire the design and feel almost unconsciously that it is worthily embodied in its material exhibition.'[108] Some of the correspondent's statements, which may have been prompted by his conversation with the owner of the quarry, but which may also have been taken from books dealing with this subject, are reminiscent of the arguments advanced by French architectural theorists. Having pointed out that good masonry was an essential of all great architectural epochs, he went on:
'Suffice it to say that it is now becoming generally acknowledged that

there is a great difference between Pointed and Classical masonry, and that the smaller size of the stones and the irregularity in laying them are main characteristics of the former style.'[109]

However, he was not at all satisfied with the kind of irregular masonry that had been introduced to date, although he welcomed the growing use of native stones, such as Kentish rag, which had featured in some attractive rubble work in London:
'In effect, a random wall, properly treated, is far better than one of squared blocks.'[110]

Another correspondent censured Robert Dennis Chantrell (1793–1872) on this account, complaining that the stones used by Chantrell for St Philip's, Leeds (Yorkshire) were 'very regularly squared', which *The Ecclesiologist* regarded as a serious artistic error.[111]

What concerned *The Ecclesiologist* at that time was not so much that monumental buildings should be constructed of stone – the material *par excellence* of Gothic architecture – but that such buildings should reproduce, by a process of mimicry, the 'picturesque' properties of Gothic craftsmanship. That is why Butterfield used old tiles for St Augustine's, a College for Anglican Missionaries which Beresford Hope asked him to build in Canterbury, and why *The Ecclesiologist* recommended that ivy should be allowed to grow on church walls.[112]

In themselves bricks possessed none of the picturesque qualities which *The Ecclesiologist* found so desirable. But it was a simple matter to produce picturesque effects, without transgressing against the requirements of architectural 'reality', by using different kinds of bricks – bricks fired by different processes or made from different clays or finished in different colours and with different glazes – in order to create contrasting patterns. And, in fact, we find that in the late 1840's *The Ecclesiologist* began to consider such possibilities. In 1848 the October issue contained an article entitled 'On Tiles';[113] and two years later, in a review of *The Seven Lamps of Architecture*, a contributor referred at some length to Ruskin's preference for mosaic facing,[114] while one of his colleagues, who had written a piece on 'Mr Pugin and *The Rambler*', accused Pugin of having disregarded the question of constructional polychromy.[115]
'We are every day more and more convinced that this is one of the problems, which the revived Pointed architecture of the nineteenth century, enterprising and scientific as it is, will have chiefly to work out, if it means to vindicate its position of being a living and growing style.'[116]

Butterfield's All Saints, Margaret Street, London was to become a test case,[117] and as a test case it acquired considerable celebrity.[118] Because of this we tend to forget that the leading Continental architects, who were not inhibited by ecclesiological considerations, had tackled the problem of constructional polychromy long before. In 1839 the Coblenz architect Lassaulx, whom I have already described as a friend of Whewell, published his *Beschreibung einer neuen Art Mosaik aus Backsteinen* (Description of a New Kind of Mosaic Composed of

109 *Ibid.*, p.43.

110 *Ibid.*, p.44.

111 *Ibid.*, VIII (1848), p.110. – At first the correspondent thought that Scott was the architect; a correction appeared on p.198.

112 *Ibid.*, IX (1849), p.6; I (2nd ed. 1843), pp.47–8.

113 *Ibid.*, IX (1849), pp.81–5.

114 John Ruskin, *The Seven Lamps of Architecture* (London, 1849). – The German translation by Wilhelm Schoelermann (Leipzig, 1900) is probably the only foreign-language version of this book. – *The Ecclesiologist*, X (1850), pp.113–14.

115 *Ibid.*, pp.193–9.

116 *Ibid.*, pp.393–9.

117 *Ibid.*, X (1850), p.432.

118 Hitchcock, *Early Victorian Architecture* (1954), I, Last Chapter: 'Ruskin or Butterfield: Victorian Gothic at Mid-Century'. – Hitchcock, 'Ruskin and American Architecture, or Regeneration Long Delayed' in *Concerning Architecture, Essays on Architectural Writers and Writing Presented to Nikolaus Pevsner*, edited by John Summerson (London, 1968), pp.166–208.

58, 59

Bricks); and in 1846 he started work on the Church of St Arnulph at **85** Nickenich (Eifel, Rhineland Palatinate), where he was able to put his ideas on constructional polychromy into practice, although in this case he used different kinds of stones and not bricks.[119] The change from rough, picturesque stone walls to smooth, coloured brick walls is of significance for the development of architectural theory in so far as it prompted Gottfried Semper, who lived in London from 1851 to 1855, to advance his genetic explanation of walls, which he claimed had been derived from carpets.[120]

As early as 1845 Benjamin Webb pointed out in a lecture on 'Church Architecture in the Tropics' that, in Northern Italy at least, there were various mediaeval precedents for constructional polychromy. This was not the case where iron churches were concerned. However, although *The Ecclesiologist* insisted on stone altars, it had never established a strict hierarchy of values for the different materials used in church construction as such. Consequently, when it gave its approval to the new iron style, it was able to justify its action by reference to the ethical and aesthetic criteria of 'truth' and 'reality'. And, in fact, we find that, of all the ideas evolved by the nineteenth-century architectural theorists, the one most widely propagated at the time was the idea that every architectural style was a product of a particular region with particular building materials, climatic conditions and national characteristics.[121] The Crystal Palace building designed by Joseph Paxton (1803–65) was condemned not because it was made of iron and **60** glass, but because of its form (or lack of form). The fact that Paxton designed a number of completely conventional castles gives pause for thought in this connexion. But we should not underestimate the opposition to the Crystal Palace. This is clearly illustrated by the following excerpt, in which *The Ecclesiologist*'s critic at the Architectural Exhibition of 1852 drew attention to two new developments:

'One was the growing taste for the Gothic styles and more especially for the middle period of that sort of architecture – the Pointed of the fourteenth century ... The other most remarkable point is the growing tendency to introduce an iron style of construction – not, indeed, after the model of the Crystal Palace, which was not architecture at all, properly speaking – but as an element of architectural design.'[122]

And in the following year we are told in a report on the *Instrumenta Ecclesiastica*, in which the Ecclesiological Society published collections of designs, that Carpenter was preparing a series of drawings of an iron church.[123] But Carpenter died while still engaged on this project, which was completed by his pupil and successor William Slater (1819–72).[124] **61** The drawings were published in the *Instrumenta* in 1856, together with two separate estimates for the church: £2150 and £2500 sterling.[125] The caption for the first plate contained a summary of the views held by *The Ecclesiologist*:

'The iron structures so familiar to our eyes in railway-sheds are altogether unecclesiastical in character and associations, and, like the

119 Schwieger, *Johann Claudius von Lassaulx* (1968), pp. 33–6 and 96; figs. 42–9.

120 Gottfried Semper, *Der Stil in den technischen und tektonischen Künsten ...*, 2 vols. (I: Frankfurt am Main, 1860; II: Munich 1863); 2nd ed. (Munich, 1878–9), I, pp.213–16 (§ 62). – Ernst Stockmeyer, *Gottfried Sempers Kunsttheorie* (Zurich and Leipzig, 1939), pp.57–60, esp. pp.15–17. – L[eopold] D[avid] Ettlinger, 'On Science, Industry and Art; Some Theories of Gottfried Semper' in *Architectural Review*, CXXXVI (1964), pp.57–60, esp. pp.59–60.

121 De Zurko, *Origins of Functionalist Theory* (1957), esp. pp.119–98. – Jürgen Joedicke, 'Anmerkungen zur Theorie des Funktionalismus in der modernen Architektur' in *Jahrbuch für Ästhetik und allgemeine Kunstwissenschaft*, X (1965), pp.14–24. – Collins, *Changing Ideals* (1965).

122 *The Ecclesiologist*, XIII (1852), p.58.

123 *Ibid.*, XIV (1853), p.271.

124 *Ibid.*, XVI (1855), pp.49, 119 and 137–41; XVII (1856), p.62.

125 *Instrumenta Ecclesiastica*, II (1856), pls. LXVII ff. – Pickett, who also invented an iron style, commented on this design in *The Ecclesiologist*, XVII (1856), pp.280–1.

Crystal Palace, fall within the province of engineering rather than of architecture. But undoubtedly they show a legitimate use of that material, and develop, according to sound principles, its special properties and characteristics. The present design is an attempt to show how a churchlike building may be constructed in iron, without, on the one hand, abandoning architectural forms, or, on the other, violating the essential laws which ought to regulate the employment of this, or indeed of any, material.'[126]

It is interesting to note that, when faced with this new development, the ecclesiologists resorted to the association doctrine evolved in the eighteenth century in order to justify the pointed arches and trefoils in their iron churches. In 1858 and 1859 Beresford Hope, Slater and the iron manufacturer F. A. Skidemore pursued this matter further.[127] Others also took an active interest. But no iron churches were erected in England, for the English bishops refused to consecrate such buildings. They were tolerated in the colonies, but only in exceptional circumstances.[128]

The Ecclesiologist also took note of the uses to which cast-iron was put on the Continent. In commenting on the cast-iron spires on the towers of Sainte-Clotilde, the Paris correspondent *H* (Beresford Hope?) merely observed that they did little to improve the appearance of the church;[129] he made no reference whatsoever to the fact that, since they were imitations of stone spires, they offended against the principles of 'truth' and 'reality'. By comparison, this correspondent's criticism of the church of Sainte-Eugène in Paris, which was designed by Louis-Auguste Boileau (1812–96), was much more severe:
'A. M. Boileau, a gentleman not we believe professionally educated and who owes his present official employment to political considerations, offered his services to the projectors of the new church, and we find, in the rising structure of *S. Eugène*, the result of what he ambitiously calls a new system of construction . . . He affects to economize space and materials, and naturally, and certainly with no great powers of invention, has recourse to cast-iron. There is positively not the slightest novelty in his conception, which is only that of an iron framework with the interstices filled up with stone . . . The cost of this abominable building is a million francs – forty thousand pounds.'[130]

The Ecclesiologist's ideal solution, namely the imitation of early fourteenth-century English parish churches, was seldom practicable in the colonies.[131] But even in England this conception was to be changed or modified.

Imitating an old parish church was, of course, a complex undertaking. It was not just a question of erecting a box-shaped structure and then giving it a Gothic dress (which is how many of the Commissioners' churches had been conceived). Apart from providing a general structure in keeping with the Gothic original, the architect had to ensure that both the individual components and the relationship between those components were authentic. Great importance was attached to the chancels – which by the eighteenth century had shrunk until they were

69

126 *Instrumenta Ecclesiastica*, II (1856), pl. I (caption).

127 *The Ecclesiologist*, XX (1859), pp.52 and 261. – Skidemore also read papers on this subject; see *ibid.*, XVII (1856), pp.221–2.

128 Hitchcock, *Early Victorian Architecture* (1954), I, pp.529–30. – Schild, *Glaspalast* (1967), pp.121–4.

129 *The Ecclesiologist*, XIV (1853), p.168. – After spending six years on the design stage Franz Christian Gau (1790–1853), the Cologne architect, began to build his church in 1846; it was completed in 1857 by Théodore Ballu (1817–85), who followed Gau's original design. – In the previous year another correspondent had given an entirely negative assessment of the iron tower of Rouen Cathedral; see *ibid.*, XIII (1852), p.382. – See also Jean-Philippe Desportes, 'Alavoine et la flèche de la cathédrale de Rouen' in *Revue de l'art*, XIII (1971), pp. 48–62. (I am indebted for this reference to Andreas Hauser.)

130 *The Ecclesiologist*, XVI (1855), pp. 235–6. – In actual fact, the cost was 530,000 francs; see Bruno Foucart, 'La "Cathédrale synthétique" de Louis-Auguste Boileau' in *Revue de l'Art*, 1969, No.3, pp.49–66. – Boileau's church behind Leicester Place, London, which has recently been replaced by a new church, is discussed, with illustrations, by Nikolaus Pevsner; see N.P. 'Notre-Dame-de-France' in *Architectural Review*, CI (1947), p.111.

131 White, *Cambridge Movement* (1962), pp.105–10. – Basil F[ulford] L[owther] Clarke, *Anglican Cathedrals outside the British Isles* (London, 1958), pp.4–9.

little more than niches – and also to the various fitments in the chancels.[132] Galleries were considered to be unworthy features.[133] Even medium-sized churches had to have aisles.[134] Towers placed asymmetrically were highly esteemed, whilst centrally positioned façade towers were looked upon with distaste. This even applied to churches in Germany, where there were numerous mediaeval precedents for such structures.[135] Cruciform ground-plans were thought to be impractical,[136] whilst open roofs with 'all their honest nakedness' were regarded as an essential attribute of the all-important principle of 'reality'.[137]

These precepts were based on the findings of a large-scale enquiry carried out by Neale and Webb and their friends, who travelled far and wide in search of comparative material. Their *Church Scheme*, a kind of *aide-mémoire* listing all the different parts of buildings and all the fitments which had to be examined on such journeys, ran to seven editions.[138] Other precepts established by *The Ecclesiologist* were derived from a highly artificial form of symbolism. Thus, the Trinity was to be symbolized by the east windows in the chancel, for which triple lancet windows were prescribed.[139]

It is hardly surprising to find that in the middle of the nineteenth century the English ecclesiologists should have restricted their Gothic models to those of native provenance. This tendency was, of course, reinforced by their aversion to mixed styles. Strangely enough, it was Street – one of whose churches was mistaken by Scott for a genuine fourteenth-century building and who was, therefore, no mean performer in this sphere – who began to undermine the dogma of the national style.[140] In the very first paper that he read to the Ecclesiological Society – 'On the Probability of Certain Churches in Kent and Surrey Being by the Same Architect, with Suggestions for a Guild of Architects' of 16 May 1850 – he put forward practical proposals. Among other things, he argued that, if the regional differences found in English mediaeval churches were due to the fact that they had been designed by different Masters, then – in view of the state of nineteenth-century communications – it seemed pointless to try to reproduce specific regional styles.[141] What Street did consider important, however, was that new churches should be built from local materials. Later the same year he launched an all out attack on the mediaeval parish church, which the ecclesiologists had set up as their *beau idéal*.[142]

Rejecting the anti-urbanist Romanticism advocated by *The Ecclesiologist*, he argued that churches in urban environments were subject to their own laws and suggested that, in view of the great diversity and richness of urban settings, these laws could and should be respected. Rusticity, he insisted, must be avoided at all costs. Street also felt that the roofs of urban churches, which were less exposed to the elements and were usually well maintained, could be flatter than their rural counterparts, and that the windows in such churches, which were often surrounded by tall buildings, should be set high up in the walls. He also objected to asymmetrical designs for urban churches.

132 *The Ecclesiologist*, II (1843), pp.12–13, 20 and 34; III (1844), pp.5–7, 33–7 and 161–8; IV (1845), p.40; etc.

133 *Ibid.*, IV (1845), p.20; etc.

134 *Ibid.*, III (1844), p.22.

135 *Ibid.*, VIII (1848), p.202.

136 *Ibid.*, V (1846), p.80; VIII (1848), p.111.

137 *Ibid.*, III (1844), p.102.

138 *Ibid.*, I (2nd ed. 1843), pp.57, 71 and 123; II (1843), p.43; XIII (1852), pp.277–8. – White, *Cambridge Movement* (1962), pp.54 and 231–6 (reproduction). – The Royal Institute of British Architects, London, possesses five volumes containing questionnaires filled in between 1839 and 1841; see *ibid.*, p.56, note 5.

139 *Ibid.*, pp.68–79. – William Durandus, *The Symbolism of Churches and Church Ornaments: a Translation of the First Book of the Rationale Divinorum, written by W.D., sometime Bishop of Mende*, with an Introductory Essay by John Mason Neale and Benjamin Webb (Leeds, 1843). – *The Ecclesiologist*, III (1844), p.83; IV (1845), p.48 (announcement of Johannes Kreuser, *Kölner Dombriefe oder Beiträge zur altchristlichen Kirchenbaukunst*, (Berlin, 1844); VI (1846), pp.67–8 and 126–33 (attack on the Reverend John Lewis Petit); VIII (1848), pp.216–20 (symbolic text from Iceland); XI (1850), pp.217–26 ('chain' of symbolic texts, compiled by Neale); XII (1851), pp.3–11 (end of the 'catena'). – Precursor: G[eorge] R[obert] Lewis, *Illustrations of Kilpeck Church, Herefordshire . . .* (London, 1842) (with excerpts from Durandus, pp.19–27).

140 A. E. Street, *Memoir of George Edmund Street* (1888), p.60.

141 *The Ecclesiologist*, XI (1850), pp.31–42, esp. pp.38–40.

142 'On the Proper Charactcristics of a Town Church', *ibid.*, pp.227–33.

'Regularity of parts is essential', he said. In his view asymmetrical structures were picturesque only when they were sited in an open landscape; and for larger buildings he rejected them irrespective of the setting. As for church steeples in urban environments, he insisted that these must be imposing, even when they consisted of a plain tower, i.e. a tower without a spire, for only then could they make an impression. Having made these points, Street suggested that since the majority of her mediaeval towns had been on the small side, England probably possessed too few suitable models and that it would, therefore, be advisable for English architects to consider Continental models as well: 'My own feeling is, that a diligent study of many of the examples which the large Continental churches furnish, would, if accompanied by a thorough knowledge and respect for those Anglicanisms in art of which we have so much reason to be proud, do very much for us.'[143]

The examples listed by Street include the churches of Saint-Germain-l'Auxerrois in Paris and Saint-Pierre in Chartres. Incidentally, he considered that urban parish churches were 'quasi-collegiate-churches' and could be designed as such. Of course, the stress which Street laid on horizontal lines in his designs was not inspired by mediaeval models. On the contrary, it was a completely independent development. However, on his almost annual visits to the Continent, Street acquired an incomparable knowledge of European Gothic architecture. Present-day authors are still quoting from his book on Spain.[144]

When Scott – who once described himself as the architect 'of the multitude' – returned home from a visit to France in 1847 he was an enthusiastic admirer of the 'square abacus', and from then onwards he spoke quite openly of his preference for 'eclectic principles' and the 'square abacus manner'. But the reasons for Street's conversion to Continental models, which were explained in a lecture given to the Oxford Architectural Society and published in *The Ecclesiologist* in 1852, were much more complex.[145] The title of this lecture – 'The True Principles of Architecture, and the Possibility of Development'[146] – is reminiscent of Pugin, and it comes as no surprise to find that, in the opening section, Street repeated Pugin's contention that religious art was good art and, conversely, good art was ultimately grounded in religion. He then went on to argue that new architectural forms could only be developed if the principle of 'truth' was adhered to. He totally rejected iron buildings. These, he said, were not works of architecture but mere engineering products. And yet Street considered that construction was the whole basis of architecture:
'Now, in all architecture, the first principles are most eminently constructional, and no architecture can be good in which this is not the case. This is the great law at the foundation of all styles. And it at once resolves certain points on which the practice of the last three centuries has certainly been at variance with true principles . . . The invention of the pointed arch . . . is up to the present time the greatest invention in construction which has ever been made, and so far as we can judge, it is impossible that any further such principle of construction should be developed.'[147]

143 *Ibid.*, p.232.

144 *Some Account of Gothic Architecture in Spain* (London, 1865; latest edition 1914).

145 Scott, *Personal and Professional Recollections* (1879), pp.112, 146 and 155–7.

146 *The Ecclesiologist*, XIII (1852), pp. 247–62.

147 *Ibid.*, pp.249–50.

Such ideas were not new. Nor, indeed, were they true, unless – like Street – one rejected iron buildings and denied all possibility of constructional developments in the future. However, in advancing his principle of constructional functionalism Street was not trying to undermine the Gothic Revival as such; what he was attacking was the narrow-minded nationalism of so many of its exponents. In his view, national, climatic and historical considerations were of only secondary importance in determining the kind of style to be adopted by the Revivalists, the really crucial factor in this respect being the great technical advantages offered by the pointed arch. Towards the end of his lecture Street touched briefly upon the question of polychromy, and praised Butterfield's work in this field. He also dealt with the distribution of light in churches, recommending alternate areas of light and shade arranged in such a way as to reproduce the kind of effect found on forest paths.

The technical achievement of the Gothic architects was never completely forgotten by later generations. In England George Saunders and Samuel Ware were probably among the first to regard the arch and the vault as the genetic principle of Gothic art.[148] Some twenty years later, in 1835, Robert Willis (1800–78), who was to become Vice-President of the Cambridge Camden Society, traced even the decorative forms of Gothic architecture to a constructional source: 'This style is remarkable for the skill with which all the ornamental parts are made to enter into the apparent construction. Every member, nay, almost every moulding is a sustainer of weight, and it is by this consequent subdivision of weight, that the eye becomes satisfied of the stability of the building, notwithstanding their slender proportions.'[149]

Initially, *The Ecclesiologist* seems to have been blinded to such considerations by its preoccupation with the rural English parish church, even though, in the opening pages of his *Remarks*, Willis specifically referred to the Gothic Revival and undertook to outline principles 'by which we may be led to compose and invent Gothic buildings instead of copying them piecemeal'.[150] But as *The Ecclesiologist* came to appreciate the virtues of Continental Gothic architecture, its eyes were gradually opened to these wider issues; and in 1855, in a review of John Lewis Petit's *Architectural Studies in France*, which had been published three years earlier, we find the following comment on Willis and his views:
'A vaulted church is thus a kind of organic whole; and it is scarcely fanciful to say that a Willis – the Owen of the comparative anatomy of architecture – could reconstruct such a design from a few of its bones. Herein consists, in our opinion, the immeasurable inferiority of our English wooden-roofed churches, and we heartily wish that our church-builders would set themselves resolutely against their introduction, at least in churches of any cost or pretensions.'[151]

Beresford Hope was very proud of the fact that the idea for the vaulted choir which Butterfield designed for the Church of All Saints, Margaret Street, and which towered up above the nave in the German

148 George Saunders, 'Observations on the Origin of Gothic Architecture, with an Appendix', read 24th January, 1811, in *Archaeologia or Miscellaneous Tracts Relating to Antiquity*, published by the Society of Antiquaries of London, XVII (1814), pp.1–29, esp. pp.2–7. – Samuel Ware, 'Observations on Vaults', read 5th March, 1812, *ibid.*, pp.40–84, esp. pp.40 and 47.

149 R[obert] Willis, *Remarks on the Architecture of the Middle Ages, especially of Italy* (Cambridge, 1835), pp.20–1. – Nikolaus Pevsner, *Robert Willis . . .* (Northampton [Mass.], 1970), esp. p.12.

150 Willis, *Remarks on the Architecture of the Middle Ages* (1835), p.3.

151 *The Ecclesiologist*, XVI (1855), p.45. – Sir Robert Owen (1804–92) was a leading figure in the fields of comparative anatomy and palaeontology.

manner had come from him. Butterfield drew up the plans in 1849 whilst Hope's comment dates from 1853.[152] As early as 1872 the young Eastlake was able to observe 'a steady reaction propitious to home traditions of style'.[153] But this was a reaction that set in in every European country, and as far as England was concerned, it took place quite independently of *The Ecclesiologist*, which had ceased publication in 1868.

Meanwhile, when *The Ecclesiologist* began to promulgate its dogmas in 1841 and to subject contemporary church building to criticisms which grew progressively more severe in a column entitled 'New Churches', the majority of those buildings were already being built in a neo-mediaeval style. However, the models used by their creators ranged from the Early Christian basilicas to Perpendicular Gothic churches. Initially, as I have suggested, neither the members of the Cambridge Camden Society nor the editors of *The Ecclesiologist* were unduly severe. Thus, the two colonial churches which Salvin designed – the first in the Norman, the second in the Early English style[154] – either for, or through the agency of, the Society received quite friendly notices. Even in this early period, however, *The Ecclesiologist*'s correspondents made no attempt to disguise their annoyance at deviations from their own dogmatically held views as to what constituted an appropriate historical and regional style. A number of quite exceptional buildings – such as Christ Church, Streatham, London (architect James William Wild; 1814–92) – were rejected on these grounds:

'Streatham church is so utterly unlike every other architectural building of our own country, that it is by no means easy to describe it. The style has been called by a variety of names with more or less appropriateness: it is, in fact, a poor adaptation of the Romanesque of the south of Europe ... Why were our own ecclesiastical styles deserted for forms which are at best imperfectly developed, and which are adapted only to the necessities of a burning climate?'[155]

The Romanesque was 'at best imperfectly developed' while even the 'First-Pointed' style, i.e. thirteenth-century Gothic, was 'after all only Romanesque improved'.[156] It was evidently felt that although biological analogies might well be able to illustrate the process whereby the 'best' style was selected, they could not possibly provide logical arguments with which to justify that selection; that was more than could be expected of any analogy. Initially, *The Ecclesiologist* regarded 'Middle-Pointed' as the ideal style, but subsequently also gave its blessing, with certain reservations, to 'early Middle-Pointed'.[157] From 1848 onwards 'First-Pointed' was allowed, although 'early First-Pointed' was not.[158] The concepts 'First-Pointed', 'Middle-Pointed' and 'Third-Pointed' were coined by *The Ecclesiologist* in order to render the French conception of the *style ogivale*, and from 1845 onwards appeared regularly in the articles written for the periodical.[159]

It was in 1859 that *The Ecclesiologist* finally opted for this wider and more permissive attitude. This was the year in which it defended

152 Law/Law, *Book of the Beresford Hopes* (1925), p.176.

153 Eastlake, *A History of the Gothic Revival* (1872), p.367.

154 *The Ecclesiologist*, I (2nd ed. 1843), pp.4 and 180.

155 *Ibid.*, p.20.

156 *The Ecclesiologist*, VI (1846), p.254.

157 *Ibid.*, II (1843), pp.21 and 23; III (1844), p.134; IV (1845), p.24; V (1846), pp.66–7; VII (1847), p.203; VIII (1848), pp.54–5 and 258; X (1850), p.119; XI (1850), p.120; XIII (1852), p.58; XVI (1855), p.238; XIX (1858), p.128; etc.

158 *Ibid.*, VIII (1848), pp.191 and 198.

159 *Ibid.*, IV (1845), p.52.

62–4 Street's Church of St Philip and St James in Oxford against the negative assessment placed on it by the Oxford Architectural Society. St Philip's and St James's has been justly described as a 'test for taste' and 'Street's finest church'.[160] Externally, the church is cruciform in appearance. The tripartite nave, the long apsidal chancel and the transepts are surmounted by a crossing tower which rises up from a rectangular ground-plan and is covered by a stone spire. The general symmetry of the building is disrupted by three irregular features: a small polygonal tower containing a newel stair, which is placed between chancel and south transept at the side of the main tower; a low porch on the south side of the church, which affords access to the second bay of the aisle; and the vestry on the north side, which juts out at the end of the nave and runs parallel to the transept. Pairs of small pointed-arched windows placed between the buttresses light the aisles whilst on the clerestory walls normal tracery windows alternate with rose windows. These are balanced by the rose windows in the gables of the nave and the south transept. The coursed rubble masonry of the walls is framed by matching square stones at the corners and divided into sections by dark horizontal bands. The clerestory windows are framed by voussoirs of alternative colour. Internally, the church does *not* appear cruciform because the chancel begins beneath the crossing tower. Above the nave there is a wagon roof with tie beams. In the aisles the lean-to roofs are only partially visible, for the flying buttresses cross immediately beneath the roof. The chancel has rib vaults of stone. The design of the end bay in the nave is also highly individual: at this point the walls of the church converge with the result that the nave is noticeably narrower; and the arcades peter out in front of the enormous east wall of the nave, the end arches being attached to the wall above the level of the imposts. The arches of the nave, supported by sturdy and highly polished granite columns, are wide. There is a second arcade, partly blind, partly detached from the main wall, which frames the clerestory windows. Given the character of his own church, it comes as no surprise to find that Street objected to the 'prettiness' of Rheims Cathedral.[161]

The Committee of the Oxford Architectural Society which, like the Committee of the Ecclesiological Society, gave advice on building and restoration problems, disapproved of Street's design:
'They object chiefly to the growing taste which is so exemplified in the present drawings, for the introduction of a foreign element, to the suppression of the English, believing, as they do, that the English styles of the same centuries are quite as good as the Foreign, and much more consistent. As they believe that this general objection would be considered by many mere prejudice to foreign details, they would specially point to the preponderating influence of horizontal lines in the coloured bands, which interfere with the peculiar character of the ascending line in mediaeval English buildings. This horizontalism partakes more of Lombardic than Gothic Architecture. Again, they consider the spire too short for the very large spire lights which are set against it.

160 H[enry] S[tuart] Goodhart-Rendel, *English Architecture since the Regency, an Interpretation* (London, 1953), p.142. – Hitchcock, 'G. E. Street in the 1850's' (1960), p.155.

161 *The Ecclesiologist*, xx (1859), pp.332–3.

'In the interior, the roof is essentially of a French character, the
pillars disproportionably short, and the clerestory arranged apparently
with a disregard to the principle of placing masses over masses, and
voids over voids; the same interruption of the ascending line is visible on
the exterior, from the irregular arrangement of the clerestory windows.
They consider that the vestry is ill-placed, as breaking out beyond the
cross line of the transepts, and would suggest that it might well be
placed in the east of the organ chamber.'[162]

The Ecclesiologist, acting for the Committee of the Ecclesiological
Society, sprang to Street's defence:
'The chief gravamen of these charges is evidently the assertion that the
design is more foreign than English in its character. The answer to this is
that the design is original and no mere copy. It is not a French design,
nor an Italian one, nor a German one; nor is it, we freely confess, such
an English design as Alan of Walsingham or William of Wykeham ever
imagined. But is this a fault? We think not . . . There are still plenty of
architects who borrow their ideas and their detail form from the most
orthodox sources: and it is well that they do so. But Mr Butterfield, in
All Saints, Margaret Street; Mr Scott in Exeter College chapel; Mr
Burges in his Constantinople church; and Mr Bodley in his church of
S. Michael, Brighton, have shown us, that we have all gone long enough
to walk alone. We claim the same privilege for Mr Street . . . The time
has come when our command of new materials, our enlarged
acquaintance with foreign varieties of the style, and the necessity
of adapting the Pointed of our ancestors to new climatic and social
conditions, demand – not merely justify – some progress. It is quite fair
to criticize the manner in which this progress is attempted; but it is not
sufficient to condemn a design to say that it is not English . . . The truth
is, that assuming our premises of the expediency of an eclectic
development of the style, the present design will be considered a very
remarkable instance of success.'[163]

On the face of it, this excerpt would suggest that I may perhaps have
exaggerated *The Ecclesiologist*'s predilection for 'copyism' and that I
was at error in claiming that it was only in respect of the colonies, where
conditions were exceptional, that this periodical was prepared to deviate
from its strictly dogmatic approach. But despite the reference in this
excerpt to 'new social . . . conditions', I still stand by my assessment.
What is apparent, however, is that, having dealt with the development
of the architectural theories underlying the selection of building
materials and of ideal historical and regional styles, we will shortly have
to consider the attitude adopted by *The Ecclesiologist* to the question
of artistic licence.

But before we do so, there is one last factor to be considered, which
has to do with the distinction between ecclesiastical and domestic
architecture. The fact of the matter is that the question of artistic
licence was felt to be far more important in the sphere of domestic
architecture, in which the relatively few surviving models were largely
late mediaeval, and which was faced with different and, in some cases,

162 *Ibid.*, p.418.

163 *Ibid.*, xx (1859), p.390.

completely new tasks. As early as the 1790's a few English architects were advocating the use of the Gothic for churches, parsonages, castles, and country houses. John Claudius Loudon (1783–1843) was one of this small group, which urged the universal application of the Gothic before Pugin.[164] Initially, the members of the Cambridge Camden Society wanted to restrict the use of the Gothic to ecclesiastical buildings, and stipulated that parsonages and church school houses should not be fitted with tracery windows lest they should look too much like churches. (Not surprisingly, they objected strongly to the appearance, in an English seaside resort, of a commercial building rejoicing in the name of the 'GOTHIC TEA SHOP'.)[165] But although secular buildings had to be clearly distinguishable from churches, it was none the less felt that a parsonage 'ought to be distinctly religious in its character'.[166] A parsonage designed by Butterfield, one of his early works which has been highly praised by modern writers,[167] was also well received by *The Ecclesiologist* in July 1845:

'A very unaffected parsonage is building by Mr Butterfield, at Coalpit Heath, near Bristol. We think he has quite succeeded in giving the peculiar character required for such a building.'[168]

In the following year Butterfield's school house in East Farleigh (Kent) was also favourably reviewed:

'The whole is treated in a bold and masterful way, with a happy avoidance of any mere chapel effect. We fully expect to see a characteristic style arise for our church schools.'[169]

Although it was widely believed that buildings of the 'Middle-Pointed' period should not be used as models for domestic architecture, the ecclesiologists did not subscribe to this belief, and so introduced their ideal style into this field as well.[170] As late as 1850 Street was still of the opinion that ecclesiastical architecture and domestic architecture were two quite distinct professions.[171] But three years later he read a paper in Oxford 'On the Revival of the Ancient Style of Domestic Architecture'[172] which appeared in print, in a revised and enlarged version, under the title *An Urgent Plea for the Revival of True Principles of Architecture in the Public Buildings of the University of Oxford*. In this publication Street tried to bring influence to bear on the building committee responsible for the University Museum by drawing attention to examples of secular buildings of the High Gothic period – such as the Palais Synodale in Sens (Yonne) – and by producing a sketch of a museum executed in this style.[173] John Ruskin (1819–1900) launched a similar campaign. Between them, Street and Ruskin won the day: the museum, which was built by the firm of Dean & Woodward between 1855 and 1868, was executed in 'early Middle-Pointed'. In 1857 George Gilbert Scott published a lengthy book entitled *Remarks on Secular and Domestic Architecture, Present and Future*, which *The Ecclesiologist* unreservedly recommended even though it was able to find little in it that was new.[174] Scott's book was the opening shot in the 'battle of the styles', as the competition for the new Government Offices was soon to be called. In the end Scott obtained the commission but was forced to

65, 66 (margin reference)

67 (margin reference)

164 See Note 74 for Part II above.

165 *The Ecclesiologist*, II (1843), p.10.

166 *Ibid.*, p.147; for a similar comment see *ibid.*, VIII (1848), p.321.

167 Hitchcock, *Early Victorian Architecture* (1954), I, p.144: 'Deriving from the Tudor Parsonage models of the 20's and 30's, the plan looks forward to the innovations of Philip S. Webb (1831–1915), W. Eden Nesfield (1835–1888), and R. Norman Shaw (1831–1912) in the 60's ... This is an early instance of that "agglutinative" domestic planning (so to call it) which was transmitted from England to America in the 70's and which has there a real place in the genealogy of the modern house.'

168 *The Ecclesiologist*, IV (1845), p.189.

169 *Ibid.*, V (1846), p.159.

170 *Ibid.*, VIII (1848), p.258.

171 *Ibid.*, XI (1850), p.41.

172 *Ibid.*, XIV (1853), pp.70–80, see also *ibid.*, p.140.

173 George Edmund Street, *An Urgent Plea* ... (Oxford and London, 1853), pp. 14–15. – Peter Ferriday, 'The Oxford Museum' in *Architectural Review*, CXXXII (1962), pp.409–16. – For further information see Ruskin literature.

174 *The Ecclesiologist*, XIX (1858), pp.16–23.

abandon his mediaeval design.[175] In the nineteenth issue of *The Ecclesiologist* the contributors canvassed fiercely for Scott. In its twentieth issue the periodical declared the Gothic Revival universally valid:

'Mr W. M. Teulon has designed a by no means unsuccessful Butcher's Shop, for Rossington, in Yorkshire . . . We are glad to see Pointed features impressed on buildings for every-day use.'[176]

In this issue a new column was started under the title 'Secular Pointed Works'.[177]

On 1 June 1858 William Scott wrote a review of Street's paper 'On the Future of Art in England' in which he claimed that 'the Society had from the first advocated *principles*, not mere imitations of old examples'; this was an exaggeration.[178]

In the very first issue of *The Ecclesiologist* one of the periodical's reviewers launched an attack on the eclectic opinions of John Lewis Petit (1810–68). The reviewer referred to 'our national cathedrals and parish churches' as 'our own most pure and beautiful models, so admirably adapted to, because reared by, the genius of our church, our nation, and our climate', and insisted that if complete artistic licence were allowed, this must inevitably lead to 'solecism and absurdity'.[179] For the kind of partial licence which it was prepared to endorse *The Ecclesiologist* coined the phrase 'inventive imitation'.[180] Eclecticism was condemned because it was felt that it indicated a lack of certainty, a kind of 'homelessness'.[181] Another anti-eclectic contributor to *The Ecclesiologist* regarded Cologne Cathedral as the foremost example of Gothic architecture and maintained that although future generations might one day produce even better buildings, what was required of contemporary architects was painstaking imitation.[182] In 1848 Henry Woodyer (1816–96), a pupil of Butterfield, received a favourable notice for his Christ Church in Kibworth (Leicestershire), the small octagonal tower which rises from the pediment on the main façade, where it is flanked by flying buttresses, being singled out for special commendation: 'The idea is very original, and originally treated.'[183]

And the reviewer went on to say:

'On the whole we are greatly pleased with the want of commonplace in this church. It is a great thing to be at once original and correct.'

This was why *The Ecclesiologist* was so annoyed when it was able to recognize the source of individual parts of a church.[184]

Butterfield was the first practising architect to free himself from 'copyism'. This prompted Edward Augustus Freeman (1823–92), a great lover of the Perpendicular style, to accuse *The Ecclesiologist* of defending this architect even when he violated the dogmas laid down by the Society;[185] and it could well be that the gentle criticism of Butterfield's crotchets, which appeared in 1850, was simply an attempt to placate Freeman.[186]

Scott must have been the most prolific architect of his day; in 1858 he employed twenty-seven assistants, who produced working drawings with estimates from his rapid and expressive sketches.[187] Occasionally,

175 The most entertaining account of this competition has been given by Kenneth Clark in his *Gothic Revival* (1964), pp.167–72.

176 *The Ecclesiologist*, xx (1859), p.74.

177 *Ibid.*, p.211.

178 *Ibid.*, xix (1858), pp.232–40 and 266. – In Vol. iv (1845), p.124 there is a different formulation: 'What we want is principles.'

179 *Ibid.*, i (2nd ed. 1843), p.88.

180 *Ibid.*, p.135.

181 *Ibid.*, iv (1845), p.58.

182 *Ibid.*, v (1846), pp.48–53.

183 *Ibid.*, viii (1848), p.189.

184 *Ibid.*, ix (1849), pp.162–3.

185 *Ibid.*, xi (1850), pp.209–10.

186 *Ibid.*, x (1850), p.68.

187 Thomas Graham Jackson, *Recollections of T.G.J., Bart., R.A. . . . 1835–1924*, arranged and edited by Basil H. Jackson (Oxford [etc.], 1950), pp.58–9.

188 *The Ecclesiologist*, XI (1850), p.63.

189 *Ibid.*, XIII (1852), p.58.

190 Viktor Kotrba, 'Die Anfänge der Neugotik in den böhmischen Ländern' in *Alte und moderne Kunst*, XX (1965), No.81 (July/August), pp.35–44, esp. p.44. – For an account of Lamb as a theorist see Stanton, *Gothic Revival and American Church Architecture* (1968), p.175. – Latest assessment: John Summerson, *Victorian Architecture: Four Studies in Evaluation* (New York and London, 1970), pp.47–76.

191 Pugin, *The True Principles* (1841). – Alfred Bartholomew, *Specifications for Practical Architecture, Preceded by an Essay on the Decline of Excellence in the Structure and in the Science of Modern English Buildings; with the Proposal of Remedies for those Defects* (London, 1840; 2nd ed. 1846). – Edward Lacy Garbett, *Rudimentary Treatise on the Principles of Design in Architecture as Deducible from Nature and Exemplified in the Works of the Greek and Gothic Architects . . .* (London, 1850; 2nd ed. 1863).

192 *The Ecclesiologist*, II (1843), pp.146–7.

193 See Notes 44, 74 and 86 for Part II above.

194 *The Ecclesiologist*, XIX (1858), p.198. – For a similar statement see *ibid.*, VIII (1848), p.111.

195 *Ibid.*, XII (1851), p.69; XIV (1853), pp.71–2 and 78; XV (1854), p.137.

196 *Ibid.*, XII (1851), p.152.

197 Carroll L[ouis] V[anderslice] Meeks, *The Railroad Station, an Architectural History . . .* (New Haven and London, 1956; 2nd ed. 1964), Introductory Chapter. – For the twentieth-century ramifications of the picturesque see Banham, 'Revenge of the Picturesque' (1968).

Scott's productivity had unfortunate results. One of his church projects was censured by a reviewer in *The Ecclesiologist*, who said it was like 'a prize poem' and as such had nothing in common with genuine poetry.[188]

But if Scott was thought to be commonplace, Edward Buckton Lamb (1806–69) was written off as 'crazy':
'All his works appear to us to fail for want of attention to precedents. Originality is dearly purchased at the expense of conformity to the necessary laws and standards of architectural styles.'[189]

Notwithstanding *The Ecclesiologist*'s poor opinion of his work, Lamb was a successful architect, and received commissions from as far afield as Bohemia.[190]

It was not until the 1850's that *The Ecclesiologist* finally threw off its dogmatic and casuistic attitudes. The credit for this must go to Street, who suggested that the principles laid down by Pugin, Bartholomew, and Garbett should be taken as a general guideline.[191] To a limited extent, of course, these principles had already been taken into account in the reviews of parsonages and school houses printed in the early 1840's:
'The exterior ought to be adapted to the requirements of the internal arrangement, instead of the latter being made to accommodate . . . a preconceived uniform shell.'[192]

The practical advantages of an irregular ground-plan, which was quite permissible in terms of Gothic architecture, had already been recognized in *c*.1800 by the early advocates of a Gothic Revival.[193] *The Ecclesiologist* was even prepared to accept utilitarian buildings with 'little or no characteristic Pointed character'. The parsonage designed by William White (1825–1900) for the village of Hooe in the parish of Plymstock (Devonshire) is a case in point:
'. . . a parsonage of average size, commodiously and judiciously arranged, and of very modest but picturesque cottage-like style, with little or no characteristic Pointed character; but the details have evidently been carefully studied, and though simple, are quite in keeping.'[194]

The chief dangers, as far as parsonages were concerned, were the overemphasis of irregularity for the sake of picturesque effects and the nineteenth-century mania for gables.[195] The best contemporary formulation of this problem – which, as it happens, was prompted by a church – appeared in *The Ecclesiologist*:
'We are more and more convinced by experience that the true picturesque follows the sternest utility.'[196]

All architectural theorists have tended to regard utility as the most important aspect of architectural design. What was new about nineteenth-century theory was the belief that beauty was a concomitant of utility. The 'picturesque' referred to above was the highest commendation known to nineteenth-century architectural criticism.[197]

When the designs submitted by the participants in the competition for the Lille Cathedral commission were put on show – before the jury convened to decide the winner – Street, accompanied by his pupil William Morris (1834–96), set off post haste for France, where he quickly, and erroneously, concluded that his design was bound to win. But Street was not the only English visitor to France on that occasion. Two of *The Ecclesiologist*'s critics – possibly Webb and Beresford Hope – also crossed the Channel.[198] The review of the competition designs which they subsequently wrote is the only one ever published in *The Ecclesiologist* to list precise critical criteria:

'We call those the best plans, not which show the smartest façade, but which most resolutely fulfil the conditions: which display the largest combination of artistic requisites, design, skill in combination, practical acquaintance with building as well as with water-colour drawing; which to a sense of the beautiful add technical familiarity with the useful; which display artistic morality as well as aesthetic; which show a large familiarity with and learned love of archaeology and the whole circle of Christian art and symbolism; which display a knowledge of religious literature, and a practical knowledge of painting, sculpture, enamelling; which prove an eye skilled in colour, a hand practised in composition, a mind imbued with the sense of the beautiful, and a soul possessed of religious sentiment: in a word, which show the artist to be truthful as well as picturesque.'[199]

What is remarkable about this criticism is not the insistence on the essentially religious nature of art – a consequence of eighteenth-century 'Enthusiasm' – but the importance attached to craftsmanship. This reflects the widely held nineteenth-century view that, to be acceptable, a building must function as a *Gesamtkunstwerk*, in other words it must be a product of 'allied arts'.[200]

With its multiplicity of styles the nineteenth century posed a special threat to unity of design. Various safeguards were suggested. The first of these we have already considered in some detail: the selection of the best and most appropriate historical model to the exclusion of all other models. In *The Ecclesiologist*'s view this was 'early Middle Pointed'. A second safeguard envisaged a system of central control whereby the architect would make himself personally responsible for every aspect of the design programme. During the Gothic Revival the principal exponent of this method, which was first proposed by Jacques-François Blondel (1705–74) in 1738,[201] was Street. Richard Norman Shaw (1831–1912), who was Street's chief draughtsman before he embarked on his own brilliant career, once said:

'The charm of his work is that when looking at it you may be certain that it is entirely his own, and this applies to the smallest detail as to the general conception.

'I am certain that during the whole time I was with him I never designed one single moulding.'[202]

Street modelled details of his decor in clay,[203] and recommended this practice to his students.[204] He also produced perspective sketches which he used instead of models. But he would have nothing to do with coloured drawings,[205] preferring to develop his own form of cross-

198 A. E. Street, *Memoir of George Edmund Street* (1888), p.25. – *The Ecclesiologist*, XVII (1856), pp.84 and 133.

199 *Ibid.*, p.85.

200 *The Ecclesiologist*, XVI (1855), pp.2–4. – *Annales archéologiques*, XIV (1854), pp.386–8. – *Organ für christliche Kunst*, V (1865), pp.10–11. – See also [L. Détrez,] *Notre-Dame de la Treille*, III: *Ses chantiers, la genèse d'une cathédrale . . .*, 2nd ed. (Lille, n.d. [1944?]).

201 J.-F.B., *De la distribution des maisons de plaisance et de la décoration des édifices en général*, 2 vols. (Paris, 1737–8), II, pp. 127 and 159. – Dr Alain Gruber kindly drew my attention to this passage. – The term *Gesamtkunstwerk* was first used by Richard Wagner in 1850 in an article entitled 'Kunstwerk der Zukunft'. What Wagner understood by this term was a work of art produced by a combined effort on the part of several different disciplines; see R.W., *Gesammelte Schriften und Dichtungen*, hrsg. von Wolfgang Golther (Berlin, Leipzig, Vienna and Stuttgart, n.d. [1913]) III, p.60. – Nicoletta Birkner kindly drew my attention to this source.

202 A. E. Street, *Memoir of George Edmund Street* (1888), p.284.

203 *Ibid.*, p.136.

204 *Ibid.*, p.329.

205 *Ibid.*, pp.321–2.

68

54 hatching. When Scott won the competition for St Nicholas, Hamburg in 1844, he gratefully acknowledged his indebtedness to Street, who had joined his staff shortly before and had helped with the design work. Distinguishing between Street's approach and his own, Scott remarked: 'He gives drawings, while I do my work by influence.'[206] Incidentally, it was probably Street whom Burges had in mind when he said: 'What a pity that he cannot build his cross-hatching.'[207] Sarcastic observations of this kind were commonplace in nineteenth-century architectural circles, for there were many who used 'showy views'[208] for competition purposes, which was felt to be dishonest.

It is quite evident from *The Ecclesiologist*'s criticism of the Lille competition entries, that architects with over-all responsibility for a particular design were not only expected to be proficient in other branches of the fine arts but also in the various crafts. Many were. Street, for example, once decorated the ceiling of a schoolroom with motifs taken from Overbeck[209] whilst Butterfield had tried his hand as a smith.[210]

Scott, who was a past master at delegating responsibility, proposed a different way of safeguarding unity of design; namely, by founding a new industrial school with a curriculum specially drawn up to meet the needs of craftsmen engaged on Gothic buildings. Significantly, Street tried to dissuade Scott from this project whilst Butterfield gave him only nominal support.[211] But Scott went ahead none the less, and his school was eventually founded as part of the 'Architectural Museum', which housed collections of casts, models, and photographs. But in 1857, within five years of its official opening, Scott's foundation ran out of funds and was merged with Henry Cole's Museum in South Kensington, the forerunner of the Victoria and Albert Museum. Incidentally, one of the reasons for the foundation of the Victoria and Albert Museum was the poor quality of some of the English craftsmanship at the Great Exhibition of 1851.[212] That the decline in English craftsmanship was due not only to the 'depraved taste' of the eighteenth and the stylistic diversity of the nineteenth century, but also to the divorce of craftsmanship from industry and the growing practice of delegating individual parts of the work programme, was well known to the editors of *The Ecclesiologist*.[213] After all, Beresford Hope was President of the Architectural Museum, for which Scott acted as treasurer and actuary. Moreover, Ruskin produced casts for the Museum and lectured to its members, while Charles Barry sat on its Committee.

But although the Architectural Museum held craft competitions for which prizes were awarded, its influence was small compared with the kind of influence brought to bear by enterprises such as Barry's Houses of Parliament. This particular project took thirteen years to complete, and the details on the façades and the interior fitments were created by

32 Pugin; with ample time at their disposal and with such designs to work from, it is hardly surprising that the craftsmen employed at Westminster should have achieved high standards. The mediaeval precedent for this kind of practical training was provided by the

206 Scott, *Personal and Professional Recollections* (1879), pp.118 and 216.

207 Charles Handley-Read, 'William Burges' in *Victorian Architecture*, edited by Peter Ferriday ... (London, 1963), pp. 185–220; quotation taken from *ibid*., p.190. – Charles Handley-Read is at present preparing a Burges monograph.

208 This expression can be found in *The Ecclesiologist*, III (1844), p.111.

209 In Wantage (Oxfordshire) in 1850; see A. E. Street, *Memoir of George Edmund Street* (1888), p.13.

210 Paul Thompson, 'William Butterfield' in *Victorian Architecture*, edited by Peter Ferriday ... (London, 1963), pp.165–84; reference to *ibid*., p.168.

211 Scott, *Personal and Professional Recollections* (1879), pp.165–70. – *The Ecclesiologist*, XII (1851), pp.390–4; XIII (1852), pp.277–8 and 280–2; XIV (1853), pp.24–8 and 84–6; XIX (1858), pp.116–17.

212 W. Papworth, *John B. Papworth* (1879), pp.31, 89, 97, and 106–14. – Alf Bøe, *From Gothic Revival to Functional Form* (1957).

213 *The Ecclesiologist*, X (1850), p.117; XIV (1853), p.423; XVI (1855), p.265.

Bauhütten, the masonic guilds responsible for the construction of the great Gothic cathedrals. Thus, in the very first issue of *The Ecclesiologist* we read:

'We must see a kind of Freemasonry revived, before we can recover the amount of skill which distinguished the church-builders of former days. Why should not every Cathedral be made a school of art in these and other departments?'[214]

This rhetorical question was answered in a reader's letter, which was published in the periodical under the title 'Freemasonry Revived: or, Working Models' and whose author suggested that the Cambridge Camden Society should set up its own workshop in order to undertake restorations on its own account. He also proposed that the Society should consider the possibility of commissioning stained-glass windows against future use.[215] But very little came of these suggestions. True, the Society gave John Keith, the London silversmith, a licence authorizing him to produce silver articles from Butterfield's designs,[216] and demonstrated its keen interest in stained-glass window design by making the glass painter Thomas Willement (1785–1871) an honorary member as early as 1841. (Later the Gérente brothers were also made honorary members.) Moreover, the Society paid close attention to Didron's efforts to set up a workshop for the production of stained glass, although it made no attempt to emulate him.[217]

But since we are investigating the development of architectural theory, we are not really concerned with the renewal of art in general as a result of improved standards of craftsmanship. What interests us is the renewal of architecture as a result of improved standards of masonry. In so far as the English exponents of the Gothic Revival preferred rubble- and brick-work structures to ashlar structures, it comes as no surprise to find that the French and German masons were more highly skilled than their English counterparts. This was not disputed by *The Ecclesiologist*.[218] But the fact that Zwirner's annual reports on the progress of the Cologne Cathedral project were regularly translated and published in this periodical reflects a persistent belief in the desirability of a Christian-based masonic association that would be able to fulfil its functions without being subjected to the competitive pressures of nineteenth-century industrial life.[219]

The 'College of the Freemasons of the Church', a Christian architectural association founded by Alfred Bartholomew (1801–45) and dedicated to the rediscovery, conservation and promotion of the true principles and practices of architecture, was only a pale shadow of this ideal conception. Bartholomew, the editor of *The Builder*, believed that all architects should undergo a full course of training, with special emphasis on structural engineering, and should, where appropriate, be taught by master craftsmen.[220] Papworth, whose agitation led to the foundation of the first state-financed industrial school, of which he was the original director, was made an honorary member of Bartholomew's College in 1846.[221] Street also advocated the establishment of a religious architectural community, but the sort of thing he had in mind was more

214 *Ibid.*, I (2nd ed. 1843), p.150.

215 *Ibid.*, p.169.

216 *Ibid.*, II (1843), pp.117 and 126; III (1844), p.95; XVIII (1857), p.49; etc.

217 *Report of the Cambridge Camden Society*, 1841, p.45. – *The Ecclesiologist*, X (1850), p.168; XVI (1855), pp.282–3.

218 *Ibid.*, IV (1845), p.242 (Cologne); VIII (1848), p.62 (Cologne); XVI (1855), p.297 (France). – Street did not have a very high opinion of the workmanship in Cologne; see *ibid.*, XVI (1855), p.365; XX (1859), pp.339–40.

219 Street stresses the religious aspect; see *ibid.*, XI (1850), pp.40–1.

220 George G. Pace, 'Alfred Bartholomew, a Pioneer of Functional Gothic' in *Architectural Review*, XCII (1942), pp.99–102.

221 W. Papworth, *John B. Papworth* (1879), p.97.

like the painters' communities founded in Germany during the Romantic period.[222]

Ever since the Romantic period certain German and English scholars had taken a keen interest in the 'early freemasons' because they hoped to rediscover the lost secrets to which, they believed, these mediaeval craftsmen had had access. The Gothic law of proportion (based on triangulation), to which Cesare Cesariano had drawn attention in the commentary to his translation of Vitruvius's *De Architectura*, was known to late eighteenth-century observers; and this, combined with the preference for pyramidal structures established in *c.* 1800, gave rise to wild rumours about ancient Egyptian rituals which were allegedly performed by the new freemasons. Incidentally, the Gothic system of triangulation was also linked with the Christian doctrine of the Trinity.[223] But the Gothic Revival, which had developed as a reaction to what was regarded as the excessive regimentation of Palladian architecture, was not really compatible with any theory of proportions,[224] and it comes as no surprise to find that only one contributor to *The Ecclesiologist* ever attempted to explain the system of triangulation. This was the architect William White (1825–1900) who, incidentally, appears to have been unaware of the extensive German literature on this subject.[225] When the competition designs for Lille Cathedral were put on public display the English observers were impressed by a design submitted by the Swiss architect Ferdinand Stadler (1813–70), which contained triangulation lines; and yet despite this distinctive feature, they mistook Stadler's design for the work of an Englishman.[226] They also took note of the *vesica piscis* in the design produced by Vincenz Statz (1819–98), an architect from Cologne. Commenting on this mouchette or 'fish bladder' form in 1809, Thomas Kerrich had described it as a combination of an Early Christian fish symbol, a Gothic seal, a pointed arch, and a Vitruvian triangle.[227]

But it should not be thought that White's paper, which he read to the Ecclesiological Society in 1853, was devoted to ritual mysteries. On the contrary, it dealt with a theory of proportions, which White presented as a viable basis for the Gothic Revival, and appeared in *The Ecclesiologist* under the title 'Modern Design'.

In considering the question of modern design in this period we have to ask ourselves whether *The Ecclesiologist* and its supporters were initiators of a new English architectural theory or mere imitators. How progressive was *The Ecclesiologist* by comparison with men like Pugin, Batholomew, Garbett, Petit, and Ruskin, whose names have appeared from time to time in the course of this study, or men from the anti-Gothic camp such as James Fergusson (1808–86)?[228]

Of course, most of the articles and reviews written for *The Ecclesiologist* were published anonymously, and so, as a rule, attribution can only be made to the periodical, not to individual contributors. This process is not without its dangers, for it tends to gloss over contradictory opinions and to present a kind of consensus view, as if the periodical had always pursued a single line of development. But if due

222 A. E. Street, *Memoir of George Edmund Street* (1888), pp.38 and 56. – *The Ecclesiologist*, XI (1850), p.41.

223 Murphy, *Plans, Elevations . . . of the Church of Batalha* (1795), pp.2–3, 14, 16–18.

224 P[eter] H[ugh] Scholfield, *The Theory of Proportion in Architecture* (Cambridge, 1958), pp.83–9.

225 Paul Thompson, 'The Writings of William White' in *Concerning Architecture, Essays on Architectural Writers and Writing Presented to Nikolaus Pevsner*, edited by John Summerson (London, 1968), pp.226–37. – *The Ecclesiologist*, XII (1851), pp.305–13; XIV (1853), pp.313–30.

226 *Ibid.*, XVII (1856), p.96.

227 *Ibid.*, p.101. – Kerrich, 'Some Observations' (1812), pp.292–325, see esp. pp.313–14. – For an account of Kerrich's later theories see Scholfield, *Theory of Proportion* (1958), pp.88–9.

228 The best account is in Stanton, *Gothic Revival and American Church Architecture* (1968).

allowance is made for this proclivity, it will be found that the architectural theory propagated by *The Ecclesiologist* was more diversified, more objective and more consistent than that propounded by the individual writers listed above.

The most difficult comparison to make is that between *The Ecclesiologist* and Pugin, for in their case there was a constant process of give and take.[229] The fact of the matter is that both theoretically and, more especially, liturgically there was a great deal of common ground between the Anglicans and the Catholic. In 1844 Pugin was even asked to design the Ecclesiological Society's signet.[230] Scott commented on Pugin's influence at that time (the early 1840's) in his memoirs, which he started to write in 1864:

'In 1841 . . . I had awakened to a truer sense of the dignity of the subject. This awakening arose, I think, from two causes operating almost simultaneously: my first acquaintance with the Cambridge Camden Society, and my reading Pugin's articles in the *Dublin Review*. I may be in error as to their coincidence of date.'[231]

Scott was probably not in error: Pugin began his series of articles in 1840, and *The Ecclesiologist* was launched in 1841. Scott also read publications by Petit, which **may** well have been drawn to his attention by a review in *The Ecclesiologist*. But like the reviewer, Scott may also have been attracted by Petit's drawings, which gave a general impression of architectural arrangements, and his eclecticism, which was completely non-doctrinaire. It is unlikely that he will have noted the evident pleasure which Petit derived from industrial buildings. Considering that he was writing in 1841, Petit's attitude to such buildings seems quite remarkable:

'If it were asked which of the buildings of the present day bid fairest to command the admiration of posterity, I should answer, without hesitation those connected with our railways. I do not speak of the ornamental, but the essential parts, as the bridges and viaducts, – many of which may be pronounced the very perfection of mechanical beauty . . . Here is a field, not for the mere display of fancy, but for the application of practical science. The beauty resulting from it will always please and interest us, as being grounded in physical facts; and we may therefore consider it as in a manner dictated by nature herself. But it speaks ill for the spirit of an age when buildings which owe their existence to the highest motive and feeling of all – Piety – shew a decidedly inferior character.'[232]

Although Petit approved of the revival of mediaeval design, especially for church architecture, he avoided the rigid attitude adopted by the Gothic Revivalists, who were convinced of the technical excellence of Gothic architecture but refused to acknowledge any architectural qualities in modern industrial buildings.

This kind of attitude is even found in Bartholomew's writings which, with the single exception of Pugin's *Contrasts*, are the most stimulating of all the theoretical publications to appear at that time. In his *Specifications for Practical Architecture* Bartholomew suggested that

229 In the first twenty volumes of *The Ecclesiologist* Pugin is mentioned more often than any other architect. For example, he appears in: I (2nd ed. 1843), p.179; II (1843), pp.141–4 and 184–5; V (1846), pp.3 and 10–16; VI (1846), p.84; VIII (1848), pp.26, 79, 116, 132, 242, 327, and 399; IX (1849), pp.152, 163, 212, 289–90, and 369–70; X (1850), pp.204, 206, 322–6, and 393–9; XI (1850), pp.44, 235 and 271; XII (1851), pp.205–11 and 355–6; XIII (1852), pp.58, 278 and 352–7; XIV (1853), pp.25 and 76; XVI (1855), p.139; XVII (1856), pp.87 and 185; XX (1859), p.268. – This list is not complete.

230 *Ibid.*, III (1844), p.184. – See also Stanton, *Gothic Revival and American Church Architecture* (1968), pp. ix and xi.

231 Scott, *Personal and Professional Recollections* (1879), p.87.

232 J[ohn] L[ewis] Petit, *Remarks on Church Architecture*, 2 vols. (London, n.d. [1841]), II, p.151. – It was some time before *The Ecclesiologist* came to appreciate railway architecture; see *The Ecclesiologist* X (1850), pp.121–2.

Greek, Roman, and Gothic architecture were all 'purely structural' (thus anticipating the assessment made by Viollet-le-Duc in his *Entretiens*). But having done so, he then went on to devote five sections to Gothic architecture and only three to the whole of Antique architecture.[233] Moreover, although he cited the Old Testament as one of the authorities for his functionalist doctrine, in actual fact – and unlike Pugin and Street – he did not expect to see an architectural renaissance brought about by ecclesiastical reform but by the integration of architecture and engineering:

'Formerly, every architect was a civil engineer, and every civil engineer was an architect; but from the vast employment in modern times, in the making of canals, docks, bridges and rail-roads, the profession has become split into two; and this has tended, perhaps more than any other circumstance, to the ruin of real practical science in architecture.'[234]

If we disregard the initial reference to happier times, this passage is not at all what we would expect from a Gothic Revivalist. But let us look at Bartholomew's examples:

'The beautiful forms of the new London Bridge, of the new Bridge at Turin, and of the Eddystone Lighthouse, shew of what Civil Engineering is capable without sacrifice of practical utility.'[235]

Both of these bridges are of stone, a material which Bartholomew loved. 'Let us', he said, 'become once more REAL FREE-MASONS.'[236] But when Bartholomew enumerates the principles underlying the use of materials – 'simple repose, equipoise, tie' – we are also reminded of iron architecture.[237] Copyism Bartholomew found objectionable. 'One thing for which we modern English architects are eminent, is for the servile copying of ancient works [238] ... *Second-handedness* in architecture is the peculiar folly of modern England: it is wasteful pedantry of the worst kind: it leads men to prefer things unstable, inconvenient, and tasteless, – for taste has always relation to the age, the climate, and the destination.'[239]

The same Bartholomew dismissed the Elizabethan style as corrupt and the 'transition style' as impure, which was of course in keeping with his aversion to 'second-handedness'. But having done so, he then called for 'chronological symmetrie' and ridiculed any architect who had failed to master the syntax of Gothic architecture as a 'refined antiquary'. Finally, he proclaimed the Gothic not just as an ecclesiastical, but as a universal style, which could be mastered only by those who had grasped its manner and developed a genuine feeling for it.[240]

Edward Lacy Garbett made a similar distinction between 'false (i.e. acquired) expression' and 'natural expression'. At the same time he insisted that 'the province of expression must not be overrated'.[241] Under 'expression' Garbett understood what earlier generations had meant by 'character'; namely, the definition of an architectural project by means of particular traits or styles. Garbett pointed out that once a given style was proclaimed as a universal style, genre styles became meaningless. Consequently, if an architect wished to distinguish between a club house and a private residence he would have to use

233 Bartholomew, *Specifications for Practical Architecture* (2nd ed. 1846), § XVIII ff.

234 *Ibid.*, § 76.

235 *Ibid.*

236 *Ibid.*, § 331.

237 *Ibid.*, § 389.

238 *Ibid.*, § 664.

239 *Ibid.*, § 783.

240 *Ibid.*, § 622–43, 663, 763, and 766.

241 Garbett, *Rudimentary Treatise* (1850), pp. 25–6.

printed signs.[242] With this argument Garbett disposed of a theoretical problem which had arisen as a direct result of the diversification of architectural styles. By contrast, *The Ecclesiologist* continued to insist on a special style for parsonages for many years to come. Garbett, who had received a philosophical training and was adept in the definition of concepts, also clarified two other key-words which had emerged at the end of the eighteenth century:

'Whatever would be sublime or excellent in essentials, the same is picturesque in non-essentials.'[243]

Garbett held that constructive truth and constructive unity were the real basis of both Greek and Gothic architecture. And since the Gothic style had derived from the use of stone vaults he argued that all Gothic buildings must be vaulted and that consequently 'the whole of modern Gothic architecture is a constructive falsehood'.[244] Up to this point Garbett is at one with Bartholomew (whom he mentions in his writings). But whereas Bartholomew simply enumerated three principles underlying the *use* of materials – 'simple repose, equipoise, tie' – Garbett designated three constructive *styles* – based on 'cross-strain', 'compression' and 'tension', respectively. The third of these he regarded as futuristic.[245] (In justice to Bartholomew it should be pointed out that he was writing in 1841, nine years before Garbett.)

It was probably due to the influence of Garbett's *Treatise* that, from *c*.1850 onwards, Street began to dissociate himself from the view, which was still being advocated by Pugin and *The Ecclesiologist*, that the English country churches of the Middle Ages provided ideal models for ecclesiastical architecture. Garbett, for whom the Gothic was essentially a vaulted style, hated the open timber roofs in these churches; and when the Brandon brothers and the editors of *The Ecclesiologist* maintained that the 9000 country churches in England provided an inexhaustible supply of authentic precedents, he angrily accused them of self-delusion. He also poured scorn on the rural masons of medieaval England who, he claimed, had been both incompetent and insensitive.[246] According to Garbett, architecture had always been an international and an esoteric art form, which had remained impervious to popular influence.[247]

It was entirely in keeping with the intellectual climate of the mid-nineteenth century that Garbett should have developed a colour theory based partly on the odd snippets of information supplied by the eighteenth-century garden theorists and partly on the findings of the nineteenth-century physicists. In this theory Garbett equated complementary, contrasting, and harmonious colours, and compared them with the diminished sixth in music by reference to the wave theory of light.[248] Garbett was a versatile writer. Whether he was connected in any way with the architect Edward Garbett, who built the neo-Early English church at Theale (Berkshire), or with the Reverend Edward Garbett (1817–87) is not known; but judging by his writings, it seems most unlikely that Garbett was a practising architect.[249]

James Fergusson (1808–86), who spent a number of years in India as a business man and who wrote with the same brash assurance as

242 *Ibid.*, p.27.

243 *Ibid.*, p.106.

244 *Ibid.*, p.208, note, and pp.130–2.

245 *Ibid.*, pp.132, 135 and 260–4.

246 *Ibid.*, pp.238–9.

247 *Ibid.*, p.249.

248 *Ibid.*, pp.38–9.

249 Goodhart-Rendel, 'English Gothic Architecture of the Nineteenth Century' (1924), p.325. – Colvin, *A Biographical Dictionary of English Architects* (1954), p.224. – British Museum Reading Room Catalogue.

Garbett, certainly was not a practising architect. Fergusson embarked on his career as an architectural writer after his return to England in 1845, and his *Illustrated Handbook* appeared ten years later. The completely uninhibited works which Fergusson published subsequently are, of course, much more entertaining.[250] But his *Handbook* tells us more about his position *vis-à-vis* Bartholomew, Garbett and *The Ecclesiologist*.

In the opening pages of his *Handbook* Fergusson regretted the babel of styles,[251] insisting that, until the end of the mediaeval period, the true basis of all architecture had been a combination of utility and ornamental construction:
'Architecture is nothing less than the art of ornamental and ornamented construction.'[252]

Fergusson's love of ornament enabled him to follow in the steps of Robert Willis in recognizing the decorative and expressive character of the Gothic vault shafts. In fact, he went much further than Willis in this regard, for he considered that in many cases flying buttresses were used not in order to counteract the outward thrust of the vault, but simply to express it.[253]

When, as is often the case, Fergusson points to the constructive beauty of ships as an object lesson for contemporary architects, when he praises the design of the warehouses in the industrial towns of the north of England, and when he enthuses over the Crystal Palace, he seems more progressive than *The Ecclesiologist*.[254] He loses this advantage, however, when he insists on a fixed hierarchy of values for different building materials, ranging from large ashlar down to bricks, and reserves judgement on cast-iron buildings until sufficient numbers have been erected.[255] Fergusson is more or less in line with *The Ecclesiologist* when he says:
'Art, however, will not be regenerated by buildings so ephemeral as Crystal Palaces, or so prosaic as Manchester warehouses, nor anything so essentially utilitarian as the works of our engineers.'[256]

But he falls far behind *The Ecclesiologist* when he tries to show how a plain warehouse can be transformed into a stately bank by producing five sketches showing successive stages of such a conversion.[257] Fergusson was also quite capable of making contradictory statements. For example: he condemned a vast range of buildings, from St Peter's, Rome to the Houses of Parliament in Westminster, and yet he looked to a style of architecture that had been developed from the Neo-Renaissance mode of English clubs and business houses as the hope for the future;[258] his own bank sketches were executed in this Neo-Renaissance style, and yet he insisted that the Italians had never been great architects;[259] finally, Fergusson maintained that all imitations were mere masquerades,[260] and yet he himself believed in a new style, of which *The Ecclesiologist* laconically observed: 'From some period it *must* start.'[261]

Of all the English architectural theorists writing during the lifetime of *The Ecclesiologist* John Ruskin (1819–1900) was the most

250 Maurice Craig, 'James Fergusson' in *Concerning Architecture, Essays on Architectural Writers and Writing Presented to Nikolaus Pevsner*, edited by John Summerson (London, 1968), pp. 140–52.

251 Fergusson, *The Illustrated Handbook of Architecture* (1855), I, p. xxv.

252 *Ibid.*, p. xxviii.

253 *Ibid.*, p. xliii f.

254 *Ibid.*, pp. liii–lviii.

255 *Ibid.*, pp. xxxii–xxxiv.

256 *Ibid.*, p. lvii.

257 *Ibid.*, p. xxvii.

258 *Ibid.*, pp. xxvi and lvi.

259 *Ibid.*, p. xvii; II, p.765.

260 *Ibid.*, p. xxvi.

261 Review in *The Ecclesiologist*, XVII (1856), pp.23–31 and 259–67; quotation taken from *ibid.*, p.24.

contradictory and – at least as far as contemporary patrons were concerned – the most influential. He also knew less about the practical side of building than any of his colleagues. It is not only modern readers who have found Ruskin verbose, contradictory and slow to acknowledge the achievements of others.[262] All these faults were noted by the editors of *The Ecclesiologist*. But, as good Victorians, they none the less praised his 'eloquent and earnest pen'.[263]

Let us first consider Ruskin's *Seven Lamps*, as seen through the eyes of *The Ecclesiologist*.[264] The contributor who reviewed this work noted with evident satisfaction that Ruskin shared the periodical's views in all major respects. For example, he insisted on authentic materials, he was opposed to ornaments that had been pressed or cast, he liked handmade articles and wanted them to look as if they were handmade, he recognized the importance of light and shadow, he ridiculed the idea of an entirely new style, and he recommended 'the English earliest Middle-Pointed' as the most appropriate model. But the reviewer also noted certain differences of opinion. Ruskin still hoped that an acceptable style of iron architecture might be developed and that the Gothic might acquire a new and independent lease of life from the introduction of 'geometrical colour-mosaic'. Neither of these developments seemed plausible to the reviewer, who also dissociated himself from Ruskin's confusing theory of imitation.

Despite Ruskin's extreme verbosity, *The Ecclesiologist* neatly identified the one really independent and fertile argument in his book: the idea that the modern system of specialization was reducing the craftsman to a mere robot and his products to purely functional objects devoid of beauty. This Ruskin considered to be a poor substitute for independent works, i.e. works executed in their entirety by a single individual, which gave pleasure to both the craftsman and the viewer, even when their execution was clumsy.[265] The sixth chapter in the second volume of Ruskin's *Stones of Venice*, which bears the title 'The Nature of Gothic', was reprinted for the Working Men's College in 1854. Another edition, for which William Morris wrote a preface, appeared in Morris's Kelmscott Press in 1892. And finally, the Morris edition was republished in London in 1899. Incidentally, in the *Stones of Venice* Ruskin did not hesitate to draw attention to the social unrest of the late 1840's and early 1850's while in the twenty-seven years of its existence *The Ecclesiologist* only once referred to a building strike, and then only in passing.[266]

By now it should be apparent that, as far as modern design was concerned, *The Ecclesiologist* and its supporters were essentially progressive. But were they sufficiently progressive to justify the title that I have given to this part of my study? In other words, was the Gothic Revival a reform movement?

Certainly, *The Ecclesiologist* fulfilled many of the requirements of a reforming periodical. It helped to dispose of the moribund doctrine of architectural character by proclaiming the Gothic as a universal style, thus dispensing with the need for individual genre styles. It rejected the

262 *Ibid.*, XII (1851), pp.275–6; XIV (1853), p.415.

263 *Ibid.*, X (1850), p.111.

264 *Ibid.*, pp.111–20. – See also the latest work on Ruskin: George P. Landow, *The Aesthetic and Critical Theories of John Ruskin* (Princeton [N.J.], 1971).

265 John Ruskin, *The Stones of Venice*, II: *The Sea-Stories* (London, 1853); quotations taken from the *Library Edition: The Works of John Ruskin*, edited by E. T. Cook and Alexander Wedderburn, X (London and New York, 1904), pp.191–6 (= Chap. VI, § 2–16) and 202 (= Chap. VI, § 22). – *The Ecclesiologist*, XIV (1853), pp.415–27, esp. p.423.

266 *Ibid.*, XX (1859), p.427. – Ruskin, *Library Edition*, X (1904), p.195.

hierarchical values traditionally accorded to the different building materials and so was able to come to terms with the important new iron buildings erected in the nineteenth century. Within its own sphere of influence it effectively opposed the decorative mania of Victorian England by its insistence on constructive 'truth' and 'reality'. It countered the popular demand for picturesque arrangements by stipulating that all architectural arrangements must serve a functional purpose. It recognized the deep gulf which divided the traditional conception of 'original' art from the new conception of 'mass-produced' art that was gaining currency in the nineteenth century. Consequently, it was also aware of the schism between the all-powerful architect and the dedicated stone-mason, and so lent its support to the new craft school attached to the Architectural Museum. Finally, it gained the collaboration of reputable architects such as George Edmund Street, who later became the mentor of the younger generation of architects which was to resolve, for the rest of their period at least, the problem posed by the babel of styles.[267]

The Ecclesiologist was, of course, concerned primarily with churches, parsonages, and schoolhouses. It is understandable, therefore, that it should have paid little attention to general housebuilding and town-planning requirements, to new industrial projects and the special organizational problems which these involved, or to the great host of technical innovations which made their appearance in the nineteenth century. Such matters were left to the building magazines, which dealt with them in great detail. The same is true of both the *Annales archéologiques* and the *Kölner Domblatt*. Consequently, the real significance of *The Ecclesiologist* emerges when we compare it with its Continental counterparts.

3 The 'Annales archéologiques'

The *Annales archéologiques* was a private publication. It was launched by Adolphe-Napoléon Didron (1806–67), the journalist, iconographer, dealer in devotional objects, and stained-glass window designer, and his brother, the publisher. Later it was inherited by Didron's nephew, who continued to run it for a period of two years after his uncle's death.[268] Nearly all the articles in this periodical were signed; many were written by Didron himself.

Didron considered that 'archéologie' was synonymous with 'the history of mediaeval art' or, to be more precise, 'the history of mediaeval religious art'; and he regarded the 'renaissance de l'architecture ogivale' as the end object of the 'mouvement archéologique'.[269] Despite its name, Didron's *Annales archéologiques* dealt more thoroughly with the Gothic Revival than any other French periodical of its day, and provided this movement with its most effective mouthpiece.[270]

The most important of the architects who contributed to the *Annales*

267 *The Ecclesiologist*, XIX (1858), pp.46 and 172 (Philip Webb and Richard Norman Shaw).

268 For information about Didron aîné as a journalist see: *Annales archéologiques*, V (1846), p.284; VIII (1848), p.106; as a dealer in devotional objects see *ibid.*, VIII (1848) pp.61–4; IX (1849), pp.354–5; X (1850), p.162; XI (1851), pp.60 and 373; as a stained-glass designer see *ibid.*, IX (1849), pp.351–6; XII (1852), pp.97 and 336; XVII (1857), p.309.

269 *Ibid.*, VIII (1848), p.336; XVI (1856), p.185.

270 Hautecœur, *Histoire de l'architecture classique*, VI (1955), pp.292–5. – Léon, *La vie des monuments français* (1951), pp.92–7, 120–6, 214–17, and 239–40.

were Lassus (1807–57), Viollet-le-Duc (1814–79) and Alfred Darcel (1818–93); the most important of the archaeologists was Félix de Verneilh (1819–64). The Société d'Archéologie nationale, which was founded as a direct result of the Revolution of 1848, made no real impact. Didron was president of the society, the Baron de Guilhermy (1808–78) was vice-president, and Lassus and Viollet-le-Duc were *commissaires délégués* (plenipotentiaries).[271] They hoped to bring about 'la régénération de l'art par l'étude, l'enseignement et l'application de l'archéologie nationale', but their only positive act appears to have been an application to the Minister of the Interior for permission to erect an architectural museum with departments for drawings and casts on the site of the Roman baths at the Hôtel de Cluny.[272]

Neither the members of the Académie Royale des Beaux-Arts nor the countless architects – many of them in government service – who had received their training at the Academy were opposed to the study of mediaeval styles of building. But they took strong exception to their practical application. The Academy was founded in 1671. Lectures on architecture were given from then onwards, and diplomas were awarded from 1867 to 1940. Since then all French architects have had to hold a state diploma, which means that the state now has a monopoly as far as architectural training is concerned.[273] In the eighteenth century the Academy had enjoyed a virtual monopoly in this field, and had zealously guarded this privilege against would-be competitors. Thus, Jacques-François Blondel (1705–74), who founded a school of architecture in Paris in 1743, was made a member of the Academy in 1755 and appointed Professor of Architecture in 1762. In this case the opposition was simply swallowed up.[274] In 1830 Henri Labrouste (1801–75) opened a progressive atelier, where he trained a number of leading Gothic Revivalists, including Lassus and Emile Boeswillwald (1815–96), although he himself designed no buildings in the new style.[275]

Even as a boy Viollet-le-Duc had not taken kindly to school,[276] and instead of going on from school to train at the Ecole des Beaux-Arts (the Academy school), he worked, first for Jean-Jacques-Marie Huvé (1783–1858), and subsequently for Achille Leclère (1785–1853). His principal objection to the Ecole des Beaux-Arts was its uniformity: 'The Ecole is a mould for architects; by the time they leave, they are all virtually identical. M. Huyot has his mould, M. Percier has his mould, M. Lebas has his mould, etc. . . . so that if we look at the work of people who have passed through the Ecole, we are able to place them in categories – these belong to Huyot, these to Percier, these to Lebas.'[277]

But Viollet-le-Duc did not like working in architectural offices either, and eventually became a teacher himself. In 1834 he obtained a post as *professeur suppléant* at the School of Drawing in the Rue de l'Ecole de Médecine, where he continued to teach until 1850. In 1837, when the Ecole des Beaux-Arts tried to take over the School of Drawing, he helped to organize resistance;[278] and in 1856, when Labrouste closed his school of architecture, Viollet-le-Duc agreed to instruct a group of students who did not want to transfer to the Ecole des Beaux-Arts. But

271 *Annales archéologiques*, VIII (1848), pp.237–41 and 334–5.

272 2 November 1848. – For an account of the origins of the museum see R[ené] Schneider, *Quatremère de Quincy et son intervention dans les arts (1788–1830)* . . . (Paris, 1910), pp.88–90.

273 Sàndor Kuthy, *Julien Guadet (1834–1908)*, thèse de doctorat, Faculté des Lettres et Sciences humaines de l'Université de Paris, 1968 (typescript), p.11.

274 Hautecœur, *Histoire de l'architecture classique*, III (1950), pp.466–8. – Robin [D.] Middleton, 'Jacques François Blondel and the *Cours d'Architecture*' in *Journal of the Society of Architectural Historians*, XVIII (1959), pp.140–8.

275 Hautecœur, *Histoire de l'architecture classique*, VI (1955), pp.241–8. – Paul Gout, *Viollet-le-Duc, sa vie, son œuvre, sa doctrine* (= *Revue de l'art chrétien*, supplément III), (Paris, Lille, Bruges, and Brussels, 1914), pp.155–9.

276 *Ibid.*, pp.12–19.

277 *Ibid.*, p.19 (Diary entry for 3 December, 1831): 'L'Ecole est un moule à architectes; il en sortent tous presque semblables. M. Huyot a son moule, M. Percier a son moule, M. Lebas a son moule, etc. . . . De sorte que lorsque l'on sort de l'Ecole, en voyant vos œuvres, on peut vous classer soit dans les Huyot ou les Percier ou les Lebas.'

278 Gout, *Viollet-le-Duc* (1914), pp.30–1.

this venture was short-lived. The students were high-spirited, and Viollet-le-Duc walked out on them when they began painting obscene pictures on the walls.[279] Later, he invited a number of pupils to live in his house, including Anatole de Baudot (1834–1915), who proved a loyal disciple. On 15 January 1857 Viollet-le-Duc began to give lectures in his atelier, and arranged for their publication in the form, and under the title, of *Entretiens*, which appeared in instalments. Didron passed the following comment:

'We will announce their publication immediately they appear. This is the first time that anyone has tried to teach the history of mediaeval architecture and provide instruction on the maintenance and conservation of buildings in a French atelier. All honour to M. Viollet-le-Duc for his initiative. The talent and prodigious energy, the archaeological and practical knowledge of this Master, who has been entrusted with so many important and highly diverse commissions, will make his atelier a meeting place for the new generation of architects.'[280]

By 1859 Didron was able to announce the publication of the *Sixième Entretien*.[281] Four years later, in 1863, Viollet-le-Duc persuaded the Emperor, Napoleon III, with whom he was on friendly terms, to issue a decree designed to curb the power of the Academy.[282] The principal features of this decree were a reduction in the upper age limit for the coveted *Prix de Rome* and the creation of a new chair at the Ecole des Beaux-Arts in the History of Art and Aesthetics, which was given to Viollet-le-Duc, who was generally expected to concentrate on the mediaeval period in his lectures. These measures were unpopular, and Julien Guadet (1834–1908), who subsequently became a professor himself, had no difficulty in organizing student resistance. As a result, Viollet-le-Duc's lectures were so badly disrupted that he was obliged to relinquish his post. And so his attempt to take over the Ecole des Beaux-Arts, which he had always despised and frequently attacked, proved a failure.

The first of these attacks had been made in the *Annales archéologiques* in 1839 in connexion with the Gothic Revival design submitted by Franz Christian Gau (1790–1853) for the Church of Sainte-Clotilde on the Place Bellechasse in Paris.[283] Although – interestingly enough – Viollet-le-Duc's uncle and tutor Etienne-Jean Delécluze tried to persuade Gau to turn his back on the Gothic, and Didron urged him to abandon his mixed style,[284] he steadfastly refused to do so. In the end the Paris city council approved his third design, which was still based on a mixture of historical and regional styles, and so sparked off a general debate in the Academy on the merits of Gothic and Gothic Revival architecture. The majority view was subsequently reported by Raoul-Rochette (Désiré-Raoul Rochette), the permanent secretary to the Academy, in his 'Considérations sur la question de savoir s'il est convenable, au XIXᵉ siècle, de bâtir des églises en style gothique'. This report was printed, together with Viollet-le-Duc's reply, in the *Annales archéologiques*.[285]

Raoul-Rochette conceded that Gothic architecture evoked an

279 *Ibid.*, pp.158–9.

280 *Annales archéologiques*, XVII (1857), p.54. 'Nous les annoncerons lorsque la publication en sera faite. C'est la première fois qu'on enseigne en France, dans un atelier, l'histoire de l'architecture du moyen âge, et qu'on y donne des instructions sur l'entretien et la conservation des édifices. Une pareille initiative fait honneur à M. Viollet-le-Duc. Le talent et l'activité prodigieuse, la science archéologique et la science pratique du maître, auquel sont confiés des travaux si importants, si divers et si nombreux, feront de cet atelier le rendez-vous de la génération nouvelle des architectes.' – The original spelling of his name was Viollet-Leduc. I have used the modern form (Viollet-le-Duc), both for original documents and for later commentaries.

281 *Annales archéologiques*, XIX (1859), p.350.

282 *Eugène Viollet-le-Duc, 1814–1879*, [Catalogue de la] Caisse nationale des Monuments historiques (Paris, 1965), pp.140–7. – Sàndor Kuthy, 'Julien Guadet et l'enseignement de l'architecture' [extraits de la thèse de doctorat] in *Architecture – mouvement – continuité, Bulletin de la Société des Architectes diplômés par le Gouvernement*, No.176 (February 1970), pp.26–31.

283 A[uguste] Bouillet, *Sainte-Clotilde . . .* (Paris, n.d. [*c*.1900]). – Dr Peter Kurmann kindly drew my attention to this publication and also provided me with a copy. – Jacques Lethève, *Sainte-Clotilde . . .* (Paris, n.d. [1947]). – Karl Hammer, *Jakob Ignaz Hittorff, ein Pariser Baumeister, 1792–1867 . . .* (Stuttgart, 1968), pp.226–7.

284 Ernst Weyden, 'Zwei Pariser Kirchen' in *Organ für christliche Kunst*, V (1855), pp.256–7, 264–9 and 289; see esp. *ibid.*, p.268. – *Annales archéologiques*, V (1846), p.187.

285 *Ibid.*, IV (1846), pp.325–53.

69–71

emotional response: it recalled the great period of Philip Augustus and Saint Louis, aroused man's religious sense, made him reflect on the deity, called to mind the heavenly Jerusalem, and appealed to the imagination; consequently, Gothic monuments deserved to be protected and preserved. But he saw no merit in Gothic imitations, and refused to accept that Gothic architecture was the epitome of Christian architecture. If this were so, he asked, why had the Gothic failed to establish itself in Rome, the hub of the Catholic universe? Christianity, he insisted, did not need a special style:

'We would be doing an injustice to Christianity, or completely misrepresenting its spirit, if we were to assume that it had need of a special kind of art in order to express its beliefs.'[286]

The academicians' aversion to imitation was not restricted to the Gothic. They found copies of the Parthenon as objectionable as copies of the Sainte-Chapelle, since both of these buildings were symbols of societies which had long since disappeared. Where Gothic churches were concerned, however, they also criticized the use of flying buttresses on the grounds that they disrupted the visual appearance of the façades and failed to provide adequate support. The lack of a basic module in Gothic architecture was a further bone of contention. For all these reasons the Academy was not prepared to recommend the adoption of the Gothic style for public buildings, although it had no objection to its use for churches and castles built by private individuals:

'... it believes that if confronted with this plagiarized or counterfeit Gothic, people who are moved by the old, the true, Gothic would remain cold and indifferent.'[287]

Finally, Raoul-Rochette insisted that the nineteenth century would have to discover its own kind of Christian architecture. He was confident that, just as the architects of the Renaissance had evolved a new style by basing their work on the Antique, so the nineteenth-century architects would be able to develop a new style in their turn.

In his 'Réponse aux considérations de l'Académie des Beaux-Arts, sur la question de savoir s'il est convenable, au XIXe siècle, de bâtir des églises en style gothique' Viollet-le-Duc retaliated with considerable polemical skill. In assessing his remarks it should be remembered that he remained an atheist throughout his life, insisting that, when he died, no clergyman of any denomination was to accompany his coffin to the grave.[288] In his opening gambit Viollet-le-Duc drew attention to the national character of the Gothic:

'But who in their right mind would ever have maintained that the Gothic is the only form of Christian art? What we are asking, gentlemen, is that everybody should revert to an art form which originated in our country. We live on the forty-eighth parallel.'[289]

Viollet-le-Duc then suggested that the Academy was encouraging mixed styles or, to use the expression in vogue among French architects at that time, eclecticism.[290] But Viollet-le-Duc was also flippant:

'The Gothic having degenerated, the Renaissance had recourse to the

286 *Ibid.*, p.329: 'On ferait tort au christianisme, ou méconnaîtrait tout à fait son esprit, si l'on croyait qu'il ait besoin d'une forme d'art particulière pour exprimer son culte.'

287 *Ibid.*, p.331: 'Elle croit qu'en présence de ce gothique de plagiat, de contrefaçon, les populations qui se sentent émues devant le vieux, devant le vrai gothique, resteraient froides et indifférentes.'

288 Gout, *Viollet-le-Duc* (1914), p.70, note 3.

289 *Annales archéologiques*, IV (1846), p.336: 'Mais quel est l'homme sérieux qui ait jamais prétendu que le gothique résumât à lui seul l'art chrétien? Ce que nous demandons à tous, messieurs, c'est le retour à un art né dans notre pays. Nous sommes par le 48e degré de latitude.'

290 *The Ecclesiologist*, XVII (1856), pp.86–91, 284–7, 362–4, and 414–21. – *Annales archéologiques*, II (1845), pp.76–7, 305 and 333; IV (1846), pp.337–8; XI (1851), p.129; XVI (1856), p.121.

Antique. Today the Renaissance has been exhausted in its turn; and so we want to make use of the Gothic.'[291]

Viollet-le-Duc then suggested that the minor liturgical differences between thirteenth- and nineteenth-century usage should be disregarded, and pointed out that the architects responsible for the Parisian churches of Saint-Eustache and Saint-Sulpice had also based their designs on Gothic models. Finally, he observed:

'First, we want our artists to study our thirteenth-century architecture, but to study it as they would study their own language, so that they grasp, not only the words, but the grammar and spirit as well . . . if they take as their point of departure a type of art, whose principles are both simple and applicable in our country, and whose form is both beautiful and rational, then – with their undoubted talents – our architects will be able to make the kind of modifications required by present-day needs and customs. Once the basic principle has been grasped, then within certain limits everybody can be allowed a free hand; in our country, with its modern industry and activities, this national art will soon make headway.'[292]

Viollet-le-Duc regarded thirteenth-century Gothic as an entirely beautiful and rational form of architecture which, because it was based on principles instead of rules, was compatible with modern building techniques and met the requirements of modern living. And since it had originated in France, it was not only a national style of architecture in its own right, it also provided the point of departure for a new national style of the future.

Despite the influence of Chateaubriand and Hugo, French enthusiasm for the Gothic was undoubtedly inspired, above all, by the conception of the Gothic cathedrals as 'technical miracles'. This formed the whole basis of Viollet-le-Duc's doctrine. He probably acquired much of his technical knowledge from Lassus, with whom he collaborated in 1842–3 on the design for the restoration of Notre-Dame in Paris. By 1845 Lassus was classifying all stone arches as Gothic:

'The actual structure of the Madeleine [in Paris] is based on the pointed arch, its visual form on the lintel. This may seem a strange combination, admittedly, but that is the way it is; consequently, the Madeleine is a Gothic monument, and the architect was quite right to make it Gothic, for the sake of greater stability.'[293]

By way of a prelude to his famous *Dictionnaire raisonné de l'architecture française du XIe au XVIe siècle* Viollet-le-Duc published a series of articles in the *Annales archéologiques*, starting with the very first issue, under the title 'Construction des édifices religieux en France depuis le commencement du christianisme jusqu'au XVIe siècle'.[294] In the 1840's, when these articles appeared, he was still of the opinion that Greek temple design had been evolved from timber-framed buildings; consequently, the vaulted construction of the French cathedrals appeared to him to be even more striking:

'In the French cathedrals the principle of timber construction was forgotten; there the VAULT system alone was employed, on a larger scale

---

291 *Ibid.*, IV (1846), p.347: 'Le gothique étant perverti, la Renaissance s'est servie de l'antique. Aujourd'hui la Renaissance est usée à son tour; eh bien, nous voulons nous servir du gothique.'

292 *Annales archéologiques*, IV (1846), p.352: 'Nous demandons que notre architecture du XIIIe siècle soit d'abord étudiée par nos artistes, mais étudiée comme on doit étudier sa langue, c'est à dire de façon à en connaître non-seulement les mots, mais la grammaire et l'esprit . . .; partant d'un art dont les principes sont simples et applicables dans notre pays, dont la forme est belle et rationelle à la fois, nos architectes auront assez de talent pour apporter à cet art les modifications nécessitées par des besoins récents, par des coutumes nouvelles. Le principe une fois enseigné, mais sous restrictions, laissez faire chacun; dans notre pays, au milieu de l'activité et de l'industrie moderne, cet art nationale ne tardera pas à progresser.'

293 *Annales archéologiques*, II (1845), p.74: 'A la Madeleine, la construction réelle est en ogive et la forme apparente en plate-bande. Cela peut sembler étrange, nous en convenons, mais cependant cela est: par le fait, la Madeleine est un monument ogival, et l'architecte a eu raison de le faire ainsi, pour la solidité.'

294 *Ibid.*, I (2nd ed. 1854), pp.334–7; II (1845), pp.78–85, 143–50 and 336–49; III (1845), pp.321–36; IV (1846), pp.266–83; VI (1847), pp.194–205 and 247–55. – Originally, the *Dictionnaire* was planned as a two-volume work, comprising some 480 pages – see *Annales archéologiques*, XIII (1853), p.228; later, four volumes were envisaged – see *ibid.*, XIV (1854), p.146; and, in the event, ten volumes appeared (Paris, 1854–68).

and with greater consistency than anywhere else.'[295]

It was in connexion with his vault theory that Viollet-le-Duc coined the misleading term 'élasticité',[296] by which he meant the plasticity of the mortar beds, which were thicker in the Early Gothic period than they had been before and which, he maintained, provided a cushion that prevented cracks from appearing in the masonry.[297] Viollet-le-Duc rejected the practice – which had set in during the Late Gothic period – of cutting extremely intricate forms from a single block, not because he found it distasteful, but because it was a waste of good stone.[298] Not surprisingly, therefore, he preferred the stylistic confusion of the nineteenth century to those forms of Gothic Revival architecture, in which neither construction nor stone-cutting were accorded any importance.[299] Like the English Gothic Revivalists, Viollet-le-Duc considered that the only time when reality and truth had been fully realized in architecture had been in the Gothic period:

'The most important of all qualities in architecture (in our view, at least) is that it should not conceal any needs, any necessities; on the contrary, it should display them, profit from them in the happiest manner possible, and deck them out with a beautiful form. We go further: we believe that the whole object of the art of architecture is to express a need, and consequently both the totality and the details of this art, both the composition and the execution, must move in unison towards this end object. The principle that we are formulating here is more or less the same as that subscribed to by the whole of the Ecole [des Beaux-Arts], but the conclusion which we draw from that principle, although entirely logical, does not enjoy the same support. Our conclusion is quite simply that French thirteenth-century architecture, which was fashioned from our materials and in our climate to suit our character, which is beautiful, often formally admirable, and not very costly, should be the only form of architecture studied in France; and it should be approached under three different headings: construction, art, and economy. For even if we wished to study Greek architecture, for us today this is no longer a serious or technically feasible proposition; it is not practical architecture but *archaeology*, in the precise meaning of that word.'[300]

This passage contains one or two allusions which call for comment. Thus, according to Viollet-le-Duc, construction is not beautiful in itself, and has to be decked out with a beautiful form. He also points out that the Gothic Revivalists were not the only architects to preach a functionalist doctrine, although they were the only ones to trace this functionalism back to a Gothic source. Whether, in this passage, Viollet-le-Duc was directing a shaft against Labrouste's first major building – the Bibliothèque Sainte-Geneviève, which was begun in 1843 – is not clear. But Lassaulx's non-Gothic vaulting was certainly a target.[301]

Throughout the centuries the French school of stone-cutting had benefited greatly from the fact that France was so liberally provided with limestone quarries; it is no accident that, where the English speak

295 *Ibid.*, II (1845), p.79: 'Dans les cathédrales de France, le principe de la construction en bois est oublié; c'est le système de la voûte qui est seul employé, c'est son application la plus étendue, la plus vraie.'

296 Pol Abraham, *Viollet-le-Duc et le rationalisme médiéval* (Paris, 1934). – *Annales archéologiques*, II (1845), pp.143 ff.

297 *Ibid.*, p.339.

298 *Ibid.*, III (1845), p.323.

299 *Ibid.*, p.333.

300 *Ibid.*, IV (1846), p.267: 'La première de toutes les qualités en architecture (à nos yeux du moins), c'est de ne dissimuler aucun besoin, aucune nécessité; c'est au contraire de les laisser voir, d'en profiter de la manière la plus heureuse et les couvrir d'une belle forme. Nous dirons plus: nous croyons que l'art de l'architecture a pour but l'expression d'un besoin, et il faut alors que l'ensemble comme les détails de cet art, que la composition et l'exécution concourent à ce but. Nous exprimons ici un principe qui est à peu près celui de toute l'école aujourd'hui, mais nous en tirons une conclusion qui, toute logique qu'elle puisse être, ne rencontre pas la même sympathie. Notre conclusion, c'est que l'architecture française du XIIIᵉ siècle, façonnée à notre caractère, bâtie avec nos matériaux, sous notre climat, belle, admirable de forme souvent, et peu dispendieuse, est la seule qui nous paraisse devoir être étudiée en France, 1° sous le rapport de la construction, 2° de l'art, 3° de l'économie. Que l'on étudie l'architecture grèque, à la bonne heure; c'est là réellement de l'*archéologie*, dans la véritable acception du mot, mais ce n'est plus pour nous de l'architecture sérieuse, applicable, bonne à exécuter enfin.'

301 *Annales archéologiques*, VI (1847), pp.194–5, note 2.

of the 'texture of the wall', or of 'bonding', the French use the much more expressive term *appareil*. During the Gothic Revival this term, which so aptly reflects the constructive beauty of buildings, was singled out for special attention. Not surprisingly, therefore, Didron was shocked to find that T. O. Weigel, of Leipzig, the best German publisher of architectural books of his day, had brought out an illustrated archaeological work, in which there was no reproduction of bonding. In his review of this publication Didron wrote: 'In archaeology, the texture of the wall is just as important as muscular and cutaneous tissue in the human anatomy.'[302]

But although they attached such great significance to masonry, the French never made the mistake of regarding Gothic buildings as stone buildings pure and simple. Their archaeological tradition and their restoration projects had taught them the importance of wooden and iron cramps. As early as 1846, in the fourth issue of the *Annales archéologiques*, Didron published a paper by Viollet-le Duc which contains almost the same material as the article on 'chainage' in the *Dictionnaire raisonné de l'architecture*.[303] The Germans and Austrians were far less enlightened. In 1879, when the Votivkirche designed by Heinrich von Ferstel (1828–83) was consecrated in Vienna, Moriz Thausing proudly pointed out that no iron cramps or pins had been used in its construction.[304] In mediaeval buildings, of course, the cramps often run across the windows, where they are almost indistinguishable from the bars used to hold the stained-glass windows.[305]

Given the general outlook of the French archaeologists and the nature of France's extant Gothic monuments, it is understandable that Didron and his associates should have sought different models from those recommended by Pugin and *The Ecclesiologist*. For the French the Gothic style was essentially constructive, and their ideal models were the episcopal and collegiate churches or – for smaller projects – the episcopal and palace chapels dating from the first half of the thirteenth century. The English ecclesiologists, on the other hand, were more interested in functional criteria, for as churchmen they felt responsible, above all, for the preservation of the liturgy and the provision of suitable fitments.

The first new church designs published by Didron were those produced for the miniature cathedral of Saint-Nicolas in Nantes (Loire-Atlantique). Initially, this project had been undertaken by Louis-Alexandre Piel (1808–41); but when he died, Lassus took it over (in 1843) and completed it in accordance with his own ideas. The choir, which was finished in 1848,[306] was executed in the same style as the Cathedral of Chartres (commenced in 1194), which Lassus had measured in connexion with the monograph that was compiled on the cathedral. (Work started on this monograph in 1842, and it was finally published in 1881 under the name of Paul Durand.)

Didron did his utmost to blur the distinction between the Gothic and the Gothic Revival. Thus, the plates of the new church in Nantes were entitled 'église du XIIIe siècle', while detailed estimates were appended,

72–4

302 *Ibid.*, xiv (1854), p.394: 'En archéologie, l'appareil est aussi important que le tissu musculaire et cutané en anatomie humaine.'

303 *Ibid.*, iv (1846), p.281.

304 M.T., *Die Votivkirche in Wien, Denkschrift des Baucomités, veröffentlicht zur Feier der Einweihung am 24. April 1879* (Vienna, 1879), p.24.

305 Viollet-le-Duc, *Dictionnaire raisonné de l'architecture*, ii (1867 edition), p.401 (passage concerning the Sainte-Chapelle in Paris).

306 *Annales archéologiques*, i (2nd ed. 1854), pp. V and 318; ii (1845), p.48; ix (1849), pp.114–15; xii (1852), p.167; xiii (1853), p.220.

307 *Ibid.*, VII (1847), pp.169–77; XII (1852), pp.164–7, 231–3 and 367–77; XIII (1853), pp.97–8, 166 (facing), 233–8 and 289 (facing); XIV (1854), p.25 (facing); XV (1855), pp.213–22; XVII (1857), pp.162–4.

308 *Ibid.*, II (1845), p.189; X (1850), pp. 216 and 285.

309 *Ibid.*, IV (1846), p.388.

310 *Ibid.*, V (1846), p.93.

311 *Ibid.*, XVIII (1858), p.366. – The period under discussion, both here and in *The Ecclesiologist*, is 1840–59.

312 *Annales archéologiques*, II (1845), pp. 258–60; VI (1847), pp.348–9. – Durand designed the pilgrims' church in Lourdes (Hautes-Pyrénées).

313 *Ibid.*, I (2nd ed. 1854), p. V.

314 *Ibid.*, p. V; XVII (1857), pp.162–4.

315 *Ibid.*, II (1845), p.310; V (1846), p.187.

316 *Ibid.*, III (1845), pp.159–60, note.

317 *Ibid.*, VI (1847), p.3.

318 *Ibid.*, p.7: 'L'architecte protestant de la future cathédrale fera une église romane. Mieux vaut le roman que le romain, et puisqu'on ne veut pas nous donner l'ogive, nous savons nous contenter du cintre qu'on nous offre.'

319 *Annales archéologiques*, XIV (1854), p.385: 'Tout projet en style prétendu moderne sera impitoyablement refusé. Le roman, qui est l'ogival en germe, le XIVe et le XVIe siècle, qui sont l'ogival malade ou agonisant, ne seront pas admis; on ne veut, je le répète, que du XIIIe siècle mûr et solide.'

without any further comment, to the plans of genuine old churches which Didron also published in the *Annales*. These were: the Church of Montréal (Yonne), the Church of Pontaubert (Yonne), the Church of Pont-sur-Yonne, the Archbishop's Chapel in Rheims and the Chapel of Sainte-Croix in Montmajour (Bouches-du-Rhône).[307]

Didron was always ready to recommend a specific model for any new church. Thus, he advocated the Archbishop's Chapel in Rheims for the Sacré-Cœur in Moulins, although his friend Lassus, who was the architect, preferred to create a design of his own, which he based on the general *style* of a mediaeval building, namely Chartres Cathedral.[308] Didron also recommended Notre-Dame in Villeneuve-le-Comte (Seine-et-Marne) as a model for rural churches,[309] the Rheims palimpsests for Gothic-Revival façades,[310] and the Abbey Church of Saint-Yved in Braine (Aisne) for a large church (probably Saint-Léon, which was started in 1860) in Nancy.[311]

Originally Didron had hoped to produce designs for three different model churches, in collaboration with the architect Hippolyte-Louis Durand (1801–82), and publish them independently of the *Annales*. But nothing ever came of this project;[312] and if we wish to assess his *beau idéal*, we have to turn to his critical and polemical articles.

From these we discover that, although the first designs published in the *Annales* (those for Lassus's Saint-Nicolas in Nantes) were based on the style of architecture dating from the closing years of Philip Augustus's reign (d.1226),[313] Didron stated his intention, from the outset, of publishing Romanesque designs as well. He was as good as his word, for in 1857 he reproduced the plans of Sainte-Croix in Montmajour.[314] Didron criticized Gau's Sainte-Clotilde on the grounds that it lacked the austerity appropriate to the period of Philip Augustus. In his opinion Gau had created a mixed style, based partly on Saint-Ouen in Rouen and partly on Cologne Cathedral, in an attempt to please both his original compatriots in Cologne and his new compatriots in Paris.[315] Didron placed a particularly high assessment on the façades of Notre-Dame in Paris and Notre-Dame in Laon (Aisne).[316] Not surprisingly, therefore, he thought very little of the Chapelle du Saint-Sacrement in Arras, and censured its architect, Alexandre-Charles Grigny (1815–67), for having succumbed to the *beauté coquette* of the fifteenth century.[317] On the subject of Marseille Cathedral he wrote: 'The Protestant architect of the projected cathedral will create a Romanesque church. Romanesque is better than Roman, and since we are not to be given the Gothic style, we shall content ourselves with the circular style.'[318]

Didron was well pleased when thirteenth-century Gothic was prescribed for the Lille competition: 'All so-called modern designs will be rejected out of hand. Nor will the Romanesque, which is but an embryonic form of the Gothic, or the fourteenth- and sixteenth-century styles, which are a morbid or moribund form, be acceptable; the only, I repeat only, style that is desired is thirteenth-century, pure and powerful.'[319]

69–71

142

But if Didron was pleased with the conditions laid down for the competition, he was disappointed by the result. Lassus's design, which he had wholeheartedly endorsed, was placed third, the first two places going to foreign competitors. This must have been doubly galling for Didron, since it was he who had suggested that the competition should be thrown open to foreign architects.[320]

Apart from the fact that they provided for a brick building – a requirement which Lassus had simply disregarded – the conditions faithfully reflected contemporary French attitudes to architecture. Eastlake was of the opinion that, apart from Viollet-le-Duc's *Dictionnaire raisonné de l'architecture française*, the Lille competition was the greatest single factor in attracting the attention of the English Gothic Revivalists to French models.[321]

This comment of Eastlake was made following a friendly debate conducted by Didron and his English correspondents.[322] Replying to an English architect, who defended his predilection for fourteenth-century models on the grounds that these were the true basis of the English national style, Didron wrote:

'Although the beautiful thirteenth-century French style suits all climates, all countries and all nations – as is evident from the cathedrals of Uppsala, Cologne, Canterbury, Amiens, Clermont-Ferrand etc. – we cannot blame M. Longueville Jones for preferring the fourteenth-century English style for English churches. If every nation had adhered to its own style, we would not have sought out the Parthenon in Athens or the Pantheon in Rome, in order to build ridiculous churches in France.'[323]

But Didron's own feelings of patriotism did not prevent him from rating the ornamental sculptures in Lincoln Cathedral more highly than those in Rheims Cathedral.[324] He formed this assessment during his first visit to England, which he made in order to attend the consecration of Pugin's church in Cheadle, whose regional and historical style Pugin defended on the same grounds as those advanced by Jones but which Didron found unacceptable. He objected, not only to the 'style ogival fleuri du XVe siècle', but also to the admixture of French thirteenth-century motifs and the timber roof in the chancel.[325]

This attack elicited a response from Beresford Hope, who argued that, in dating Pugin's design, Didron had been unduly influenced by French monuments, and insisted that the church in Cheadle was quite clearly derived from the fourteenth-century English style.[326]

Didron followed his accounts of his travels with a bibliography of English Gothic. Like *The Ecclesiologist*, he attacked the picturesque lithographs which had become fashionable in England, insisting that these contributed nothing to the history of architecture. Having done so, he went on to reject the vast majority of English models:

'When we see these monuments executed in an inferior style of architecture being proposed as models, we find it regrettable that England does not possess chapels as beautiful as the Sainte-Chapelle in Paris, the Archbishop's Chapel in Rheims, the Chapel of Saint-Jean-en-

320 *Annales archéologiques*, XVI (1856), pp.126 and 230.

321 Eastlake, *A History of the Gothic Revival* (1872), p.317.

322 In his analysis of the differences between French and English Gothic Revival theories Nikolaus Pevsner refers to other sources; see N.P., *Ruskin and Viollet-le-Duc: Englishness and Frenchness in the Appreciation of Gothic Architecture* ... (London, 1969).

323 *Annales archéologiques*, IV (1846), p.129: 'Quoique le beau XIIIe siècle français convienne à tous les climats, à tous les sols et à toutes les nations, comme les cathédrales d'Upsal, de Cologne, de Cantorbéry, d'Amiens, de Clermont-Ferrand, etc., en sont la preuve, nous ne saurions cependant désapprouver M. Longueville Jones de préférer le style anglais du XIVe siècle pour des églises anglaises. Si chaque nation restait chez elle, nous n'aurions pas été chercher le Parthénon à Athens ou le Panthéon de Rome, pour en faire de ridicules églises en France.'

324 *Annales archéologiques*, V (1846), p.245.

325 *Ibid.*, pp.292 and 298.

326 *Ibid.*, VI (1847), pp.67–9.

l'Ile in Corbeil [Seine-et-Oise], parish or abbey churches as beautiful as those in France, or sublime cathedrals such as may be found in nearly every French province. In England – and this cannot be said too often – examples of really noble mediaeval architecture are few and far between, and the architects of England are too enamoured of the declining Gothic.'[327]

In 1850 Beresford Hope and Didron again corresponded with one another on the question of suitable models. Beresford Hope still insisted that, as far as England was concerned, the fourteenth-century parish church was the ideal solution while Didron predicted that within ten years the English would go over to thirteenth-century models.[328] The Frenchman was to be proved right.

When Didron revisited England in 1851 he did not so much as mention the Crystal Palace in his reports, but he severely criticized the English for their bad taste and their lack of archaeological knowledge. He made an exception in the case of Pugin, who seemed to him at least to be moving in the right direction:

'... because M. Pugin, who is French, not only on his father's side, but also in his affinities and his archaeological taste, is moving towards the thirteenth century, although too slowly for our liking.'[329]

The International Exhibition staged in Paris in 1855, at which designs for new churches were displayed, provided the French public with a new insight into the state of English architecture. The correspondent who reported on these designs in the *Annales* was the architect Alfred Darcel, a friend of Lassus, who frequently reviewed architectural exhibitions for Didron. After commenting on the predilection revealed by the English for coloured perspective drawings Darcel suggested that this was probably due to the picturesque functionalism that was one of the principles underlying nineteenth-century English architecture. But he showed little sympathy for this principle: 'You always find the same system of irregular buildings, whose external appearance is determined by the interior design.'[330] He also took exception to the use of polychromatic effects:

'To do what M. W. Butterfield has done in his design for the Church of All Saints, London is to misuse colour, both in terms of design and in terms of architecture. The white stone, and the bricks, which range from flame-red to the deepest black, create a kind of marquetry that is far too sensational [French *marqueterie* also implies a general muddle] ... And the whole building is decked out with harshly coloured paintings, which reveal more manual dexterity on M. Butterfield's part than moderation of taste.'[331]

And when Darcel summed up his impressions with the observation that 'in France the graphic element takes precedence over the picturesque' he was referring, not only to draughtsmanship, but also to design.[332]

However, although the French and the English were poles apart in their conception of what constituted a suitable model or an ideal style, the theoretical ideas on which imitative architecture was based in their

35, 36

58, 59

62, 69

327 *Ibid.*, p.360: 'En voyant ces monuments d'une architecture inférieure proposée comme modèle, nous regrettons que l'Angleterre n'ait pas nos belles chapelles du Palais, à Paris, de l'archevêché à Reims, de Saint-Jean-en-l'Ile, à Corbeil, nos belles églises paroissiales ..., nos belles abbatiales et nos cathédrales sublimes de presque toutes les provinces de notre pays. En Angleterre, on ne saurait trop le répéter, les exemples de la plus noble architecture du moyen âge sont assez rares, et les architectes de ce pays portent trop d'amour au gothique de décadence.'

328 *Annales archéologiques*, x (1850), pp.283–4.

329 *Ibid.*, xi (1851), pp.292–4: 'car M. Pugin, français par son père, par ses amitiés, par son goût archéologique, arrive au XIIIe siècle, mais avec trop de lenteur, à notre sens.'

330 *Ibid.*, xv (1855), pp.245–6 and 251: 'C'est toujours le même système de bâtisses sans ordres, subordonné à la distribution intérieure.'

331 *Ibid.*, p.252: 'C'est par trop abuser de la couleur, en dessin et en nature, que de faire comme M. W. Butterfield pour l'église de All-Saints, à Londres. La pierre blanche, les briques, échelonnées depuis le rouge ardent jusqu'au noir le plus sombre, y forment une marqueterie trop éclatante. ... Le tout est revêtu de peintures très montées de ton, qui dénotent chez M. Butterfield plus d'habileté de main que de modération de goût.'

332 *Annales archéologiques*, xv (1855), p.425: 'En France l'élément graphique prime l'élément pittoresque.'

respective countries were essentially the same, and underwent a similar development.

In 1844, when Viollet-le-Duc justified the historical method on the grounds that it enables us to regard historical studies and stylistic reproductions, from the Ptolemaic period in Egypt right through to the Renaissance, as an historical constant, he was advancing a purely personal opinion (one which, incidentally, failed to take account of the iconological factor).[333] In general – and notwithstanding the fact that Montalembert, like Pugin and the Ecclesiological Society, hoped to use art as a means of restoring the whole of the mediaeval world order – the French tended to regard the Gothic Revival in purely artistic terms. The Baron de Guilhermy, who was a first-rate historian, expressed the French attitude quite excellently when he described his reaction to the new church in Nantes:

72–4 'The new church of Saint-Nicolas will be the most important building of our times constructed in the Gothic style. I, for my part, await its completion with great impatience; and I am but a half-hearted protagonist of art forms which look backwards into the past, and am prepared to endorse the reproduction of the past, irrespective of the particular period involved, only in so far as it enables me to escape from the poverty of contemporary creations. Saint-Nicolas in Nantes may well provide the solution to a problem which engages many minds today.'[334]

Even Lassus, the architect of Saint-Nicolas, hesitated before deciding in favour of imitation, but was finally persuaded to do so by the constructive advantages of the Gothic style:
'For, you know, we ourselves would be extremely happy to see the emergence of a new art form; but try as we may, we can see absolutely nothing. Meanwhile, we have to take sides, because we cannot subscribe to the imitation of the Antique in our climate and with our materials.'[335]

For Lassus eclecticism was out of the question. Opposition to eclecticism, which was still considered a perfectly acceptable method for the revival of traditional forms by the authors of the *Encyclopédie*, was the kernel of Lassus's doctrine, just as the logic of Gothic construction was the kernel of Viollet-le-Duc's:
'No matter what one does, stylistic unity . . . is one of those basic rules which cannot possibly be ignored; because without this strict condition, there can be neither art nor artists. Eclecticism in architecture is completely impossible and makes no sense whatsoever.'[336]

The concept of eclecticism was revived, in its philosophical sense, by Victor Cousin, whose lectures were widely discussed in the 1830's.[337] But it was not only from the syncretists, but also from the traditionalists, that Lassus was determined to protect his conception of an ideal style. In times of change, he said, men must rely on the power of reason, not on the law of continuity.[338] That was why he dealt so leniently with the Classicists, for although they had opted for the Antique, in doing so they had also opted for stylistic unity, which meant that they had acted rationally.[339] But Lassus did not favour a purely

333 *Ibid.*, I (2nd ed. 1854), p.334.

334 *Ibid.*, II (1845), p.48: 'La nouvelle église Saint-Nicolas sera le plus important édifice construit de nos jours en style ogival. J'attends pour ma part l'achèvement avec une vive impatience, moi qui ne suis qu'un demi-partisan de tout art rétrospectif, et qui n'accepte la reproduction du passé, quel qu'il soit, que dans l'espoir d'échapper à la pauvreté des créations contemporaines. Saint-Nicolas de Nantes nous donnera peut-être la solution d'un problème qui préoccupe aujourd'hui bien des intelligences.'

335 *Annales archéologiques*, II (1845), p.76: 'Croyez-le, cependant, nous serions nous-même fort heureux de voir surgir un art nouveau; mais, malgré tous nos efforts, nous ne voyons absolument rien. Cependant il faut bien prendre un parti, puisque nous ne pouvons admettre une imitation de l'antique dans notre climat et avec nos matériaux.'

336 *Annales archéologiques*, II (1845), p.76: 'L'unité de style, par exemple et quoi qu'on fasse, est une des règles fondamen-tales dont il est impossible de se départir; car sans cette condition rigoureuse, il n'y a ni art ni artiste. En architecture, l'éclectisme est complètement impossible et ne présente aucun sense.' – For further references see Note 290 for Part III above.

337 Collins, *Changing Ideals* (1965), pp.117–18.

338 *Annales archéologiques*, II (1845), p.200.

339 *Ibid.*, p.329.

imitative style of architecture. He felt no desire to copy thirteenth-century buildings. What he wanted was to absorb the spirit of the thirteenth century and then seek solutions which would reflect that spirit while at the same time catering for modern needs and modern materials. Thus, in the case of larger churches, he recommended that **73** the axial Lady Chapel – which in the nineteenth century was used for weekday services, for holy communion, and as a place of silent worship – should be longer than the other radiating chapels, even in churches built in the style of the early thirteenth century. He himself acted upon this recommendation in his own buildings.[340]

The spirit of the Gothic cannot be expressed in the form of rules but only in the form of principles. Unlike Viollet-le-Duc (or, at least, the young Viollet-le-Duc) Lassus, who was better acquainted with the canons of Classical art, did not base his defence of the Gothic exclusively on its constructive excellence. In the first place, he opposed the practice – which was described by Vasari but which Lassus discovered in Antoine-Chrysostome Quatremère de Quincy's *Dictionnaire historique d'architecture* – of equating style with order, and order with a rigid canon of proportions.[341] If architecture were to be reduced to a set of rules, he argued, then the architect would be no more than 'une machine à bâtir' (a building machine).[342] Lassus regarded the proportions of Antique architecture as a closed system, and all buildings constructed in accordance with that system – such as St Peter's in Rome – as purely mechanical structures capable of being deduced from models. In Gothic architecture, on the other hand, the absolute dimensions of the various components remained constant, irrespective of the size of the building: 'In the thirteenth century, for example, the bases, the capitals, the columns, the mouldings, the ribs, in fact all the details are exactly the same, irrespective of whether they are found in a great cathedral or a simple church, because in all such buildings unity is provided by man himself, and man can neither grow nor shrink . . . All our monuments express rigorously, mathematically, the image of what they really are. And is that not true rationalism?'[343]

This passage is a masterly example of apologetic writing. First, Lassus ensures the concurrence of his readers by repeating the well-known criticism of St Peter's. He then demonstrates his humanist leanings by developing a *modulor* theory, which anticipates Le Corbusier, and contrasting this with the Vitruvian *module* theory. Finally, he presents Gothic design as a system of co-ordinates which enables us to establish with certainty the absolute dimensions of Gothic buildings. For Lassus the Gothic is human, true and rational.

The French *archéologues* had very little sympathy with the system of determining architectural proportions by means of triangulation, which was presented to the English public in *The Ecclesiologist* by William White (who was its only advocate among the contributors to that periodical). Lassus maintained, in contradiction of Cesariano and Boisserée, that triangulation was simply a means of measuring buildings[344] whilst Verneilh, Boisserée's implacable but ever courteous

340 *Ibid.*, p.335.

341 See Note 168 for Part I above. – Antoine-Chrysostome Quatremère de Quincy, *Dictionnaire historique d'architecture*, 2 vols. (Paris, 1832), II, p.173 ('ordre'). – Schneider, *Quatremère . . . intervention* (1910), pp.367–8. – *Annales archéologiques*, II (1845), pp.71–2.

342 *Ibid.*, p.74.

343 *Ibid.*, pp.201–2: 'Au XIIIe siècle, par exemple, les bases, les chapiteaux, les colonnettes, les meneaux, les nervures, enfin tous les détails sont exactement les mêmes, et dans la grande cathédrale et dans la simple église de campagne, et cela parce que dans tous les monuments l'homme seul sert toujours d'unité et que l'homme, lui, ne peut se grandir ni se diminuer . . . Tous nos monuments donnent rigoureusement, mathématique-ment, l'idée de ce qu'ils sont réellement. Nous demandons si ce n'est pas là du véritable rationalisme.' – Summary by Alfred Darcel, *ibid.*, XVII (1857), p.312.

344 Lassus, 'Considérations sur la renaissance de l'art français au XIXe siècle' (1858), p.9.

adversary, declared: 'Most decidedly, we have very little faith in the doctrine of the isosceles triangle.'[345] As for Didron, he undermined the theological interpretation of the triangle as a symbol of the holy trinity by stating, in his review of Neale and Webb's edition of the *Rationale* of Durandus, that 'symbolism seduces, if indeed it does not blind, the best intellects'.[346]

The French architects who contributed to the *Annales archéologiques* regarded the 'imitation of the Gothic' as a creative process. It was not a question of copying a mediaeval building, but of producing a new building that had been conceived in the spirit of the Gothic and executed in accordance with the constructive and formal principles underlying the Gothic, which these architects claimed to have recognized. There is an obvious parallel here with language, which Viollet-le-Duc was always referring to and which was also cited by Didron.[347] But Didron based his comparison on early speech training: 'So much the worse for those who do not learn to imitate by copying. If anyone were to try to speak without first concentrating, for years on end, on repeating the words uttered by his mother or nurse, he would either remain a mute for the rest of his days or would speak some incomprehensible patois. In art, and especially in architecture, even domestic architecture, we are like children, and could not do better, for a number of years at least, than to reproduce the buildings executed with such marvellous skill by our mediaeval forebears, so that we may master their manner and their techniques. For our most competent builders of churches in the Gothic style are undoubtedly those who copy our ancient monuments with most humility. Later, when we have reached man's estate, we too will invent, and we too will be able to rely exclusively on inspiration. But if we proceed differently, then for centuries to come we will build houses like those on the Rue de Rivoli, in other words ugly, heavy and pretentious buildings.'[348]

In view of his general attitude to architecture, it is hardly surprising that Didron did not hesitate to recommend individual mediaeval monuments as models.[349] And yet, within two years of writing the passage reproduced above, he had persuaded himself that the French Gothic Revivalists had in fact 'reached man's estate'. Perhaps it was the large number of impressive designs submitted by architects from so many different countries for the Lille Cathedral competition that made him change his mind. This would seem to follow from the remarks prompted by Lassus's competition design:
'Perhaps the moment really has come for us to abandon copyism and allow personal inspiration a free rein within a clearly defined art form, so that it may assimilate that art form and reproduce its spirit. In our opinion, at least, it is still a little too soon to cut the guiding reins, with whose aid we have learned to walk; but since it is generally felt that we can now dispense with this aid, let us abandon our tutelary implements and walk in the grand manner that we have been learning by heart for the past thirty years.'[350]

By the following year, 1857, the transition had been completed.

76–8

345 *Annales archéologiques*, VII (1847), p.235: 'Décidément nous croyons très peu à cette religion du triangle équilatéral.'

346 *Ibid.*, VIII (1848), p.57: 'Le symbolisme séduit, s'il ne les aveugle pas, les meilleurs esprits.'

347 *Ibid.*, II (1845), pp.80 and 308; IV (1846), p.452; and in other publications.

348 *Annales archéologiques*, XIV (1854), p.390: 'Tant pis pour ceux qui ne copieront pas d'abord, afin d'imiter ensuite. Quiconque voudrait parler sans répéter, avant tout et pendant plusieurs années, le mot à mot de sa mère ou de sa nourrice, resterait muet toute sa vie ou n'userait que d'un patois incompréhensible. En art, surtout en architecture, même domestique, nous sommes des enfants qui n'avons rien de mieux à faire, pendant quelques années du moins, qu'à reproduire, pour nous rendre maîtres de leur manière et de leurs procédés, ce que nos ancêtres du moyen âge ont si merveilleusement exécuté. Ainsi, nos plus habiles constructeurs d'églises en style ogival sont incontestablement ceux qui copient avec plus de modestie les monuments anciens. Plus tard, quand, à notre tour, nous serons devenus des hommes, nous inventerons pour notre propre compte, nous parlerons une langue à nous, et la simple inspiration pourra nous suffire. Avec la méthode contraire, nous bâtirions pendant des siècles des maisons comme celles qui bordent la rue de Rivoli, c'est-à-dire du laid, du lourd et du prétentieux.'

349 See Notes 307–10 for Part III above.

350 *Annales archéologiques*, XVI (1856), p.122: 'Peut-être, en effet, le moment est-il déjà venu d'abandonner la copie et de laisser à l'inspiration personnelle la liberté de se mouvoir dans un art bien déterminé, pour se l'approprier, pour se l'assimiler, pour en reproduire l'esprit. C'est sans doute, à notre avis du moins, couper un peu trop tôt les lisières à l'aide desquelles nous avons appris à marcher; mais enfin, puisque l'on croit pouvoir s'en passer, abandonnons ces instruments tutélaires de notre éducation, et marchons librement dans le grand art que nous apprenons par cœur depuis une trentaine d'années.'

351 *Annales archéologiques*, XVII (1857), p.253. – The church was finally designed by Stadler, who is mentioned by Lille; see Dorothea Christ, *Die St. Elisabethenkirche in Basel . . .* (Basle, 1964).

352 He even praises Les Halles in Paris, which were built by Victor Baltard (1805–74), who intrigued against him in Rome and clouded his friendship with Ingres; see Viollet-le-Duc, *Entretiens sur l'architecture*, I (1863), p.323, which contains an astonishing early attack on the modern conception of art: 'Là, on s'est soumis aux nécessités du programme et de la matière employée; il en est résulté, à mon sense, un très bel édifice. Peut-être n'a-t-on pas pensé qu'il fallût *faire de l'art*. Il faudrait donc souhaiter qu'on n'en voulût plus faire aujourd'hui; ce serait peut-être le plus court chemin pour arriver à nous donner des œuvres d'art, expressions de notre civilisation.' – The Baltard episode is described in E[ugène-Emmanuel] Viollet-le-Duc, *Lettres d'Italie, 1836–1837, adressées à sa famille*, annotées par Geneviève Viollet-le-Duc (Paris, 1971), pp.271–2.

353 *Annales archéologiques*, III (1845), p.72: '. . . matière qui semble exiger indispensablement le style ogival'.

354 *Ibid.*, XIII (1853), p.229: 'C'est l'architecture antédiluvienne, plus monstrueuse et plus bossue que les mastodontes les plus rébarbatifs,' – See also Foucart, 'La "Cathédrale synthé-tique"' (1969), pp.52 and 58.

355 *Annales archéologiques*, XIII (1853), p.103 (Rouen Cathedral and Sainte-Clotilde); *ibid.*, p.260 (St Apollinaris near Remagen); XVII (1857), pp.132–4 (iron roof girders in Cologne Cathedral).

356 *Ibid.*, III (1845), p.333.

357 *Ibid.*, VI (1847), p.4: 'Je crois pouvoir démontrer qu'il existait pour les campagnes un style ogival aussi simple que l'ordre *paestum* et toscan de l'architecture classique. Nous avons en Picardie de jolies églises ogivales en briques; ces briques sont placées avec une rare intelligence dans les renforcements des murs et dans les pendentifs des voûtes d'arêtes. Nos pères avaient assez de bon sens pour faire, avec économie, de la bonne architecture dans les pays qui offraient peu de ressources.'

358 Quotation taken from Mallion, *Victor Hugo et l'art architectural* (1962), p.594. – See also *Annales archéologiques*, II (1845), p.336.

Didron himself may still have had his doubts; but Alfred Darcel, who was a practising architect, had begun to criticize the contemporary mania for copyism most severely. His special target was the competition design for the Elisabethenkirche in Basle produced by the Dusillion brothers, which was modelled on the Sainte-Chapelle.[351]

There were a number of issues which featured regularly in *The Ecclesiologist* but were seldom mentioned in the *Annales archéologiques*. Iron for example, which elicited such an enthusiastic but ill-informed response from Viollet-le-Duc in the *Entretiens*, was discussed only on rare occasions.[352] One of these occurred in 1845, when Antoine-Guillaume-Bernard Schayes (1808–59) observed that, in the Quartier Louise in Brussels, a new church was to be built in iron, 'a material which would undoubtedly seem to call for the Gothic style'; and Didron, who was no laggard when it came to providing corrective, explanatory or disapproving footnotes, printed this observation without comment.[353] Are we to assume from this that Didron was essentially in favour of the constructive iron style? Eight years later, when he reviewed Boileau's pamphlet *Nouvelle forme architecturale*, in which Boileau described a 'cathédrale synthétique', a cruciform pyramidal structure with vessels of different heights and measuring 892 feet, Didron waxed indignant over what he regarded as 'antediluvian architecture, more monstrous and more mis-shapen than the most repellent mastodons', but he passed no comment whatsoever on Boileau's suggestion that iron should be used in preference to stone.[354] On the other hand, Didron's contributors mercilessly castigated the substitution of iron for stone.[355]

Apart from iron and ashlar, very few building materials were mentioned in the *Annales archéologiques*. In an article published in 1845, Viollet-le-Duc discussed the use of stucco, cast metal and terra-cotta,[356] which he rejected, and two years later the archaeologist Antoine Goze, a native of Amiens, referred to the bricks employed in French rural churches:

'I believe I can show that a Gothic style was used for rural areas that was just as simple as the Doric Order of Classical architecture used in Paestum and Tuscany. In Picardy we have some pretty Gothic churches made of bricks, the bricks being arranged with unusual skill in the buttresses and the webs of the vaults. Our forebears had enough common sense to be able to create good, economical architecture in districts that were short of natural resources.'[357]

This is an interesting passage, for it shows not only that the French – like the English – attached considerable importance to rural churches, and to their local peculiarities and the local materials from which they were built, but also that there was a definite link between the preference for the Doric Order shown by the French Classicists and the predilection for the Early Gothic style (dating from the reign of Philip Augustus) revealed by the Gothic Revivalists. It was not by chance that Victor Hugo used the term 'majestueuse simplicité', which would normally have been applied to Doric temples, in his description of Sainte-Philibert in Tournus (Saône-et-Loire).[358]

84 Reichensperger and Lassus were also attracted by local peculiarities and local materials. It will be remembered that they reacted enthusiastically to the timber buildings designed by Friedrich Eisenlohr (1808–55) for the Badische Eisenbahnen.[359]

Although the revival of art through craftsmanship was a theme that the *Annales archéologiques* failed to take up either in the 1840's or in the 1850's, the stonemason's craft was discussed on various occasions. This was, of course, a natural consequence of the great interest shown by French archaeologists in construction and stone cutting. Not surprisingly, Viollet-le-Duc, who was an inveterate opponent of academic knowledge, praised the practical skills and intelligence of the stonemasons; he had an almost archaic reverence for large stone blocks and would quite literally stand over his masons to ensure that they did

81, 82 not chip away a fraction more than was necessary.[360] This was why he objected to the Renaissance architects, who demanded blocks of uniform size from their masons. Viollet-le-Duc regarded such an attitude as a sinful waste of stone and an abuse of the mason's craft: 'They have turned the workman into a machine, in the name of unity.'[361] The articles written by the French contributors to the *Annales archéologiques* were invariably objective accounts of historical developments.[362] The view advanced by Carl Schnaase (1798–1875) and shared by – among others – Viollet-le-Duc, that in the twelfth and thirteenth centuries the artistic leadership in Europe had passed to the laity was repudiated in a footnote by Didron, who insisted that the Gothic was the very epitome of a Christian style.[363] And Reichensperger's conviction – which he acquired in Cologne – that, not only the Gothic, but art in general, and even the social order, could be regenerated by the *Bauhütten* formed for the construction of large churches, i.e. by craftsmen's guilds, went unheeded in France. Reichensperger hoped that the competition for the Votivkirche in

90 Vienna, in which his protégés Vincenz Statz (1818–98), Friedrich von Schmidt (1825–91) and Georg Gottlob Ungewitter (1820–64) were rightly awarded the second prize, would create a new atmosphere conducive to the propagation of the Gothic:

'It is not on the buildings that I place the principal stress but on the "ateliers" [*Bauhütten*], from which these buildings will emerge. In them a new generation of artists and artisans is gradually being formed, without whom the regeneration of art would be impossible. Because of the completely disorganized state in which they find themselves – a legacy of the Revolution – and because of the competition provided by the factories, our crafts – especially those connected with the arts – have degenerated to the point of idiocy; they can only be rejuvenated in these immense ateliers, which will be organized along university lines and independently of the industrial movement. The atelier attached to Cologne Cathedral has already produced offshoots: firstly, in the town where M. Statz, whom I have already mentioned, and his colleague

88, 89 M. Schmidt employ, for their private commissions, a dozen stonemasons who were trained in the Cathedral school; and then in Hamburg, in

359 *Ibid.*, IX (1849), p.349; XIII (1853), p.259.

360 *Ibid.*, III (1845), p.330.

361 *Ibid.*: 'On a fait de l'ouvrier une machine, sous prétexte d'unité.'

362 *Ibid.*, V (1846), pp.274–5; VIII (1848), pp.147–54 and 185–93; IX (1849), pp.10–11.

363 Carl Schnaase, 'Les francs-maçons du moyen âge' [translation of part of C. S., *Geschichte der bildenden Künste*] in *Annales archéologiques*, XI (1851), pp.325–34, note p.326. – See also Notes 179–80 and 185 for Part II above.

Soest and other towns, where there are important restorations to be carried out in the Gothic style. Just another three or four of these central ateliers, operating in the close proximity of as many cathedrals, and we shall see what happens!'[364]

Unlike *The Ecclesiologist*, the *Annales archéologiques* was not controlled by churchmen; and it was partly for this reason that the question as to whether the Gothic was – and should again become – a Catholic, a Christian, or a universal style was answered only in glosses. For Didron it went without saying that a Gothic Revival church was an 'édifice en style vraiment chrétien', a building executed in a truly Christian style.[365] He also received, and printed, a letter from the Bishop of Langres, Parisis, dated 3 October 1844, in which the work of the *Annales archéologiques* was described as a sacred cause.[366] Certainly, Didron thought of himself as a champion of religion:
'The struggle in which we have engaged against foreign art and in the interests of our national art, against pagan art and in favour of Christian art, against death and for life, this struggle is still entirely fresh and still extremely vital.'[367]

Viollet-le-Duc did not try to publish his ideas on the predominance of the laity during the Gothic period in the *Annales archéologiques*. It would have been surprising if he had. But by a nice coincidence, the first French secular structure in the Gothic style mentioned in the *Annales*, the façade of the Préfecture in Auxerre (Yonne), was also the first of Viollet-le-Duc's independent works to be mentioned. The style of this façade was not discussed.[368]

In 1852 Aymar Verdier (1819–80) began to publish his *Architecture civile et domestique*, a serial publication which consisted largely of reproductions of original models, and so enabled Didron to concentrate exclusively on ecclesiastical art.[369] In his publication which began to appear at virtually the same time as the pamphlets in which George Edmund Street argued the case for a Gothic Revival Museum in Oxford,[370] Verdier drew attention to the brick buildings erected in Italy in the thirteenth century. This line of enquiry, which was similar to that pursued by contemporary English architects, met with the approval of Didron.[371]

The attitude of the *Annales archéologiques* to the Gothic was based on three principal factors. These were: firstly, the constructive and technical mastery of the Gothic architects; secondly, the national character of Gothic architecture; and thirdly, its Christian character. As far as the national character of the Gothic was concerned, the French encountered opposition from the Germans, who had regarded the Gothic as *deutsche Baukunst* ever since Goethe had written his essay in 1772, and were loath to accept the arguments advanced by reputable historians in every country of Europe in favour of its French origin. But we shall be dealing with this question in the section on the *Kölner Domblatt*.

79, 80

364 *Annales archéologiques*, XIII (1853), pp.347–8: 'Ce n'est pas aux édifices que je mets le principal poids, mais aux "ateliers" d'où ces édifices sortent. Là se forme peu à peu une nouvelle génération d'artistes et d'ouvriers, sans laquelle la restauration de l'art est impossible. Par suite de leur désorganisation totale, fruit de la révolution, et par la concurrence des fabriques, les métiers, ceux spécialement qui se rattachent aux arts, se sont dégradés jusqu'à l'imbécillité; ils pourront seulement être rajeunis dans ces vastes ateliers, pour ainsi dire universitaires et indépendants du mouvement industriel. L'atelier de notre cathédrale de Cologne a déjà ses colonies: d'abord dans la ville même où M. Statz, dont j'ai parlé plus haut, et son collègue M. Schmidt, occupent à leurs entreprises privées une douzaine de tailleurs de pierre, élevés dans l'école de la cathédrale; puis à Hamburg, à Soest et ailleurs, où il y a des restaurations importantes à faire en style gothique. Encore trois ou quatre de ces ateliers centraux, travaillant au pied d'autant de cathédrales, et nous verrons.' – Reichensperger's article appeared in a series entitled 'L'art et l'archéologie en Allemagne' (1849, 1850, 1853, and 1857); for futher information on this series see Pastor, *Reichensperger* (1899), II, pp.449 ff. (with an almost complete bibliography of Reichensperger's publications).

365 *Annales archéologiques*, I (2nd ed. 1854), p.106.

366 *Ibid.*, p.413.

367 *Ibid.*, II (1845), p.309: 'La lutte que nous avons ouverte contre l'art étranger au profit de l'art national, contre l'art païen en faveur de l'art chrétien, contre la mort pour la vie, cette lutte est toute nouvelle encore et cependant des plus vives déjà.'

368 *Ibid.*, VI (1847), p.6.

369 *Ibid.*, XII (1852), p.58.

370 See Notes 172–3 for Part III above.

371 *Annales archéologiques*, XII (1852), p.343.

4 The 'Kölner Domblatt'

At the beginning of 1843 the Secretary of the *Zentral-Dombauverein* (Central Association for the Cathedral Project) in Cologne called for the establishment of branch associations throughout the country in the *Kölner Domblatt*, and sought to inspire his compatriots with the following stirring words:

'The Catholics are building a house to their God, in which the genius of art is soaring on the wings of religion into the highest heaven; but all our people are helping to promote this glorious monument to Christian feeling, German strength and German concord . . . We are concerned with the most sacred and most beautiful of all things: Religion, Fatherland, and Art; they call to us in unison.'[372]

'Religion, Fatherland, and Art.' With these three expressions Reichensperger summed up the Romantic attitude which had prompted the completion of Cologne Cathedral, and provided a series of catchwords for the Gothic Revival in Germany, which were still being used there in the twentieth century, and which were also recognized by foreign archaeologists as significant concepts.[373]

In 1814, when Joseph Görres urged that the Cathedral should be completed as a national monument to commemorate the successful outcome of the War of Liberation he honestly believed that the Gothic was a German style of architecture and that Cologne Cathedral was the major example of that style. This is hardly surprising, for those were early days. What is rather surprising, however, is that Sulpiz Boisserée should have failed to visit the French Cathedral of Amiens, which bears a striking resemblance to Cologne, even though he had procured a copy of the plans in 1811.[374] Whether he recognized the truth and purposely suppressed it in order to realize his life's ambition – the completion of Cologne Cathedral – or whether he was blinded by the exalted conception of the *Gesamtkunstwerk* as an individual creation, which was fashionable in his day, and so was unable to grasp the idea of historical evolution, we are unable to determine with any degree of certainty.[375] At all events, it came as a rude shock to the Germans when they discovered the similarity between the two cathedrals, and learned that Amiens was the earlier. But it would be a mistake to think that all German scholars were afflicted by this chauvinistic scotoma. Two of them, Johannes Wetter (1807–97) and Franz Mertens (1808–97) were well informed about the French origins of the Gothic and helped to open up this particular field of study. As early as September 1841 Mertens issued a twelve-page programme giving details of a projected series of lectures *Über den Dom zu Köln und die französische Bauschule in Deutschland* (On Cologne Cathedral and the French School of Architecture in Germany).[376] Félix de Verneilh (1819–64), one of the best French architectural historians of the period, publicly acknowledged the contribution made by both Wetter and Mertens.[377] Incidentally, it was Verneilh who so accurately defined Cologne Cathedral as 'the work which resumed, not the work which inaugurated, the most beautiful period of Christian art'.[378]

372 Pastor, *Reichensperger* (1899), I, p.170: 'Der Katholik baut an seinem Gotteshause, in welchem der Genius der Kunst auf den Schwingen der Religion den höchsten Flug angenommen; alle aber fördern das herrliche Baudenkmal christlichen Sinnes, deutscher Kraft, deutscher Eintracht . . . Es gilt ja das Heiligste und Schönste: Religion, Vaterland, Kunst, sie rufen mit vereinter Stimme.'

373 *The Ecclesiologist*, VII (1847), p.157 (translation from the *Kölner Domblatt*, 27 December, 1846): 'There are three principal elements at work to which we may refer the active sympathy shown in the erection of our cathedral: Religion, Fatherland, and Art.'

374 Sulpiz Boisserée, 'Über das Verhältnis des Domes von Amiens zu dem kölner Dom', in *Kölner Domblatt*, 29 March, 1846.

375 *Ibid.*, 30 November, 1845; etc. – *Annales archéologiques*, VII (1847), pp.178–87 and 225–6. – *Briefwechsel Sulpiz Boisserées* (typescript): Zwirner to Boisserée, 12 January, 1844; etc.

376 J[ohannes] Wetter, *Geschichte und Beschreibung des Domes zu Mainz, begleitet mit Betrachtungen über die Entwicklung des Spitzbogenstyls, das neugothische Constructionssystem in Deutschland und Frankreich und den Einfluss der lombardischen und byzantinischen Kunst auf diese Länder* (Mainz, 1835), pp. V and 47–52, note. – Franz Mertens, *Über den Dom zu Cöln und die französische Bauschule in Deutschland, Programm zu den neuen Vorlesungen über Monumentalgeschichte, welche in besonderem Bezuge auf jenen Gegenstand zu Cöln im Locale des Städtischen Gesangvereins sollen abgehalten werden* (Cologne, 1841), pp.9–10. – According to an Editor's Note Mertens recorded his observations in 1840 but was unable to find a publisher until 1843. The title of his article runs as follows: Franz Mertens, 'Paris baugeschichtlich im Mittelalter' in *Allgemeine Bauzeitung*, VIII (1843), pp. 159–67 and 253–60.

377 *Annales archéologiques*, II (1845), p.138, note; IX (1849), p.14.

378 *Ibid.*, VII (1847), p.57: '. . . l'œuvre qui a résumé et non celle qui a ouvert la plus belle période de l'art chrétien'.

51

379 *Ibid.*, pp.179–80.

380 Also in Reichensperger, *Vermischte Schriften* (1856), pp.381–99. – As early as March 10, 1844 Johannes Kreuser had written in the *Domblatt*: 'Dieser für den kölner Dom so wichtige Dom von Amiens, angefangen 1220, beendet 1280, kann auch wohl den jetzigen Portalstreit entscheiden.'

381 [August Reichensperger,] *Einige Worte über den Dombau zu Köln, von einem Rheinländer an seine Landsleute gerichtet; der Ertrag ist für den Dombau bestimmt* (Coblenz, 1840; facsimile reprint 1948), p.25: 'Der Kölner Dom ist ein kern-deutscher Bau, ein Nationaldenkmal im vollsten Sinne des Wortes, und dazu noch das glänzendste vielleicht, was uns die Vergangenheit vermacht hat.'

382 August Reichensperger, 'Die christlich-germanische Baukunst und ihr Verhältnis zur Gegenwart' in *Katholische Zeitschrift für Wissenschaft und Kunst*, I, 2nd half-vol. (1844), pp.275–307; II, 2nd half-vol. (1845), pp.267–305; book edition (Trier, 1845); quotation taken from 3rd ed. (Trier, 1860), p.9: '... unter der Botmässigkeit der germanischen Race stand, die ihm in mehr als einer Beziehung ihr Gepräge aufdrückte und Institutionen dort einpflanzte, welche, wie die gleichzeitig gegründeten Dome, den Stürmen der Jahrhunderte Trotz geboten haben.'

383 See Note 22 for Part III above.

384 *Annales archéologiques*, VII (1847), p.225.

385 *Ibid.*, IX (1849), p.26: 'Non, pour que des savants illustres et des observateurs consciencieux osent appeler du nom de leur pays l'art universel, l'art chrétien par excellence, il faut qu'ils soient aveuglés par ce germanisme jaloux dont l'Allemagne est aujourd'hui possédée et qui la rend injuste en histoire aussi bien qu'en politique.'

The Germans felt doubly embarrassed by their belated discovery because it was made shortly after the funds for the Cologne project had been sanctioned by the King of Prussia and the Dombauverein. When they realized the nature of the relationship between Amiens and Cologne – in 1842 – Lassaulx, Reichensperger, Zwirner, and Baron Ferdinand de Roisin kept the matter secret.[379] But eventually Reichensperger found the courage to discuss it in the *Domblatt* (on 30 November 1845). He was prompted to do so because, at that time, certain details of the transept, for which there were no mediaeval designs, had to be determined, and he felt that it would be ridiculous to arrive at a decision without first inspecting the transept of the related cathedral in Amiens.[380] But it was not easy for Reichensperger to acknowledge this relationship, for in 1840, just five years before, he had proudly proclaimed:

'Cologne Cathedral is German to the core, it is a national monument in the fullest sense of the word, and probably the most splendid monument to be handed down to us from the past.'[381]

He solved his dilemma – honestly and without equivocation – by coining the concept 'Christian-Germanic architecture'. The Gothic, he said, was a Germanic art form because in *c.*A.D.1200 northern France 'stood under the dominion of the Germanic race, which left its mark in more ways than one, and established institutions which, like the cathedrals founded at that time, have withstood the tempests of time.'[382]

Both as a lawyer and (subsequently) as the founder of the Zentrumspartei, whose policies were similar to those of the French catholicisme libéral, Reichensperger tended to think in terms of legal customs and prescriptive rights, and in identifying the border line between Germanic and Roman law he cited Alexis de Tocqueville as his authority. It is hardly surprising that Reichensperger really felt himself 'to be in the grip of Germanic influences' in England.[383] Verneilh congratulated Reichensperger on having freed himself from the twin tyrants of popular opinion and patriotism;[384] and although Verneilh launched a fierce attack on the more extreme forms of nationalism, this was not intended as a rebuke to Reichensperger, for as an historian he was well aware of the wide difference between linguistic borders, mediaeval territorial borders, and modern political borders. Verneilh wrote:

'No, for famous scholars and conscientious observers to dare to call this universal art, this Christian art *par excellence*, by the name of their country, they must have been blinded by the envious "Germanism" with which the Germans are now obsessed and which makes them behave unjustly in both the historical and political spheres.'[385]

But Verneilh went on to point out that France, which had been so favoured by history and was so well provided with good quality quarries, could not lay claim to the Gothic either, since it belonged to the whole of Christian Europe. Finally, he paid high tribute to the new project in Cologne:

'What M. Zwirner has designed and built has seemed to us to be every bit as good as the best work produced both here and in England.'[386]

The idea of historical development also toppled the second cornerstone of Boisserée's much admired critical system. We have already seen that Cologne Cathedral could no longer be regarded as the origin and apogee of German architecture; but neither could it be regarded as a uniform work built in accordance with an original design created by Master Gerhard. Boisserée had interpreted the obvious differences between the east and the west sides, and between the lower and upper sections, of the cathedral as brilliant variations within an integral plan. But the new generation insisted that the different stages of the cathedral had been executed in different historical styles. In his review of Jacob Burckhardt's *Conrad von Hochstaden*, which appeared in the *Kölner Domblatt* in 1843, Ernst Weyden had identified three separate structures dating from different periods: the lower part of the choir, the choir clerestory, and the main façade with the towers.[387] The sense of outrage felt in Cologne could not have been more complete. The lawyer Friedrich Blömer summed up popular feeling in a letter published in the following issue of the *Domblatt*:

'The sacred figure of the great master of Cologne Cathedral, as created by our feelings of veneration, must now descend from his throne of honour on to the common ground, and the marvellous work of genius is transformed into a mere epiphenomenon produced by general historical trends . . . The work . . . as a total creation is no longer the canon of our national architecture, no longer a building *sans pareil* . . . the seal of a unique and divine invention, which had been stamped on all its parts, has been broken; and whilst we had thought we were revering something extraordinary, all that had really happened was that, in our fondness, we had failed to note the gradual development of the cathedral design from different cultural stages.'[388]

As one of the really great mediaeval buildings Cologne Cathedral was, of course, far too big to be used as an exact model, although there was no reason why Gothic Revival buildings should not have been designed in the same style. This was precisely what Zwirner did when he built his church on the Apollinarisberg near Remagen (Rhineland Palatinate; 1839–43).[389] But Zwirner's solution was attacked by three different groups. The first of these, which consisted of young German architects, was opposed to the use of details of specific models, and – like Pugin and the members of the Cambridge Camden Society – argued that complex building *types* should be used instead; the second objected to the perfection of Cologne Cathedral, because it militated against inventive design; and the third favoured a moderate form of eclecticism. Lassaulx belonged to this third group, as is quite evident from the following observation:

'[As far as his buildings in the circular style are concerned, the author has recently been censured] for his failure to produce designs in accordance with a consistent and historically based conception; and . . . in point of fact he honestly believes that it is permissible to employ, and to combine, the good elements of all periods, provided they are basically

86, 87

386 *Ibid.*, VIII (1848), p.133: 'Ce que M. Zwirner a dessiné et bâti nous a paru aussi bien que ce que l'on fait de mieux parmi nous et en Angleterre.'

387 *Kölner Domblatt*, 22 October, 1843. – See also Note 270 for Part II above.

388 *Kölner Domblatt*, 29 October, 1843: 'Die heilige Gestalt des grossen Dombaumeisters, wie unsere Verehrung sie sich schuf, muss von dem Throne ihrer Ehre auf den Boden der Gewöhnlichkeit herabsteigen und das wundervolle Werk des Genius wandelt sich zur blossen Erscheinung allgemeiner Zeitbestrebungen . . . Das Werk . . . hat in seiner Totalität aufgehört, der Canon vaterländischer Baukunst, der Bau ohne Gleichen zu sein . . .; das Siegel einer einigen göttlichen Erfindung, das allen Theilen aufgedrückt war, ist gebrochen, und wo wir Ausserordentliches verehrten, hat unsere Befangenheit nur die allmähliche Entwicklung aus gegebenen Culturstufen übersehen.'

389 August Reichensperger, 'L'art et l'archéologie sur les bords du Rhin' in *Annales archéologiques*, IX (1849), pp.335–58; reference to p.342.

compatible, and that consequently we should now be engaged in tracking down such elements as a matter of urgency.'[390]

The truth of the matter was that Lassaulx's circular style was among the most arbitrary products of ecclesiastical architecture in the period around 1840; and his polychrome work – mostly masonry designs composed of small stone blocks of various colours but with a sprinkling of rosette and shark skin patterns – anticipated English constructional polychromy by more than a decade. Lassaulx, who was born in 1781, was still able to treat mediaeval models with a licence that was denied to Pugin and the architects of his generation. True, Didron was wont to refer to Lassaulx as the 'German Pugin', but this was because, in their respective spheres, both men were pioneers of the constructive approach to mediaeval architecture. In fact, of the two, Didron probably preferred Lassaulx, who was a specialist in mediaeval vaulting techniques. And, of course, Didron was in any case more easily reconciled to a style that was 'too early' than to one that was 'too late'.[391]

Pastor Heinrich Wilhelm Prisac (1802/3–70) was a frequent contributor to the *Kölner Domblatt*, in which he propagated the views of an archaeological group, which considered that the Romanesque provided a better basis for nineteenth-century architecture than the Gothic, a view also urged by Heinrich Hübsch (1795–1863).[392] In considering this proposition we must bear in mind that the Rhenish territories were unusually well endowed with Late Romanesque buildings. Prisac, who subscribed to the evolutionary conception of architecture but was unaware that the Gothic had originated in France, referred to the Late Romanesque as the 'transitional style' and recommended that it be adopted as the 'future architectural style in the Prussian territories on the Rhine' because:

'1. this style was developed to meet specific needs, i.e. climatic and other local conditions;

2. it is highly suitable for the purposes of a Christian church;

3. it is a vehicle of great beauty;

4. with its emphasis on stone construction, it provides the basis for the reintroduction of the pointed arch style or of some new, perfected style that would be in keeping with our times, our needs and our building techniques . . . The suitability of this style of architecture for Christian, and especially Catholic, worship is also undeniable. It is immediately apparent, from both their external and internal appearance, that buildings executed in this style are dedicated to the service of the creator; this is vouchsafed by their rich and dignified construction, which is not found in other buildings, by their graceful forms, their high towers, their noble windows and portals, and by their cruciform ground-plan, and the semicircular or octagonal chancels, which are situated in the east and, in some cases, in the west as well.'[393]

The model recommended by Prisac (with acknowledgement to Hübsch) was the monastery church of Maria Laach in the Rhenish Palatinate. Prisac's patriotic attachment to his native district is reminiscent of contemporary English clerics, who expressed similar

390 *Kölner Domblatt*, 23 February, 1845: '[Für seinen Rundbogenstil ist dem Verfasser] neuerlich der Vorwurf gemacht worden, dass er nirgends nach einem durchgreifenden Plane geschichtlich bedingt geschaffen habe: er . . . glaubt auch in der Tat ernstlich, dass man das Gute aus allen Zeiten benutzen und vereinigen dürfe, sobald es sich sonst zusammen verträgt, dass man daher nur recht emsig dem Guten überall nachspüren solle.'

391 See Note 32 for Part III above.

392 Termehr, *Romanische Baukunst* (typescript, 1950), pp.150–71. – Albrecht Mann, *Die Neuromanik, eine rheinische Komponente im Historismus des 19. Jahrhunderts* (Cologne, 1966). – Michael Bringmann, *Studien zur neuromanischen Architektur in Deutschland* (Heidelberg thesis, 1968; n.p., n.d.).

393 *Kölner Domblatt*, 2 October, 9 October and 16 October, 1842; quotation taken from issue of 16 October: '1. hat sich dieser Styl rein aus dem Bedürfnisse, den klimatischen und örtlichen Verhältnissen entwickelt; 2. ist er den Zwecken eines christlichen Kirchengebäudes höchst angemessen, 3. eines hohen Grades von Schönheit fähig, 4. durch die Ausbildung der Steinconstruction die Brücke entweder zur Wiedereinführung des Spitzbogenstyles oder irgend eines vollendeten neuen, der Zeit, den Bedürfnissen und Mitteln entsprechenden . . .
'Auch die Zweckmässigkeit dieses Baustyls für den christlichen Gottesdienst, namentlich für den katholischen, kann nicht geläugnet werden. Das in diesem Style errichtete Gebäude charakterisiert sich von aussen und von innen auf den ersten Anblick als ein dem Dienste des Schöpfers gewidmetes, durch eine den übrigen Bauwerken fremdartige, reichhaltige und würdevolle Construction, gefällige Formen, hohe Thürme, erhabene Fenster und Portale, endlich die Kreuzform im Grundrisse, den halbrunden oder achteckigen Chor in Ost oder in Ost und West zugleich.'

394 Gottfried Semper, *Über den Bau evangelischer Kirchen (mit besonderer Beziehung auf die Frage über die Art des Neubaues der Nikolaikirche in Hamburg und auf ein dafür entworfenes Projekt* (Leipzig, 1845); reprinted in G. S., *Kleine Schriften*, hrsg. von Manfred und Hans

85

Semper (Berlin and Stuttgart, 1884), pp. 443–67; quotations taken from *ibid.*, pp. 461, 463, 464, and 465, note: 'Der germanische Baustil gestattet keine Emporkirchen ... Es ist falsch, wenn der mittelalterliche Baustil des 12., 13. und 14. Jahrhunderts als der *ausschliesslich* nationale bezeichnet wird. Vielmehr ist der Rundbogen dem Boden Deutschlands ebenso vertraut wie ein anderer ... ; ebenso wahr ist es, dass die vorgotische Rundbogenarchitektur unserer Zeit näher steht als der Spitzbogen. Dieser Baustil, dessen echt nationale Entwicklung durch das hinzugekommene Element des Spitzbogens gestört wurde, hat sich selbst nicht überlebt wie der gotische, er ist teils aus diesem Grunde einer ferneren Ausbildung fähiger, teils an sich biegsamer und weniger exklusiv ... Unsere Kirchen sollen Kirchen des 19. Jahrhunderts sein ... Das Gewölbe ist der eigentliche Träger des Kirchenstils, so wie der Plafonds den Hörsälen zukommt.'

395 *Organ für christliche Kunst*, II (1852), pp.203–4; quotation taken from reprint in *Kölner Domblatt*, 30 April, 1854: 'Es ist allerdings nicht zu läugnen, dass viele im romanischen Style ausgeführte Kirchen einen allzu düstern und schwerfälligen Eindruck auf den an die leichteren und freieren Formen des gothischen Styles gewohnten Beschauer machen; dieses gilt namentlich von den älteren Bauwerken, während die grossen Fortschritte, die derselbe in wenigen Jahrhunderten gemacht hat, den Beweis liefern, welcher hohen Ausbildung dieser Styl fähig ist. Überhaupt eignet sich derselbe, eben weil noch nicht völlig ausgebildet, recht eigentlich dazu (wenigstens neben dem gothischen), zum Kirchenstyle bei Neubauten wieder erhoben zu werden, da er nicht bloss an und für sich ein echt christlicher Styl ist, sondern auch dem eigenen Denken und Schaffen des Künstlers noch einen hinreichend freien Spielraum lässt. Bei dem Neubau einer gothischen Kirche dagegen ist der Künstler mehr darauf angewiesen, das aus der gothischen Zeit Vorhandene treu zu copiren.' – The editor of the *Organ für christliche Kunst* made the following comment: 'Der romanische Styl ist keineswegs in seiner Entwicklung der Art unterbrochen worden, dass er bei weiterm Fortschreiten ganz andere Resultate gezeigt hätte, als jetzt noch in den vollendetsten Bauten vor uns stehen ... Es war ... ein naturgemässer Fortschritt, den der christliche Kirchenbau machte, als er in den Spitzbogenstyl überging und selbst die Bruchtheile romanischer Bauten im Gothischen vollendete. Darum ist es auch kein richtiger Schluss, dass der romanische Styl dem Denken und Schaffen des Künstlers einen freien Spielraum lasse.'

particularist sentiments in *The Ecclesiologist*.

In 1845, when it looked as if George Gilbert Scott might carry off the commission for the church of St Nicholas in Hamburg, Gottfried Semper published an article in which he argued the case for his own competition design. This case was based partly on the findings of recent research into the Gothic, partly on the technical problems posed by the project, and partly on the kind of considerations advanced by Prisac:
'Germanic architecture does not allow for galleries above the aisles ... It is wrong to regard the mediaeval style of architecture of the twelfth, thirteenth, and fourteenth centuries as *the* national style. The truth of the matter is that the circular arch is quite as familiar in Germany as any other ... and it is equally true that pre-Gothic circular arch architecture is more in keeping with our own period than the pointed arch. This style of architecture, whose development as a genuine national style was disrupted by the introduction of the pointed arch, has not outlived itself, as has the Gothic, so that – partly for this reason and partly because it is more adaptable and less exclusive – it lends itself better to further development ... Our churches should be nineteenth-century churches ... The vault is the whole basis of the ecclesiastical style, just as ceilings are the epitome of secular auditoria.'[394]

And so Semper came out in favour of the Romanesque on the grounds that it was a more truly national style and lent itself more readily to further development. Both of these arguments were discussed over a long period and, on occasions, were mentioned in the *Kölner Domblatt*. Thus, in 1854, one of the periodical's correspondents (*B*) appended the following general observation to his assessment of the Church of St Quirin in Neuss:
'It is of course undeniable that many of the churches executed in the Romanesque style make a far too sombre and heavy impression on viewers accustomed to the lighter and freer forms of the Gothic; this is especially true of the older [Romanesque] buildings, but the great progress made by this style in just a few centuries shows that it is still capable of a great and noble development. In fact, it is precisely because it has not yet been fully developed that it is particularly suitable (certainly, as an adjunct to the Gothic) for new ecclesiastical buildings; because not only is it a genuine Christian style in its own right, it also gives the architect ample opportunity to express his own creative ideas. In the case of a new church built in the Gothic style, on the other hand, the architect is obliged, to a far greater extent, to produce a faithful copy of extant Gothic buildings.'[395]

Here the Romanesque is not presented as a style whose development was prematurely broken off, but as a preliminary stage in the emergence of the Gothic, whose ultimate perfection called for the reproduction of Gothic models or, alternatively, the creation of new buildings conceived in the spirit of its Romanesque roots.

Although this article was not printed in the *Kölner Domblatt* until 1854, it had already appeared two years earlier in the *Organ für christliche Kunst*, whose editor (Baudri) made the following comment in a footnote:

396 August Reichensperger, *Die Kunst Jedermanns Sache* (Frankfurt am Main, 1865); 2nd ed. (Wegberg, 1891), pp.VI–VII.

397 *Kölner Domblatt*, 1 June, 1856 and 30 June, 1865 (Report of a paper read by Reichensperger in Bonn): '. . . gerade in dem echtgermanischen Wesen der Gotik, dass jedes Erzeugnis derselben ein *Individuum* sei, einen ganz *besonderen* Charakter an sich tragen müsse, wesshalb kein Baudenkmal alle denkbaren Vorzüge an sich vereinigen könne . . . So stehe auch der kölner Dom allerdings in mancher Beziehung hinter anderen Domen zurück.'

398 Quotation taken from Hans Vogts, *Vincenz Statz (1819–1899), Lebensbild und Lebenswerk eines Kölner Baumeisters . . .* (Mönchengladbach, 1960), p.21: '. . . dass die Neugotiker vielfach Zwergdome an Stelle ländlicher Kapellen setzen.'

399 H[einrich] von Dehn-Rotfelser, 'Vortrag, gehalten im kasseler Architekten- und Ingenieurverein' in *Kölner Domblatt*, 31 October, 1866, 31 December, 1866 and 31 March, 1867; first printed in *Literatur- und Anzeigeblatt für das Baufach* (subtitle: Beilage zur *Allgemeinen Bauzeitung*), VII (1861–1865), pp.45–9; quotations taken from *ibid.*, pp.45–6: 'Nur im Volke lebte noch halb unbewusst die Liebe zu den in den mittelalterlichen Bauwerken so charakteristisch ausgeprägten örtlichen Eigenthümlichkeiten fort . . . Sorgfältiges Vermeiden jedes grellen Widerspruches gegen die besonderen Eigenthümlichkeiten eines Ortes wird hierbei jedem mit feinem Gefühl begabten Künstler oft der beste Leiter für die Wahl des bei seinen Werken zu beobachtenden Stiles sein.'

400 [August Reichensperger,] 'Welby Pugin' in *Organ für christliche Kunst*, II (1852), pp.196–9 and 205–6; quotation taken from *ibid.*, p.199 ('Private Letter' of 1851 or 1852): 'Sorgen Sie, dass Ihre Kirchen den Bedürfnissen der Religion vollkommen angemessen sind, und dass die Gläubigen alles sehen können; ahmen Sie nicht *alle* alten Muster nach, aber folgen Sie *guten* alten Mustern.'

401 August Reichensperger, *Georg Gottlob Ungewitter und sein Wirken als Baumeister, zumeist aus Briefen desselben dargestellt* (Leipzig, 1866), p.7.

'The development of the Romanesque style was certainly not broken off in the sense that, if it had been allowed to continue, it would have produced quite different results than are to be found in the most perfect extant examples of this style . . . It was . . . a natural progression when Christian ecclesiastical architecture went over to the pointed arch, and even unfinished Romanesque buildings were completed in the Gothic style. Consequently, it is wrong to assume that the Romanesque style allows the architect to express his own creative ideas.'

This doubtless reflected the consensus of opinion in Cologne. The editor, Friedrich Baudri, was the brother of the coadjutor Johann Anton Baudri; and men like Johannes Kreuser (1795–1870), Reichensperger, and Statz all contributed to Baudri's periodical. Reichensperger rejected Neo-Romanesque architecture on similar grounds.[396]

In 1856 Zwirner referred to Cologne Cathedral as 'the canon of Gothic architecture'. This view was not shared by Reichensperger, who maintained that 'because the Gothic is so quintessentially Germanic, every building designed in this style is an *individual* creation with a very *special* character, and consequently no Gothic architectural monument can contain every conceivable virtue . . . By the same token Cologne Cathedral is inferior to other cathedrals in certain respects.'[397] Like his friends on *The Ecclesiologist* Reichensperger disapproved of the contemporary nineteenth-century practice of building 'dwarf cathedrals instead of rural chapels'.[398] It is significant in this connexion that Reichensperger's friend, the architect Georg Gottlob Ungewitter, had promised to contribute to an inventory of the historical monuments in the Electorate of Hesse, whose editor attached great importance to 'the local peculiarities of mediaeval buildings' and recommended that contemporary architects should 'do their utmost to avoid clashing with the peculiarities of individual locations'.[399]

And so in the *Kölner Domblatt* we find the monastery church of Maria Laach advocated as a mediaeval model, Cologne Cathedral referred to as the canon of Gothic architecture and local peculiarities being singled out as an important factor in determining contemporary architectural design. Clearly, therefore, the *Domblatt* differed from both *The Ecclesiologist* and the *Annales archéologiques* in that it was not bound to a particular historical type or style. Like the *Organ für christliche Kunst*, the *Domblatt* followed the rule of thumb which Pugin had outlined in a letter to one of its contributors (presumably Reichensperger):

'Take all necessary steps to ensure that your churches meet the needs of religion and that the congregation can see what is happening; do not imitate *all* old models, but follow *good* old models.'[400]

But despite this rather functional approach, Reichensperger none the less noted with satisfaction that Ungewitter was revealing a growing preference for the thirteenth century.[401]

Ungewitter, who – like Reichensperger – wanted to see the Gothic adopted as a universal style, sought in vain for High Gothic models of private residences in Germany. He finally concluded that the only course open to him was to imitate the numerous extant Late Gothic models and then to use the knowledge gained in this way to reconstruct fourteenth- and thirteenth-century types.[402] This method of procedure, whereby Early or High Gothic forms were evolved from Late Gothic models, appeared perfectly viable to Didron. Commenting on a confessional, which he and Lassus had designed between them, he suggested that 'if the artists of Nuremberg had lived in the thirteenth century and had been asked to produce a confessional, they would probably have made one similar to that which we are now presenting', because they (Didron and Lassus) had based their design on the Late Gothic confessionals in the Liebfrauenkirche.[403] At that time Nuremberg was regarded as the epitome of a mediaeval town, and even in England was invariably cited by Gothic Revival architects as the principal centre of Gothic secular architecture.[404]

But let us return to the *Kölner Domblatt*. In 1853 the art historian Anton Springer (1825–91), who subsequently acquired a considerable reputation, read a paper to the general assembly of the *Akademischer Dombauverein Bonn*, which was reported in the *Domblatt* as follows: 'After indicating that the popular misconception of the Gothic – as the perfect expression of Germanic art and as a style of architecture that would always be dominant in our nordic climes and among the Germanic peoples – he [Springer] went on to point out that, quite apart from the fact that it appeals to our general conception of beauty, Gothic or, to be more precise, Germanic art enjoys one great advantage over Antique art in the sphere of secular architecture. Antique art provides us with no pure models of domestic buildings; during its best period it was simply temple architecture, and its forms are comprehensible only in terms of a temple installation. Germanic art, on the other hand, embraced both monumental and domestic architecture from its very inception, and provides us with perfect models, not only for splendid cathedrals, but also for the most insignificant functional buildings.'[405]

We see, therefore, that the dogmatic Gothic Revivalists of the 1840's and 1850's were not satisfied with just any kind of Gothic secular architecture. As in the ecclesiastical sphere, they insisted that it should be modelled on complex building *types*. Meanwhile, the Antique domestic buildings, which had been found from the eighteenth century onwards in an excellent state of preservation beneath the lava of Vesuvius, were brushed aside because they did not come from the 'best period' of Antique architecture. The fact that the secular buildings of the Gothic Revival would also have failed such a test, since they did not come from the 'best period' of the Gothic, was simply disregarded. This kind of ideological attitude is reminiscent of Andrea Palladio, who argued the same case in reverse in 1570, when he defended the temple façades which he had used for his villas on the grounds that the temples and public buildings of Antiquity had been derived from domestic buildings.[406]

The Cologne Museum and the Hamburg Town Hall corresponded to the Oxford Museum and the Government Offices in so far as they too

402 *Ibid.*, p.36 (Letter of 23 December, 1850).

403 *Annales archéologiques*, I (2nd ed. 1854), p.464 (and following plates): 'Si les artistes de Nuremberg avaient vécu au XIIIᵉ siècle, et avaient été chargés d'un confessional, nul doute qu'ils ne l'eussent exécuté comme celui que nous offrons aujourd'hui...'

404 *The Ecclesiologist*, XIV (1853), p.78 (Street); etc. – Ludwig Grote, *Die romantische Entdeckung Nürnbergs...* (Munich, 1967).

405 *Kölner Domblatt*, 4 September, 1853: 'Schon längst sei das Vorurtheil verschwunden, als wäre die Geltung des gothischen Styles der Herrschaft in nordischen Landschaften und bei den germanischen Völkern unvergänglich. Was aber insbesondere die Verwendbarkeit der gothischen oder richtiger germanischen Kunst für den Privatbau betrifft, so hat sie ausser ihrem, unserem Schönheits- gefühl am meisten zusagenden Charakter im Allgemeinen noch folgende Vorzüge vor der antiken Kunst: Diese liefert uns keine reinen Vorbilder für den Privatbau, sie war in ihrer besten Zeit blosse Tempel- Architektur, und ihre Formen sind nur bei einer Tempel-Anlage verständlich. Dagegen umfasst die germanische Kunst seit ihrem Beginn gleichmässig den monumentalen wie den Privat-Bau und liefert uns vollendete Vorbilder für die grossartige Kathedrale wie für den geringfügigen Nutzbau.'

406 Palladio, *I Quattro libri dell' architettura* (1570), Book I, p.6; Book II, p.69.

407 Volker Plagemann, *Das deutsche Kunstmuseum (1790–1870)*; *Lage, Baukörper, Raumorganisation, Bildprogramm...* (Munich, 1967), pp.169–75; figs.197–210. – Heinz-Jürgen Brandt, *Das Hamburger Rathaus: eine Darstellung seiner Baugeschichte und eine Beschreibung seiner Architektur und künstlerischen Ausschmückung* (Hamburg, 1957), see esp. pp.18–19 and 49–50; fig.71.

408 A[ugust] R[eichensperger,] 'Der Rathaus-Bau in Hamburg und der Museums-Bau in Köln' in *Kölner Domblatt*, 5 November, 1854; reprinted in Reichensperger, *Vermischte Schriften* (1856), pp. 457–9; quotation taken from *Domblatt*: 'Das Rathaus wurzelt seinem Wesen und seiner Bestimmung nach im Mittelalter; das sogenannte classische Alterthum kennt solche Bauten nicht, liefert uns also keinerlei Muster, während die Kunst des Mittelalters hier eben so Grosses und Schönes geleistet hat wie in der kirchlichen Baukunst... Doppelt unbegreiflich wäre es, wenn in einer freien Stadt, deren Grösse im Mittelalter wurzelt, dasjenige Monument, in welchem sich die Gemeinde gleichsam verkörpert, dessen Ideen durch und durch germanischer Natur ist, eine fremde und dazu noch eine todte Sprache sprechen sollte.'

409 Georg Germann, 'Melchior Berris Rathausentwurf für Bern (1833)' in *Basler Zeitschrift für Geschichte und Altertumskunde*, LXIX (1969), pp.239–319, esp. p.260.

410 A[ugust] R[eichensperger,] 'Besprechungen, Mittheilungen etc.' (deals with the Hamburg Town Hall) in *Organ für christliche Kunst*, V (1855), pp.79–80; quotation taken from *ibid.*, p.80: 'In diesem Fall sollte man lieber dem glattesten Modernismus die Sache in die Hand legen...; ein gothisch costumirter Koloss.'

411 *Kölner Domblatt*, 2 March, 1856: 'Wer Deutschlands altehrwürdige Städte besucht, dem fällt nichts so sehr auf, als die Pracht ihrer vormaligen Baukunst. Wo nur der Handel blühte, da blühte auch die Kunst, und jedes Gebäude, mochte es kirchlichen oder weltlichen Zwecken dienen, legte Zeugniss ab von den edlen Gesinnungen, von denen die bürgerliche Gesellschaft durchdrungen war...
'Dennoch fühlte ich recht wohl, dass kein Plan dem von Ihnen beabsichtigten Zwecke würdig entsprechen wird, der nicht durchwegs ausdrucksvoll im Charakter ist, der Sie nicht auf gleiche Stufe mit der Vergangenheit stellt und Sie mit jenen alten Handelsplätzen in geistige Verbindung setzt, welche Deutschland vormals so sehr verherrlicht haben, und als deren Gesammt-Repräsentanten Ihre Stadt angesehen werden kann.

were test cases for the Gothic Revival. If anything, the events leading up to the erection of the two German buildings were even more significant because they were concentrated within such a brief period (1854–56).[407] In his propaganda campaign Reichensperger spoke out loud and clear:

'A town hall is a mediaeval building, in both character and function; so-called Classical Antiquity produced no buildings of this kind, and so provided us with no models, whereas the achievements of mediaeval artists were as great in this sphere as in the sphere of ecclesiastical architecture... It would be doubly incomprehensible if in a Free Imperial City whose greatness originated in the Middle Ages, the one monument in which the community is, so to speak, embodied, the very idea of which is so completely Germanic, should speak to us in a foreign and, what is more, a dead language.'[408]

Reichensperger insisted that the Town Hall must produce a 'picturesque effect' and argued that this could be achieved by a Gothic Revival, but not by a Classical, design. He mentioned the town halls in Danzig, Breslau, Brunswick, Cologne, and Lübeck as possible models. Although Reichensperger was mistaken in thinking that the architects of Classical Antiquity had produced no town halls, it must be said in his defence that, at that time, the form of the Greek *Buleuteria* was still unknown.[409] As for his pathos, this is perhaps understandable if we remember that he regarded the Free Imperial City of Hamburg, with its mediaeval associations, as a counterpoise to the centralized state, as embodied in nineteenth-century France and, more especially, Prussia.

But Reichensperger was not an uncritical Gothic Revivalist. Although he considered it even more imperative that the Wallraf-Richartz-Museum in Cologne should be executed in a Gothic style than the Hamburg Town Hall, he rejected the design submitted by Joseph Felten out of hand. 'A colossus decked out in Gothic costume' was how he described this project, and added that he would prefer even the 'smoothest Modernism'.[410]

The memorandum which George Gilbert Scott submitted with his competition design for the Hamburg Town Hall seemed to Reichensperger so important that he reproduced it verbatim in the *Domblatt*. This document was addressed to the German commission which had organized the competition:
'The visitor to Germany's old and venerable cities notices, above all else, the splendour of their ancient architecture. Where trade flourished, art also flourished, and every building, whether it served an ecclesiastical or a secular purpose, testified to the lofty ideals with which the citizens of those days were imbued...
'And yet I have the definite feeling that no design would meet your requirements unless it were completely expressive in character, and reconciled those requirements with the past, by creating spiritual links with the old market places which were one of the great glories of Germany in times gone by and are so perfectly represented in your own city.

'Diesem Gedanken kann kein Gebäude entsprechen, dem nicht mehr oder minder die in den alten Städten Deutschlands herrschende Bauweise zu Grunde liegt . . .
'Wahr ist's, jedes Zeitalter, so wie jedes Land sollte besondere unterscheidende Kennzeichen im Baustyle haben; ich führe daher hier auch nicht das Wort dafür, dass die Bauart unserer Vorfahren *unverändert* herüberzunehmen sei, sondern dafür, dass sie als die Grundlage gelten soll, worauf wir die Baukunst der Zukunft zu entwickeln versuchen sollten . . .
'Schon die Idee eines Rathauses oder Stadthauses ist gothisch. Die städtischen Regierungen, welche sie versinnbildlichen, sind ihrem Ursprung und Dasein nach wesentlich teutonisch und unter die ruhmwürdigsten Denkmäler des deutschen Volkes zu rechnen . . .
'Die Phase der gothischen Baukunst, welche ich mir angeeignet, die ich als leitendes Vorbild betrachtet habe, ist die, welche der Periode angehört, wo die Gothik ihre höchste Vollkommenheit erreicht; sie concentrirt sich in dem Jahre 1300. Diese Periode fällt etwas früher, als die meisten der noch übrig gebliebenen städtischen Gebäude, weil die höchste Höhe des Wohlstandes der Municipalitäten in den meisten Städten durchweg erst erstiegen ward, als die Architektur bereits in absteigender Bewegung begriffen war – ein zufälliger Umstand, der keinen Grund darbietet, warum *wir* nicht das Beste als Ausgangspunkt für unsere eigene Entwicklung wählen sollten. Halten wir uns an diese frühere Periode, so gewinnen wir dadurch auch grössere Einfachheit, und tritt das Phantastische zurück, was zu dem Ernst des Gegenstandes besser stimmt . . .
'Im vorliegenden Falle habe ich die mehr symmetrische Weise der Behandlung gewählt, weil ich fühlte, dass Einheit und Grossartigkeit mehr durch die Natur und Stellung des Gebäudes erfordert sei und besser mit den umgebenden Gegenständen stimme, als malerische Unregelmässigkeit.'

412 See Note 40 for Part III above. – See also the article signed *S*. 'Über eine neuerdings im gothischen Style erbaute evangelische Kirche' in *Organ für christliche Kunst*, v (1855), pp.177–9 and 189–91.

413 Quoted from Pastor, *Reichensperger* (1899), I, pp.602–3: 'Es möge nur ein einziger Punkt namhaft gemacht werden, in betreff dessen bei einem Theaterbau der gotische Stil nicht ausreiche oder bloss hinter irgend einem andern Stil zurückstehe! Auch die gotischen Rathäuser erklärten die nämlichen Stimmen für unverträglich mit dem Geiste und den Bedürfnissen des neunzehnten Jahrhunderts – und doch stehen gegenwärtig zwei Hauptstädte,

'No building can express this conception unless it is based, more or less, on the dominant style of architecture in Germany's historic towns . . .
'The plain truth of the matter is that the architecture of any given period, and of any given country, should possess specific and distinctive characteristics; consequently, I have no intention of advocating that the architectural style favoured by our forebears should be adopted *unmodified*, but merely that it should serve as the basis on which we should endeavour to develop the architectural style of the future . . .
'The very idea of a town hall or a civic hall is Gothic. The town councils which they symbolize are essentially teutonic, in terms of both origin and character, and must be regarded as one of the most worthy German institutions and one that deserves to be commemorated . . .
'The phase of Gothic architecture which I have made my own and which I regard as the ideal model, is one which forms part of the period in which the Gothic reached its peak of perfection; the focal point of this phase was the year 1300. Most of the urban buildings to have survived from the Gothic era are rather later than this period, for the simple reason that the municipalities in most mediaeval towns did not reach the peak of their affluence until Gothic architecture had begun to decline. This was a purely fortuitous circumstance, and is no reason why *we* should not choose the best period as the point of departure for our own architectural development. If we adhere to this earlier period, we will also find greater simplicity, and a diminution of the phantastic, which is more in accord with the serious character of our project . . .
'In the present case I have used a rather more symmetrical method, because I felt that the character and the position of the building called for unity and splendour, which would be more in keeping with the neighbouring buildings than picturesque irregularity.'[411]

Let me recapitulate a few of the key concepts in this long-winded memorandum: *Captatio benevolentiae* (vintage Scott!) – the resurgence of trade leads to the resurgence of art – historical settings call for historicizing architecture – town halls are essentially teutonic and German – town halls are essentially Gothic – the peak of Gothic architecture was *c*.1300 – monumental buildings call for symmetrical design.

We find that, at first, the idea of building Protestant churches in a Gothic Revival style was received just as coolly in Cologne as it was in England, where *The Ecclesiologist*'s initial reaction to Scott's competition entry for the church of St Nicholas in Hamburg had been decidedly negative.[412] But as far as Reichensperger was concerned, the Gothic was quite simply a universal style:
'As for the assertion that the Gothic style is unsuitable, or less suitable than other styles, for a theatrical building, this is easily rebutted. The fact of the matter is that the people who claim this are the same people who maintained that Gothic town halls were incompatible with the spirit and the needs of the nineteenth century – and yet two major cities, Vienna and Munich, are about to erect such buildings.'[413]

Reichensperger was probably the only person to insist that, as a

91, 92

159

Wien und München, im Begriffe, sich
solche zu errichten.' – The Town Hall in
Vienna: built 1872–83 by Friedrich von
Schmidt; the Town Hall in Munich: built
1867–74, 1888–93 and 1899–1908 by
Georg von Hauberisser.

414 Erwin Hainisch, *Der Architekt Johann
Ferdinand Hetzendorf von Hohenberg*
(offprint from *Wiener Jahrbuch für
Kunstgeschichte*; Innsbruck and Vienna,
1949), p.65; pls. XXII–XXIII. –
Bringmann, *Studien zur neuromanischen
Architektur* (1968), pp.313–16.

415 Pastor, *Reichensperger* (1899), I, pp.
520–2.

416 Friedrich Hoffstadt, *Gothisches
A-B-C-Buch, das ist: Grundregeln des
gothischen Styls für Künstler und
Werkleute* (Frankfurt am Main, 1840);
French translation by Théodore
Aufschlager (Liège, 1851); Italian
translation by F. Lazzari (Venice, 1858). –
Kölner Domblatt, 23 October, 1842.

417 Reichensperger, *Ungewitter* (1866),
pp.150–3 (letters of 1856).

418 *Ibid.*, p.126 (Ungewitter to
Reichensperger, 25 January, 1855);
'Nachbildungen alter ausgeführter
Sachen'.

419 V[incenz] Statz and G[eorg Gottlob]
Ungewitter, *Gotisches Musterbuch*,
herausgegeben von V. Statz und G.
Ungewitter, mit einer Einleitung von A.
Reichensperger, 2 vols. (Leipzig, 1856–61),
II, p.50, note: 'In den verschiedenen in
diesem Heft enthaltenen Figuren kam es
nur darauf an, die geometrischen Systeme
der einzelnen Werke darzutun.' – There
were two further German editions, one
English (1858), and one French (1855–6).

420 See Note 76 for Part III above.

421 Carl [Alexander von] Heideloff, *Die
Bauhütten des Mittelalters in Deutschland,
eine kurzgefasste geschichtliche Darstellung
mit Urkunden und andern Beilagen, so wie
einer Abhandlung über den Spitzbogen in
der Architektur der Alten als Vorläufer der
Grundzüge der altedutschen Baukunst und
auch an des Verfassers Werk 'Die
Ornamentik des Mittelalters' sich anreihend*
(Nuremberg, 1844). – Mathias Roriczer,
*Das Büchlein von der Fialen Gerechtigkeit
von Mathias Roriczer, weiland
Dombaumeister in Regensburg; nach einem
alten Drucke aus dem Jahre 1486 in die
heutige Mundart übertragen und durch
Anmerkungen erläutert . . . Mit einem
Vorwort von A. Reichensperger* (Trier,
1845); the Foreword also in Reichensperger,
Vermischte Schriften (1856), pp.55–71.

422 See Note 364 for Part III above.

universal style, the Gothic Revival must even be capable of catering for
the needs of the theatre. This, after all, was the ultimate demand. The
only other designs for theatre buildings in a mediaeval style were
prompted by considerations of conformity. There were two of them.
Johann Ferdinand Hetzendorf von Hohenberg designed an annexe
containing a theatre for the Gothic Revival building of Franzensburg in
Laxenburg, near Vienna; but this design, which probably dates from
1807, was never executed. And in 1889 Otto March (1845–1913)
designed and built the Festival Theatre in Worms, which was given a
Romanesque appearance so that it would blend with the general
townscape, whose dominant feature is the Romanesque cathedral.[414]

Faced with the great dearth of original Gothic models for secular
buildings, Reichensperger and Statz tried to overcome this problem by
publishing enlarged copies of the town views drawn by Matthäus
Merian the Elder (1593–1650).[415]

In Germany, and especially in Reichensperger's circle, the processes
of triangulation and quadrature played a similar role in the theory of
Gothic Revival design as the concepts of the 'picturesque' in England
and 'visual construction' in France. In 1840 the lawyer Friedrich
Hoffstadt (1802–46) published a book dealing with these processes,
which was warmly welcomed in the *Kölner Domblatt*. The reviewer,
Ernst Weyden, referred to Hoffstadt as 'the Vitruvius of the German
style', adding that his book was clearer and more easily understandable
than the *De Architectura*.[416] Subsequently, when Statz and Ungewitter
joined forces to produce the *Gotisches Musterbuch*, Ungewitter objected
strongly to Hoffstadt's 'mania for figures', which he attributed to his
preoccupation with Late Gothic models, although Reichensperger, who
wrote the introduction for this book, was quite convinced of the
intrinsic value of architectural geometry.[417] Ungewitter then proposed
a section entitled 'Nachbildungen alter ausgeführter Sachen' (Copies of
Old Executed Projects),[418] and pointed out that for a number of the
illustrations all they would have to do was 'represent the geometrical
systems on which the various works were based'.[419] This type of
presentation was similar to that used by the Brandon brothers in
England.[420] Meanwhile, two new editions of Mathias Roriczer's
Fialengerechtigkeit, which had first been published in 1486 and which is
still an indispensable aid in the assessment of the geometry used in
Gothic architecture,[421] had appeared in 1844 and 1845, respectively.
The first of these was edited by Carl Alexander von Heideloff
(1789–1865), the second by Reichensperger.

Reichensperger's interest in the geometry of Late Gothic architecture
was linked with his interest in the organization of the Late Gothic
52 *Bauhütten*, whose revival formed the cornerstone of his whole theory of
architecture.[422] According to the *Kölner Domblatt*, Reichensperger made
the following prediction in a speech delivered in Bonn in 1850:
'It could well be that the whole future of art and its general viability
depend on whether it can forge new links with craftsmanship and
whether – as has always been the case in great creative periods – the

various branches of art are able to reunite within the ambiance of architecture, in which they all had their origin. When art and craftsmanship were divorced, art became too ethereal and was lost from sight in a remote and tenuous realm; it lost its popular and historical base. As for craftsmanship, that has become a mechanized and inferior form of factory work, with which it cannot hope to compete. Art must once again speak to the people of the people, it must become flesh of their flesh, life of their life.'[423]

Reichensperger reminded his audience that the mediaeval *Bauhütten* should on no account be confused with the freemasons' lodges of the nineteenth century. After pointing out that the masons of the Middle Ages were organized in societies based on a complex body of rules and regulations and were subject to disciplinary measures, he explained that these rules had nothing to do with 'police regulations' since their sole purpose was to create an environment in which theory and practice, art and craftsmanship, could interact and so produce a complete and unique fusion.[424]

This theory of Reichensperger received almost daily confirmation from Zwirner, the head of the Cathedral *Bauhütte* in Cologne, and his disciples Statz and Schmidt, who had risen from the ranks of the German craftsmen to become architects of international renown. But Reichensperger was not the only Rhinelander to take pride in the Cathedral *Bauhütte*. In the obituary which he composed on Zwirner's death, Johannes Kreuser wrote:
'If the Rhineland now sees its resurgent craftsmanship forging new links with art, it is the Cologne *Bauhütte*, i.e. Zwirner's *Bauhütte*, that is the matrix of all such phenomena.'[425]

As for Statz, he was once accorded the honorary title of *Kunsthandwerker* (artistic or creative craftsman) in the *Organ für christliche Kunst*; and Schmidt, who was elevated to baronial rank in Vienna, asked for the following simple but moving inscription to be placed on his gravestone:
'Here lies Friedrich Schmidt, a German mason.'[426]

In Reichensperger's thinking the concept of 'truth' merged with his conception of the relationship between mediaeval art and craftsmanship to form a unique combination. In discussing the forms of mediaeval buildings he wrote:
'Everything, from the rake of the turrets and roofs down to the fittings on the doors, shows how the men who created this building tried to transform technical and mechanical features into a vehicle for art, and to engender beauty from necessity.'[427]

He then contrasted these mediaeval practices with the state of affairs in his own day:
'Academic examinations have now replaced the traditional "masterpieces"; instead of training in a *Bauhütte*, our architects attend lectures; the guilds, which emerged and developed as a normal part of everyday life, have been disbanded, and the sense of craftsmanship and discipline which they instilled in their members destroyed; apprentices

423 *Kölner Domblatt*, 1 December, 1850: 'Überhaupt ist vielleicht die ganze Zukunft der Kunst und ihre Lebensfähigkeit dadurch bedingt, dass die höhere Kunstübung sich wieder mit dem Handwerk verbinde, und dass die Künste überhaupt sich wieder – wie solches in allen grossen schöpferischen Kunstperioden der Fall gewesen – auf dem Boden der Architektur sammelten, auf welchem sie auch sammt und sonders entsprossen seien. Durch die Lostrennung der Kunst vom Handwerke sei erstere in den höheren Regionen verdunstet, sie habe ihre geschichtliche, volkstümliche Unterlage eingebüsst, während das Handwerk mechanisch und dem Fabrikwesen leibeigen geworden sei, mit dem es die Concurrenz unmöglich aushalten könne; es müsse die Kunst wieder vom Volk zum Volke reden, Fleisch von seinem Fleische, Leben von seinem Leben werden.'

424 *Ibid.*, 2 March, 1851.

425 *Ibid.*, 1 December, 1861: 'Wenn endlich das Rheinland das aufstrebende Handwerk wieder zur Kunst zurückkehren sieht, so ist die kölner d.h. Zwirner's Hütte, die Mutter aller dieser Erscheinungen.'

426 *Organ für christliche Kunst*, IV (1854), p.159. – August Reichensperger, *Zur Charakterisierung des Baumeisters Friedrich Freiherrn von Schmidt* (Düsseldorf, n.d. [1891]), p.19: 'Hier ruhet in Gott Friedrich Schmidt, ein deutscher Steinmetz.'

427 Reichensperger, *Die christlich-germanische Baukunst* (3rd ed., 1860), p.15: 'Alles, von den Neigungswinkeln der Thurmspitzen und Dächern an bis zu den Beschlägen der Thore herab, zeigt das Bestreben, das Technische und Mechanische zum Vehikel der Kunst zu machen und das Schöne aus dem Nothwendigen erwachsen zu lassen.'

and journeymen have been promoted to *élèves* and *conducteurs* and every last man Jack has become a "gentleman". These gentlemen have learned a vast number of Greek and Latin names; they can produce the most sensitive drawings with a proper distribution of light and shade; they have a working knowledge of physics, chemistry, mineralogy and botany, hydraulics and hydrostatics, pneumatics, mechanics and perspective, integral and differential calculus, plane and spherical trigonometry; in fact they have learned everything – everything except the art of building. But the art of building is the one thing that was fully understood by our simple and uneducated masters in their leather aprons.'[428]

Whereas in the eighteenth century the academics had proudly proclaimed their internationalism,[429] in the nineteenth century nationalism was the order of the day, and went hand in glove with a new anti-academic trend. True, there was a lively interaction between the ecclesiologists, the *archéologues* and the *Neugotiker* which transcended national borders. But in showering one another with eulogies and in handing out honorary memberships to one another with such abandon, these groups were motivated primarily by the desire to form an alternative society that would replace the Classically oriented society of the academies. This was one of the reasons for the paradoxical situation whereby the Gothic was regarded as both a national or indigenous and an international or Christian style. The international view found its most powerful advocates during the 1850's and 1860's when – as we have seen from the contemporary quotations, especially those taken from *The Ecclesiologist* – it influenced the choice of Gothic models.

But during this period there was also a growing tendency for the Gothic and Classical camps to merge. In 1855 George Gilbert Scott was made an Associate of the Royal Academy; and the Institute of British Architects had numbered quite a few Gothic Revivalists among its members ever since its inception. In France, Viollet-le-Duc failed in his attempt to gain control of the Ecole des Beaux-Arts; but Guadet, who led the students' revolt against the Emperor's protégé, won a prize at the Ecole with a design for a 'mediaeval' monastery. None the less, the struggle between the Classical and the Gothic Revival schools was more protracted in France than elsewhere. With his essentially political and rather aggressive outlook, Reichensperger often tended to characterize the conditions obtaining in Germany and, more especially, Prussia (which, at that time, included the Rhenish territories) in the light of his experience of France. When the lawyer and art historian Carl Schnaase (1798–1875), a native of Berlin, described, in an article in the *Annales archéologiques*, what was happening in Prussia at the beginning of the 1850's, he pointed out that a large Gothic Revival church was under construction, and then went on to correct the impression created by Reichensperger:[430]

'But, in point of fact, our German taste and attitudes differ somewhat from yours. We do not have this exclusive predilection for Gothic art; our inclinations and our sympathies are more likely to be roused by the

428 *Ibid.*, p.24: 'Die gelehrten Examina haben die Meisterstücke verdrängt; statt in den Bauhütten werden unsere Architekten vor dem Katheder gebildet; die mitten aus dem Leben erwachsenen Zunftgenossenschaften sind zersprengt und ihre Standesehre wie ihre Disziplin zu Grunde gegangen; die Lehrjungen und Gesellen sind zu Eleven und Konduktoren avancirt und damit alle sammt und sonders "Herren" geworden. Diese Herren wissen dann eine Unzahl griechischer und lateinischer Wörter auswendig; sie können die feinsten Gefühlslinien, Licht- und Schattenstriche machen, sie verstehen mehr oder weniger von Physik, Chemie, Mineralogie und Botanik, Hydraulik und Hydrostatik, Pneumatik, Mechanik und Perspektive, Integral- und Differential-Rechnung, ebene und sphärische Trigonometrie, kurz Alles, Alles, nur nicht – die Kunst des Bauens. Die aber gerade verstanden die schlichten, alten, ungelehrten Meister im Schurzfell.' – For a similar account see Reichensperger's 'Aphorismen über Kunst' in *Kölner Domblatt*, 30 September, 1863, 31 August, 1864, 28 February, 1865, and 30 November, 1865. An earlier series of aphorisms had already appeared in *The Ecclesiologist*, XVII (1856), p.367; XVIII (1857), pp.179–80; German version in Reichensperger, *Vermischte Schriften* (1856), pp.513–40.

429 Werner Oechslin, 'Internationalismus im 18. Jahrhundert: Aspekte der italienischen Architektur des Settecento' in *Neue Zürcher Zeitung*, 4 January, 1970, pp.37–8.

430 [Carl] Schnaase, 'Mouvement archéologique en Prusse' in *Annales archéologiques*, XI (1851), p.129. – This must be St Peter's in Berlin, built in 1846–50 by Johann Heinrich Strack (1805–80), which was destroyed in 1943.

Romanesque art of the Middle Ages. We do not believe that the restoration of Gothic art pure and simple is possible, or even desirable. We would prefer, so to speak, to revive the ideas evolved in the Middle Ages; to vivify and christianize (if we may be allowed to use such expressions) our national taste by study and, within certain limits, by the imitation of mediaeval art. We hope that, as a result, a style will emerge that will be partly new and partly a mediaeval revival. We do not have this struggle between the academic school and the Christian and French school, which is being conducted in your country and in which you and your friends have achieved so much that is memorable and that will also been of benefit to us. Our architects, certainly the vast majority of our architects, are admirers and connoisseurs of both mediaeval and Antique art; but we have no school that consciously tries to obliterate the memory of either one or the other.'[431]

The quiet tone of Schnaase's article survived Didron's forthright postscript, in which the Frenchman insisted that German eclecticism was a bad method.

Reichensperger and his associates had three principal aims: to ensure that artists and architects received a predominantly practical training, to create a bourgeois Christian society based on the cellular formation of the mediaeval guilds, and to establish the Gothic Revival as a universal style. None of these was achieved in their lifetime.

Although Viollet-le-Duc was ridiculed by his compatriots for his attachment to the Gothic, his rationalism and his unbiased approach to the new iron style have ensured his *Entretiens* an astonishing reputation among twentieth-century scholars.[432] It was, of course, the excessive attachment of the German Gothic Revival movement to the techniques of the traditional stonemason that prevented it from making any real headway. Reichensperger was so opposed to iron that he conducted a bitter and completely hopeless campaign to try to dissuade Zwirner from his declared intention of building an iron roof for Cologne Cathedral;[433] and when Bötticher had predicted the development of a new iron style in 1846, he had dismissed the possibility as a foolish notion.[434] But Reichensperger's party, which pursued both political and artistic objectives, was taken seriously. In the Communist Party Manifesto of 1848 we read:

'The bourgeoisie has discovered how the brutal expression of strength, which the reactionary forces so greatly admire about the mediaeval period, found its perfect complement in absolute sloth.'[435]

And when the authors of the Manifesto included the Gothic cathedrals in their list of technical 'miracles' which far excel anything produced in the bourgeois period, there can be little doubt but that they were having a jibe at Reichensperger and his Cologne circle.

Semper, who met Marx when he went to London as a political refugee, wrote in *Der Stil*:

'The zealots in that proselytizing artists' party regard the north western and northern territories of Europe as a pagan land that has to be reconquered for Christianity, and they recommend the same methods

431 *Ibid.*: 'Mais, en effet, le goût et les allures de l'Allemagne diffèrent un peu des vôtres. Nous n'avons pas cette prédilection exclusive pour l'art gothique; notre tendence et notre sympathie sont peut-être plus dirigées vers l'art roman du moyen âge. Nous ne croyons pas que le rétablissement de l'art gothique pur et simple soit possible, ni même qu'il soit à désirer. Nous tendons plus à faire revivre les idées du moyen âge dans un certain sens; de vivifier et christianiser (si l'on peut dire ainsi) le goût national par l'étude et, dans certaines limites, par l'imitation de l'art du moyen âge. Nous espérons que par cette infusion un style, en partie nouveau, en partie régénérateur du moyen âge, naîtra, Nous n'avons pas cette lutte entre l'école académique et l'école chrétienne et française qui existe sur le sol de votre patrie, et dans laquelle, vous et vos amis, avez fait tant d'exploits, dont nous profiterons à notre tour. Nos architectes, ou du moins l'immense majorité de nos architectes, sont admirateurs et connaisseurs de l'art du moyen âge autant que de l'antique, mais il n'y a pas d'école qui ait la tendance d'écarter de l'art actuel les reminiscences de l'un et de l'autre.'

432 John Summerson places Viollet-le-Duc on a par with Alberti and regards him as the last great architectural theorist; see J. S., *Heavenly Mansions and Other Essays on Architecture* (London, 1949), p.135.

433 *Kölner Domblatt*, 4 September, 1853; for Zwirner's reply see *ibid.*, 3 June, 1855. – *Annales archéologiques*, XVII (1857), pp. 132–4. – *The Ecclesiologist*, XVII (1856), pp.349–52 (with commentary, in which the editor considered the pros and cons of this design).

434 See Note 95 (last section) for Part III above. – Reichensperger, *Die christlich-germanische Baukunst* (1860), p.66.

435 Karl Marx and Friedrich Engels, *Manifest der Kommunistischen Partei* (1848); quotation taken from Leipzig edition (1959), p. 127 (= Part I, §17).

of conversion as those already employed in France for a similar purpose (see Reichensperger's *Fingerzeige*).

'The determination and calculation of this movement, the principle of constraint which has been clearly and precisely formulated in its programme and which was drawn up by archaeologists and priests, are the best guarantee that those who deny it a future role, even if its achievements should be properly appreciated and its plans well conceived, are in the right.'[436]

As a political revolutionary, as a practical architect who had travelled the world, and as an archaeologist, Semper had a thorough knowledge of production conditions, both past and present, and in two sections of *Der Stil* entitled 'Der Kautschuk das Faktotum der Industrie' (Rubber: the Factotum of Industry) and 'Jetziger Stil, der bei den Kautschuk-produkten vorherrscht' (The Dominant Style Used at Present for Rubber Products) he had begun to consider an entirely new type of material at a time when Reichensperger was still attacking cast-iron products.[437] 'Faced with such a material', Semper wrote, 'a stylist's mind ceases to function.'[438] But Semper's mind did not cease to function. On the contrary, he applied it to good purpose. He had long since realized, from his investigation of polychromy in Antique architecture, that the artistic form of a building is not determined by the materials and the construction alone. To some extent Semper's ideas resembled those advanced by Fergusson, although it is arguable that, of the two, he was the more influential.

The Gothic Revival movement in Germany did not possess a theorist of his calibre; and it was this, more than anything else, that was to prove its downfall.

Could it be that I have overestimated the importance of the *Kölner Domblatt* in placing it on a par with *The Ecclesiologist* and the *Annales archéologiques*? To nineteenth-century scholars, certainly, this assessment would have seemed perfectly valid. On the other hand, it must be admitted that the *Domblatt*'s close links with a daily newspaper and with the Dombauverein, which was interested only in matters that had a direct bearing on the completion of Cologne Cathedral, prevented it from developing its potential to the full. Incidentally, this was the reason for the foundation of the Christlicher Kunstverein für das Erzbistum Köln (Association for the Development of Christian Art in the Archbishopric of Cologne) and the publication of the *Organ für christliche Kunst*. But although it was intended to supplement the *Domblatt*, this periodical was really no more than a news sheet. In addition to the *Domblatt*, which he edited, and the *Organ*, Reichensperger had many other forums at his disposal. His later writings and parliamentary speeches were remarkable for their novel and trenchant maxims, but they contained no new arguments.

In my analysis of the *Kölner Domblatt* I have restricted myself to three principal points: nationalism, stylistic ideal, and *Bauhütte*. It should be pointed out, however, that Reichensperger and the other contributors to this periodical also referred to the great majority of the

436 Semper, *Der Stil*, I (1878), pp. XVII–XVIII: 'Die Eiferer in jener tendentiösen Künstlerpartei behandeln das nordwestliche und nördliche Europa geradezu wie ein dem Christenthum neu zu eroberndes Heidenland und bringen dieselben Mittel der Bekehrung in Vorschlag, wodurch bereits schon einmal über Frankreich dasselbe Ziel erreicht wurde (*vide* Reichensperger's *Fingerzeige*). 'Das Absichtsvolle und Studirte, was dieser Richtung anhaftet, das Prinzip der Unfreiheit, das in dem von Priestern und Archäologen entworfenen Programm derselben mit klaren und bestimmten Worten ausgesprochen ist, sind die sichersten Bürgschaften für die Ansicht derer, die ihr die Zukunft absprechen, mögen ihre Leistungen an sich auch wohlverstanden und ihre Pläne gut berechnet sein.'

437 *Ibid.*, pp.105–11 (= §§32–3).

438 *Ibid.*, p.109: 'Bei einer solchen Materie steht einem Stilisten der Verstand still!' – See also Günter Bandmann, 'Der Wandel der Materialbewertung in der Kunsttheorie des 19. Jahrhunderts' in *Beiträge zur Theorie der Künste im 19. Jahrhundert*, I, hrsg. von Helmut Koopmann und J. Adolf Schmoll gen. Eisenwerth . . . (Frankfurt am Main, 1971), pp.129–57.

topics discussed in *The Ecclesiologist* and the *Annales archéologiques*. Meanwhile, if we wish to assess the importance of the project for the completion of Cologne Cathedral, of the Cathedral's *Bauhütte*, and of the *Bauhütte* conception propagated in the *Domblatt*, we need only consider the way in which the twentieth-century Bauhaus developed, both as a word and as an idea, from the nineteenth-century *Bauhütte*.

IV The Influence exerted by the Gothic Revival

1 The Gothic Revival as the Basis of a New Style

1 Paul Clemen, 'Strawberry-Hill und Wörlitz: von den Anfängen der Neugotik' in *Neue Beiträge deutscher Forschung, Wilhelm Worringer zum 60. Geburtstag*, hrsg. von Erich Fidder (Königsberg, 1943), pp.37–60; quotation (for which no source is given) taken from *ibid.*, p.37: '... dass er am liebsten eine neue Baukunst *erfinden* würde, die aber gewiss mehr Fortsetzung der gotischen wie der griechischen wäre.'

2 Heinrich Hübsch, *In welchem Style sollen wir bauen? Beantwortet von Heinrich Hübsch* (Karlsruhe, 1828). – Robert Dale Owen, *Hints on Public Architecture, Containing among other Illustrations, Views and Plans of the Smithsonian Institution ...* (New York and London, 1849). – See also Carroll L[ouis] V[anderslice] Meeks, 'Romanesque before Richardson in the United States' in *Art Bulletin*, XXXV (1953), pp.17–33.

3 Eisenlohr, *Ausgeführte oder zur Ausführung bestimmte Entwürfe* (1852), II, § 6: 'System ... über welches hinaus kein wesentlich anderes und neues aufgefunden werden kann'.

4 *Ibid.*: 'Es muss aber freilich dieses urbildliche Wesen der deutschen Baukunst von der örtlichen und zeitlichen Erscheinung unterschieden werden ... Einer Wiederaufnahme dieser Architektur im streng archäologischen Sinn soll hier keineswegs ausschliesslich das Wort geredet sein, wohl aber einem künstler-ischen Schaffen innerhalb ihres Prinzips und urbildlichen Wesens, von einer Wiedergeburt und Erneuerung im Sinne freier Entfaltung des Prinzipmässigen.'

5 Herman Lotze, *Geschichte der Aesthetik in Deutschland ...* (Munich, 1868); facsimile reprint (New York, 1965), p.549: 'Betrachten wir das religiöse Leben als den Mittelpunkt unserer idealen Cultur, so würde nur der gothische Styl, und vielleicht der romanische, die nöthige Biegsamkeit besitzen, um allen unsern verschiedenen Lebensinteressen zu entsprechen.'

We are told that, after visiting the Gothic cathedral in Meissen, Philipp Otto Runge (1777–1810) said that 'he would like best of all to *invent* a new style of architecture but that this would be a continuation of the Gothic rather than the Grecian'.[1] This statement, which reverberated throughout the whole of the nineteenth century, posed a problem. It was, after all, one of the basic tenets of nineteenth-century architectural theory that a new style could not be 'invented'. On the contrary, this 'new style' had to emerge 'organically' from one of the mediaeval styles imitated by contemporary architects. If we disregard the Romanesque Revival – which was particularly strong in Germany and which also gained a foothold in the United States – we are left with the Gothic Revival, Neo-Classicism and Eclecticism; and of these three movements the Gothic Revival undoubtedly made the greatest contribution to the subsequent development of architectural theory in the first half of the twentieth century.[2] The deterrent effect of 'copyism' on 'organic' development had been recognized by the 1850's.

Friedrich Eisenlohr (1805–55) regarded the Gothic as an architectural system 'which could not be bettered by any fundamentally different or new system'.[3] This assessment, which was based on a constructive view of architecture, was of course invalidated by the subsequent introduction of iron and reinforced concrete, which led to the development of entirely new methods of construction. Meanwhile, however, the primacy accorded to construction by Eisenlohr and others obviated the necessity for imitative ornamentation:
'We must of course distinguish between the essential character of Gothic architecture [deutsche Baukunst] and particular geographical and temporal examples ... We are certainly not recommending the readoption of this architecture in a strictly archaeological sense, but what we do advocate is the implementation of artistic activity in accordance with its underlying principle and original character.'[4]

In his *Geschichte der Aesthetik*, which appeared in 1868 and reached a very wide public, Hermann Lotze (1817–81) argued the same case from a cultural point of view:
'If we regard the religious life of the nation as the focal point of our intellectual culture, then really only the Gothic or, conceivably, the Romanesque would be flexible enough to cater for our many different interests.'[5]

Although Lotze considered that stone was the perfect material for all

84

60

architectural purposes, he none the less preferred the light timber structures built by men like Eisenlohr in the early days of the railways to the massive stone buildings of the Neo-Romanesque school.[6] He defended Paxton's Crystal Palace on the same grounds, arguing that the extraordinarily slender supports provided for this building did not detract from its architectonic quality, since 'aesthetic sensitivity is a product of experience'.[7] This insight was to enable the next generation to appreciate the value of reinforced concrete.

We have already seen, from the excerpts reproduced from *The Ecclesiologist*, that the English theorists investigated the problem of imitation more thoroughly than their Continental counterparts. At first only a few outsiders were prepared to go against the imitative creed evolved by the Gothic Revivalists. One of these was Thomas Harris (1829–1900):

'An Architecture, to be national, must be strictly the outgrowth of the wants and feelings of the age and country . . . We must no longer grope about amongst the mazes of former ages, but must ascend to clear first principles, and with strong faith chisel out for ourselves new expressions, being content with simple and, it may be, rude achievements at the outset.'[8]

But in fact, if we look at Harris's own buildings, we find that they have their roots in the Gothic Revival.[9] This is hardly surprising for, as *The Ecclesiologist* once observed in another connexion: 'From some point it *must* start'. Harris tried to find his new expressions by stipulating that each different material must have its own style or character.[10] This was not a new idea, but the way in which Harris expressed it was new. He said that the material demanded its own style. In other words, the material was the active agent, not the architect. This passive attitude of Harris, which was in marked contrast to the direct and active approach adopted by the High Victorian architects, was characteristic of his generation. In his *History of the Gothic Revival*, Charles Locke Eastlake (1836–1906), who was a personal friend of many of the Late Victorian architects, praised the dexterity of men like Richard Norman Shaw (1831–1912) and William Eden Nesfield (1835–88) who, he said, 'can acquire so speedily and so thoroughly the special characteristics of any style which they may select for imitation'.[11]

In his assessment of Nesfield's Cloverly Hall, Whitchurch (Shropshire; 1862–70) Eastlake was more specific:

'To describe a modern building by the general remark that its style can be properly referred to no precise period in the history of styles, would, not many years ago, have been equivalent to pronouncing its condemnation, and even at the present time there are but few designers who can depart from recognized canons of taste without arriving at a result more original than satisfactory.'[12]

Small wonder that Eastlake made no reference to architects like Edward Buckton Lamb and Thomas Harris. He did not share the view held by many of his contemporaries that the historical approach to

6 *Ibid.*, pp.507–8 and 544.

7 *Ibid.*, p.545: '. . . unser ästhetisches Gefühl ist hier abhängig von der Erfahrung.'

8 Thomas Harris, *Victorian Architecture: a Few Words to Show that a National Architecture Adapted to the Wants of the Nineteenth Century is Attainable* (London, 1860), pp.3 and 5. – Harris seems to have been the first person to use the concept 'Victorian architecture'; see Goodhart-Rendel, *English Architecture since the Regency* (1953), p.135.

9 Eastlake, *A History of the Gothic Revival*, additional plates in the 1970 edition, fig.22.

10 Harris, *Victorian Architecture* (1860), p.6.

11 Eastlake, *A History of the Gothic Revival* (1872), p.339.

12 *Ibid.*, p.340.

architecture should be thrown overboard. On the contrary, he considered that a national style of architecture would emerge from the Gothic Revival, provided English architects achieved complete mastery over the architectural forms of the Gothic:

'Then and not till then shall we possess – if it be worth possessing – a really national architecture. Then and not till then will the Gothic Revival be complete.'[13]

No sign here of Pugin's and Street's thesis that a good Gothic Revival architect must first be a good Christian!

Not only the architectural historians, but many of the architectural theorists writing in the last thirty years of the nineteenth century, were preoccupied with the question of form. Sir Thomas Graham Jackson (1835–1934), who was a pupil of Sir George Gilbert Scott and who, incidentally, recorded the most delightful anecdotes about his famous teacher, is a particularly suitable author to consider in this connexion, for he wrote on the question of form both as an historian and as a theorist. The table of contents in his *Modern Gothic Architecture*, which appeared in 1873, lists catch phrases which cover every aspect of this problem, while the first chapter of this book, which bears the significant title 'The Proper End of the Gothic Revival', contains subtitles such as: 'Anomalous history of Architecture during the last four centuries, and especially since the revival of the Gothic style . . . – No style is quite suitable to any other country or age than that which produced it – Gothic, therefore, is not quite suitable to us, and a new style is wanted –Why, then, revive Gothic at all? – Because a new art must be developed out of an older one . . . – The real object of the revival of Gothic is to revive, not Gothic art, but Art itself: it is a means, not an end – True definition of Modern Gothic Architecture from a practical instead of an antiquarian point of view – The revival of Gothic has failed hitherto to effect the recovery of Art . . . '[14]

In his second chapter Jackson castigates 'Formalism and Purism', and maintains that 'modern Gothic is concerned with the principles rather than the forms of ancient Gothic' and that 'Art in England, when we recover it, will necessarily be Gothic, but it will be Gothic without mediaevalism'.[15]

In the third chapter Jackson criticizes false originality and the public that demands it, and in the fourth he breaks with the preceding generation:

'The partial unsuitability of Gothic need not discourage us: its very defects serve to suggest those modifications which will lead to its development into the art we want – But in order to detect and remedy every defect we must apply the style universally to all our buildings, and this we have never yet done – absurdity of the popular idea that it is an ecclesiastical style . . . – Used in the middle ages by men of all creeds, and in all buildings – "Christian architecture" a misnomer – Danger lest universal application of the style should betray us into Purism – Eclecticism suggested as a safeguard . . . – Eclecticism will not make our work less Gothic in the true modern sense.'[16]

13 *Ibid.*, p.372.

14 T[homas] G[raham] Jackson, *Modern Gothic Architecture* (London, 1873), p. v.

15 *Ibid.*

16 *Ibid.*, pp. vi–vii.

Although Jackson was convinced that there was a basic affinity between all good architecture, irrespective of the style in which it was executed, he none the less believed that the English architects of the nineteenth century should base their work on the Gothic style, which had been developed on English soil.[17] Jackson regarded the Carolingian Renaissance, the mediaeval preoccupation with Latin studies, which had resulted in the resurgence of a predominantly literary culture, and the Humanist Renaissance as precedents; and, like Erasmus before him, he warned his compatriots to avoid Ciceronianism.[18] Jackson's predilection for the Queen Anne style is explained partly by his eclecticism and partly by the kind of buildings being designed in his day: 'If men could be taught that simplicity is not destructive of originality, and that there is more that is really original in the plainest old farm-house of Queen Anne's time than in a whole "park" of showy modern Gothic villas; very little encouragement would be given to the vicious affectation of originality.'[19]

Unlike the Continental Neo-Baroque – which followed an ornate Neo-Renaissance period and, during its initial phase at least, was chiefly remarkable for its ostentation – the specifically English Queen Anne Revival was a simple style which anticipated the German Neo-Biedermeier of the period preceding the First World War. We shall see on a later page how Jackson assessed the outcome of the Gothic Revival in his day.[20]

Philip Webb (1831–1915) was not an architectural theorist, and refused to write for periodicals. But partly through his buildings, which he planned with great care, and partly through his conversations, he exerted a considerable influence. 'He thought more of stone than of style' William Richard Lethaby (1857–1931) said of him. Lethaby also recorded various laconic statements made by Webb which are completely in line with Jackson's theoretical views. For example: 'Architecture is building traditionally'; 'I never begin to be satisfied until my work looks commonplace'; 'Saw many of the old Swiss houses, very sober, useful, dignified and even beautiful.'[21] Although he was a pupil of George Edmund Street, Webb did not approve of the condition whereby the entrants in the competition for the Anglican Cathedral in Liverpool were required to submit a Gothic design. The cornerstone of this cathedral was laid in 1904, and it is only now being completed in accordance with the Gothic plans drawn up – and frequently revised – by Sir Giles Gilbert Scott (1880–1960), the original prizewinner.[22]

William Morris (1834–96) was a lifelong friend of Webb, whom he first met in Street's Oxford office. Later Morris asked Webb to build a house for him – the celebrated Red House in Bexleyheath (Kent; 1859) – and when he founded the firm of Morris, Marshall, Faulkner & Co. in 1861 he commissioned Webb for numerous projects. In his theoretical pronouncements at least, Morris – who was largely responsible for the emergence of the Arts and Crafts movement – remained true to the Gothic.[23] What he looked for in an architectural project was 'a harmonious co-operative work of art', in other words a *Gesamtkunstwerk*.[24]

97

17 *Ibid.*, pp.6 and 11.

18 *Ibid.*, pp.14–31.

19 *Ibid.*, p.85.

20 See Note 33 below.

21 W[illiam] R[ichard] Lethaby, *Philip Webb and His Work* (London, 1935), pp.118, 136 and 162. – Lethaby's monograph was first printed in 1925 in *The Builder*.

22 Letter of 18 October, 1901 in Lethaby, *Philip Webb* (1935), p.121. – See also Vere E[gerton] Cotton, *The Book of Liverpool Cathedral* (Liverpool, 1964).

23 Of the recent works on Morris the one with the greatest biographical detail is Philip Henderson, *William Morris, His Life, Work and Friends* (London, 1967).

24 William Morris, *Gothic Architecture: a Lecture for the Arts and Craft Exhibition Society* (London, 1893), p.24. – The lecture was given in 1889.

'Now, that Harmonious Architectural unit, inclusive of the art in general, is no mere dream. I have said that it is only in these later times that it has become extinct: until the rise of modern society, no Civilization, no Barbarism has been without it in some form; but it reached its fullest development in the Middle Ages ... Remote as those times are from ours, if we are ever to have architecture at all, we must take up the thread of tradition there and nowhere else, because that Gothic Architecture is the most completely organic form of the Art which the world has seen; the break in the thread of tradition could only occur there: all the former developments tended thitherward, and to ignore this fact and attempt to catch up the thread before that point was reached, would be a mere piece of artificiality, betokening, not new birth, but a corruption into mere whim of the ancient traditions.'[25]

In this passage Morris considered Gothic architecture in the light of his 'Harmonious Architectural unit'. Later, he adopted a constructive approach:

'To my mind, organic Architecture, Architecture which must necessarily grow, dates from the habitual use of arch, which, taking into consideration its combined utility and beauty, must be pronounced to be the greatest invention of the human race.'[26]

He then went on to argue that although the arch was known to the Romans, their architecture remained mere 'engineering' because 'the construction and ornament did not interpenetrate'.[27] Consequently, he insisted, the Roman style was 'inorganic'.[28]

Morris's thesis that the renewal of art must be preceded by a process of social renewal was a secular version of the creed preached by Pugin and Street, and constituted a further development of Ruskin's ideas. The Gothic, he said, had reached its peak at the same time as the mediaeval guilds, and until such time as the artisans of the nineteenth century had regained their traditional liberties, there could be no question of a new architectural style:

'The form, as well as the spirit, must be Gothic; an organic style cannot spring out of an eclectic one, but only from an organic one. In the future, therefore, our style of architecture must be Gothic Architecture.'[29]

If we were to judge Morris solely on the basis of his writings, we might be tempted to classify him as a purist. But in the light of his works it is clear that such a classification would be quite wrong.

As in England, so too in Germany, the generation that followed the dogmatists of the 1840's and 1850's tried to extend the existing repertoire of architectural styles. (Incidentally, the dogmatists' insistence on a 'pure' style taken from the 'best' period reveals clear traces of Vitruvian thinking.) There are numerous representatives of this younger generation of architects, whose writings could be quoted to demonstrate the change which had taken place in German attitudes to the Gothic. I have chosen Rudolf Redtenbacher (1840–85), a pupil of Friedrich Schmidt, whose *Leitfaden zum Studium der mittelalterlichen Baukunst* appeared in 1881. Although written primarily for architects, this book was based on an evolutionary view of history, which was in

25 *Ibid.*, pp.6–8.

26 *Ibid.*, p.16.

27 *Ibid.*, pp.19–20.

28 *Ibid.*, p.23.

29 *Ibid.*, p.66.

itself a considerable advance.[30] From Redtenbacher we learn that the members of his generation had acquired an entirely new conception of both the early and the late Gothic styles:

'It is wrong to think of the Late Gothic simply as a decadent style; unprejudiced observers with a keen eye will be able to discover in it various embryonic forms capable of further development, which might even provide a point of departure for present-day architecture.'[31]

Redtenbacher's reference to 'embryonic forms capable of further development', a phrase which was still being used in the early twentieth century, indicates the emergence of a new attitude to mediaeval models.

Soon after the turn of the century Gothic Revival architecture was restricted to ecclesiastical buildings. As late as 1912 a decree was promulgated in the Archdiocese of Cologne which stated that in future building permits would be issued only for those churches which conformed to specific stylistic requirements:

'In general *new* churches should be built in the Romanesque or the Gothic, or the so-called Transitional, style. For our locality the Gothic style is normally the most suitable. Recently, however, some of our architects have tended to chose later and, in some cases, even distinctly modern styles. In future – unless there are highly exceptional circumstances – permission will not be given for such buildings.'[32]

But this extreme attitude was not entirely characteristic of the 1910's. Sir Thomas Graham Jackson adopted a more balanced view. Although a typical theorist of the historical school, Jackson regarded the changes in architectural practice which had taken place during his lifetime with benevolence, and tried to come to terms with them as fairly and as honestly as he could. In his *Gothic Architecture in France, England and Italy*, which appeared in 1915, he assessed the contemporary state of English architecture in the light of past events, and also looked to possible future developments:

'It will be admitted even by those who deplore it that the Revival of Gothic was the great artistic event of the 19th century . . . In architecture the neo-Goth broke the chain of Classic tradition, and showed the way to freedom, though at first only dimly, for brought up as he had been in the worship of the five orders, his first idea was that the Gothic had its rules and formulas like Classic . . . Let our architects, fully stored with knowledge of the past, but regarding the bygone art as their tutor rather than their model, bend themselves resolutely to the problems of the day, to novel modes of construction, to the use of novel materials, to new habits of life and new social needs, and let them satisfy these demands in the most direct and common-sense way, regardless of precedent and authority, and they will be working in the true Gothic spirit.'[33]

This might be dismissed as empty rhetoric but for the fact that, in the appendix to his book, Jackson made a serious attempt to assess the significance of reinforced concrete. He defined this new material as one whose skeletal frame had to be concealed; and he pointed out in this

30 Rudolf Redtenbacher, *Leitfaden zum Studium der mittelalterlichen Baukunst: Formenlehre der deutschen und franzö-sischen Baukunst des romanischen und gothischen Stiles auf Grundlage ihrer historischen Entwicklung* (Leipzig, 1881).

31 *Ibid.*, p.22: 'Mit Unrecht sieht man in der Spätgotik bloss einen Verfall, man wird mit scharfen und vorurtheilsfreien Augen nicht wenige entwicklungsfähige Keime in ihr entdecken, an welche sich heutzutage noch anknüpfen lässt.'

32 First published in *Kirchlicher Anzeiger für die Erzdiözese Cöln*, LII (1913), No.31; quotation taken from Willy Weyres, *Neue Kirchen im Erzbistum Köln, 1945–1956* . . . (Düsseldorf, 1957), p.27: '*Neue* Kirchen sind der Regel nach nur im romanischen oder gotischen bzw. sog. Übergangsstile zu bauen. Für unsere Gegend empfiehlt sich durchgängig am meisten der gotische Stil. In letzterer Zeit geht das Bestreben mancher Baumeister dahin, spätere Stilarten, selbst ganz moderne Bauarten zu wählen. In Zukunft wird dazu – es müssten denn ganz eigentümliche Verhältnisse obwalten – keine Genehmigung erteilt werden.'

33 Thomas Graham Jackson, *Gothic Architecture in France, England, and Italy*, 2 vols. (Cambridge, 1915), II, pp.316 and 318.

172

connexion that the mediaeval craftsmen had often had recourse to iron clamps, which they had also concealed in the walls of their buildings, a fact that the Gothic Revivalists were loath to concede, since it clashed with their cherished conception of a pure stone or brick style.[34]

Constructive 'truth', which presupposed visible structures and the interpenetration of construction and form (i.e. expression), had always been an immutable principle of Gothic Revival architecture. Jackson realized, quite rightly, that this principle was threatened by the introduction of reinforced concrete, even though he failed to recognize the full potential of this material. His belief that it would lead to the emergence of a 'trabeated style' shows that he had not really grasped its essential character.[35] He also considered that it was unlikely to prove successful. But it would be asking too much of Jackson to have expected him to foresee the widespread application of reinforced concrete in the twentieth century for in 1915, when his book appeared, he was a man of 80. Basically, he shared the view expressed by Shaw, who was four years his senior:

'It is, as I remember my friend Richard Norman Shaw once saying to me, either the beginning or the end of architecture.'[36]

Of course, even when using reinforced concrete, the architect can express a kind of 'truth': he can show the marks of the shuttering. And so the history of the Gothic Revival is seen to play its part even in the development of concrete surfaces. The delight taken by Ruskin in the precise blows of the stonemason's chisel, Morris's 'Anti-Scrape' movement, whose object was to prevent the renewal of visible surfaces in restoration projects, and Rodin's annoyance whenever original stones in his beloved cathedrals were replaced, all reflect the intense interest taken, in the late nineteenth and early twentieth centuries, in the surface texture of stone, an interest which should not really surprise us since this was, after all, the age of Impressionism.[37] Later, Le Corbusier also paid homage to the texture of mediaeval buildings in his account of the visit which he made with Fernand Léger to the United States and to which he gave the curious title *Quand les cathédrales étaient blanches*:

'I believe in the *skin* of things, just as I believe in the skin of women.'[38]

Incidentally, it was in this book that Le Corbusier wrote the sentence which finally disposed of one of the central topics of architectural theory:

'Let us stop talking about styles, either modern or ancient; style is the event itself.'[39]

2 Functionalism

Although the architectural theories of the Gothic Revival are an important link in the chain of functionalist theories, that is all they are.[40] Our understanding of this development has been confused by the

34 See Note 433 for Part III above.

35 Jackson, *Gothic Architecture* (1915), II, p.320.

36 *Ibid.*

37 Ruskin, *The Seven Lamps* (1849), § 15. – Martin S[haw] Briggs, *Goths and Vandals: a Study of the Destruction, Neglect, and Preservation of Historical Buildings in England* (London, 1952), pp.203–19. – August Rodin, *Les cathédrales de France ...; introduction par Charles Morice* (Paris, 1914).

38 Le Corbusier, *Quand les cathédrales étaient blanches: voyage au pays des timides* (Paris, 1937), p.18: 'Je crois à la *peau* des choses, comme à celle des femmes.'

39 *Ibid.*, p.50: 'Ne parlons plus de styles, ni modernes, ni anciens; le style est l'événement même.' – The affinity with Buffon's dictum 'Le style est l'homme même' is unmistakeable; see Note 101 for Part II above.

40 The development of functionalism has been pursued with particular interest in Italy. Liliana Grassi has produced an anthology with an excellent commentary; see L. G., *Razionalismo architettonico dal Lodoli a G. Pagano con appendice antologica* (Milan, 1966). – Pietro Scurati Manzoni has also provided an anthology; see P. S. M., *Il Razionalismo: l'architettura dall'illuminismo alla reazione neoespressionista* (*XVIII – XIX – XX secolo*) (Milan, 1966). – There is also a *florilegium* in the Exhibition Catalogue *Die verborgene Vernunft: funktionale Gestaltung im 19. Jahrhundert* (Munich, 1971), pp.31–75.

introduction of countless metaphorical expressions, the most popular being that of the 'organic whole'.[41] Nor has the situation been improved by the great proliferation of theoretical postulates, many of which are contradictory. The following maxims, for example, were all advanced by Gothic Revivalists:

1. Functional things are beautiful.
2. All functional things are beautiful.
3. Only functional things are beautiful.
4. Functional things are necessarily beautiful.
5. Only things that are expressively functional are beautiful. (Contradicts 2 and 4.)
6. Only things that are intrinsically functional are beautiful. (Contradicts 2 and 4.)
7. Function is related to materials, construction and purpose.
8. Things that are beautiful have style.
9. Style is determined exclusively by materials.
10. Style is determined by construction. (Contradicts 9.)
11. Style is determined exclusively by purpose. (Contradicts 9 and 10.)
12. For each material there is only one functionally apposite method of construction.

Matters become even more complicated if we try to establish a hierarchy of materials, and to assess the relative significance of character and beauty, or truth and expression. And then again, what is the relationship between seeing and knowing in truth and expression? Such questions were of course fully investigated by the generation of architects after the Second World War, which eventually turned away from functionalism. But long before this, they were considered by the architectural theorists of the nineteenth century. Friedrich Weinbrenner (1766–1826), a member of the Classicist camp, dealt with them in some detail in his *Architektonisches Lehrbuch*:[42]
'And so beauty lies in the complete concurrence of form and purpose, and the form is perfect when the object appears to have been perfected within it, so that we are unable to think of anything that might be added to, or taken away from, the given form.'[43]

In this concept of form Weinbrenner includes the expression of the architectural purpose:
'Consequently, a form is beautiful if its outline is seen to be functionally perfect. Function is itself determined by the concept of form.
'From this it would also follow that there are different types of beauty for men and women, for young and old, and for temples and palaces.'[44]

Weinbrenner recognized a fixed hierarchy of architectural purposes. Thus, he considered that a temple was functionally more important than a pigsty and consequently more beautiful.[45] He also considered that the new concept of functionalism invalidated the old canon of the Classical orders:
'According to the Ancient Greek and Roman conception of the architectural orders, the beauty of the orders is to be found simply in the proportions of their component parts, the materials of which they are

41 Collins, *Changing Ideals* (1965), pp. 149–58.

42 Friedrich Weinbrenner, *Architektonisches Lehrbuch*, 13 (individually numbered) issues in 3 vols. (Tübingen, 1810–25). – For bibliographical details see Arnold Pfister, 'Melchior Berri: ein Beitrag zur Kultur des Spätklassizismus in Basel' (Part II) in *Basler Jahrbuch*, 1936, pp.179–223.

43 Weinbrenner, *Architektonisches Lehrbuch*, III, 1st issue (1819), p.6: 'Die Schönheit liegt somit in der vollkommenen Übereinstimmung der Form mit dem Zweck, und vollkommen ist die Form, wenn das Objekt in ihr als vollendet erscheint, so dass wir für die gegebene Gestalt nichts dazu oder davon denken können.'

44 *Ibid.*: 'Schön ist demnach die Gestalt, in deren Umrissen sich durchaus eine zweckmässige Vollendung zeigt. Die Zweckmässigkeit selbst wird durch den Begriff der Gestalt bestimmt. 'Hieraus ergiebt sich dann auch, dass es für weibliche und männliche Schönheit, für Jugend und Alter, für Tempel und Palläste, verschiedene Schönheits-Typen geben müsse.'

45 *Ibid.*, p.8.

made being of no consequence; but if we imagine three columns, one of stone, one of wood, and one of iron, each of the same length and each required to bear the same load, the mind baulks at the idea that the iron column should be as thick as the wooden column, and the wooden column as thick as the stone column, etc, etc.

'However, if we paint or cover these different columns in the same colour, so that visually the different materials are reduced to a single material, we are no longer disturbed by this idea.'[46]

Weinbrenner was not just theorizing, for the design of his own buildings was always dictated by the nature of the materials used in their construction. The wooden portico which he designed for the Kurhaus in Baden-Baden (1821–3) with unusually wide intercolumniation ratios and slender columns is a good example. But then Weinbrenner had an excellent eye for materials and construction, as is apparent from the following passage in which he compares Classical and Gothic architecture:

'Incidentally, if we compare the principal characteristics of these two kinds of architecture in terms of ornamentation, we find that whereas Greek and Roman architecture sought to achieve perfection by the use and adaptation of wooden structures, Gothic architecture sought to do so by building in stone from the outset.'[47]

For Weinbrenner ornamentation was not a superficial attribute. He regarded it as the outward symbol of an inner condition:

'Just as the skeletal structure of the human body denotes its principal parts, and is clearly visible on the surface of the body, where the individual parts are seen to terminate and articulate with one another, thus forming an organic structure, so too the principal parts which constitute the forms of a building must reveal themselves to the human eye in a harmonious and articulated structure within the "material-construction" [i.e. within the general framework of the materials and the type of construction used in the building].'[48]

The 'types of ornamentation' defined by Weinbrenner in his antiquated language include an 'artistic material-construction that is pleasing to the eye'.[49]

But both the Classicists – as represented here by Weinbrenner – and the Gothic Revivalists were far too preoccupied with their formal canons to realize that the purpose for which a building is designed, whether utilitarian or structural, is only one of the factors which determine its form.

Let me illustrate what I mean by a practical example. Between 1818 and 1821 the architect Wilhelm Tappe published a treatise entitled *Darstellung einer neuen, äusserst wenig Holz erfordernden und höchstfeuersicheren Bauart* (An Account of a New Kind of Architecture Requiring Very Little Timber and Highly Resistant to Fire).[50] This new kind of architecture was a very simple affair. By constructing vaulted structures based on the catenary principle it was possible to build without rafters, and by starting the arches either at ground level or on low piers, buttresses and braces could be dispensed with. Formally, this

46 *Ibid.*, p.9: 'Nach der alt griechischen und römischen Säulenordnung will man zwar annehmen, dass die Schönheit der Säulen blos in den richtigen Verhältnissen der einzelnen Theile ohne Rücksicht auf das Material zu suchen sei, allein wenn man sich einen Säulenstamm von Stein, Holz, Eisen in gleicher Dicke und Höhe für eine gleich grosse Last zu tragen denkt, so streitet es wohl gegen den gesunden Menschenverstand, wenn wir den eisernen so dick wie den hölzernen, und diesen wieder so dick wie den steinernen etc. etc. annehmen.
'In so fern man diese verschiedenen Säulen mit einer gleichen Farbe anstreicht oder bekleidet, und wenn dadurch die verschiedenen Materien für das Auge gleichsam in eine verwandelt werden, findet diese Störung nicht mehr statt.'

47 *Ibid.*, III, 2nd issue (1819/20), pp.4–5: 'Wenn man übrigens das Hauptcharakteristikum dieser zwei Bauarten in Hinsicht der Verzierung näher mit einander vergleicht, so findet man, dass die griechische und römische Architektur ihre Vollkommenheit auf dem Wege und in der Übertragung des Holzbaues, die gothische hingegen unmittelbar in der Construction des Steinbaues zu erhalten suchte.'

48 *Ibid.*, p.5: 'Wenn bei dem menschlichen Körper der Knochenbau die Hauptbestandtheile desselben angibt, und auf der Oberfläche überall zu erkennen ist, wo die einzelnen Theile sich begränzen und organisch verbinden, so müssen auf ähnliche Weise in der Material-Construction die Haupttheile, welche die Form der Gebäude bilden, auf der Oberfläche unserm Auge sich in harmonischer Fügung zeigen.'

49 *Ibid.*, p.19: 'Verzierungsarten ... eine für das Auge angenehme und künstliche Material-Construction.'

50 Eight issues (Essen, 1818–21).

94

system was a development of the 'architecture ensévelie' (sunken architecture) that was evolved during the revolutionary period in France; structurally, it was based on the catenary principle, which had been evolved in the early eighteenth century and had been consistently applied ever since.[51] One would have thought that the Gothic Revivalists, who recognized a certain structural affinity between the pointed arch and the catenary arch, would have had some sympathy with Tappe's rather unconventional designs. But they did not. When the evangelical community in Lüdenscheid (Westphalia) wanted to build a church designed by Tappe with transverse arches on the catenary principle, Schinkel wrote a lengthy report as a member of the Prussian *Oberbaudeputation* (Building Office), in which he castigated Tappe's ideas.[52] He rightly pointed out that such arches were by no means easy to construct and called for craftsmanship of a high order. But what really bothered him was that, in his view, this system posed a threat to the 'legitimate development of art'.[53]

Heinrich Hübsch (1795–1863), the principal theorist of the Neo-Romanesque school in Germany, adopted quite a different attitude to the catenary. He regarded it simply as a useful means of representing in graphic form the distribution of the static load in vaulted buildings, such as basilicas. Hübsch recommended that a cross-section of any building that was to be investigated in this way should be inverted and pinned to the wall. A cord (or chain) could then be attached to the foundations of the aisles so that it passed through the centre of the vault above the nave, after which suitable weights could be attached at those points where the cord passed loadbearing walls. Thus, the cord would effectively demonstrate the distribution of the static load.[54] But Hübsch drew no formal conclusions from this experiment, and continued to favour the Romanesque basilica.

In his *Eléments et théories de l'architecture*, which was based on a series of lectures and was still being used as a text-book until the outbreak of the Second World War, Julien Guadet (1834–1908), Viollet-le-Duc's erstwhile opponent, also dealt with the question of vaulted churches.[55] In this book Guadet juxtaposed two sketches, each representing a cross-section of the Gothic Church of Saint-Ouen in Rouen. The first of these showed the mediaeval buttresses in their original condition; the second showed gently curving buttresses designed on the basis of new and mathematically precise calculations.[56] In presenting these contrasting designs Guadet's immediate object was to undermine the doctrine preached by Viollet-le-Duc, in which the Gothic had been presented as a completely rational style of architecture. Quite apart from this, however, Guadet had an inveterate aversion to Gothic buttresses, which he considered to be an unseemly device. This attitude was shared by many of his compatriots, and had been for generations.

Whilst Guadet was preparing his lectures for the press Anatole de Baudot (1834–1915) was completing Saint-Jean de Montmartre (Paris; 1894–1901), probably the first church to be built in reinforced concrete throughout. This church looks more modern than the relatively small

marginal note: 93

marginal note: 95, 96

51 See Notes 40–1 for Part II above. – Samuel Ware, *A Treatise of the Properties of Arches and Their Abutment Piers . . .* (London, 1809).

52 Ludwig Schreiner, 'Wilhelm Tappe (1769–1823), ein Architekturtheoretiker des 19. Jahrhunderts' in *Niederdeutsche Beiträge zur Kunstgeschichte*, IX (1970), pp.195–234, esp. p.214.

53 The whole report is reproduced *ibid.*, pp.225–7; quotations taken from *ibid.*, p.227: '. . . tausendjährige Kunstbestrebungen . . . anzuwenden versteht. Er geht dann den Weg, auf welchem der Phantasie gerade so viel Freiheit erlaubt wird, als . . . einer gesetzmässigen Entwicklung der Kunst nicht hinderlich ist.'

54 Heinrich Hübsch, *Bau-Werke* (1st series), 1 vol. text ('Text zum ersten und zweiten Heft') and 1 vol. plates ('Atlas'), (Karlsruhe and Baden-Baden, 1838); see vol. of text, pp.44–53.

55 J[ulien] Guadet, *Eléments et théories de l'architecture: cours professé à l'Ecole nationale et spéciale des Beaux-Arts*, 4 vols. (Paris, n.d. [1901–4]), III (1903), pp.81–283. – The first edition was soon followed by five further editions.

56 Guadet, *Eléments*, III (1903), pp.200–1, fig.1076.

number of buildings designed by Guadet, although Baudot, who was a former pupil of Viollet-le-Duc, employed both circular and pointed arches in its decoration.[57]

Meanwhile, Antonio Gaudì (1852–1926) was working on the Church of the Sagrada Familia in Barcelona. This building had been conceived in a conventional Gothic Revival style by the Diocesan architect Francisco de Paula del Villar y Lozano, who had started to build it in 1882. Gaudì had modified Villar's design on repeated occasions, moving farther and farther away from the original style. Both in this church and in other buildings he replaced pointed arches by parabolic arches, which were based on the catenary principle. He also employed Hübsch's method of calculating static loads, and built large three-dimensional models especially for this purpose.[58] Gaudì first used parabolic arches for the Casa Vicens in Barcelona, which he built between 1878 and 1880.[59] Although he started out as a Gothic Revivalist Gaudì subsequently came to share Guadet's view that the Gothic style was 'technically imperfect and had not fully matured.'[60]

This whole development, which led from the French discovery, in the seventeenth and eighteenth centuries, of the outstanding technical qualities of Gothic ecclesiastical architecture to Wilhelm Tappe's catenary style and, finally, Antonio Gaudì's parabolic arches, might best be described as constructive functionalism. It was basically a French development, and was accompanied by a parallel development in England, which was based on the concept of architectural purpose and stressed the importance of asymmetrical composition. This English development might be defined as picturesque functionalism.

Both these forms of functionalism, which had their origins in the Gothic Revival, are still influencing architectural theory in our day.

3 'Bauhütte' and Bauhaus

With their great love of secret societies, which was perhaps prompted by a mixture of fear and admiration, the Romantics regarded the freemasons – which was the name they gave to the stonemasons who worked in the mediaeval *Bauhütten* – as men possessed of strange powers who had been elected as the custodians of secret architectural laws.[61] This view, which was inspired in part by the development of eighteenth-century freemasonry but which was also advanced in the masonic literature of the times, was particularly widespread in Germany, where it was encouraged, rather than discouraged, by the ready availability of early records. Even after the historians had begun to establish the factual situation, the word *Bauhütte* still retained a mythical connotation. In point of fact, this word had been used in Germany during the late mediaeval period to denote either a yard next to a large building site, especially a church building site, or the men who worked in the yard, or their official organization, which differed, due to the special nature of the building trade, from the urban guilds in that

57 Schild, *Glaspalast* (1967), pp.132–7 (with ill.).

58 This is dealt with in some detail in James Johnson Sweeney and Josep Lluìs Sert, *Antoni Gaudì* (London, 1960; New York, 1961); German version (Stuttgart, 1960). – It is not despite, but because, he used traditional masonry techniques that Gaudì's work became progressively more constructive; prefabrication and reinforced concrete are not conducive to pure constructivism; see Dietmar Grötzebach, *Der Wandel der Kriterien bei der Wertung des Zusammenhanges von Konstruktion und Form in den letzten hundert Jahren* (Technische Universität Berlin thesis; Berlin, 1965), pp.79–80.

59 Calle de Las Carolinas 24–6; conversion 1925–6. – The dates are taken from Francesco Camprubì Alemany, *Die Kirche der Heiligen Familie in Barcelona, das Hauptwerk des spanischen Architekten Antonio Gaudì* . . . (Barcelona, 1960), p.13.

60 *Ibid.*, pp.13–14.

61 For specific instances see Stieglitz, *Von altdeutscher Baukunst* (1820), pp.8 and 191. – Heideloff, *Die Bauhütten des Mittelalters* (1844), p.17. – Heinrich Hübsch, *Die Architectur und ihr Verhältnis zur heutigen Malerei und Sculptur* (Stuttgart and Tübingen, 1847), pp.86–7.

its jurisdiction extended beyond its own immediate region.

But August Reichensperger and the members of his circle shared the Romantic conception of the mediaeval *Bauhütte*. For them this institution had many different facets. Thus, it facilitated the creation of a *Gesamtkunstwerk*, it provided practical – i.e. non-academic – training, it was a Christian working community within a hierarchical society, and it was a bulwark, for both artists and craftsmen, against the threat of industrialization.[62] However, it did not fulfil the demand made by John Ruskin and William Morris, who insisted that craftsmen should be unhampered by working drawings since this was the only way in which they could find fulfilment.

Morris, for his part, stripped the concept of the *Bauhütte* of its religious connotations and removed it from its traditional association with specific buildings. The largest Gothic Revival project undertaken in England, in which Morris's ideas were put into practice, was for a secular building: Barry's and Pugin's Houses of Parliament in Westminster. As for Ruskin's conception, that was realized in connexion with the Oxford Museum, which was also a secular building. But while a canteen was provided in Oxford to cater for the physical needs of the workmen, their spiritual welfare was also provided for by means of daily prayers.[63] Henry Wentworth Acland (1815–1900), a pioneer of scientific education at Oxford and a friend of Ruskin, described the close collaboration between the architect and the workmen on the Museum project in words which might well have come from Ruskin's own pen:

'The temper of the architect has reached the men. In their work they have had pleasure. The capitals are partly designed by the men themselves, and especially by the family of O'Shea, who bring wit and alacrity from the Emerald Isle to their cheerful task.'[64]

Although Morris's firm also produced fitments for churches, it was in the provision of hand-made articles for country houses that English craftsmanship reached its apogee at the end of the nineteenth century. Shortly afterwards, Morris's fame spread to Germany, thanks to Hermann Muthesius (1861–1927).[65] When he noted the connexion between Morris's work in England and the German *Bauhütte* tradition, Muthesius was prompted to compare Morris with the 'brilliant teacher Karl Schäfer' (1844–1908).[66] Schäfer, a pupil of Reichensperger's friend Ungewitter, completed the façade of Meissen Cathedral, and taught in Berlin (from 1878) and Karlsruhe (from 1894). Hugo Hartung once described him as 'the most celebrated professor in the technical colleges of Germany'.[67] From Muthesius and the German Werkbund the craftsmanship ethos passed to Walter Gropius (1883–1969) and the Bauhaus. Gropius wanted to reconcile craftsmanship and industry. But despite this laudable ambition, the real *leitmotif* in Weimar was provided by the mediaeval *Bauhütten*. Ludwig Grote, a contemporary of Gropius, wrote in 1965:

'The Bauhaus regarded itself as a [*Bau-*] *Hütte* at the foot of the cathedral which Feininger had glorified in crystalline visions.'[68]

62 See Notes 422–8 for Part III above.

63 Henry W[entworth] Acland and John Ruskin, *The Oxford Museum: from the Original Edition, 1859; with Additions in 1893* (4th ed.), (London and Orpington, 1893), p.41.

64 *Ibid.*, p.42.

65 The most important German and English texts (in German translation) have been compiled and commented by Julius Posener; see J. P., *Anfänge des Funktionalismus: von Arts and Crafts zum Deutschen Werkbund* . . . (Berlin, Frankfurt am Main and Vienna, 1964). – See also Dennis Sharp, *Sources of Modern Architecture: a Bibliography* . . . (London, 1967).

66 Muthesius, *Stilarchitektur* (1902), p.33.

67 Hugo Hartung, 'Zu Carl Schäfers Gedächtnis' in *Festschrift zur Feier der Weihe der Glocken in den erneuerten Türmen des Domes zu Meissen am 27. Oktober 1908*, hrsg. von dem Vorstande des Meissner Dombauvereins . . . (Meissen, 1908), pp.5–7; quotation taken from *ibid.*, p.6: '. . . der gefeiertste Professor an den technischen Hochschulen Deutschlands'. – Dr. Günter Krüger, the authority on the Brücke painters, kindly drew my attention to this work.

68 Ludwig Grote, 'Funktionalismus und Stil' in *Historismus und bildende Kunst* . . . (Munich, 1965), pp.59–72; quotation taken from *ibid.*, p.63: 'Das Bauhaus sah sich als Hütte am Fuss der Kathedrale, die Feininger in gläsernen Visionen verherrlicht hat.'

69 Ludwig Grote, 'Zum Gestaltwandel des Bauhauses' in *Eberhard Hanfstaengl*

zum 75. Geburtstag (Munich, 1961), pp.178–85; quotation taken from *ibid.*, p.179: 'In dem Manifest von 1919 und in der Namensgebung hat Gropius sein Ziel in die Vision des grossen Einheitswerkes gebannt, zu dessen Errichtung sich alle Künste in gemeinsamer Arbeit vereinigten. Feininger hat dazu in einem Holzschnitt, den die vorderste Seite des Programms aufnimmt, dem Ideal kommender Baukunst die Gestalt einer dreitürmigen gotischen "Kathedrale des Sozialismus", wie sie genannt wurde, verliehen. Die Revolution von 1918 spricht aus dem Manifest in der Absage an die klassentrennende Anmassung der Akademien und in dem Bekenntnis zum Handwerk und seiner Lebensweise in der Werkstatt und auf dem Bauplatz.'

70 See Note 253 for Part II above.

71 Quotation taken from Hans M[aria] Wingler, *Das Bauhaus: 1919–1933, Weimar – Dessau – Berlin* (n.p. [Bramsche and Cologne], 1962), p.30: 'In ihrem Kreise könnte eine ähnlich glückliche Arbeitsgemeinschaft wiedererstehen, wie sie vorbildlich die mittelalterlichen "Hütten" besassen, in denen sich zahlreiche artverwandte Werkkünstler – Architekten, Bildhauer und Handwerker aller Grade – zusammenfanden und aus einem gleichgearteten Geist heraus den ihnen zufallenden gemeinsamen Aufgaben ihr selbständiges Teilwerk bescheiden einzufügen verstanden aus Ehrfurcht vor der Einheit einer gemeinsamen Idee, die sie erfüllte und deren Sinn sie begriffen. Mit der Wiederbelebung jener erprobten Arbeitsweise, die sich der neuen Welt entsprechend anpassen wird, muss das Ausdrucksbild unserer modernen Lebensäusserungen an Einheitlichkeit gewinnen, um sich schliesslich wieder in kommenden Tagen zu einem *neuen Stil* zu verdichten.' – The second edition of Wingler's work (1968) contains an additional section on the Chicago Bauhaus; apart from this section, the pagination of the two editions is identical. – English translation from the second edition (Cambridge [Mass.], 1969).

72 Helmut von Erffa, 'Das frühe Bauhaus: Jahre der Entwicklung, 1919–1923' in *Wallraf-Richartz-Jahrbuch*, XXIV (1962), pp.413–14; quotation taken from *ibid.*, p.413: 'In der Aula begrüsste Gropius uns Neulinge. Er sprach von Zusammenarbeit, vom Gefühl der Zusammengehörigkeit im Sinne der mittelalterlichen Baugilden. Daraus sollte sich eine Erneuerung der Kunst unserer Zeit bilden.'

73 Marcel Franciscono, *Walter Gropius and the Creation of the Bauhaus in Weimar* ... (Urbana, Chicago and London, 1971), p.96.

Grote also considers that Gropius consciously derived the name Bauhaus from the term *Bauhütte*:

'Both in the manifesto of 1919 and in the name he chose for his institute Gropius conjured up the vision of a great corporate undertaking, in whose development all the arts would work in unison. Feininger designed a woodcut, which was reproduced on the first page of the Bauhaus programme, and in which he expressed this idealistic conception of architecture in the form of a triple-towered cathedral called the "Cathedral of Socialism". The manifesto reflected the revolution of 1918 by rejecting the arrogance of the Academies, which was dividing the nation, and by paying homage to craftsmanship and the craftsman's way of life, both in the workshops and on the building sites.'[69]

The *Bauhütte* concept was already evident in the 'Proposals for the Establishment of a Training Institute as an Advisory Centre for Industry, Trade and Craft' which Gropius submitted to the local authorities on 25 January 1916. These proposals were written in a style that is reminiscent of the memorandum which Schinkel submitted with a competition design for a memorial cathedral,[70] and shows quite clearly that Gropius had something more in mind than a simple school of arts and crafts:

'In this environment we could revive the happy working community that was one of the characteristic features of the mediaeval *Bauhütten*, in which numerous allied *Werkkünstler* – architects, sculptors and craftsmen of all grades – joined forces and, inspired by the same corporate spirit, were able to make their individual and modest contribution to the communal tasks which they were required to perform, out of reverence for the unity of a corporate idea which filled their minds and whose significance they had understood. With the revival of this trusted working method, which will be adapted to meet the requirements of our new world, the artistic statements which we make about life today will become more and more unified, and will eventually be condensed into a *new style*.'[71]

In an article which he wrote for the annual report of the Wallraf-Richartz-Museum in 1962, Helmut von Erffa recalled the opening address delivered by Gropius to new entrants at the Bauhaus in 1921. 'Gropius welcomed the new entrants in the assembly hall. He spoke to us of communal work, of a sense of belonging similar to that found in the mediaeval building guilds, and suggested that this would lead to a renewal of art in our day.'[72]

The members of the Bauhaus generation looked with longing eyes to Spain, where Gaudì, as we have seen, appeared to be creating both the new style and the new community to which they aspired.[73]

But despite strenuous efforts to develop the Bauhaus institute in other directions, it remained a mere school. Shortly after its foundation in 1919 a heated discussion was conducted in Weimar over the correct form of address to be adopted *vis-à-vis* the members of the teaching staff: 'master' or 'professor'.

V Conclusion

1 The Events Leading up to the Gothic Revival

Between the sixteenth and eighteenth centuries there were three principal factors which foreshadowed the emergence of the Gothic Revival. First, there were the buildings which, having been started during the Gothic period, were completed in the Gothic style. Second, there were the new buildings which were designed and executed in the Gothic style. And third, there were the various written accounts and assessments of mediaeval Gothic buildings, which were supplemented and elucidated by accounts of the post-Gothic projects for the completion of mediaeval churches such as San Petronio in Bologna, Sainte-Croix in Orleans and Westminster Abbey in London.

In these completion projects the reason why the Gothic style was chosen was, invariably, to ensure stylistic unity or, to use the phrase favoured by contemporary authors, for the sake of conformity. In the 'Vitruvian period' stylistic unity was often considered more important than the Classical canon. Unfortunately, it would seem that no attempt was made by contemporary authors to establish the reasons for the choice of the Gothic style for new buildings during this period.

In this study I have tried to show, in terms of both architectural theory and architectural history, how the Vitruvians of the sixteenth, seventeenth and eighteenth centuries tried to interpret mediaeval architecture in the light of their own architectural theory and concepts. In this connexion the analysis of the term 'Gothic style' seemed to offer the most promising line of enquiry. As far as we know, the word 'style', which Filarete applied to painting and sculpture as early as 1460, was not applied to architecture until 1578, when it appeared in the documents relating to the San Petronio project in Bologna. However, there were only three occurrences, and until well into the eighteenth century mediaeval architecture and the various types of Vitruvian architecture – Doric, Ionic and Corinthian – were all described as 'orders'. But for as long as mediaeval architecture was regarded as the epitome of all that was barbaric, the term 'Gothic order' was felt to be inappropriate. This was clearly indicated by Baglione in 1642 and Baldinucci in 1681.

The word 'style' became fully established in the mid-eighteenth century, apparently as a result of the introduction of the new key concept of the fine arts, under which architectural theory and the theories of the other artistic disciplines were subsumed and integrated. This development probably set in earlier in England than in France, Italy and Germany.

181

In the early sixteenth century Gothic architecture was generally thought to be of German origin, and in Northern Italy it was actually called 'German architecture'. But the more disreputable it became, the more the Italians tended to refer to it as 'barbaric' or 'Gothic' architecture, these two terms being virtually synonymous at that time. In 1550 Vasari evolved a theory to explain the development of the Gothic, in which the Goths were represented as the originators of mediaeval architecture. But precisely when the expression 'Gothic style' was first used is not known.

The essentially modern character of Vitruvianism becomes apparent when we consider that the members of this movement were by no means prepared to accept either the master's doctrine or the architectural monuments of Antiquity as they stood. Among other things, they seized upon a number of incidental remarks in the *De Architectura*, and from them fashioned an entirely new doctrine of architectural mimesis that was very much in line with similar doctrines already established in the other fine arts. They then argued that the Antique orders had been derived from an original primitive hut made of tree trunks, and that they were, therefore, 'imitations' of a natural prototype. At a surprisingly early date – 1510 – the author of a letter addressed to Pope Julius II (an author who has been identified, on different occasions, as Count Castiglione, as Raphael, and as Bramante) derived the pointed form of Gothic vaults from the interlocking branches of living trees. This particular interpretation may have been prompted either by the new mimesis theory or by the 'branch forms' of the Late Gothic period. Subsequently, the eighteenth-century theorists combined the 'natural' and 'barbaric' origins when they suggested that the Gothic churches had been derived from the forest sanctuaries of Celtic or Germanic antiquity.

With the growth of natural science in the second half of the eighteenth century the expression 'organic whole', which was probably coined by the Swiss scientist Charles Bonnet in 1769, made its way into architectural theory. In 1809 Alois Hirt maintained that, with its integrated and functional character, a building which constituted an organic whole was analogous with an animal or vegetable organism. Later, the Gothic Revival theorists adopted this expression and used it in an extended sense in their evolutionary conception of historical development. It was not until the 1950's that it began to disappear from the architectural scene.

2 The Beginnings of the Gothic Revival

In the eighteenth century the attitudes adopted to Gothic architecture in England, France and Germany were very different.

With their associationist tradition, the English stressed the emotional properties of the Gothic. They pointed to its links with nature, and to the sombre, mysterious and awesome atmosphere of mediaeval churches, which they found so conducive to feelings of piety; and they insisted on the essentially national character of this style of architecture, which was so very different from what they regarded as the international, or alien, character of Classical architecture.

The French, on the other hand, were attracted primarily by the lightness of Gothic churches, and held them up as an example to those architects who continued to build heavy Italianate churches supported by massive pillars. In 1741 the architect Soufflot who, according to Chambers, produced numerous drawings of Gothic buildings, analysed the optical processes whereby the structure of Gothic buildings appeared to be even lighter than it actually was, and infinitely lighter than that of traditional pillar churches. Later, when Boffrand evolved his theory of architectural character, the French also came to appreciate the emotional properties of Gothic churches, which were of course partly induced by their lightweight construction. In 1790 Boullée spoke in this connexion of the 'magic of art'.

Meanwhile, the German landscape theorists of the 1770's and 1780's tried to form a synthesis from the English theory of association, the French theory of character, and the Vitruvian theory of architectural proportions. At the same time, German writers like Goethe, Forster and Tieck, who were unencumbered by considerations of traditional architectural theory, enthused over Strasbourg Cathedral and Cologne Cathedral. Finally, as a result of the growing influence of the English theorists, the Germans declared the Gothic to be a national style and suitable for both churches and castles.

After the Gothic conversion of Walpole's country house (Strawberry Hill, 1750–70) Gothic villas became socially acceptable. Incidentally, it would seem that the example set by Walpole in commissioning this project exerted greater influence than the random remarks which he passed on the Gothic and its revival. In 1777 John Carter, who occasionally worked for Walpole, suggested that a comparison should be made between St Paul's and Westminster Abbey in order to demonstrate the excellence of the Gothic style for ecclesiastical architecture. Shortly afterwards, in c.1800, the landscape theorists reconciled the French theory of character with the Gothic by distinguishing between House Gothic, Abbey Gothic, and Castle Gothic. And all the time the archaeologists were probing more and more deeply into the historical development of the Gothic. In 1806 Loudon, who was perturbed by the great number of different styles in use during the early years of the nineteenth century, suggested that the Gothic should be adopted as a universal style. He was probably the first person to recommend this course, and one of the reasons why he did so was that, because of its picturesque character, the Gothic allowed the architect to create irregular and functional ground-plans. From 1835 onwards Pugin also advocated the universal application of the Gothic. Pugin, who collaborated with Barry on the greatest Gothic Revival project undertaken in England, the new Houses of Parliament, considered that the affinity between Gothic architecture, the Catholic Church and the mediaeval world order was so great that the revival of the one would automatically lead to the revival of the others. Meanwhile, far and away the largest number of Gothic Revival buildings were commissioned by Churches of all denominations.

Although French enthusiasm for the technical expertise of the Gothic architects led to the construction of numerous colonnade churches in the eighteenth century, Gothic forms were seldom found outside the walls of English-style gardens, many of which were laid out in France at that time. And after the Revolution those interested in Gothic architecture in France concentrated their efforts on the restoration or preservation of Gothic buildings which had escaped destruction. Many of these were badly damaged whilst others had been abandoned and so had fallen into neglect, or else were threatened by new traffic routes. Such conservation projects benefited greatly from the splendid work of contemporary French archaeologists such as Arcisse de Caumont. Prior to 1840 the French undertook very few new buildings in the Gothic style.

After the War of Liberation the Germans were determined to erect a national monument. Of the numerous proposals put forward to this end in 1814 and 1815, the one finally adopted was for the completion of Cologne Cathedral. The original idea for this project, which was supposed to symbolize the unity of 'Religion, Fatherland, and Art', would seem to have come from Crown Prince Ludwig of Bavaria. Work began on the completion in 1841 and was finished in 1880. Not only in Germany, but also in England, Cologne Cathedral was regarded as the greatest extant example of Gothic architecture; and even in France it was classified as one of the greatest. Those responsible for the completion of the cathedral attached great importance to the practical craft training provided in the Cathedral's *Bauhütte*. Schinkel also drew attention to this development in connexion with the design which he submitted to the King of Prussia for a Gothic Revival cathedral in Berlin. This too was intended to celebrate the victorious outcome of the War of Liberation.

The Gothic was proclaimed as a national style in England, France and Germany, and in each of these countries three architectural camps began to form, all of which were dedicated to the restoration of stylistic unity, which by the beginning of the nineteenth century had been lost from view. These three camps were: the Gothic, the Eclectic, and the Classical. The people living at that time were preoccupied with the problem of personal and national identity; their great fear was that they might lose their identity, and many of the arguments conducted by the members of these rival camps were overshadowed by that fear.

3 Doctrinal Aspects of the Gothic Revival

Although the Gothic Revival was generally acclaimed as a universal style, it was not universally applied. Basically, it remained an ecclesiastical style. It was no accident that the 'ecclesiological movement' or 'gotische Bewegung' or 'mouvement archéologique', which were the names given to the Gothic Revival in the 1840's, was led by ecclesiastically oriented periodicals – *The Ecclesiologist*, the *Kölner Domblatt*, and the *Annales archéologiques* – whose editors and correspondents maintained close contact with one another. We have, of course, already seen that the contributors to two of these periodicals, *The Ecclesiologist* and the *Annales*, included a number of celebrated architects, namely Scott, Street, Lassus, and Viollet-le-Duc.

There were three principal factors for which the Gothic Revivalists had to provide a theoretical justification: the imitation of the Gothic; the particular type of Gothic model to be imitated; and the way in which it was to be imitated. *The Ecclesiologist* was particularly successful in this respect. Numerous discussions were conducted in its columns, and as a result the English archaeologists were able to evolve a comprehensive but flexible doctrine.

As far as the imitation of the Gothic was concerned, it was argued that Gothic architecture was a true, functional and national style, and so was the perfect vehicle, not only for ecclesiastical buildings, but for all buildings in a Christian land. This view was held by the Gothic Revivalists of England, France and Germany.

But when they came to consider the type of Gothic model to be imitated, there was a divergence of opinion amongst these different national groups. It was generally conceded that, in view of the evolutionary nature of historical processes, it was impossible to regard Gothic architecture, the Christian Church or Christian peoples as fixed constants, and it was assumed, therefore, that if the Gothic Revival was to succeed as a reform movement, it must revive the best style of Gothic architecture and reconcile that style with modern building techniques. It was here that the divergence occurred, for whereas the English and Germans favoured the early fourteenth century, the French preferred the early thirteenth. But, although important, this was essentially a matter of detail; in principle, it was agreed that the revival of the best Gothic style was a necessary condition for the emergence of a new style.

As for the way in which Gothic models were to be imitated, this was not just a question of reproducing the decorative appearance of Gothic buildings. On the contrary, Gothic Revival architects were expected to create buildings which not only reflected the complexity of mediaeval design – hence the importance attached by English archaeologists to their picturesque and asymmetrical rural churches – but which also incorporated its underlying principles. Consequently, they had to produce plans which stressed the structural characteristics of their buildings, which reflected the nature of the materials used in each case, and which provided for a functional lay-out. (This last requirement was of English provenance, but was subsequently adopted by Continental archaeologists as well.) 'Inventive imitation' was the ideal, and 'copyism' was frowned upon; but, initially at least, the dogmatists were liable to see heresy in every original design.

In the 1850's this dogmatism was gradually relaxed. By then it was felt that enough was known about the Gothic for it to be permissible to invent new forms. Foreign models were sanctioned; so too was the use of polychromatic effects, which were obtained by the introduction of different coloured stones or bricks; and in England serious consideration was given to the possible use of prefabrication in cast-iron construction, which Rickman had been employing for church buildings as early as 1813.

Although there were many English nineteenth-century theorists who did not belong to the group centred on *The Ecclesiologist*, their publications were fully reported in the periodical. One of these outsiders was Ruskin, who tried to counteract the growing alienation being induced by industry and the decline of the traditional crafts by promoting the idea of a new Arts and Crafts movement, in which craftsmen would be encouraged to produce articles of artistic value based on their own designs. Ruskin found willing disciples among the former pupils and employees of the architect George Edmund Street, who held a completely opposite view, insisting that the architect must design everything in his building himself, even down to the keyholes in the doors. The best known of these disciples was William Morris.

In France, Viollet-le-Duc based the whole of his architectural theory on the constructive and material character of buildings. Although he considered that Greek and Roman architecture were also constructive, Viollet-le-Duc ascribed this quality primarily to the Gothic, which he regarded as the rational style of architecture *par excellence*. Not surprisingly, the high-minded conception of art entertained by the majority of his contemporaries seemed to him quite bogus.

The most fertile idea conceived by the German Gothic Revivalists was probably their conception of the *Bauhütte*. For Reichensperger, the editor of the *Kölner Domblatt*, the *Bauhütte* served a dual purpose, for it not only provided practical, i.e. non-academic, training in the various building crafts and so ensured that architecture retained its links with the people, it also provided a nucleus for an ideal Christian and bourgeois state.

4 The End of the Gothic Revival

For as long as the bulk of our buildings were made of stone or brick, Gothic architecture seemed the logical point of departure for a new style because, with its combination of constructive and decorative form, it constituted a genuine organic whole. As late as 1939 Frank Lloyd Wright referred to it as a perfect example of an organic style.

During the early period of the Gothic Revival great importance was attached to the associative character of the Gothic. But from 1860 onwards this approach was abandoned, and attention was focused instead on the basic architectural principles derived from the Gothic. Once this shift had taken place, no architect was ever accused of having designed a profile in a style that was 'an hour too early', which was the bitter comment passed by Sir George Gilbert Scott on one of his critics. On the other hand, virtually no established architects made any really serious attempt to abandon their tried and trusted historical styles prior to 1890. Contemporary critics, it is true, were wont to accuse architects of building in 'a style that defies description'; but this censure was reserved, almost without exception, for outsiders.

Functional principles were identified for far too long with the Gothic style. The realization that, with the development of reinforced concrete, the old conception of the pointed arch as the greatest constructive invention of all time might no longer be tenable was not made until 1915, when Jackson drew attention to this possibility. At about the same time, in Barcelona, Gaudì switched from the pointed arch to the parabolic arch, which was based on the catenary principle, and invented a system of ramified supports which enabled him to dispense with external buttresses.

Meanwhile, in Germany the ideas emanating from the Arts and Crafts movement and the ideas evolved by the *Bauhütten* of the Gothic Revival were combined in the Bauhaus at Weimar, where they helped to promote the Romantic conception of a self-contained community, the Gothic Revival conception of craftsmanship, and a modern school of design intended to cater for industrial products.

5 The Historical Significance of the Gothic Revival

The only effective way of assessing the significance of the Gothic Revival and its theoretical premises is by comparing them with other movements and other theories. The Gothic Revival could, for example, be compared with the 'Renaissances' of the ninth, twelfth and fifteenth centuries, or with the Neo-Classical or Eclectic movements of the nineteenth century. Gothic Revival theory might also be compared with the architectural theory of the mid-twentieth century, which would show how certain ideas and certain groups of words had developed in the interim.

But although in the course of this study I have made a number of comparisons of this kind in order to elucidate the theoretical premises of the Gothic Revival, these have necessarily been extremely brief. I am not, therefore, in a position to assert that these theoretical premises provide the main link between the Vitruvianism of the sixteenth, seventeenth and eighteenth centuries and the architectural theory of the twentieth century, and consequently are more important than either Neo-Classical or Eclectic theory. And yet I would suggest that this is the case. I would also suggest that the reason why the theories underlying the Gothic Revival were so influential is that they all but succeeded in reconciling an ideal conception of architectural style with firm principles of architectural practice.

Even in the British Isles it is noticeable that at no time did the production of genuine Gothic Revival buildings account for even half of the total production of new buildings. And so the Gothic Revivalists failed to achieve their objective, which was the establishment of the Gothic Revival as a universal style. But then that is the usual fate of a reform movement: it fails to achieve its objective, but it does establish its principles.

Plates

1

1
The Cathedral of Sainte-Croix in Orleans: façade of the south transept; 17th century.

2
The Cathedral of Sainte-Croix in Orleans; design for the principal façade by Guillaume Hénault and Robert de Cotte in *c.*1708 (Chenesseau).

3
The Cathedral of Sainte-Croix in Orleans; design for the façade of the transept created by Etienne Martellange in 1624 or 1627.

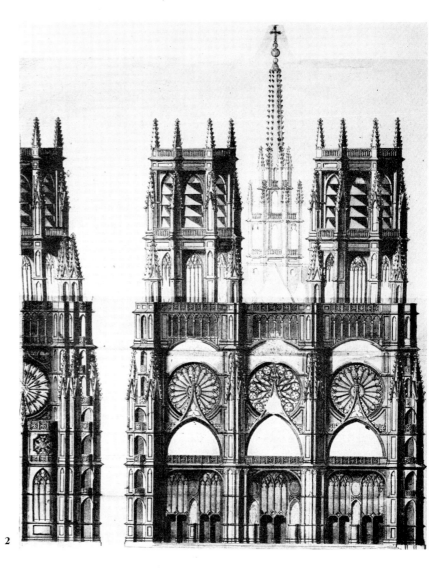

2

3

191

The Fifth Order of the Gothick Architecture. *Plate* **XIII**.

4

4
'The Fifth Order of the Gothick Architecture'; as proposed by Batty and Thomas Langley in 1741 (T. and B. Langley, *Gothic Architecture Improved*).

5
'Gothick Temple'; design created by Batty and Thomas Langley in 1741 (T. and B. Langley, *Gothic Architecture Improved*).

6
'Gothic Cathedral'; designed for Kew Gardens by Johann Heinrich Müntz in *c*.1758; now demolished (Chambers, *Plans, Sections, Elevations, and Perspective Views of the Gardens and Buildings at Kew*).

5

6

193

7
Human Figure with Geometrically
Determined Proportions; reproduction
taken from the Cesariano edition of
Vitruvius (Como, 1521).

8
Milan Cathedral: section (Cesariano, 1521).

9
Milan Cathedral: section (Cesariano, 1521).

10
Monastery Chapel of Batalha: section
(Murphy, 1792–5; R.I.B.A.).

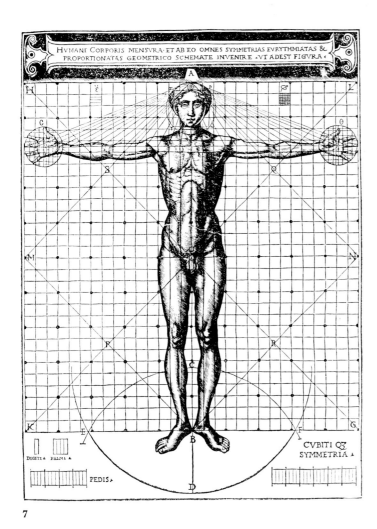

7

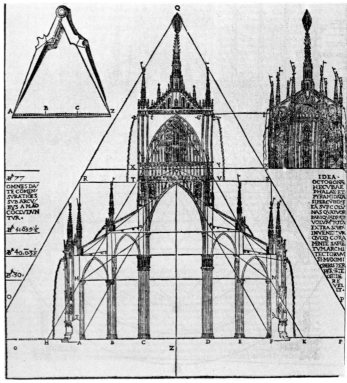

8

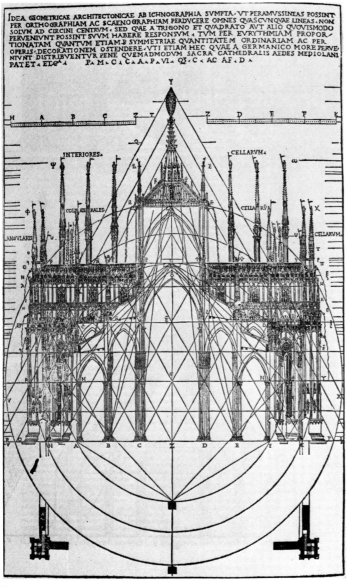

9

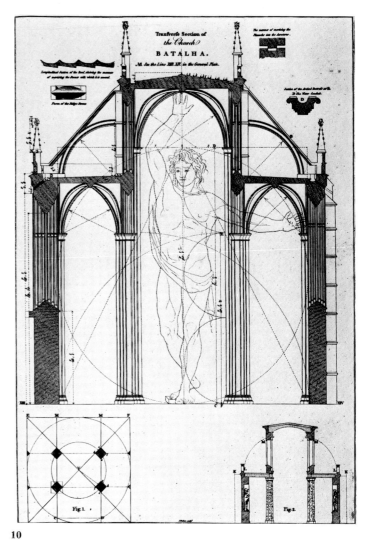

10

11

11
Primitive Hut; reproduction taken from
Laugier (1753).

12
Blaise Castle Estate, Henbury, Bristol;
garden building designed by Humphrey
Repton in 1791.

12

13
Strawberry Hill, Twickenham; Gothic
Revival conversion carried out by various
architects in collaboration with the owner,
Horace Walpole, from 1750 onwards
(Walpole, *Description of the Villa*).

14
'Wicker Cathedral'; experimental
structure and garden building designed by
Sir James Hall in 1792–3 (Hall, *Essay on the
Origin, History and Principles of Gothic
Architecture*).

13

14

15

15
Fonthill Abbey; designed by James Wyatt in 1796; now derelict: staircase (Britton, *Graphical and Literary Illustrations of Fonthill Abbey*).

16
'Pavilion and Green House for a Gothic Mansion'; design created by J. Adey Repton in 1802 (H. Repton, *Observations*).

17
'Hall for a Gothic Mansion'; design created by J. Adey Repton in 1802 (H. Repton, *Observations*).

16

17

18
'A Villa Designed as the Residence of an Artist' by John B. Papworth (Papworth, 1818).

19
'Gothic Cottage'; designed by John B. Papworth (Papworth, 1818).

20
'Gothic Church'; design created by John Carter in 1777: window tracery (*The Builder's Magazine*).

21
'Gothic Church'; design created by John Carter in 1777: façade (*The Builder's Magazine*).

18

19

200

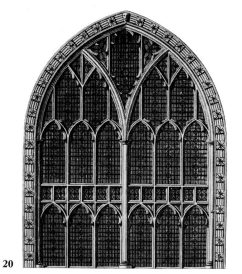

20

overleaf pp.202–3:

22
Church of St Paul, Portland Square, Bristol; designed by Daniel Hague; built 1789–94: façade.

23
Church of St Paul, Portland Square, Bristol; designed by Daniel Hague; built 1789–94: window tracery.

24
Church of St Paul, Portland Square, Bristol; designed by Daniel Hague; built 1789–94: view from the east.

25
Holy Trinity, Cloudesley Square, Islington, London; designed by Charles Barry; built 1826: interior.

26
Church of St George, Everton, Liverpool; designed by Thomas Rickman; built 1813–14: view from the south-west.

27
Church of St George, Everton, Liverpool; designed by Thomas Rickman; built 1813–14: interior.

28
Church of St Luke, Chelsea, London; designed by James Savage; built 1820–4: view from the west.

29
Church of St Luke, Chelsea, London; designed by James Savage; built 1820–4: interior.

21

201

22

23

24

25

26

28

27

29

30
The Houses of Parliament, London;
designed by Sir Charles Barry in
collaboration with A. W. N. Pugin, in
1835; started in 1840; Victoria Tower
completed in 1860: view from the river.

31
The Houses of Parliament, London;
designed by Sir Charles Barry and A. W.
N. Pugin: The Victoria Tower (completed
in 1860).

32
The Houses of Parliament, London;
designed by Sir Charles Barry and A. W.
N. Pugin; started in 1840: view from the
north-west.

33
St Mary's Cathedral, Killarney (Eire);
designed by A. W. N. Pugin in 1842;
completed in 1912: columns.

34
St Mary's Cathedral, Killarney (Eire);
designed by A. W. N. Pugin in 1842;
completed in 1912: interior.

33

34

35
Church of St Thomas of Canterbury,
Fulham, London; designed by A. W. N.
Pugin; built 1847–9: window tracery.

36
Church of St Thomas of Canterbury,
Fulham, London; designed by A. W. N.
Pugin; built 1847–9: interior.

35

36

37
Convent of the Sisters of Mercy,
Handsworth, Birmingham; design created
by A. W. N. Pugin in 1840.

38
'Contrasted Residences for the Poor';
etching executed by A. W. N. Pugin in
1836 (Pugin, *Contrasts*).

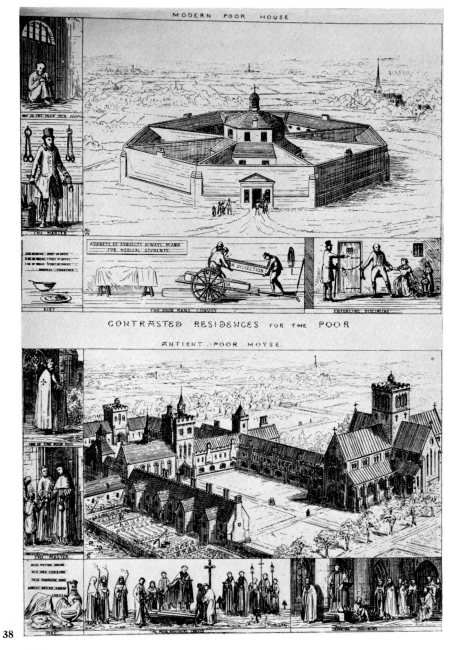

37

38

39

39
St Patrick's College, Maynooth (Eire);
design created by A. W. N. Pugin in 1845:
west front.

40
St Patrick's College, Maynooth (Eire);
design created by A. W. N. Pugin in 1845:
quadrangle.

40

42

41
Panthéon, Paris (formerly Sainte-
Geneviève); designed by Jacques-Germain
Soufflot; started in 1757: interior (Carl).

42
The Cathedral of Saint-Vaast, Arras;
designed by Constant d'Ivry; started
c.1760: interior.

43

212

43
Gothic ruins in Betz (Oise) ; built *c*.1780
(Laborde, *Description*).

44
Gothic ruins in Betz (Oise); built *c*.1780
(Hauser).

45
Castle on the Pfaueninsel, Berlin;
built by Brendel in 1794–6: view from the
north-east.

44

45

213

46
The Walhalla at Donaustauf near
Regensburg; designed by Leo von Klenze;
built 1830–42: view from the north-west.

47
The Walhalla at Donaustauf near
Regensburg; designed by Leo von Klenze;
built 1830–42: view from the west.

48
The National Monument, Edinburgh;
designed by Charles Robert Cockerell and
William Henry Playfair; started in 1822;
unfinished.

47

48

49

216

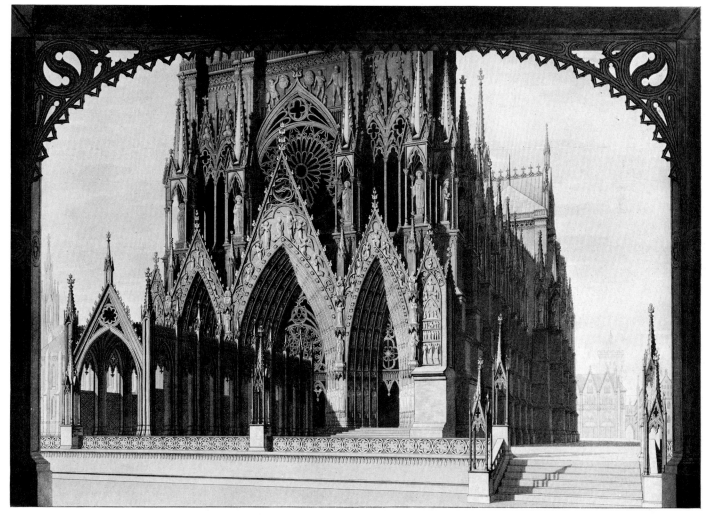

50

49
Mausoleum for Queen Luise of Prussia;
design by Karl Friedrich Schinkel
(Staatliche Museen zu Berlin, National-
galerie).

50
Rheims Cathedral; stage design for
Schiller's *Jungfrau von Orleans* created by
Karl Friedrich Schinkel, probably in 1817
(Schinkel, *Sammlung von Theater-
Decorationen*).

51
Cologne Cathedral as it was at the end of
the mediaeval period; drawing executed
by Angelo Quaglio in *c.*1820 (Boisserée,
*Geschichte und Beschreibung des Doms von
Köln*, 2nd ed.).

52
Cologne Cathedral *Bauhütte* in 1846;
drawing by Vincenz Statz (Cologne,
Collection of Dombaumeister Willy
Weyres).

53
Mariahilfkirche in der Au, Munich;
designed by Daniel Ohlmüller; built
1831–39; badly damaged in the Second
World War: façade (*Allgemeine
Bauzeitung*, VII).

53

54
Church of St Nicholas, Hamburg; designed
by Sir George Gilbert Scott in 1844–5;
completed in 1863; badly damaged in the
Second World War: principal façade
(*Allgemeine Bauzeitung*, XIII).

54

55

56

55
Church of St Paul, Brighton;
designed by Richard Cromwell Carpenter;
built 1846–8: view from the east.

56
Church of St Paul, Brighton;
designed by Richard Cromwell Carpenter;
built 1846–8: porch.

57
Church of St Paul, Brighton;
designed by Richard Cromwell Carpenter;
built 1846–8: interior.

58 (overleaf, p.224)
Church of All Saints, Margaret Street,
St Marylebone, London; designed by
William Butterfield in 1849–50;
built 1850–9: view from the south-east.

59 (overleaf, p.225)
Church of All Saints, Margaret Street, St
Marylebone, London; designed by William
Butterfield in 1849–50; built 1850–9:
interior.

57

60
The Crystal Palace, Hyde Park, London;
designed by Joseph Paxton in 1850–1;
built 1850–1, destroyed by fire in 1936
(*Allgemeine Bauzeitung*, XV).

60

61
Iron church; design created by
William Slater in 1856
(*Instrumenta Ecclesiastica*, II).

61

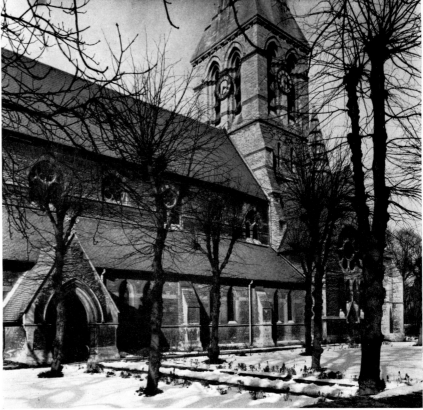

62
Church of St Philip and St James, Oxford;
designed by George Edmund Street in
1859; built 1860–2: view from the south-
east based on Street's drawing (Eastlake,
History of the Gothic Revival).

63
Church of St Philip and St James, Oxford;
designed by George Edmund Street in
1859; built 1860–2: view from the south-
west.

64
Church of St Philip and St James, Oxford;
designed by George Edmund Street in
1859; built 1860–2: interior.

63

65
St Mary's Vicarage, Coalpit Heath, near
Bristol; designed by William Butterfield in
1845: view from the south-east.

66
St Mary's Vicarage, Coalpit Heath, near
Bristol; designed by William Butterfield in
1845: west window.

67
University Museum, Oxford; designed by
Deane & Woodward in 1854: view of the
west façade.

68
The Law Courts, London; designed by
George Edmund Street in 1866; built
1871–82: view from the south-west.

69
Sainte-Clotilde, Paris; started in 1846 by
Franz Christian Gau, completed in 1857 by
Théodore Ballu: base of pillar in the porch
(Hauser).

70
Sainte-Clotilde, Paris; started in 1846 by
Franz Christian Gau, completed in 1857 by
Théodore Ballu: elevation of the principal
façade (*Revue de l'art chrétien*, I).

71
Sainte-Clotilde, Paris; started in 1846 by
Franz Christian Gau, completed in 1857 by
Théodore Ballu: interior.

69

70

71

235

72
Saint-Nicolas, Nantes; designed by Jean-
Baptiste-Antoine Lassus in 1843; built
1844–69: principal façade.

73
Saint-Nicolas, Nantes; designed by Jean-
Baptiste-Antoine Lassus in 1843; built
1844–69: the radiating chapels (Hauser).

236

74
Saint-Nicolas, Nantes; designed by Jean-
Baptiste-Antoine Lassus in 1843; built
1844–69: interior.

75
Lille Cathedral (Notre-Dame de la Treille);
joint design created by Père Arthur
Martin and others, and incorporating
features from the entries in the 1856
competition; the architect in charge of this
unfinished project was Charles Leroy:
interior.

76
Church in Aillant-sur-Tholon; designed by
Viollet-le-Duc in 1865; built by A. A.
Lefort 1865–7: view from the south-east.

77
Church in Aillant-sur-Tholon; designed by
Viollet-le-Duc in 1865; built by A. A.
Lefort 1865–7: capital (Hauser).

78
Church in Aillant-sur-Tholon; designed by
Viollet-le-Duc in 1865; built by A. A.
Lefort 1865–7: interior (Hauser).

78

79
Cathedral and Préfecture in Auxerre
(Yonne): view from the east in *c.*1820
(Laborde, *Monumens*, II).

80
Cathedral and Préfecture in Auxerre; the
latter converted by Viollet-le-Duc
1847: view from the north.

79

80

240

81
Castle of Pierrefonds; restored from a ruin
by Viollet-le-Duc 1858–70: view from the
north.

82
Castle of Pierrefonds; restored from a ruin
by Viollet-le-Duc 1858–70: view of the
courtyard from the entrance.

81

82

241

83
St Johanniskirche, Berlin-Moabit;
designed by Karl Friedrich Schinkel in
1834; rebuilt in 1957: drawing by
Schinkel (Schinkel, *Architektonische
Entwürfe*, XXIV).

84
The Railway Station of Freiburg
(Breisgau); designed by Friedrich Eisenlohr
in 1845; now replaced by a modern station
(Eisenlohr, *Ausgeführte und zur
Ausführung bestimmte Entwürfe*).

85
St Arnulph at Nickenich; designed by
Johann Claudius von Lassaulx; built
1846–9: view from the north-east

86
Church on St Apollinarisberg, near
Remagen; designed by Ernst Friedrich
Zwirner in 1839: doorway.

87
Church on St Apollinarisberg, near
Remagen; designed by Ernst Friedrich
Zwirner in 1839: interior.

88
St Stephan in Krefeld; designed by
Friedrich von Schmidt; built 1854–9;
tower completed in 1881: façade.

89
St Stephan in Krefeld; designed by
Friedrich von Schmidt; built 1854–9;
tower completed in 1881: interior.

90
Votivkirche in Vienna; competition design
submitted by Vincenz Statz in 1854:
façade (*Allgemeine Bauzeitung*, XXII).

91

91
Town Hall in Vienna; designed
by Friedrich von Schmidt in 1868;
built 1872–83: south front.

92
Town Hall in Munich; designed
by Georg von Hauberisser: east wing
(built 1867–74).

92

93
Section of a church with tripartite nave showing the disposition of the buttressed vault; drawing by Heinrich Hübsch (Hübsch, *Bau-Werke*).

94
Gateway, Houses, and a Church executed in the 'Parabolic Style'; design by Wilhelm Tappe (*Karl Friedrich Schinkel: Lebenswerk*, XIII).

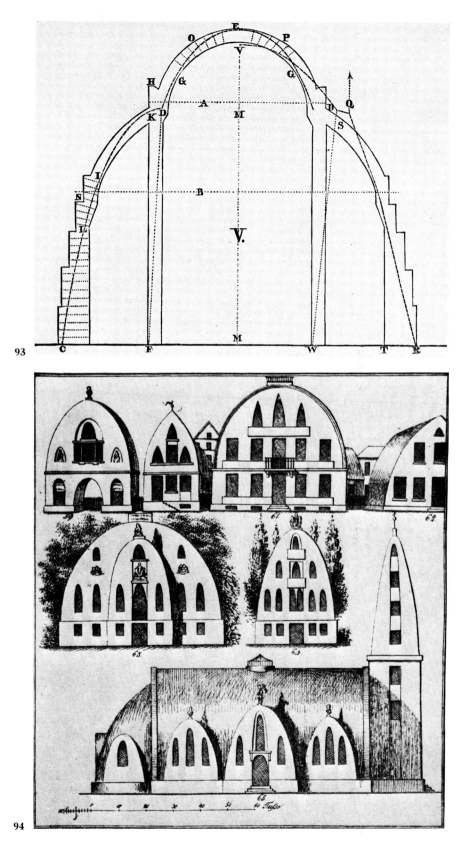

93

94

95
Saint-Jean de Montmartre; designed by
Anatole de Baudot; built 1894–1901:
principal façade.

96
Saint-Jean de Montmartre; designed by
Anatole de Baudot; built 1894–1901:
interior.

97
Anglican Cathedral in Liverpool; general
design created in 1902, tower design in
1924, by Sir Giles Gilbert Scott; building
work has been going on since 1904: view of
the crossing from the south.

98
Cathedral of the Future; woodcut
by Lyonel Feininger in 1919
(*Bauhausprogramm*).

Index

263